Speaking into the Air

Speaking into the Air

A History of the Idea of Communication

JOHN DURHAM PETERS

The University of Chicago Press Chicago and London

The University of Chicago Press, Chicago 60637
The University of Chicago Press, Ltd., London
© 1999 by The University of Chicago
All rights reserved. Published 1999
08 07 06 05 04 03 02 01 00 99   1 2 3 4 5
ISBN: 0-226-66276-4 (cloth)

Peters, John Durham.
    Speaking into the air : a history of the idea of communication /
John Durham Peters.
        p.   cm.
    Includes bibliographical references and index.
    ISBN 0-226-66276-4 (alk. paper)
    1. Communication—Philosophy—History.   I. Title.
P90.P388 1999
302.2′01—dc21   98-50308
                                                          CIP

∞ The paper used in this publication meets the minimum requirements of the American National Standard for Information Sciences—
Permanence of Paper for Printed Library Materials, ANSI Z39.48-1992.

To my mentors at four universities

HAL MILLER, LEN HAWES, DON ROBERTS, *and* SAM BECKER

So likewise ye, except ye utter by the tongue words easy to be understood, how shall it be known what is spoken? for ye shall speak into the air. There are, it may be, so many kinds of voices in the world, and none of them is without signification. 1 COR. 14:9–10 KJ

Written kisses don't reach their destination, rather they are drunk on the way by the ghosts. It is on this ample nourishment that they multiply so enormously. Humanity senses this and fights against it and in order to eliminate as far as possible the ghostly element between people and to create natural communication, the peace of souls, it has invented the railway, the motor car, the aeroplane. But it's no longer any help, these are evidently inventions being made at the moment of crashing. The opposing side is so much calmer and stronger; after the postal service it has invented the telegraph, the telephone, the wireless. The spirits won't starve, but we will perish. FRANZ KAFKA TO MILENA JESENSKÁ

It is a question whether the obvious increase of overt communication is not constantly being corrected, as it were, by the creation of new obstacles to communication. EDWARD SAPIR, "COMMUNICATION"

If communication bears the mark of failure or inauthenticity in this way, it is because it is sought as a fusion. EMMANUEL LEVINAS, "THE OTHER IN PROUST"

Contents

Introduction:
The Problem of Communication

When you take a word in your mouth you must realize that you have not taken
a tool that can be thrown aside if it will not do the job, but you are fixed in a
direction of thought which comes from afar and stretches beyond you.

HANS-GEORG GADAMER

Though humans were anciently dubbed the "speaking animal" by Aristotle, only since the late nineteenth century
have we defined ourselves in terms of our ability to *communicate* with one another. The intellectual, ethical, and political implications of this revolutionary change in self-
description have not been sufficiently traced. This book
attempts to begin such a tracing. It is at once a critique of
the dream of communication as the mutual communion
of souls, a genealogy of sources and scenes of the pervasive
sense that communication is always breaking down, and a
reclamation of a way of thinking that avoids both the
moral privilege of dialogue and the pathos of breakdown.
I aim to trace the sources of modern ideas of communication and to understand why the modern experience of
communication is so often marked by felt impasses.

"Communication" is one of the characteristic concepts
of the twentieth century. It has become central to reflections on democracy, love, and our changing times. Some
of the chief dilemmas of our age, both public and personal,
turn on communication or communication gone sour. A
diverse company of thinkers—Marxists, Freudians, existen-
tialists, feminists, anti-imperialists, sociologists, and phi-

1

losophers of language, to name a few—have dealt with the tragedy, comedy, or absurdity of failed communication. The difficulty of communication across various social boundaries—gender, class, race, age, religion, region, nation, and language—confronts us daily. But horizons of incommunicability loom beyond the merely human world as well, in the vexing question of communication with animals, extraterrestrials, and smart machines. Much in the century's popular culture, especially science fiction, plays on how new symbol-processing machines allow for such dangers and delights as mind control or bodily transport. Likewise, much twentieth-century drama, art, cinema, and literature examines the impossibility of communication between people. One need only mention such playwrights as O'Neill, Beckett, Sartre, Ionesco, Albee, or Havel or filmmakers such as Bergman, Antonioni, or Tarkovsky to evoke scenes of stammering face-to-face relations. Intellectuals of all kinds have likewise found in communication a topic with which to explore the outer limits of human connection and to weigh the demands we place on one another. Strother Martin's line from the 1967 film *Cool Hand Luke,* starring Paul Newman, has assumed an epochal significance: "What we have here is failure to communicate."

"Communication" is a registry of modern longings. The term evokes a utopia where nothing is misunderstood, hearts are open, and expression is uninhibited. Desire being most intense when the object is absent, longings for communication also index a deep sense of dereliction in social relationships. How did we get to the pass where such pathos attaches to the act of speaking with another person? How did it become possible to say that a man and woman "are tuned to different frequencies"?[1] How did a term once associated with successful transmission by telegraph, telephone, or radio come to carry the political and intimate aspirations of so many people in this age? Only moderns could be facing each other and be worried about "communicating" as if they were thousands of miles apart. "Communication" is a rich tangle of intellectual and cultural strands that encodes our time's confrontations with itself. To understand communication is to understand much more. An apparent answer to the painful divisions between self and other, private and public, and inner thought and outer word, the notion illustrates our strange lives at this point in history. It is a sink into which most of our hopes and fears seem to be poured.

---

1. Deborah Tannen, *You Just Don't Understand: Men and Women in Conversation* (New York: Ballantine, 1990), 288.

The Historicity of Communication

My aim is not to explore the full variety of communication problems as reflected in the thought and culture of the twentieth century, but rather to tell the story of how communication became such trouble for us. My strategy follows a distinction Walter Benjamin made between modes of historical narration. One mode he called historicism: it regarded history as preconstituted and given, a continuous chain of causes and effects existing in a homogeneous space-time continuum. The past waited demurely for the historian to conjure it up. The scholar needed only to call (with sufficient patience and rigor) and history would respond, telling of things as they really were. The other mode—the one Benjamin preferred, as I do—saw in every act of historical narration a constructivist principle. The historian did not wait for the past to speak its fullness but was an activist who brought ages into alignment with each other. Time, for Benjamin, is not just a continuum; it is full of ruptures and shortcuts—"wormholes," we might say. Benjamin is thinking of the medieval notion of time as *nunc stans,* an eternal present (*Jetztzeit* in his German), but as is always true in his work, the mystical sources are not wifty dreaming but have shrewd relevance to concrete concerns. The present becomes intelligible as it is aligned with a past moment with which it has a secret affinity. There is a simultaneity not only across space, but across time as well. The Roman Republic and the French Revolution, though nearly two millennia apart, are more closely linked than 1788 and 1789, separated by only a year. Fashion illustrates such simultaneity: in some periods past styles (swing music, sideburns, bell-bottoms) are dead and off-limits, and in others they are suddenly current again. The past lives selectively in the present. History works not in a solely linear way but by being arranged into various constellations.[2]

What these reflections mean for this book is that I try to illuminate the present by excavating several past moments with which I believe it has an affinity. There is little here that is directly about television, cinema, or the Internet, and not much beyond the mid-twentieth century. Yet late nineteenth-century studies in psychical research (chapters 2 and 5) or 1930s worries about how to create a warm human presence over radio (chapter 5), I believe, illuminate with some precision the questions—virtual reality, cloning, cyborgs, and global ethernets—facing us

2. Walter Benjamin, "Theses on the Philosophy of History," in *Illuminations,* trans. Harry Zohn (1940; New York: Schocken, 1968).

at the turn of the millennium. In the same way, such figures as Socrates and Jesus (chapter 1) or Augustine and John Locke (chapter 2) might not have a demonstrable role in the historical semantics of "communication," but they are good to think with. With brilliance and articulateness, they lay out arguments and concerns that in current thinking are often muffled at best. Such thinkers as these make our own thoughts more fluent. All history writing, of course, is a commentary on its own age, even (or especially) that which claims to be most true to the past. Benjamin simply makes the historian's role in creating the alignments explicit.

One might ask, Why my insistence on the historicity of "communication"? Isn't communication an issue that mystifies people everywhere? That communication troubles are written into the human condition is in one sense surely true. William James put it well in his *Principles of Psychology* (1890):

One great splitting of the whole universe into two halves is made by each of us; and for each of us almost all of the interest attaches to one of the halves; but we all draw the line of division between them in a different place. When I say that we all call the two halves by the same names, and that those names are "*me*" and "*not me*" respectively, it will at once be seen what I mean. The altogether unique kind of interest which each human mind feels in those parts of creation which it can call *me* or *mine* may be a moral riddle, but it is a fundamental psychological fact. . . . Each of us dichotomizes the Kosmos in a different place.[3]

Our sensations and feelings are, physiologically speaking, uniquely our own. My nerve endings terminate in my own brain, not yours. No central exchange exists where I can patch my sensory inputs into yours, nor is there any sort of "wireless" contact through which to transmit my immediate experience of the world to you. James took the mutual insulation of consciousness to be given in the human condition. Of the isolation of different people's streams of thought, James wrote: "The breaches between such thoughts are the most absolute breaches in nature."[4] In this view, humans are hardwired by the privacy of their experience to have communication problems.

James may well be right that all humans naturally have a privileged relation to themselves such that direct sharing of consciousness is im-

3. William James, *The Principles of Psychology*, Great Books of the Western World, ed. Robert Maynard Hutchins, vol. 53 (1890; Chicago: Encyclopaedia Britannica, 1952), 187.
4. James, *Principles of Psychology*, 147.

possible. Even though the impossibility of immediate communication between minds may be a fundamental psychological fact (or at least the fundamental fact of the field of psychology), it is important to note that we have not always talked this way about our mutual relations. Even though people's eyes and ears had been receiving apparently "private" data for thousands of years, James lived in a world in which breaches between individual minds had wider social and political relevance. There is, in other words, something historical and contingent about James's discovery of something transhistorical and given. Even though today "communication" might seem a fixed problem for the human species, from cave dwellers to postmoderns, only in James's lifetime (1842–1910) did communication acquire its grandeur and pathos as a concept. Two words coined in the late nineteenth century mark his intellectual horizon well: "solipsism" in 1874 and "telepathy" in 1882. (The latter was a brainchild of James's colleague in psychical research, Frederic W. H. Myers). Both reflect an individualist culture in which the walls surrounding the mind were a problem, whether blissfully thin (telepathy) or terrifyingly impermeable (solipsism). Since then, "communication" has simultaneously called up the dream of instantaneous access and the nightmare of the labyrinth of solitude.

This dualism of "communication"—at once bridge and chasm— arose from new technologies and their spiritualist reception, which capped a long tradition of speculating about immaterial mental contact (chapter 2). Briefly, technologies such as the telegraph and radio refitted the old term "communication," once used for any kind of physical transfer or transmission, into a new kind of quasi-physical connection across the obstacles of time and space. Thanks to electricity, communication could now take place regardless of impediments such as distance or embodiment. The term conjured up a long tradition of dreams about angelic messengers and communion between separated lovers. "Communication" seemed far superior to the age-old grubby face-to-face work of making lives together in language. It was swift as lightning, subtle as the ether, and wordless as thoughts of love. Interpersonal relations gradually became redescribed in the technical terms of transmission at a distance—making contact, tuning in or out, being on the same wavelength, getting good or bad vibes, or "Earth to Herbert, come in please!" Communication in this sense makes problems of relationships into problems of proper tuning or noise reduction.

As I examine such media of transmission and recording as the post office, telephone, camera, phonograph, and radio in later chapters, my focus will be not on how they affected face-to-face communication as an already constituted zone of human activity, but rather on how such media made "communication" possible as a concept in the first place, with all its misfires, mismatches, and skewed effects. The potentials for disruption in long-distance "communication"—lost letters, wrong numbers, dubious signals from the dead, downed wires, and missed deliveries—have since come to describe the vexations of face-to-face converse as well. Communication as a person-to-person activity became thinkable only in the shadow of mediated communication. Mass communication came first. Already in what is perhaps the first, and certainly the most articulate, account of communication as an ideal of interpersonal understanding—Plato's *Phaedrus*—communication is defined in contrast to its perversion (by manipulation, rhetoric, and writing). Communication is a homeopathic remedy: the disease and the cure are in cahoots. It is a compensatory ideal whose force depends on its contrast with failure and breakdown. Miscommunication is the scandal that motivates the very concept of communication in the first place.[5]

The Varied Senses of "Communication"

One might fairly object that I have unfairly narrowed the meaning of "communication." The term deserves a closer analysis. Like many notions hailed as unmixed goods, it suffers from the misfortune of conceptual confusion. Confusion, if it suggests the mixing of well-defined intellectual contours, may even be too precise a term, since "communication" in much contemporary discourse exists as a sort of ill formed, undifferentiated conceptual germ plasm. Rarely has any idea been so infested with platitudes. Communication is good, mutuality is good, more sharing is better: these seemingly obvious dicta, because unexamined, sweep too much under the rug. I wish it were easier to find arguments by thinkers defending such propositions explicitly and rigorously. Because "communication" has become the property of politicians and bureaucrats, technologists and therapists, all eager to demonstrate their rectitude as good communicators, its popularity has exceeded its clarity. Those seeking to make the term theoretically precise for academic study have sometimes ended up only formalizing the miasma from the culture more generally.[6] The consequence is that the

5. See Briankle G. Chang, *Deconstructing Communication: Representation, Subject, and Economies of Exchange* (Minneapolis: University of Minnesota Press, 1996), chap. 5.

6. One example would be Wilbur Schramm, one of the institutional founders of communication studies as an academic field. See "How Communication Works," in *Processes and Effects of Mass Communication*, ed. Wilbur Schramm (Urbana: University of Illinois Press, 1954).

philosophically richest thinking about communication, taken as the problem of intersubjectivity or breakdowns in mutual understanding, is often found in those who make little use of the word.[7]

"Communication" is a word with a rich history. From the Latin *communicare*, meaning to impart, share, or make common, it entered the English language in the fourteenth and fifteenth centuries. The key root is *mun-* (not *uni-*), related to such words as "munificent," "community," "meaning," and *Gemeinschaft*. The Latin *munus* has to do with gifts or duties offered publicly—including gladiatorial shows, tributes, and rites to honor the dead. In Latin, *communicatio* did not signify the general arts of human connection via symbols, nor did it suggest the hope for some kind of mutual recognition. Its sense was not in the least mentalistic: *communicatio* generally involved tangibles. In classical rhetorical theory *communicatio* was also a technical term for a stylistic device in which an orator assumes the hypothetical voice of the adversary or audience; *communicatio* was less authentic dialogue than the simulation of dialogue by a single speaker.[8]

As in Latin, one dominant branch of meaning in "communication" has to do with imparting, quite apart from any notion of a dialogic or interactive process. Thus communication can mean partaking, as in being a communicant (partaking of holy communion). Here "communication" suggests belonging to a social body via an expressive act that requires no response or recognition. To communicate by consuming bread and wine is to signify membership in a communion of saints both living and dead, but it is not primarily a message-sending activity (except perhaps as a social ritual to please others or as a message to the self or to God). Moreover, here to "communicate" is an act of receiving, not of sending; more precisely, it is to send by receiving. A related sense is the notion of a scholarly "communication" (monograph) or a "communication" as a message or notice. Here is no sense of exchange, though some sort of audience, however vague or dispersed, is implied. Communication can also mean connection or linkage. In the nineteenth-century United States, "steam communication" could mean the railroad. In Hawthorne's *House of the Seven Gables* we read: "She approached

7. My views on communication studies as a field can be found in John Durham Peters, "Institutional Sources of Intellectual Poverty in Communication Research," *Communication Research* 13, 4 (1986): 527–59; "The Need for Theoretical Foundations: Reply to Gonzalez," *Communication Research* 15, 3 (1988): 309–17; "Genealogical Notes on 'The Field,'" *Journal of Communication* 43, 4 (1993): 132–39; and "Tangled Legacies," *Journal of Communication* 46, 3 (1996): 85–87.

8. Cicero, *De Oratore*, trans. H. Rackham (Cambridge: Harvard University Press, 1942), 3.204, and Heinrich Lausberg, *Handbuch der literarischen Rhetorik: Eine Grundlegung der Literaturwissenschaft* (Munich: Hueber, 1960), 379–84. Thanks to Donovan Ochs for help on this point.

the door that formed the customary communication between the house and garden." In the sense of linkage, communication could also mean coitus.[9] Curiously, "communication" once meant what we now call intercourse, while "intercourse" once meant what we now call communication (the varieties of human dealings). The ambiguous term "relations" underlies both.

Another branch of meaning involves transfer or transmission. The sense of physical transfer—such as the communication of heat, light, magnetism, or gifts—is now largely archaic, but it is the root, as I argue in chapter 2, of the notion of communication as the transfer of psychical entities such as ideas, thoughts, or meanings. When John Locke speaks of "Communication of Thoughts," he is taking a term with a physical acceptation and appropriating it for social uses. Here too there is nothing necessarily two-way about communication. One can speak of the one-way transmissions of advertising and public relations as communications, even if no response is possible or desired. One senses that the purveyors of these things would like them to work like communicable diseases, another transmissive sense of the term.

A third branch of meaning is communication as exchange, that is, as transfer times two. Communication in this sense is supposed to involve interchange, mutuality, and some kind of reciprocity. The nature of the exchange can vary. Communication can mean something like the successful linkage of two separate termini, as they say in telegraphy. Here simply getting through, as in delivery of mail or e-mail, is enough to constitute communication. If both ends know the message has arrived, then communication has occurred. A further, colloquial sense of communication calls for the exchange of open and frank talk between intimates or coworkers.[10] Here communication does not mean simply talk; it refers to a special kind of talk distinguished by intimacy and disclosure. An even more intense sense of communication as exchange dispenses with talk altogether and posits a meeting of minds, psychosemantic sharing, even fusion of consciousness. As Leo Lowenthal put it, "True communication entails a communion, a sharing of inner experience."[11] Although Lowenthal is not necessarily saying we can share inner experience without the materiality of words, he nicely states the high-stakes definition of communication as contact between interiori-

9. *Oxford English Dictionary*, s. v. "communication," 5b.
10. Tamar Katriel and Gerry Philipsen, "'What We Need Is Communication': 'Communication' as a Cultural Category in Some American Speech," *Communication Monographs* 48 (1981): 301–17.
11. Leo Lowenthal, "Communication and Humanitas," in *The Human Dialogue: Perspectives on Communication*, ed. Floyd W. Matson and Ashley Montagu (New York: Free Press, 1967), 336.

ties. And though clearly not the only definition of communication, it is the one that has risen to prominence in the past century. Here the normative pathos is most intense.

"Communication" can also serve, in a much more modest way, as a blanket term for the various modes of symbolic interaction. Here communication is free of special pleading about what we humans should be capable of but is a descriptive term for our relations in signification. There is something of this in the King James translation of Matt. 5:37, "But let your communication be, Yea, yea; Nay, nay: for whatsoever is more than these cometh of evil." Here communication translates *logos,* one of the richest words in the Greek lexicon. Ranging across such senses as word, argument, discourse, speech, story, book, and reason, *logos* served as an overall term for the capacities that followed from the fact that humans, as Aristotle said, are animals possessing the word. Matt. 5:37 suggests that our speech be simple, but the usage suggests a general policy about humans and the *logos.*

"Communication" can mean something similarly general. As Charles Horton Cooley wrote in 1909, "By Communication is here meant the mechanism through which human relations develop—all the symbols of the mind, together with the means of conveying them through space and preserving them in time." In this book I will use "communications" in the plural in this sense. As Raymond Williams puts it in a serviceable but too psychological definition, communications are "the institutions and forms in which ideas, information, and attitudes are transmitted and received."[12] They might include tombs, hieroglyphics, writing, coins, cathedrals, stamps, flags, clocks, the press, the post, telegraphy, photography, cinema, telephony, phonography, radio, television, cable, computer, the Internet, multimedia, virtual reality, or any other signifying medium.[13] "Communication," in contrast, I take as the project of reconciling self and other. The mistake is to think that communications will solve the problems of communication, that better wiring will eliminate the ghosts.

Although I am skeptical that the word "communication" can ever fully shake the ghosts of wordless contact, the term marks out a marvelous zone for inquiry: the natural history of our talkative species. Communication theory claims this zone. As I argue below, the notion of communication theory is no older than the 1940s (when it meant a mathematical theory of signal processing), and no one had isolated

---

12. Raymond Williams, *Communications* (London: Penguin, 1962), 9. In contrast to the common usage that calls the academic field "communications," I will use "communication studies."

13. The motley list is a standard genre in treatises on media that I have no intention of omitting.

"communication" as an explicit problem till the 1880s and 1890s. Throughout I use "communication theory" not to refer to any extant practice of inquiry, but in a loose, ahistorical sense for a vision of the human condition as in some fundamental way communicative, as anchored in the *logos*. In this way communication theory becomes consubstantial with ethics, political philosophy, and social theory in its concern for relations between self and other, self and self, and closeness and distance in social organization. Though few of the figures examined in this book had any notion of "communication theory," our current situation allows us to find things in their texts that were never there before. As Benjamin knew, the present can configure the past so as to open up new points of rendezvous.

Sorting Theoretical Debates in (and via) the 1920s

These terminological distinctions do not exhaust the variety of conceptions about communication. At two points in the twentieth century, communication was an especially hot topic of intellectual debate: after World War I and after World War II. These debates clarify the varieties of this plastic concept and also provide a more contemporary window for approaching the rest of the book.

All the intellectual options in communication theory since that time were already visible in the 1920s. In philosophy, "communication" was a central concept. Major works probing the possibilities and limits of communication include Karl Jaspers, *Psychologie der Weltanschaaungen* (1919); Ludwig Wittgenstein, *Tractatus Logico-philosophicus* (1922); Martin Buber, *I and Thou* (1923); C. K. Ogden and I. A. Richards, *The Meaning of Meaning* (1923); John Dewey, *Experience and Nature* (1925); Martin Heidegger, *Being and Time* (1927); and Sigmund Freud, *Civilization and Its Discontents* (1930). In social thought more generally, large-scale communication to the many, be they "crowd," "mass," "people," or "public," was a theme in such works as Walter Lippmann, *Public Opinion* (1922); Ferdinand Tönnies, *Kritik der öffentlichen Meinung* (1922); Edward Bernays, *Crystallizing Public Opinion* (1923); Georg Lukács, *History and Class Consciousness* (1923); Carl Schmitt, *The Crisis of Parliamentary Democracy* (1923, 1926); Dewey, *The Public and Its Problems* (1927); Harold Lasswell, *Propaganda Technique in the World War* (1927); and Freud, *Group Psychology and the Analysis of the Ego* (1922). Modernist masterpieces by Eliot, Hemingway, Kafka, Proust, Rilke, and Woolf all explored breakdowns in communication. The dada movement, at its height during the war, actively provoked such breakdowns. Surrealism countered by finding connection everywhere. Everywhere, "communication" was on the agenda. "Communication" meant very different things in this highly diverse body of work. In one view, communication signified something like the dispersion of persuasive symbols in order to manage mass opinion. Such theorists as Lippmann, Bernays, and Lasswell all offered a historical narrative about the increasing importance of "communication" and "propaganda" in modern society. Industrialization, urbanization, societal rationalization, psychological research, and novel instruments of communication all provided unprecedented conditions for the manufacture of consent among dispersed populations. The experience of the First World War, moreover, proved that symbols are not just aesthetic ornaments but prime movers of social organization. Strategically cultivated perceptions lost or won battles and sent men in the trenches to their graves. Lasswell, for one, argued the inevitability of manipulation as a principle of modern social order and its superiority to the earlier reliance on more brutal forms of social control: "If the mass will be free of chains of iron, it must accept its chains of silver."[14]

The scale, systematicity, and putative effectiveness of mass-communicated symbols raised tough questions for the future of democracy. If the will of the people, the *feste Burg* of democratic theory, was little more than a bog of stereotypes, censorship, inattention, and libido to be manipulated by experts or demagogues, what did that say about the rationality of the public? Different authors had different answers to this question. Walter Lippmann argued for the obsolescence of popular sovereignty and its replacement by expert rule. His belief in the manipulability of the many, however, was tempered by an equally strong sense of the impenetrability of the people: popular irrationality could be both malleable and intransigent. Carl Schmitt, the brilliant conservative political theorist who was later briefly *Kronjurist* for the Nazis, thought people's faith that government business got done through public discussion in a parliament that reflected public opinion in general was little more than a joke. It is "as though someone had painted the radiator of a modern central-heating system with red flames in order to give the appearance of a blazing fire."[15] At the opposite end of the political spectrum, Marxist theoretician Georg Lukács saw the art of party organiza-

14. Harold D. Lasswell, *Propaganda Technique in the World War* (London: Kegan Paul, Trench, Trübner, 1927), 227.
15. Carl Schmitt, *The Crisis of Parliamentary Democracy,* trans. Ellen Kennedy (1923; Cambridge: MIT Press, 1985), 6.

tion as not just a technical but an intellectual (*geistige*) issue for the revolution. The revolutionary process was inseparable from the development of class consciousness on the part of the proletariat and hence involved choosing the right slogans and rallying cries.[16] Whereas Lippmann saw the calculated production of public opinion as proof of the unfeasibility of popular democracy, Lukács saw such production as precisely the necessary prelude to revolutionary action. Neither, however, believed in the spontaneous self-organization of popular will; each gave a major role to a "vanguard," whether of social-scientific experts (Lippmann) or intellectual party leaders (Lukács). Communication, in short, was conceived of as the power to bind a far-flung populace together for good or ill; it had the stuff to make or break political order, a notion that also informs, alas, another book of the period, Adolf Hitler's *Mein Kampf* (1925).

A second vision saw communication as the means to purge semantic dissonance and thereby open a path to more rational social relations. It is closely related to the propaganda view as cure is related to disease. *The Meaning of Meaning* (1923) by the Cambridge critics C. K. Ogden and I. A. Richards is probably the best exhibit of this view and, even more, of the dominant view of communication as the accurate sharing of consciousness. Their twin enemies were "the impasse of solipsism" and the "veritable orgy of verbomania" in the modern world, classic 1920s worries about inaccessible individuality and mass gullibility. (These concerns recapitulate the solipsism/telepathy dualism.) Their project was a "science of symbolism" that would have widespread application in clearing up controversy and confusion in human intercourse. Ogden and Richards believed that many troubles resulted from mixing the symbolic and emotive functions of language, "the same words being used at once to make statements and to excite attitudes." (There's the old bugaboo: one word, many uses.) Their diagnosis of modern democracy could be Lippmann's: "New millions of participants in the control of general affairs must now attempt to form personal opinions upon matters which were once left to only a few. At the same time the complexity of these matters has immensely increased." But their remedy differed. Lippmann argued that such complexity required shifting the burden of rule from the people to experts, but Ogden and Richards called for an educated public: "The alternative [to elite rule] is to raise the level of

---

16. Georg Lukács, *Geschichte und Klassenbewusstsein* (1923; Neuwied: Luchterhand, 1968), 452, 495.

communication through a direct study of its conditions, its dangers, and its difficulties. The practical side of this undertaking is, if communication be taken in its widest sense, Education."[17]

Communication, for Ogden and Richards, thus has both a macro and a micro application. Their purification of the language of the tribe would help at both international and interpersonal levels. In a long British tradition distrusting the deceit of words found in such thinkers as Bacon, Hobbes, Locke, Hume, Bentham, and Russell, Ogden and Richards viewed language as a necessary but flawed instrument: "Words . . . are at present a very imperfect means of communication." Indeed, Ogden spent three decades proselytizing on behalf of "Basic" English (British American Scientific International Commercial), a proposed universal language consisting of 850 English words. (Note that each word in the acronym represents an empire.) Language ties us dangerously to our primeval origins: "Tens of thousands of years have elapsed since we shed our tails, but we are still communicating with a medium developed to meet the needs of arboreal man." Indeed, the word-magic so prominent in early human cultures—the belief that the name gives power over the thing—has not declined but increased in the twentieth century, thanks to the ability of the "symbolic apparatus" to disseminate clichés. Whereas propaganda preyed on atavistic word madness, semantic analysis would provide a medium of communication for the needs of modern scientific men and women.[18]

At the interpersonal level, the chief danger was the mismatching of intention: "Normally, whenever we hear anything said we spring spontaneously to an immediate conclusion, namely, that the speaker is referring to what we would be referring to were we speaking the words ourselves." This conclusion they thought especially dubious where sharing ideas is the aim. Since meaning is in the mind of the beholder, the labyrinth of solipsism always looms. "In most matters, the possible treachery of words can only be controlled through definitions, and the greater the number of such alternative locutions available the less is the risk of discrepancy, provided that we do not suppose symbols to have 'mean-

17. C. K. Ogden and I. A. Richards, *The Meaning of Meaning: A Study of the Influence of Language upon Thought and of the Science of Symbolism*, 8th ed. (1923; New York: Harcourt, Brace and World, 1952), 20, 40, viii, x. Ludwig Wittgenstein, to his credit, thought it a "miserable book." "I have seldom read anything so foolish," he wrote to Russell; he thought it offered far too easy an answer. Ray Monk, *Ludwig Wittgenstein: The Duty of Genius* (New York: Free Press, 1990), 214.

18. Ogden and Richards, *Meaning of Meaning*, 15, 26, 29. See also W. Terrence Gordon, "Undoing Babel: C. K. Ogden's Basic English," *Etc.* 45 (winter 1988): 337–40, and Gordon, "From *The Meaning of Meaning* to Basic English," *Etc.* 48 (summer 1991): 165–71.

ing' on their own account, and so people the world with fictitious entities." The fear of fictions, the risk of discrepancy, the need of a scientific metalanguage, and the horror of populating the universe with anchorless meanings—these positions resound in later semantic views of both communication and its failures.

Communication for Ogden and Richards was not the coordination of action or the revelation of otherness, but a matching of minds, a *consensus in idem:* "A language transaction or a communication may be defined as a use of symbols in such a way that acts of reference occur in a hearer which are similar in all relevant respects to those which are symbolized by them in the speaker." This formulation, to be sure, makes pragmatic allowance for slippage ("similar in all relevant respects"), but the criterion of successful communication remains the identity of consciousness between speaker and hearer. Psychology therefore remains the best science for studying communication: "It is evident that the problem for the theory of communication is the delimitation and analysis of psychological contexts, an inductive problem exactly the same in form as the problems of the other sciences." Compared with other positions we will examine, theirs is squarely in the tradition of communication as contact between minds via some delicate and error-prone sign medium. Communication is as rare and fragile as crystal. Their mentalism logically entails the specter of miscommunication, for if meanings inhere not in words but in minds or references to objects, nothing can guarantee successful transit across the distance between two minds. They are the true heirs of John Locke, whose notion of communication I discuss in chapter 2. Their utopia of a concourse of consciousnesses can become the maze of isolated souls whose gestures of communication are nothing but impossible gambits. Little wonder this lonely crowd is so vulnerable to the wiles of propaganda![19]

Ogden and Richards's fear of solipsism was echoed in the modernist masterworks of the 1920s, which gives us a third conception: communication as an insurmountable barrier. Propaganda analysis was driven by the modernization of society and politics; the sense of impossibility was at the heart of literary and aesthetic modernism. One worried about one-way communication, the other about no-way communication. Dramas of interpersonal desolation, for example, are at the core of T. S. Eliot's enormously influential poem *The Waste Land* (1922). The poem's once notorious difficulty forces communication breakdown in the very act of reading and consists, in large part, of a series of tableaux of com-

19. Ogden and Richards, *Meaning of Meaning,* 15, 205, 206.

THE PROBLEM OF COMMUNICATION

munication breakdown, usually figured as sexual malfunction. The desire to connect always fails:

—Yet when we came back, late, from the hyacinth garden,
Your arms full, and your hair wet, I could not
Speak, and my eyes failed, I was neither
Living nor dead, and I knew nothing,
Looking into the heart of light, the silence.
(LINES 37–41)

I have heard the key
Turn in the door once and turn once only
We think of the key, each in his prison
Thinking of the key, each confirms a prison.
(LINES 411–14)

Kafka's posthumous *The Castle* (1926) is a novel of shadowboxing with an institutional other whose identity and motives remain forever enigmatic. For Kafka, as I will argue in chapter 5, interpersonal communication is no different from mass communication: both are broadcasts to invisible, absent, or veiled audiences. Virginia Woolf's *To the Lighthouse* (1927) probes the gendered dimension to the modernist soul box by playing the oceanlike, infinitely sympathetic and mutable consciousness of Mrs. Ramsay off the cold, scimitarlike, logical mind of Professor Ramsay. Lukács's *History and Class Consciousness,* in turn, gives a class analysis. He sees solitary selfhood not as a general existential condition but as a specifically bourgeois plight: the system of private property creates souls who know only the freedom of preying on other isolated individuals. Solipsism in philosophy is the correlate of lived conditions. "Capitalist reification brings about simultaneously an overindividualization and a mechanical objectification of people." Lukács's analysis gives us a way to see 1920s worries about isolation and propaganda as two sides of the same coin.[20] Much of the dark side of communication was first traced not in Ingmar Bergman's films or Samuel Beckett's plays, but in Weimar Germany and by writers of the lost generation. In any case, the specter of claustrophobic selfhood has resonated through the art and social thought of the twentieth century, with its accompanying fear of the impossibility of communication.

Thus far, these three visions show important continuities with the

20. Lukács, *Geschichte und Klassenbewusstsein,* 480, 507.

late nineteenth century. The dream of perfect communication through semantics recapitulates the dream of telepathy, a meeting of minds that would leave no remainder. The fear of inescapable solipsism recurs in the microdramas of modernist literature. Again, communication as bridge always means an abyss is somewhere near. And even in the propaganda view, the antinomy recurs: communication working telepathically has an evil twin in the specter of the mesmerized mass in the clutches of the leader, just as the fear of closed consciousness appears at the mass level as the fear of the lonely crowd, atomized and mutually oblivious. As I will argue in chapter 2, the dream of mental contact sets up the nightmare of mutual isolation. Longing for shared interiority, the horror of inaccessibility, and impatience with the humble means of language—these are the attitudes that "communication" typically instills and that I want to combat.

Two other visions of communication from the 1920s remain: those of Martin Heidegger and John Dewey. These are paths less taken but are fertile sources of communication theory that I want to rehabilitate. Despite their profound differences, each rejects the mentalist vision and its accompanying subjectivization of meaning; each makes an end run around the solipsism/telepathy couplet. Heidegger's *Being and Time* (1927), perhaps the single most influential work in twentieth-century philosophy, announced its distaste for any notion of communication as mental sharing: "Communication [*Mitteilung*] is never anything like a transportation of experiences, such as opinions and wishes, from the interior of one subject into the interior of another."[21] The transmission of messages or assertion of facts was for Heidegger a special case; more fundamentally, *Mitteilung* is the interpretive articulation of our "thrownness" into a world together with other people. Being with others is fundamental to our existence. To be human is to be linguistic and social. Speech can make our relations explicit, but there is no question for Heidegger of communication's failing between people any more than there is of people's ceasing to dwell in societies and in language. We are bound together in existential and lived ways before we even open our mouths to speak. Communication here does not involve transmitting information about one's intentionality; rather, it entails bearing oneself in such a way that one is open to hearing the other's otherness. As in Jaspers's *Psychology of World-Views* (1919) or Buber's *I and Thou* (1923), here communication is about the constitution of relationships,

21. Martin Heidegger, *Sein und Zeit* (1927; Tübingen: Niemeyer, 1962), 162.

the revelation of otherness, or the breaking of the shells that encase the self, not about the sharing of private mental property.

Certainly communication has its dangers for Heidegger. Whereas for Ogden and Richards the chief worry is discrepancy or clouded meaning, for Heidegger it is inauthenticity. The chatter of the crowd and the brooding omnipresence of "das Man"—a coinage variously translated as the "anonymous anyone" or the "they-self"—threatens to drown out "the call of conscience" and the care (*Sorge*) of being. The dictatorship of "das Man" is inconspicuous and hard to detect, but it can swallow up authentic selfhood.[22] Heidegger claimed to be describing a perennial existential possibility in human life—the descent into distraction—but in fact it has a clear historical and political dimension. As Peter Sloterdijk puts it, "Everything we have heard about [das Man] would be, in the final analysis, inconceivable without the precondition of the Weimar Republic with its hectic postwar life feeling, its mass media, its Americanism, its entertainment and culture industry, its advanced system of distraction."[23]

The political dimension is also clear in Heidegger's disdain for the public sphere. Like his fellow Nazi Carl Schmitt, Heidegger took politics as a matter of sorting out friends and enemies, not of compromise and discussion. Government by public opinion was a prescription for the reign of chatter. In contrast to Ogden and Richards, Lippmann, and Dewey, Heidegger found the question of how to provide accurate information to the citizenry all but irrelevant. He wasted no love on the democratic public. His notion of communication was neither semantic (meanings exchanged) nor pragmatic (actions coordinated) but world disclosing (otherness opened).[24] Communication as the revelation of being to itself through language resounds variously through those influenced by Heidegger—Sartre, Levinas, Arendt, Marcuse, Leo Strauss, Derrida, Foucault, and many more. Some took his vision as an agonistics of impossible dialogue, others as a mode of authentic encounter, but no one in the Heideggerian inheritance has any time for communication as information exchange.

John Dewey, also writing in 1927, was equally concerned with distraction: "No one knows how much of the frothy excitement of life, of

22. Heidegger, *Sein und Zeit*, 126.

23. Peter Sloterdijk, *Critique of Cynical Reason*, trans. Michael Eldred (Minneapolis: University of Minnesota Press, 1987), 199.

24. Stephen K. White, *Political Theory and Postmodernism* (Cambridge: Cambridge University Press, 1992).

mania for motion, of fretful discontent, of need for artificial stimulation, is the expression of frantic search for something to fill the void caused by the loosening of bonds which hold persons together in immediate community of experience." Dewey's historical account of such froth is more precise than Heidegger's: the conquest of scale through technology and industry and the subsequent disappearance of the face-to-face community. Like Heidegger, Dewey eschewed a semantic view of language as intermental plumbing, carrying "thought as a pipe carries water." The mediation of thought by language was not dangerous, but fruitful and necessary. He viewed as folly the attempt to create a *consensus in idem* between isolated individuals, in either a spiritualist or a scientific guise. In his educational ambition, however, he was more like Ogden and Richards than Heidegger: he aimed for the reinvigoration of communication on a large scale to correct for the loss of "immediate community of experience."[25] Dewey's conception of communication as pragmatic making-do in community life represents a final strand for analysis.

Like the other pragmatists, and like Hegel, Dewey regarded the universe as more than matter and mind: it was also the worlds that open up between people. What Hegel called *Geist,* Peirce called "thirdness," and Royce called "the world of interpretation," Dewey called "experience"; in his very old age he proposed the term "culture" instead. For Dewey, communication went on in the public world of experience interwoven through shared signs and practices; it could not be reduced to reference to objects without or psychic states within. To be sure, he thought the discovery of individual private experience "great and liberating," but it was also misleading if it painted communication as the junction of two sovereign egos. With Heidegger he viewed language as the precondition of thought: "Soliloquy is the product and reflex of converse with others; social communication not an effect of soliloquy."[26] Thus solipsism would be the luxury of already socialized individuals who had forgotten their histories.

Next to his onetime colleague George Herbert Mead, Dewey is perhaps the best exemplar of a theorist of communication as partaking. Like Mead, Dewey thought the ability to place oneself "at the standpoint of a situation which two parties share" was the distinctive gift of humanity. Communication meant taking part in a collective world, not sharing the secrets of consciousness. It involved the establishment of

25. John Dewey, *The Public and Its Problems* (New York: Henry Holt, 1927), 214; Dewey, *Experience and Nature,* ed. Jo Ann Boydston (1925; Carbondale: Southern Illinois University Press, 1988), 134.
26. Dewey, *Experience and Nature,* 136, 135.

a setting in which "the activity of each is regulated and modified by partnership." Meaning was not private property: rather, meaning was a "community of partaking," "method of action, "way of using things as a means to a shared consummation" or "possible interaction."[27] Misunderstanding meant upset interaction, not minds failing to meld. Dewey's analysis features the smoothness with which things get done in language: we attend meetings, play games, pay bills, arrange rides, make promises, and get married. The splendid weirdness of being (Heidegger) or the danger of populating the universe with fictions (Ogden and Richards) seems remote indeed from the busy world of Mr. Dewey. Yet Dewey is quite close to Heidegger's term *Mitteilung: mit* = with, *teilen* = to share or divide. Communication in Dewey's sense is participation in the creation of a collective world, which is why communication for Dewey always raises the political problem of democracy.[28]

Dewey took the disappearance or distortion of participatory interaction as the most alienating feature of the age. Heidegger's notion of the fall from authentic encounter was not entirely different. The notion that grace is found in dialogue was widely shared in social thinkers of the 1920s: Buber wanted to replace I-It relationships with I-Thou ones; Heidegger called for authentic confrontations; Lukács called for a joyful reconciliation of subject and object. That face-to-face dialogue or at least confrontation offered a way out from the crusts of modernity is one of the key themes in thinking about communication since the 1920s, in antimodern thinkers such as Wittgenstein, Arendt, and Levinas, all of whom recognize the ultimate impossibility of dialogue, and in a host of lesser figures who do not.

In sum, five intertwined visions are clear in the 1920s: communication as the management of mass opinion; the elimination of semantic fog; vain sallies from the citadel of the self; the disclosure of otherness; and the orchestration of action. Each captures a particular practice. The variety of visions may be due in part to the variety of practices. Heidegger wants uncanny poetry in the woods, Ogden and Richards want universal clarity of meaning, Dewey wants practical participation and aesthetic release, Kafka narrates nightmares of interpersonal asymptotes, and Bernays wants to manufacture goodwill as Hitler wants to manufacture bad will. Heidegger's celebration of language's uncanniness lives on in deconstruction's repeated exposé of the impossibility of communication; Ogden and Richard's project survives in semantics and in the cul-

27. Dewey, *Experience and Nature*, 140, 141, 146, 147, 148.
28. John Durham Peters, "Democracy and American Mass Communication Theory: Dewey, Lippmann, Lazarsfeld," *Communication* 11, 3 (1989): 199–220.

ture of scientific research more generally and informs what is probably still the dominant view of communication, the successful replication of intentions; and Dewey's vision anticipates language pragmatics and speech act theory's interest in language's seemingly modest, but astounding, ability to bind people in action. For Heidegger communication revealed our simultaneous togetherness/otherness as social beings; for Ogden and Richards it allowed a clean meeting of minds; and for Dewey it sustained the building of community and the dance of creation.

Each of these five views is also anticipated in earlier doctrines. Communication as propaganda was famously captured in the quip of Juvenal, the Roman satirist, that it takes nothing more than *panem et circenses* to satisfy the masses—bread and circuses.[29] The dream of mental conjunction via semantic agreement was traced by John Locke, and the dream of shared consciousness reaches to medieval angelology and mysticism. The breakdown of communication was explored by Kierkegaard and Emerson, and Hegel saw communication as the staking of an existential claim to recognition as a human among other humans. Finally, communication as the coordination of action appears in the British empiricists and is a central theme in pragmatism before Dewey's *Experience and Nature*.[30] The 1920s serve as a window for both what has come since and what went before.

Today the most influential thinkers about communication are probably Jürgen Habermas and Emmanuel Levinas. Certainly each has much of originality. But their lineages are clear enough. Habermas, like Dewey (though it is Mead he more frequently invokes), takes communication as a mode of action that not only implicates a morally autonomous self but is also a process that, if generalized, entails the creation of a democratic community. Habermas is emphatic that communication is not the sharing of consciousness but rather the coordination of action oriented to deliberation about justice. The term has for him an undeniable normative tint.[31] Levinas, in turn, builds on the phenomenological inheritance of Husserl and Heidegger to understand communication not as fusion, information exchange, or conjoint activity but as a caress.

29. A richer genealogy can be found in Salvador Giner, *Mass Society* (New York: Academic Press, 1976).

30. For an empiricist forerunner, see George Berkeley, *The Principles of Human Knowledge* (1710), section 20: "Besides, the communicating of ideas marked by words is not the chief and only end of language, as is commonly supposed. There are other ends, such as the raising of some passion, the exciting to or deterring from an action, the putting the mind in some particular disposition."

31. See especially Jürgen Habermas, *Theory of Communicative Action,* trans. Thomas McCarthy, 2 vols. (1981; Boston: Beacon Press, 1987).

The failure to communicate is not a moral failure, it is a fitting demise for a flawed project. As he wrote in 1947 of modernist isolation: "The theme of solitude and the breakdown of human communication are viewed by modern literature and thought as the fundamental obstacle to human brotherhood. The pathos of socialism breaks against the eternal Bastille in which each person remains his own prisoner, locked up with himself when the party is over, the crowd gone, and the torches extinguished. The despair felt at the impossibility of communication . . . marks the limits of all pity, generosity, and love. . . . But if communication bears the mark of failure or inauthenticity in this way, it is because it is sought as a fusion."[32] The failure of communication, he argues, allows precisely for the bursting open of pity, generosity, and love. Such failure invites us to find ways to discover others besides knowing. Communication breakdown is thus a salutary check on the hubris of the ego. Communication, if taken as the reduplication of the self (or its thoughts) in the other, deserves to crash, for such an understanding is in essence a pogrom against the distinctness of human beings.

The task today, I will argue, is to renounce the dream of communication while retaining the goods it invokes. To say that communication in the sense of shared minds is impossible is not to say that we cannot cooperate splendidly. (This was precisely Dewey's point.) On the other hand, to point to the pervasiveness of pragmatic coordination is also not to say that no abysses loom in the self and the other. (This was precisely Heidegger's point.) Habermas, to my taste, underplays the strangeness of language; his French foes such as Derrida (himself importantly influenced by Levinas) underplay its instrumentality. Each of the Dewey-Habermas and Heidegger-Levinas-Derrida lineages grasps important truths about communication that are inaccessible to the propagandists, semanticists, and solipsists in our midst, but neither has quite the full palette of colors. The one position has too much gravity while the other floats in a zero-gravity chamber. Habermas's sobriety misses what Charles Sanders Peirce called the play of musement; Derrida's revelry misses the ordinariness of talk.

The task is to find an account of communication that erases neither the curious fact of otherness at its core nor the possibility of doing things with words. Language is resistant to our intent and often, in Heidegger's phrase, speaks us; but it is also the most reliable means of persuasion we know. Though language is a dark vessel that does not quite

32. Emmanuel Levinas, "The Other in Proust" (1947), in *The Levinas Reader*, ed. Seán Hand (Oxford: Blackwell, 1989), 164.

carry what I, as a speaking self, might think it does, it still manages to coordinate action more often than not. This middle position is represented in recent debates by Paul Ricoeur and Hans-Georg Gadamer, but I also want to identify it with a pragmatism open to both the uncanny and the practical. Pragmatism, in its Emersonian lineage, remembers both the wildness of the signs and tokens around us and the massively practical fact that we must find ways to get on with business. Dewey and Habermas know the latter but generally forget the former, an oblivion that stains their vision of democracy through dialogue.

Technical and Therapeutic Discourses after World War II

A key feature of 1920s thinking was the lack of any distinction between face-to-face and mass communication. "Mass media," a term freshly minted in the 1920s, constituted a vague horizon: the shadow of "the symbolic apparatus" (Ogden and Richards), "distraction" (Heidegger), "instrumentalities of communication" (Dewey), "advertising mediums" (Bernays), or "chains of silver" (Lasswell) loomed. The idea of "mass media" as a distinct field of institutional and discursive activity, however, had not yet appeared. "Communication" was a term without specifications of scale. It could occur in mass education or in a dyad. In the 1930s, the basis for contrast between mass communication and interpersonal communication began to develop; communication began to split off from communications. The 1930s saw the rise of an empirically oriented social research tradition—often with commercial relevance—on the content, audiences, and effects of new mass media, especially radio, Paul F. Lazarsfeld being the key figure; a sustained body of social theory and social criticism, much of it concerned with communication and its distortion in mass culture, from the German Jewish émigrés of the Frankfurt school; and the brief heyday of propaganda analysis, which aimed to slice through the cognitive smokescreens abroad in the land. Though characteristic attitudes developed in the 1930s about the social meaning of the mass media—as relatively harmless providers of entertainment or powerful consciousness industries—and much work of importance was done in addition to that mentioned, such as in Antonio Gramsci's *Prison Notebooks,* Q. D. Leavis's *Fiction and the Reading Public* (1932), Dewey's *Art and Experience* (1934), Rudolf Arnheim's *Radio* (1936), and works by Kenneth Burke, the next explosion of intellectual and public interest in "communication" came after the war.

The late 1940s was probably the single grandest moment in the century's confrontation with communication. One source was the excitement around information theory (originally in fact known as communication theory). Information theory developed from what might be called the "information practice" of telecommunications, specifically from research on telephony at Bell Laboratories starting in the 1920s and on cryptography during the war. Claude Shannon's *Mathematical Theory of Communication* (1948) was many things to many people.[33] It gave scientists a fascinating account of information in terms of the old thermodynamic favorite, entropy, gave AT&T a technical definition of signal redundancy and hence a recipe for "shaving" frequencies in order to fit more calls on one line, and gave American intellectual life a vocabulary well suited to the country's newly confirmed status as military and political world leader. "Communication theory" was explicitly a theory of "signals" and not of "significance." But as the terms diffused through intellectual life—and they did so at violent speed—these provisos were little heeded.[34] "Information" became a substantive and communication theory became an account of meaning as well as of channel capacity. Indeed, the theory may have seemed so exciting because it made something already quite familiar in war, bureaucracy, and everyday life into a concept of science and technology. Information was no longer raw data, military logistics, or phone numbers; it was the principle of the universe's intelligibility.

One consequence of the impure diffusion of information theory was the rewriting of the great chain of being. On the smallest level, where the secrets of life are "coded, stored, and transmitted," we find J. D. Watson and F. H. Crick, discoverers of the double helix, viewing DNA as a code of genetic information. Neural synapses became switchboards and nerves telephone lines (reversing the metaphor from that of the nineteenth century, when telegraphs and telephones were "nerves"); messenger RNA proteins were dubbed "informosomes." Moving up the chain, hormones and enzymes were couriers and the brain an "information processor." In the social world, we learned that marriages will work better when men and women "communicate more" and "share information about their feelings" with each other; that good managers must communicate effectively (that is, share information) with employees; and internationally, that better flows of information between nations

33. Claude Shannon, *The Mathematical Theory of Communication* (Urbana: University of Illinois, 1949). Warren Weaver is listed as a coauthor, but the theory was Shannon's. The more socially astute text of the same moment was Norbert Wiener, *Cybernetics; or Communication and Control in the Animal and Machine* (New York: Wiley, 1948).
34. For the diffusion of information theory, see Randall Louis Dahling, "Shannon's Information Theory: The Spread of an Idea" (master's thesis, Stanford University, 1957).

aid worldwide peace and understanding. From the blueprint of life itself to the world political order, communication and information reigned supreme.

The academy is another clear example of the infiltration of the discourse of information. Several specialties define themselves in terms of the production, manipulation, and interpretation of information: computer science, electrical engineering, statistics, expository writing, library science, psycholinguistics, management science, and much of economics, journalism, and communication research. (People studying communication still sometimes have to explain that they are not in electrical engineering.) The recent booming interdisciplinary confluence under the name "cognitive science" would not be possible, one senses, without *information* as intellectual connective tissue. Some have gone so far as to suggest that all inquiry into human affairs should redescribe itself in terms of a new trinity of concepts: information, communication, and control.[35] Such schemes are the latest in the dream of unified science that runs from René Descartes to Rudolf Carnap; information was a stimulant to such dreams, just as geometry, evolution, thermodynamics, statistics, and mathematical physics each, in its heyday, promised to unify all human knowledge. The postwar fallout of information theory is still with us.

Resulting from this heady mix was a notion of communication as information exchange, a notion most closely related to the semantic view of Ogden and Richards and more distantly related to the long angelological tradition of instantaneous contact between minds at a distance. More important, this new view effaced the old barriers between human, machine, and animal. Anything that processed information was a candidate for "communication." The wild shape of this category is evident in the first paragraph of a text that did much to make information theory available for interdisciplinary poaching, Ford Foundation physicist Warren Weaver's commentary on Shannon:

The word *communication* will be used here in a very broad sense to include all the procedures by which one mind may affect another. This, of course, involves not only written and oral speech, but also music, the pictorial arts, the theatre, the ballet, and in fact all human behavior. In some connections it may be desirable to use a still broader definition of communication, namely, one which would include the proce-

35. James R. Beniger, *The Control Revolution* (Princeton: Princeton University Press, 1986). My critique: John Durham Peters, "The Control of Information," *Critical Review: A Journal of Books and Ideas* 1, 4 (1987): 5–23.

dures by means of which one mechanism (say automatic equipment to track an air-plane and compute its probable future positions) affects another mechanism (say a guided missile chasing this airplane).[36]

An extraordinary category, this, including music and missiles, speech and servomechanisms. Weaver takes us from the preferred communication situation of the semanticists (one mind affecting another) through language and the fine arts to human behavior (the ride is getting bumpy). Then he "broadens" his definition to include Korean War–vintage military technology. What made this string of sentences, this patch of discourse, intelligible—and exciting—to so many thinkers in the 1950s? For one thing, it fit the age. The two great technologies of the Second World War—the computer and the bomb—share more than a common origin. They share a common cultural space and symbolism. Information is often spoken of in nuclear terms: its half-life (as it decays like radioactive matter), its fission, and its molecular or granular quality. It shares semiotic space with subatomic physics, coming in bits, flashes, bursts, and impulses, and is often treated as mental photons: the minimal quanta of the cognitive stuff. Both the bomb and information cater to a secret pleasure in possible apocalypse, the exhilaration moderns (so used to the thrill of the new) feel in contemplating self-destruction. The computer stands at the latest moment of history and the bomb at the last one.

Less speculatively, communication was a concept able to unify the natural sciences (DNA as the great code), the liberal arts (language as communication), and the social sciences (communication as the basic social process, as Wilbur Schramm put it). By finally removing communication as an activity from any privileged anchor in the human body or soul, communication became a site for exploring posthuman couplings with aliens, animals, and machines (chapter 6). Ordinary interaction seems a frail and inadequate attempt to reach across the void compared with the speed and accuracy of servomechanisms. But the quest for authentic connection with other people, perhaps as if in compensation, was also of huge cultural moment. Communication as therapeutic self-expression, a warmed-over descendant of the existentialist call for authentic disclosure, also spread through the culture like wildfire after the war.

The therapeutic project forms the second site of the postwar buoy-

36. Warren Weaver, "Recent Contributions to the Mathematical Theory of Communication," in *The Mathematical Theory of Communication,* by Claude Shannon and Warren Weaver (1949; Urbana: University of Illinois Press, 1964), 1.

ancy about communication. As in Ogden and Richards, "communication" here was a dream of a clarifying method that would work at both interpersonal and international levels. More specifically, the formation of the United Nations, especially UNESCO, gave some intellectuals enormous hope about "communication" as an agent of global enlightenment. Psychiatrist Harry Stack Sullivan, who coined the term "interpersonal" in 1938, worked at UNESCO with the idea that the same kinds of disturbances that inhibited communication between two or a few people could also be treated on a much larger scale.[37] Julian Huxley, biologist and first leader of UNESCO, had the dream of employing mass media to spread secular scientific humanism (as a successor to religion) across the globe.[38] Gregory Bateson, who had feet in both the cybernetic excitement of information theory and the psychiatric vision of communication as therapy, is another key figure.[39]

Carl R. Rogers, the leader of person-centered, humanistic psychology in the postwar era, is perhaps the best example of a therapeutic theorist of communication. As he put it in a talk given in 1951, "The whole task of psychotherapy is the task of dealing with a failure in communication." Communication breakdown for him was the fate of the neurotic, whose communication both with himself and with others was in some way damaged—blockage of communication occurring between the unconscious and the ego, for instance. "The task of psychotherapy is to help the person achieve, through a special relationship with a therapist, good communication within himself." Good communication with others would follow. As Rogers summarized, "We may say then that psychotherapy is good communication, between and within men. We may also turn that statement around and it will still be true. Good communication, free communication, within or between men, is always therapeutic."

Rogers's argument mixes a rigorous recognition of the real difficulty of taking the place of the other together with the happier therapeutic talk of mutual understanding that a whole culture industry would later make pervasive. A chief virtue required for good communication, he argued, was the courage to get out of one's emotion-laden private perspective and restate the views of one's opponent; this is exactly the stan-

37. Harry Stack Sullivan, *The Interpersonal Theory of Psychiatry*, ed. Helen Swick Perry and Mary Ladd Gawel (New York: Norton, 1953).

38. Julian S. Huxley, *UNESCO: Its Purpose and Philosophy* (Washington, D.C.: Public Affairs Press, 1948).

39. An able treatment of the intellectual and political scene of the American social sciences in the postwar era, and of the formative years of cybernetics in particular, is Steve Joshua Heims, *The Cybernetics Group* (Cambridge: MIT Press, 1991).

dard that John Stuart Mill laid down for public discussion in his *On Liberty* (1859) and a piece of practical advice offered in communication seminars ever since. Rogers recommended expanding the method of small group understanding to much larger forums, such as the strained relations between the Americans and the Russians (this is a cold war text, of course). If both parties attempted to understand rather than to judge, important political fruit might result. An all but messianic vision of therapeutic communication as the balm of souls, couples, groups, and nations pervades the text: putting it to use, he suggested, was worth trying, given "the tragic and well-nigh fatal failures of communication which threaten the existence of our modern world."[40]

As with information theory, high hopes about communication as an agent of global education and therapy were accompanied by a foreboding sense of danger, the "well-nigh fatal failures" that Rogers had in mind. Postwar communication theory was decisively shaped, at least in its social-scientific guise, by the cold war. In the 1950s, specters of lonely selves and manipulated masses reappeared in texts confronting the postwar prosperity and its centerpiece, television. As in the 1920s, part of the story was the fear that communication could go bad, mesmerizing masses or isolating individuals. The telescreens and Big Brother in Orwell's *1984* (1948) have become staples in commentary on the meaning of mass media, but similar concerns can be found in David Riesman, *The Lonely Crowd* (1950), C. Wright Mills, *The Power Elite* (1956), Günther Anders, *Die Antiquiertheit des Menschen* (1956), Richard Hoggart, *The Uses of Literacy* (1957), Hannah Arendt, *The Human Condition* (1958), Aldous Huxley, *Brave New World Revisited* (1958), Raymond Williams, *Culture and Society* (1958), and Jürgen Habermas, *Structural Transformation of the Public Sphere* (1962). Mass society imagery in the 1950s American intellectual life was, at one level at least, a coded version of the paranoia that it could indeed happen here: television viewers might turn out to be the secret siblings of the red zombies on the other side of the Iron Curtain, whose lifeline to liberty in this narrative was, significantly, a radio station, Voice of America (the good and evil twins of communication again). Though it is unclear whether mass society theory ever was an articulate program (in retrospect the notion seems as much the invention of its detractors as of its supposed proponents), it is not hard to identify a certain sensibility in 1950s deliberations on the state of the many in a mediated world: the democratic public as crowd;

40. Carl R. Rogers, *On Becoming A Person: A Therapist's View of Psychotherapy* (Boston: Houghton Mifflin, 1961), 330, 337.

consumer pleasures stultifying public engagement; and the five A's of mass society theory—alienation, anomie, anonymity, apathy, and atomization.

Just as the bomb shaped the imagery of information in communication theory, so it made palpable the potential of communication gone wrong. As Chicago sociologist Louis Wirth argued in his 1947 presidential address to the American Sociological Association, the effort to use mass media to create a worldwide consensus was not guaranteed to succeed: "Along with the perfection of these means of human intercourse science has also perfected unprecedented means of mass destruction. But in the case of neither the instruments of mass communication nor of atomic energy do the inventors of the instrument dictate the use to which they shall be put."[41] For both information theory and the dream of a worldwide communication therapy, the bomb was a spur to the imagination, evoking both excitement about the release of new energies and anxieties about the extermination of the species.

Not only the bomb, however, shaped communication theory; as Kenneth Cmiel has shown, the fear of democratic disaffection and the moral enigma of the Holocaust presided over efforts to think through communication in the 1940s. Cynicism and evil were the fundamental problems that Robert Merton, Hannah Arendt, and Emmanuel Levinas faced first in the 1940s, and in each case the resultant vision of communication was some kind of answer to the intractable questions. Merton saw communication as an agency of national community building; Arendt as a means of discovering truth and, later, of giving birth to new political orders; and Levinas as an ethical obligation to the otherness of the other person. This threefold crossing of modernization, antimodern, and postmodern theorists is fateful for the rest of the century's social thought.[42] Merton saw communication as a kind of Durkheimian social glue; Arendt as a disclosure of the political potentials of human association; and Levinas as a respect for the autonomy of others, a respect that made communication in an instrumental sense all but impossible.

———

In the postwar ferment about "communication," then, two discourses were dominant: a technical one about information theory and a thera-

41. Louis Wirth, "Consensus and Mass Communication," *American Sociological Review* 13 (February 1948): 1–15.

42. Kenneth Cmiel, "On Cynicism, Evil, and the Discovery of Communication in the 1940s," *Journal of Communication* 46, 3 (1996): 88–107.

peutic one about communication as cure and disease. Each has deep roots in American cultural history. The technicians of communication are a diverse breed, from Samuel F. B. Morse to Marshall McLuhan, from Charles Horton Cooley to Al Gore, from Buckminster Fuller to Alvin Toffler, but they all think the imperfections of human interchange can be redressed by improved technology or techniques. They want to mimic the angels by mechanical or electronic means. When AT&T boasted a few years back that "telecommunity is our goal; telecommunications is our means," it stated the technical vision of communication with remarkable economy. The therapeutic vision of communication, in turn, developed within humanist and existentialist psychology, but both its roots and its branches spread much wider, to the nineteenth-century attack on Calvinism and its replacement by a therapeutic ethos of self-realization, and to the self-culture pervading American bourgeois life.[43] Both the technical and therapeutic visions claim that the obstacles and troubles in human contact can be solved, whether by better technologies or better techniques of relating, and hence are also latter-day heirs to the angelological dream of mutual ensoulment.

The message of this book is a harsher one, that the problems are fundamentally intractable. "Communication," whatever it might mean, is not a matter of improved wiring or freer self-disclosure but involves a permanent kink in the human condition. In this James was right. That we can never communicate like the angels is a tragic fact, but also a blessed one. A sounder vision is of the felicitous impossibility of contact. Communication failure, again, does not mean we are lonely zombies searching for soul mates: it means we have new ways to relate and to make worlds with each other. My emphasis on the debt that the dream of communication owes to ghosts and strange eros is intended as a corrective to a truism that is still very much alive: that the expansion of means leads to the expansion of minds.

The therapists miss the eccentricity of the self to itself and the public character of signs. They imagine the self as a holder of private experiential property and language as a courier of its messages. Their cure is often

43. See Christopher Lasch, *Haven in a Heartless World: The Family Besieged* (New York: Basic Books, 1977); Lasch, *The Culture of Narcissism* (New York: Norton, 1979); Lasch, *The Minimal Self* (New York: Norton, 1984); Ann Douglas, *The Feminization of American Culture* (New York: Knopf, 1977); T. J. Jackson Lears, *No Place of Grace: Antimodernism and the Transformation of American Culture* (New York: Pantheon, 1981); and Lears, "From Salvation to Self-Realization: Advertising and the Therapeutic Roots of the Consumer Culture, 1880–1930," in *The Culture of Consumption: Essays in American History, 1880–1980,* ed. Richard Wightman Fox and T. J. Jackson Lears (New York: Pantheon, 1983). A fine recent radical critique of therapeutic culture in the United States is Dana L. Cloud, *Control and Consolation in American Culture and Politics: Rhetoric of Therapy* (Thousand Oaks, Calif.: Sage, 1998).

as bad as the disease. As Theodor W. Adorno wrote, "No less indiscriminate and general than the alienation between people is the longing to breach it."[44] The technicians, in turn, miss finitude, the fact that any prosthesis meant to restore damaged communication will be an imperfect fit that chafes the stump. As Kafka notes in an epigraph to this book, those who build new media to eliminate the spectral element between people only create more ample breeding grounds for the ghosts. A cheerful sense of the weirdness of all attempts at communication offers a far saner way to think and live. The achievements that technical and therapeutic talk usually ascribes to "communication"—understanding, cooperation, community, love—are genuine human goods. Even information exchange is indispensable, in its place. But the attainment of communicative goods can never be easy or formulaic; so much depends on dumb luck, personality, place, and time.

Communication, in the deeper sense of establishing ways to share one's hours meaningfully with others, is sooner a matter of faith and risk than of technique and method. In the thinner sense of tuning to the same frequency, the concept is ultimately unhelpful as a solution to our most vexing puzzles. It makes knowing into the governor of our dealings with others. It puts the burden on husbands and wives, diplomats and colleagues to dial in: yet once the parties face each other in the same language, the adventure has not ended, but only begun. The dream of communication stops short of all the hard stuff. Sending clear messages might not make for better relations; we might like each other less the more we understood about one another. The transmission of signals is an inadequate metaphor for the interpretation of signs. "Communication" presents itself as an easy solution to intractable human troubles: language, finitude, plurality. Why others do not use words as I do or do not feel or see the world as I do is a problem not just in adjusting the transmission and reception of messages, but in orchestrating collective being, in making space in the world for each other. Whatever "communication" might mean, it is more fundamentally a political and ethical problem than a semantic one, as I argue with respect to Hegel and Marx (chapter 3). In renouncing the dream of "communication" I am not saying that the urge to connect is bad; rather, I mean that the dream itself inhibits the hard work of connection. This book bids us out of Wittgenstein's fly-bottle. Too often, "communication" misleads us from the task of building worlds together. It invites us into

44. Theodor W. Adorno, *Minima Moralia: Reflections from Damaged Life*, trans. E. F. N. Jephcott (1944–51; London: Verso, 1974), 178.

a world of unions without politics, understandings without language, and souls without bodies, only to make politics, language, and bodies reappear as obstacles rather than blessings.

Instead, the most wonderful thing about our contact with each other is its free dissemination, not its anguished communion. The ultimate futility of our attempts to "communicate" is not lamentable; it is a handsome condition. The notion of communication deserves to be liberated from its earnestness and spiritualism, its demand for precision and agreement, demands whose long history I attempt to illustrate in this book. The requirement of interpersonal mimesis can be despotic. Ralph Waldo Emerson and William James struck the right note: acknowledging the splendid otherness of all creatures that share our world without bemoaning our impotence to tap their interiority. The task is to recognize the creature's otherness, not to make it over in one's own likeness and image. The ideal of communication, as Adorno said, would be a condition in which the only thing that survives the disgraceful fact of our mutual difference is the delight that difference makes possible.

ONE

Dialogue and Dissemination

In certain quarters dialogue has attained something of a holy status. It is held up as the summit of human encounter, the essence of liberal education, and the medium of participatory democracy. By virtue of its reciprocity and interaction, dialogue is taken as superior to the one-way communiqués of mass media and mass culture. In 1956 the psychiatrist Joost Meerloo voiced a complaint against television that recurs like the locust with every new medium: "The view from the screen doesn't allow for the freedom-arousing mutuality of communication and discussion. Conversation is the lost art."[1] Leo Lowenthal likewise singled out the media: "True communication entails a communion, a sharing of inner experience. The dehumanization of communication has resulted from its annexation by the media of modern culture—by the newspapers first, and then by radio and television."[2] Media, of course, have long served as scapegoats for worries, many of them quite legitimate, about unaccountable power or cultural debasement. Criticism of the media for perpetuating structural inequalities and spiritual tawdriness is both perfectly fair and urgently needed. But such criticism ought not to overlook the inequalities that exist outside media or the tawdriness that fills our hearts unbidden.

---

1. Joost A. M. Meerloo, *The Rape of the Mind: The Psychology of Thought Control, Menticide, and Brainwashing* (1956; New York: Grosset and Dunlap, 1961), 210.
2. Leo Lowenthal, "Communication and Humanitas," in *The Human Dialogue: Perspectives on Communication*, ed. Floyd W. Matson and Ashley Montagu (New York: Free Press, 1967), 336. Obviously, dialogism has an elective affinity with the self-definition of professional humanist educators.

To blame media for distorting dialogue is to misplace pathos. First, media critique has bigger fish to fry: the concentrations of political economy and the inherent list to perversity in human appetites. Second, media can sustain diverse formal arrangements. It is a mistake to equate technologies with their societal applications. For example, "broadcasting" (one-way dispersion of programming to an audience that cannot itself broadcast) is not inherent in the technology of radio; it was a complex social accomplishment (see chapter 5). The lack of dialogue owes less to broadcasting technologies than to interests that profit from constituting audiences as observers rather than participants. Third and most important, dialogue can be tyrannical and dissemination can be just, as I will argue throughout this chapter. The distortion of dialogue is not only a form of abuse but one of the distinctive features of civilization, for better and for worse. Distortions of dialogue make it possible to communicate across culture, across space and time, with the dead, the distant, and the alien.

The strenuous standard of dialogue, especially if it means reciprocal speech acts between live communicators who are present to each other in some way, can stigmatize a great deal of the things we do with words. Much of culture is not necessarily dyadic, mutual, or interactive. Dialogue is only one communicative script among many. The lament over the end of conversation and the call for refreshed dialogue alike miss the virtues inherent in nonreciprocal forms of action and culture. Life with others is as often a ritual performance as a dialogue. Dialogue is a bad model for the variety of shrugs, grunts, and moans that people emit (among other signs and gestures) in face-to-face settings. It is an even worse normative model for the extended, even distended, kinds of talk and discourse necessary in large-scale democracy. Much of culture consists of signs in general dispersion, and felicitous communication—in the sense of creating just community between two or more creatures— depends more basically on imagination, liberty, and solidarity among the participants than on equal time in the conversation. Dialogue, to be sure, is one precious part of our tool-kit as talking animals, but it ought not to be elevated to sole or supreme status.

Rather than survey contemporary dialogians (a term to rhyme with theologians) and their intellectual roots—the various liberals, communitarians, Deweyans, Habermasians, radical democrats, plus occasional postmodernists and feminists (not necessarily mutually exclusive categories, these) who prescribe conversation for our political and cultural woes—my plan in this chapter is to sketch a deep horizon against which to set contemporary controversies. In staging a debate between the greatest proponent of dialogue, Socrates, and the most enduring voice for dissemination, Jesus, I aim to rediscover both the subtleties of what can count as dialogue and the blessedness of nondialogic forms, including dissemination. The rehabilitation of dissemination is not intended as an apology for the commissars and bureaucrats who issue edicts without deliberation or consultation; it is to go beyond the often uncritical celebration of dialogue to inquire more closely into what kinds of communicative forms are most apt for a democratic polity and ethical life.

Socrates and Jesus are the central figures in the moral life of the Western world. Their points of contact and difference have long been debated. They were both ironists or counterquestioners; martyrs whose kingdom was not of this world; teachers from whom we possess not a single word unrefracted by the interests of their disciples; and consequently personalities whose historical actuality has aroused enormous puzzlement and interest. Both of them taught about love and the dispersion of seeds, but to different effects. "Socrates" in Plato's *Phaedrus* offers one horizon of thinking about human discursive activity since then: the erotic life of dialogue. Parables attributed to "Jesus" by the synoptic Gospels provide a countervision: invariant and open dissemination, addressed to whom it may concern. These two conceptions of communication—tightly coupled dialogue and loosely coupled dissemination—continue today. The *Phaedrus* calls for an intimate love that links lover and beloved in a reciprocal flow; the parable of the sower calls for a diffuse love that is equally gracious to all. For Socrates, dialogue between philosopher and pupil is supposed to be one-on-one, interactive, and live, unique and nonreproducible. In the synoptic Gospels of Matthew, Mark, and Luke (I take up John later), the Word is scattered uniformly, addressed to no one in particular, and open in its destiny. Socrates sees writing as troubling delivery and cultivation: his vision is sender oriented. The question for him is the care of the seeds and their proper nurturing, not what the recipient might add to the process. Jesus, in contrast, offers a receiver-oriented model in which the sender has no control over the harvest. The pervasive sense of communication disturbance in the twentieth century, I argue, finds a wellspring in the Socratic privilege of soul-to-soul connection and an antidote of sorts in Jesus' sense of the necessary looseness of any communicative coupling.

My aim here is to contrast two *Grundbegriffe* in communication theory, dialogue and dissemination, as they have since taken historically effective shape in European thought. The focus is not the historical Socrates or Jesus but rather the afterlife of these figures in specific texts written by their canonical disciples, Plato and the synoptic evangelists.

Plato may have invented much of Socrates as he lives today, and Jesus of Nazareth's doctrinal originality may fade once placed in the context of first-century nascent rabbinical culture, but my focus is the intellectual and moral shadow those personages have cast, not their precise historicity. In the fusion of horizons I hope to orchestrate, the point is less to illuminate Plato or the Gospels than to let them instruct us, by their distance and familiarity. Thus we may discover what it might look like if we took communication theory seriously as an open field for reflection.

Dialogue and Eros in the Phaedrus

Nominating Plato as a source of communication theory might seem simply an act of grasping for a noble lineage if the *Phaedrus* were not so astoundingly relevant for understanding the age of mechanical reproduction. There is a partial precedent for this argument.[3] Eric Havelock has argued that Plato's work should be read against the transition in Greek culture from a dying world of orality to a nascent one of literacy. Since then many have taken Socrates' critique of the written word at the end of the *Phaedrus* as prophetic of worries about new media more generally, including recent tectonic shifts in forms of communication.[4] Walter J. Ong, for instance, has argued that Socrates' complaints about writing—that it diminishes memory, lacks interaction, disseminates at random, and disembodies speakers and hearers—are similar to late twentieth-century worries about computers as well as fifteenth-century concerns about printing.[5] The deprivation of presence, in one way or another, has always been the starting point of reflection about communication, and the *Phaedrus* has taken its place as the Platonic text most likely to be studied by those interested in media today.

Taken as a whole, the *Phaedrus* is much more than a compendium of anxieties about technology's effects on human intercourse. The critique of the written word is only part of a larger analysis of the gaps in soul

3. In 1935 Paul Lazarsfeld claimed the *Phaedrus* for social research: "The Art of Asking Why," in *Public Opinion and Propaganda: A Book of Readings,* ed. Daniel Katz (New York: Dryden Press, 1954), 675. Other invocations of the *Phaedrus* in mass communication theory include Paul F. Lazarsfeld, *Continuities in the Language of Social Research* (New York: Free Press, 1972), 153; Robert K. Merton, *Mass Persuasion: The Social Psychology of a War Bond Drive* (New York: Harper, 1946), 108; and Lowenthal, "Communication and Humanitas," 338–40.

4. Eric Alfred Havelock, *Preface to Plato* (Cambridge: Harvard University Press, 1963). An illuminating discussion, focusing on book 10 of Plato's *Republic* rather than the *Phaedrus,* is Alexander Nehamas, "Plato and the Mass Media," *Monist* 71 (1988): 214–34.

5. Walter J. Ong, *Orality and Literacy: The Technologizing of the Word* (London: Routledge, 1982), 79–81.

and desire that inform any act of communication. By focusing on the problem of when one should yield to or abstain from a suitor's entreaties and exalting an erotically charged but disembodied union of souls, "Socrates" explicitly articulates what is implicit in most twentieth-century worries about communication: the fierce longing for contact with an untouchable other. In the *Phaedrus* the question is not about media, but about love; not techniques, but mutuality. The dialogue's sensitivity to the wrinkles in new forms of inscription grows from an appreciation of the potential for distance and gaps between people, even in the supposedly immediate situation of face-to-face interaction. The dialogue contrasts modes of distribution (of words, of seeds, of love) that are specifically addressed and reciprocal in form to those that are indifferent to the receiver's person and one-way in form. Socrates' critique of writing is part of a larger deliberation on the varying tightness of the coupling between person and person, soul and soul, body and body. For Socrates the issue is not just the matching of minds, but the coupling of desires. Eros, not transmission, would be the chief principle of communication. In this the *Phaedrus* is far richer than the long spiritualizing trend in the intellectual history of communication theory—the dream of angel-like contact between souls at any distance—a trend that Plato, to be sure, indirectly contributes to.

The dialogue sketches both the dream of direct communication from soul to soul and the nightmare of its breakdown when transposed into new media forms. Both in its dramatic form and in its famous conclusion, the *Phaedrus* unites the hope of soul-to-soul contact with worries about its distortion. Facing the new medium of writing, Plato was haunted by multiplication, a term that ought to be taken in its double sense of simple copying and sexual reproduction.[6] Whereas oral speech almost invariably occurs as a singular event shared uniquely by the parties privy to the discussion, writing allows all manner of strange couplings: the distant influence the near, the dead speak to the living, and the many read what was intended for the few. Socrates' interpretation of the cultural and human significance of the new medium of writing is governed by worries about erotic perversion; writing disembodies thought, thus forging ghostly sorts of amatory and intellectual linkage. His sense that new media affect not only the channels of information exchange but the very embodiment of the human foreshadows similar anxieties in the nineteenth century, when the concept of "communication" first took its current shape.

6. Plato's *Seventh Letter* gives evidence specifically of Plato's interest in writing as a cultural form.

In later antiquity the *Phaedrus* was variously taken to have such central aims as "love," "rhetoric," "the soul," "the good," and "the altogether beautiful."[7] Indeed, the coherence and central theme of the work have long puzzled commentators, especially given Socrates' point in it that "any speech ought to have its own organic shape [*sōma*], like a living being; it must not be without either head or feet; it must have a middle and extremities so composed as to fit one another and the work as a whole."[8] The dialogue's first half consists of a series of three speeches of increasing splendor on the subject of love, a structuring device reminiscent of the *Symposium*. The second half concerns, in a much less elevated register, speechwriting or rhetoric, and it concludes with Socrates' famous critique of the written word. Scholars have adduced a variety of ingenious ways to account for the unity of the dialogue.[9] For my part, I read the dialogue as an analysis of communication in its normative and distorted forms that has not yet been surpassed.[10] "Great havoc he makes among our originalities," as Ralph Waldo Emerson wrote of Plato.[11]

All the themes are announced in the opening scene. Phaedrus, an eloquence junkie and impresario of the great speakers of the day—it is Phaedrus who gets the speechmaking rolling and serves as toastmaster general in the *Symposium*—happens upon Socrates outside the walls of Athens.[12] The pastoral setting of the dialogue—with its brooks, plane trees, cicadas, and grass—is described in unusual detail for Plato and is an unusual setting for Socrates, clearly a man of the city (cf. 230d); this is a place of abduction and inspiration, a place to have one's soul swept

7. Gerrit Jacob de Vries, *A Commentary on the "Phaedrus" of Plato* (Amsterdam: Hakkert, 1969), 22.
8. *Phaedrus*, 264c. Hereafter I cite the Greek text parenthetically by the standard Stephanus numbering, using the translation of Alexander Nehamas and Paul Woodruff, *Phaedrus* (Indianapolis: Hackett, 1995).
9. Jacques Derrida, *Dissemination*, trans. Barbara Johnson (Chicago: University of Chicago Press, 1981), 74–75; Mary Margaret Mackenzie, "Paradox in Plato's *Phaedrus*," *Proceedings of the Cambridge Philological Society* 28 (1982): 64–76; G. R. F. Ferrari, *Listening to the Cicadas: A Study of Plato's "Phaedrus"* (Cambridge: Cambridge University Press, 1987), 30–34; and Jesper Svenbro, *Phrasikleia: Anthropologie de la lecture en Grèce ancienne* (Paris: Éditions la Découverte, 1988), 219–38; see chart on 228. A splendid summary of the question of the unity of the *Phaedrus* and of recent scholarship generally is Alexander Nehamas and Paul Woodruff, "Introduction," in *Phaedrus* (Indianapolis: Hackett, 1995), ix–xlvii.
10. Needless to say, my reading omits much: the dialogue's intertextual resonance within Plato's opus, the architectonic use of myth, sly commentaries on historical persons, vegetation imagery, and plays on names, for instance.
11. Ralph Waldo Emerson, "Plato, or The Philosopher," in *The Selected Writings of Ralph Waldo Emerson*, ed. Brooks Atkinson (New York: Random House, 1950), 471. Great havoc Emerson thus makes among Harold Bloom's originalities.
12. The characterization of Phaedrus as an "impresario" is found in Ferrari, *Listening to the Cicadas*, 5–9.

away by words or love. When Phaedrus raves about a speech on the subject of love he has just heard that morning from Lysias, a distinguished non-Athenian resident politician and teacher of rhetoric, Socrates' interest perks up. Phaedrus offers to recite its major points, since he has not yet committed it to memory. But Socrates, who gushingly calls himself a man "who is sick with passion for hearing speeches" (228b), asks just what Phaedrus is holding in his left hand under his cloak. On discovering that he has the text of the speech tucked inside his tunic, Socrates loses interest in Phaedrus's version when he can have "Lysias himself." Here, already, the written word is figured as an erotic object, concealed close to the body.[13]

Socrates thereupon settles down to hear the discourse as a whole, which Phaedrus proceeds to read aloud. The mise-en-scène of the dialogue thus sketches the theme of the transgressive circulation of the written word, its ability to wander beyond the original context of its oral, interactive presence, just as Phaedrus and Socrates circulate outside the bounds of the city. Socrates' possibly ironic comment about "Lysias himself" being present (*parontos de kai Lusiou,* 228e) suggests the ghostly way that recording media can summon the absent. It also suggests a preference for the superior playback mechanism of the new medium of recording (writing) over the limited power of memory. The disembodied presence of an absent other turns out to be a theme of the dialogue, and of almost all thinking about communication since; so is the notion that what new media gain in fidelity, they lose by conjuring a new spirit world.

The speech by "Lysias" (a speech whose singular aptness for the purposes of the dialogue is perhaps the best evidence that it in fact is a parody composed by Plato) advances the paradox that a suitor moved not by the "madness" of love but by the calculation of self-interest should be preferred by a youth to one who is genuinely in love. Like the dialogue between Socrates and Phaedrus, the love in question is an affair between men.[14] Love is a *mania,* goes the argument, that can damage reason, friendship, reputation, and health. A coolly rational approach, by contrast, can spare both parties the sorrows of love. The suitor gains the sexual favors of a youth, and the youth gains the protection and counsel of an experienced older man. For young men of the elite classes in this era of Athenian history, the royal road to education (*paideia*) came through attachment to an older man in the institution known as

---

13. Svenbro, *Phrasikleia,* 220.

14. For a reading of the dialogue as female friendly, see Page DuBois, "Phallocentrism and Its Subversion in Plato's *Phaedrus,*" *Arethusa* 18 (1985): 91–103.

synousia. Love for Lysias can be distinguished from the concord of the lovers' souls; it is an instrumental good better handled without any accompanying frenzy.

The speech by Lysias is a rhetorical exercise, perhaps an advertisement of his argumentative powers, consciously contrary to received wisdom but perhaps vaguely reminiscent of views earlier espoused by Plato.[15] It celebrates impersonality as a rational way to avoid the madness of love. *Erastēs* (lover) and *eromenos* (beloved) should contract amicably, neither being moved by passion. For if love is the sole arbiter of one's potential lovers, the choice is restricted to the comparative few who also happen to be mutually afflicted. Calculation, in contrast, yields a much greater array of choices of potential lovers. Lysias banishes any vulnerability, passion, or loss from love. He calls for exchange over expenditure.

The dialogue again presents a double drama in which performance and content coincide: the setting of Phaedrus's reading to Socrates involves an erotic relation as lopsided as that proposed by Lysias. Phaedrus, as it happens, is the intended of Lysias. More specifically, reading for the ancient Greeks was often figured as the sexual relation between penetrator and penetrated. Since reading was almost always vocal, to write was to exert control over the voice and body of the eventual reader, even across distances in time and space.[16] To read—which meant to read aloud—was to relinquish control of one's body to the (masculine) writer, to yield to a distant dominating body. To write was to act as an *erastēs;* to read, as an *eromenos.* The writer was commonly understood to be dominating and active and the reader passive and defeated.[17] In the opening scene of the dialogue, then, an absent author, Lysias, exerts remote control over a reader's body and voice, and in the process his words come to unintended ears, those of Socrates. Writing allows distortions of address: words meant for two ears only are overheard by others. To record is to relinquish control over the confidentiality and personal destination of the message. Phaedrus's reading of words from his suitor that momentarily take possession of his physical being mirrors Lysias's argument that an asymmetrical relationship between a rational controller and a submissive beloved is best. Lysias wants to love Phae-

---

15. Martha C. Nussbaum, *The Fragility of Goodness: Luck and Ethics in Greek Tragedy and Philosophy* (Cambridge: Cambridge University Press, 1986), 203ff., argues that we miss something if we take the Lysian position on love as simply disgusting. It resembles in a distorted way middle period Platonic positions, as in the *Republic.* Clearly, however, Lysias's mode of rationalist rhetoric is distinct from Plato's mode of dialectical reason!

16. Svenbro, *Phrasikleia,* 157.

17. Svenbro, *Phrasikleia,* 213.

drus in the way a book loves its readers: openly, without regard to particularities, and for the use of the reader.

When Phaedrus finishes reading, he asks Socrates what he thinks of the speech. Socrates jokes by overpraising it, hemming and hawing when pressed, hiding his evident distaste for the speech's form and content. He coyly hints that he might know a better speech on love. Phaedrus's curiosity is aroused, and as a dealer in speeches and "father of the logos," he forces Socrates to deliver the goods, first by bribery, then by threat of force, and finally by a threat to take away Socrates' access to his abundant supply of philosophical discussion. Socrates is thus compelled to argue the superiority of the nonlover to the lover. Phaedrus thus assumes the stance of Lysias's nonloving "lover" to Socrates. "Phaedrus makes use of Socrates as an instrument, as an *instrumentum vocale* or an *organon empsukhon* [animate tool], which is to say, as an object."[18] The dramatic movement of the dialogue again mimes its topic: the conditions of the word and the mutuality of love. Can love be love when one partner is a subject and another an object? For Lysias, and Phaedrus at this point, the answer is yes.

Socrates then delivers a speech on love, with his face covered; it is unclear whether he does so to cover his embarrassment or his arousal.[19] Socrates has already complimented Phaedrus, whose name means something like "the shining one"—Martha Nussbaum translates it as "Sparkling"—on how glowing he looked while reading Lysias's speech. He begins by unmasking Lysias's speech as a ruse of a lover—not a nonlover—trying to win the affections of a youth pursued by many suitors. Socrates thus refuses to grant the premise of Lysias's speech, that such a thing as a nonloving lover is even possible. For him the stance of nonlover is a pretense, since no seduction would have been attempted without love.

Then Socrates characteristically turns to definitions. Love is desire (*epithumia*), he says (237d). There are two kinds of desire: an irrational desire for pleasure and a rational desire for excellence. Eros is the desire for physical beauty—the beauty of bodies (*sōmatōn kallos*) (238c). Eros can lead to a dangerous madness. Socrates plays along with the notion that love is destructive to the welfare of the beloved. The lover who is a slave to pleasure may twist the beloved to his own ends, not tolerating any superiority (238e). As Lysias argued, the *erastēs* either conquers or ignores the beloved's otherness. The lover may cultivate not the best

---

18. Svenbro, *Phrasikleia*, 226.
19. DuBois, "Phallocentrism," sees the veiling of Socrates as flirting with a feminine position.

but the worst in the beloved, sequestering him from philosophy and all that is good for him, making him into a sex slave. Taking a lover exposes a young man to all kinds of potential harm. When the lover is in a passionate mood, the beloved must put up with the disgusting effects of his age; when not, he risks being abandoned. Socrates paints the fickleness of love with an agile brush! Contrary to his own sensibility as a famously erotic man, here Socrates treats love as an evil, practicing the willing suspension of truth in the fine Sophist's manner. He shows his talent at argumentative stunt pilotry. His description of love gone sour—from jealousy, neglect, abuse, and refusal to allow the other autonomy—has a perennial ring.

The first two speeches are both delivered under compulsion. In the first, Phaedrus is under the spell of Lysias's text, which governs every syllable he speaks and every breath he takes. The text of the speech exerts a kind of remote control over his body. In the second, Phaedrus compels Socrates to speak against his will. Socrates even ascribes authorship of the speech to Phaedrus: though it was spoken through Socrates' mouth, it was, he claims, the result of a drug—a *pharmakon*—slipped him by Phaedrus (242e). Both are the fruit of some *pharmakon* or another: the first the written text, the second the compulsion of Phaedrus. Neither was the free or direct utterance of a soul. At stake in both is the question to whom and in what circumstances the *eromenos* should yield, a question "characteristic of an erotics conceived of as an art of give and take between the one who courts and the one who is courted."[20] Both speeches concern mutual usage without mutual love. Both enact asymmetrical communicative relations: the dictation of Lysias's text in the first speech, the dictatorship of Phaedrus's threat in the second. Both speeches strip love of sorrow and danger. Plato's implied critique of discourse here turns not on the medium (such as writing per se) but on constraints against the voluntary utterance of a soul.

Socrates, on rising to leave, is prohibited by his *daimonion* and stays to recite a third speech, a *palinode* (recantation) intended to atone for the blasphemy against the god of love done by the first two speeches. His second speech offers much of great resonance in the subsequent history of Western thought: the blessed madness of love (contra the denigration of madness in the previous two speeches); the battle among reason (*logos*), will (*thumos*), and appetite (*epithumia*) within each soul, as exemplified in the myth of the chariot pulled by a noble white steed and a base black one; the unique vocation of humans to know the eter-

20. Michel Foucault, *The Use of Pleasure,* trans. Robert Hurley (New York: Vintage, 1986), 231.

nal truths behind the passing shows; and bodily beauty as a clue to divine truth. In this great discourse, Socrates invents both a new kind of love and a new vision of communication. After two visions of systematically distorted communication, Socrates offers a conception without master or slave, dominant or subordinate—Platonic love, as we have come to call it, love without penetration. Two of the most characteristic Socratic gestures are the refusal to write and the refusal to penetrate, the latter described in Alcibiades' speech in the *Symposium*. In the *Phaedrus* we discover the intimate connection between the two refusals.[21] Both renounce asymmetrical relations. Socrates eliminates much of the customary inequality between *erastēs* and *eromenos*.[22] In contrast to the common view that symmetry in love could occur only when the heat of passion had cooled enough to allow former lovers to become asexual friends in old age, the *Phaedrus* describes a reciprocal kind of eros, the love of philosophical lovers. Philosophy, explains Socrates, is love (of wisdom); it can be pursued only with another human, one's beloved.[23] It takes two to philosophize.

In his vision of philosophical lovers collecting themselves as they recollect their divine origin, Socrates sketches an ideal of communication that retains force to this day: souls intertwined in reciprocity. This intertwining, however, is more than a melding of minds. Bodily beauty is at its heart, which Socrates views not as a hindrance to recollecting the truth, but as a reminder that transports the forgotten glory to presence. To one who has seen heavenly beauty, Socrates instructs, a beautiful face and form recall the vision. In the presence of a beautiful person, a lover who has not seen much of heaven "shudders and a fear comes over him" with such dread that he is willing to offer sacrifices to the beautiful beloved (251a). Eros is not just a beastly and sensual pulsation; it is the soul's quest to reunite with the celestial ocean of beauty. Continuing with the theme of *mania*, Socrates says the sight of the beloved bathes the lover in floods that cause his pores to begin sprouting the feathers the soul sported in its original divine state. To look upon a beautiful person is to be filled with a stream of beauty radiating from him (or *her*, we would want to add, though here Plato does not).[24] Apart from the sight of the beloved, the lover suffers a sickness, an itching

---

21. Svenbro, *Phrasikleia,* 232.

22. Foucault, *Use of Pleasure,* 239.

23. Of course, "philosophy" comes from the root of *phileo;* perhaps Socrates espouses an eros-sophy (or in more proper Greek, erotosophy).

24. Plato, with some serious stretching, can be read as a feminist; see Dubois, and the point that he was the first critic of generic masculine pronouns: Nussbaum, *Fragility,* 3–4.

longing, that only the sight and presence of the beloved can cure (251e). The lover is in a sorry state of mixed pleasure and pain. He is wounded by the sweet grief of eros. He follows the beloved about in a frenzy, forgetting everything else, dazzled by the sight. He longs for the presence of the beloved and disdains all mediation. Sexual desire thus is not demeaned as base by Socrates but considered an intimation of cosmic homesickness. As in Aristophanes' speech in the *Symposium*, love is quite literally a quest to recollect a lost wholeness.

Thus far Socrates' description of the wonderful and painful frenzy of eros focuses on the lover. The arrows of Eros fly, at first, in one direction only. But Socrates' narration soon shifts from the lover to the beloved, a reversal in point of view that makes the larger point about reciprocity. An "anteros" (or countereros) appears in the beloved to match the "eros" of the lover. Plato coins this word: the point is to make eros as reciprocal as *philia*.[25] The beloved does not know he is in love till a stream of counterlove pierces him. The stream of beauty "enters through his eyes, which are its natural route to the soul" (255c). The beloved starts to notice the tender care bestowed by the lover, and the flow starts to go both ways: "Think how a breeze or an echo bounces back from a smooth solid object to its source; that is how the stream of beauty goes back to the beautiful boy and sets him aflutter" (255c). The beloved is stunned into love but cannot at first tell exactly its source: "He does not realize that he is seeing himself in the lover as in a mirror" (255d). Socrates, whom Lacan somewhere called the inventor of psychoanalysis, describes a transference process in which subject and object are profoundly mixed up. In the lover, the beloved catches the image of his own beauty—and falls in love with the lover.

Though the relation of lover and beloved remains that between an older and a younger man, Socrates' innovation was to forward a vision of symmetry as a criterion of genuine love. A circular and symmetrical mutuality of soul sharing is near the top of the ladder. Each lover reclaims the memory of his heavenly origin in the other's beauty. Erotic love is the path of *anamnesis* (recollection); love of the other is the way to regrow one's lost heavenly wings. Whence Socrates' lame pun that *pteros*—a word combining *pteron*, wing, and *eros*—is even higher than eros (252c). Here are no one-way deals, compulsions, or manipulations. Instead, philosophical love arises from a mutual self-control in which each evokes the heavenly idea of beauty for the other. Sexual contact is not condemned by Socrates *tout court*, but it is clearly subordinate to

25. Nehamas and Woodruff, *Phaedrus*, 46 n. 115.

the higher mutuality of abstinence. Plato's Socrates, then, begins a long tradition that sees a reciprocal encounter with another person as a way to return to the homeland whence the soul has wandered, an idea that resonates in the Christian notion of *caritas,* in romantic love, in psychoanalysis, and perhaps even in the Hegelian and Marxist conviction that the basic human unit consists of two people. The other serves as the gateway to higher knowledge and as cure for heavenly *Heimweh.* Socrates treats interpersonal communication as not only a happy mode of message exchange but, at its finest, the mutual salvation of souls in each other's love beneath the blessings of heaven. This is the legacy, filtered through Christian, courtly, and romantic notions of love, against which "communication" has been measured ever since. It is an ideal both glorious and severe.

Phaedrus is bowled over by Socrates' speech. But being the sort he is, he is not interested enough in the place beyond the heavens to stay off the subject of speeches. So he asks Socrates about a recent attack on Lysias as a *logographos,* a speechwriter for those who wish to argue eloquently in the courts and political assemblies. Socrates, in contrast to the harder line of the *Gorgias,* an earlier dialogue that treats rhetoric as a minor art like cookery or cosmetics, does not condemn such word work per se, but he seeks to distinguish good from bad. "Writing speeches is not in itself a shameful thing" (258d). The possibility of a philosophic rhetoric is the manifest topic of the rest of the *Phaedrus.* The comedown from winged love to talk about rhetoric on a lazy June afternoon while the cicadas sing overheard—fallen muses now crying in heat, in the heat—is a key source of the puzzle of the dialogue's unity.

Socrates examines Lysias's speech and finds it wanting in terms of both its grasp of the truth and its fit to audience. To be an adequate speaker, one must be an adequate philosopher. Even to deceive, one needs a grasp of the truth; and to work effects on audiences, one must theoretically know the types of souls among one's listeners and also be able to recognize them in practice. Just as love should emerge from knowledge of the heavens and from conjoint philosophizing, so good rhetoric is guided by knowledge of both the truth and the audience. As a physician ought not to dispense remedies without knowing the patient's constitution, so an orator ought not to deliver words ill suited to the audience. The medicine must fit the disease, and the rhetorician must fit the tropes and *topoi* to the listeners. Medicine's subject is the body; rhetoric's is the soul (270b). Appearances are used best by those who know realities, who can medicinally dispense them to good effect. Socrates almost thinks in the demographic terms of modern media marketing: "No one will ever possess the art of speaking . . . unless he acquires the ability to enumerate the sorts of characters to be found in any audience, to divide everything according to its kinds" (273d–e). It is foolish to indiscriminately scatter words on those who will not know what to do with them. Socrates wishes to prevent disorders of address.

Socrates' views on speechmaking, then, parallel his views on love. Just as it is wrong to yield indiscriminately, it is wrong to speak words to those not suited for them. The soul of the speaker and of the hearer need to be closely knitted. Loose coupling between soul and soul, body and body, is the problem in each case. Indiscriminate dissemination is bad; intimate dialogue or prudent rhetoric that matches message and receiver is good. Speeches not appropriate to audiences can bring dangerous harvests. For Socrates the specificity with which expression fits recipient is the criterion of goodness in communication. "Spurious rhetoric turns out to be the phantom image of justice; genuine rhetoric is the science of *eros*."[26] Bad rhetoric is a parody of justice because it is blind, like justice, to the individualities of the listeners; good rhetoric is erotic because of its care for their particular souls. Rhetoric concerns the many, eros the one, but in their true forms for Socrates, both involve a reciprocal coupling of speaker and hearer, a closed communication circuit.[27] Socrates thus conceives of mass communication as a kind of dialogue writ large: no stray messages, furtive listeners, or unintended effects are allowed.

Writing, for Plato's Socrates, creates just this kind of scatter. Writing can never achieve such a fit with its audience, and in its pretense of mutual care, writing comes in for many of the same critiques as Lysias's speech on love. Writing may claim to address its reader one-on-one, but in fact it is indiscriminate in its care. Like speeches read aloud without understanding or youths exploited for sexual favors without love, writing is ignorant of soul and careless in distribution, disseminating words insouciantly. As ever, the dramatic turns of the dialogue enact the philosophical argument itself. Socrates puts the charge that writing destroys memory in the mouth of Thamus, king of Egypt, in a dialogue with Theuth, the supposed inventor of writing, one of many acts of ventriloquistic quotation in the dialogue. For it is precisely writing's ability to throw voices that Socrates sees as most suspicious, even when speaking

26. Seth Benardete, *The Rhetoric of Morality and Philosophy: Plato's "Gorgias" and "Phaedrus"* (Chicago: University of Chicago Press, 1991), 2.

27. As Aristotle says, *Rhetoric*, 1356b, the art of rhetoric concerns itself with types, not individuals.

in his own voice. The famous long passage criticizing *graphē*, writing, spells out the themes of this book:

> You know, Phaedrus, writing shares a strange feature with painting. The offsprings of painting stand there as if they are alive, but if anyone asks them anything, they remain most solemnly silent. The same is true of written words. You'd think they were speaking as if they had some understanding, but if you question anything that has been said because you want to learn more, it continues just to signify that very same thing forever. When it has once been written down, every discourse rolls about everywhere, reaching indiscriminately those with understanding no less than those who have no business with it, and it doesn't know to whom it should speak and to whom it should not. And when it is faulted and attacked unfairly, it always needs its father's support; alone it can neither defend itself nor come to its own support. (275d–e)

Socrates provides a checklist of enduring anxieties that arise in response to transformations in the means of communication. Writing parodies live presence; it is inhuman, lacks interiority, destroys authentic dialogue, is impersonal, and cannot acknowledge the individuality of its interlocutors; and it is promiscuous in distribution. Such things have been said about printing, photography, phonography, cinema, radio, television, and computers. The great virtue of the *Phaedrus* is to spell out the normative basis of the critique of media in remarkable clarity and, even more, to make us rethink what we mean by *media*. Communication must be soul-to-soul, among embodied live people, in an intimate interaction that is uniquely fit for each participant. As Lysias's speech denies the difference between a lover and a nonlover, so writing has no notion of the receiver's soul.

Socrates' critique of writing thus is not just a flourish toward the end of an elaborate dialogue, but a logical outgrowth of the argument that good and just relations among people require a knowledge of and care for souls. The paradox of writing's being denounced in a written dialogue may in fact perform the unity of the piece.[28] Distortions in communication for Socrates arise from the disappearance of a personal nexus. Because writing can live on far beyond the situation of utterance, it can mean many things for many people. The clients of sophists such as Lysias are at best transmitters, ignorant of the messages they bear. (No wonder we call one kind of contemporary Sophists ghostwriters.)

28. Mackenzie, "Paradox in Plato's *Phaedrus*"; see also Nehamas and Woodruff, "Introduction," xlvi–xlvii.

Writing lacks the shape or *sōma* necessary for genuine speech. Writing, understood on the model of love, is fundamentally unfaithful. The dilemma ever since has been how to secure the sure signs of personal fidelity or presence in an impersonal and fickle medium.

Socrates' final critique of writing returns to the erotic subtext of the dialogue by discussing the pattern in which intellectual "seeds" (*spermata*) are implanted by various modes of discourse. To write is to broadcast; to teach via dialectic is to implant in a durable medium. The man with real knowledge will, says Socrates, carefully sow his knowledge, which he compares to seeds (276c).[29] Just so, a wise farmer sows seeds where they will bear fruit and eventually reproduce; a farmer plants "gardens of Adonis" only for amusement.[30] Wise teachers, in the same way, plant their seeds in the fertile soil of the disciple's soul, whereas a foolish teacher writes them down, which is to risk scattering them abroad. One-on-one teaching is the legitimate brother to writing. It is a "discourse that is written down, with knowledge, in the soul of the listener; it can defend itself, and it knows for whom it should speak and for whom it should remain silent" (276a). For Socrates the soul is a "medium" more durable than papyrus, which explains the notion, quite curious to our ears, that oral teaching could be a kind of writing more durable than writing per se. Words written in a disciple's soul are fertile, can take root in others via oral teaching, and defend themselves in debate; written words, in contrast, are sterile and incapable of generation. Socrates wants question-and-answer intimacy rather than broadcasting; fertilization rather than panspermia.

Socrates is worried, in short, about paternity and promiscuity. The erotic word is not the problem, just the wrong kind of eros. He does not condemn writing per se any more than he condemns rhetoric. As Derrida summarizes, "The conclusion of the *Phaedrus* is less a condemnation of writing in the name of present speech than a preference for one sort of writing over another, for the fertile trace over the sterile trace, for a seed that engenders because it is planted inside over a seed scattered wastefully outside."[31] Socrates gives a patriarchal vision of the process of reproduction, inasmuch as the key question is the seed rather than the gestation; he figures philosophical instruction as a kind of reproduc-

---

29. The comparison of words and seeds is ancient: see Pierre Guiraud, *Sémiologie de la sexualité: Essai de glosso-analyse* (Paris: Payot, 1978), and Stuart Schneiderman, *An Angel Passes: How the Sexes Became Undivided* (New York: New York University Press, 1988).

30. These gardens were cultivated during Adonis's festival in early summer, the season in which the *Phaedrus* is set; they consisted of sprouts of lettuce and fennel whose short lives symbolized the short life of Adonis and the transience of beauty more generally.

31. Derrida, *Dissemination,* 149.

tion without women.[32] In contrast to the praise of dissemination we will find in parables attributed to Jesus, Socrates is alarmed at the dispersive properties of the written word. This line of argument taps into an archaic set of anxieties: secured paternity versus polymorphous promiscuity. For Socrates, as for many thinkers since, dialogue (fertile coupling) is the norm; dissemination (spilled seed) is the deviation. As elsewhere in the Platonic corpus, Socrates appropriates images of female reproduction (calling himself a midwife who delivers the ideas with which all men are pregnant) as his preferred model of intellectual birthing over the indiscriminate irresponsibility of a Lysias. In short, Socrates faces two kinds of "AI": the artificial intelligence of the written text, which simulates a caring teacher, and the artificial insemination of its distribution, which makes paternity undecidable. Writing for Socrates is something like an intellectual sperm bank: conception can occur between anonymous partners whose junction can be manipulated across great distances of space and time. The written word unleashes a cloud of idea spores that float through space, waiting to germinate and take root wherever they can. Both kinds of AI parody the full erotic presence and mutuality that Socrates calls for in philosophical lovers. With such reproduction as writing affords, distinctly personal contact between souls can never be ensured.

Writing on papyrus, as opposed to writing on souls, is for Socrates a kind of cheating eros. It pretends to be a live presence but in fact is a kind of embalmed intelligence, like the mummies of ancient Egypt, whence writing supposedly came. As with all new media, writing opens up a realm of the living dead. The papyrus may bring "Lysias" himself, but it is a Lysias who exerts an erotic spell at a distance without any possibility of interaction. Socrates would perhaps agree with John Milton, with a shiver, that "books are not absolutely dead things, but do contain a potency of life in them."[33] Here the *Phaedrus* foreshadows the blossoming of a wide array of discourses in the second half of the nineteenth century about the leakage of the human soul into new media of recording and transmission (see chapters 4 and 5). Socrates, as much as Kafka, has discovered the ghostly element between people.

Socrates' vision of communication, again, is not simply about media—the goodness of speech versus the badness of writing—but about the symmetry and tightness of the relationships in which they are em-

---

32. In his vision of male-to-male procreation, Socrates indulges in the dream of masculine *autarkeia*, or self-sufficient reproduction: see DuBois, "Phallocentrism."

33. John Milton, *Areopagitica*, Great Books of the Western World, ed. Robert Maynard Hutchins, vol. 32 (1644; Chicago: Encyclopaedia Britannica, 1952), 384.

bedded. For Plato's Socrates, the medium is not a mere channel but a whole series of relationships. The critique of writing on papyrus as opposed to writing on souls maintains the deeper theme of the dialogue: two are needed for love or wisdom. Writing, like rhetoric, can sever this mutuality, leaving behind odd parts of the whole body of discourse: words that wander abroad like dispossessed spirits or radio broadcasts transmitted to the great audience invisible. The specter of disembodiment, like the ghostly Lysias captured on the papyrus, returns.

Though other scholars have adduced much richer accounts of the dialogue's unity than what I offer here, I read the *Phaedrus* as a normative grid of communicative forms. The first half of the *Phaedrus* concerns eros, communication to the one; the second half concerns rhetoric, communication to the many. The dialogue begins and ends with deviant forms: personal rhetoric (Lysias's speech) and mass eros (writing). Both feign care for specific individuals but are in fact indiscriminate in address, open to any comer. Neither is, to Plato's way of thinking, the utterance of a soul in freedom; they occur only under constraint. Neither is a "live" enunciation; both are curiously artificial, even inhuman. Lysias addresses his beloved as an individual, though he is really addressed only as one of a crowd of eligible lovers. His stance is that of Kierkegaard's seducer, except that the seducer's professions of unique love are done serially rather than en masse.[34] The written word is deviant for inverse reasons: even if addressed to an individual, it can couple with unspecified readers. The speech of the nonloving lover is indiscriminate in transmission; writing is indiscriminate in reception. True eros, however, is dyadic, just as philosophic rhetoric is based on knowledge of kinds of souls. In each case, soul and word must be matched. Even in public address, Socrates proposes close correlation between the speech and the audience; the careful crafting of discourse can approximate the intimacy of dialogue on a large scale. If personal rhetoric and mass eros are the deviations, personal eros and public rhetoric are the norms.

Socrates' model of the proper and pathological forms of communication resounds to this day. We are still prone to think of true communication as personal, free, live, and interactive. Communication for the *Phaedrus*, when it goes well, can be the mutual discovery of souls; when it turns bad, it can be seduction, pandering, missed connections, or the invariance of writing, "signifying the very same thing forever" (275d).

---

34. Søren Kierkegaard, "The Seducer's Diary" (1843), in *Either/Or,* trans. Howard V. Hong and Edna H. Hong (Princeton: Princeton University Press, 1987), 1:301–445.

Plato via Socrates clearly saw that a new medium is not just a matter of repackaging old contents but a shift in the meaning of voice, word, body, and love. Perhaps the first treatise on communication, the *Phaedrus* is about messages lost in transit and illegitimate couplings. Plato's Socrates is our first theorist of communication—which also means, of communication breakdown.

Dissemination in the Synoptic Gospels

The synoptic Gospels evaluate dissemination in a way quite opposite from the *Phaedrus*, and they rest on a quite different vision of love and of communication. Like the *Phaedrus*, the synoptics feature a rhetoric of sowing and harvesting; unlike that of the *Phaedrus*, this rhetoric often celebrates dissemination as desirable and just. The parable of the sower—the archparable of dissemination—presents a mode of distribution that is as democratically indifferent to who may receive the precious seeds as the *Phaedrus* is aristocratically selective. Other parables argue the deficiency of reciprocity and tight coupling compared with an undifferentiated scattering. Socrates in the *Phaedrus* favors dialogue; Jesus in the synoptics favors dissemination. Moral theory has long taken its bearings from a confrontation with these two personalities. Why not communication theory?

Jesus is represented in all three synoptic Gospels (Matthew 13, Mark 4, Luke 8) as delivering the parable of the sower by the seashore to a vast and mixed audience. A sower, he says, goes forth to sow, broadcasting seed everywhere, so that it lands on all kinds of ground. Most of the seeds never bear fruit. Some sprout quickly (in the equivalent of gardens of Adonis?) only to be scorched by the sun or overcome by weeds. Others sprout but get eaten by birds or trampled by travelers. Only a rare few land on receptive soil, take root, and bring forth fruit abundantly, variously yielding a hundredfold, sixtyfold, or thirtyfold. In a mighty display of self-reflexive dissemination, Jesus concludes, Those who have ears to hear, let them hear!

The parable of the sower is a parable about parables. Like the *Phaedrus*, but on a far more concentrated scale, the parable enacts its point in the form of its saying, performing its own modus operandi. The diverse audience members, like the varieties of soils, who hear the parable as told by the seashore are left to make of it what they will. It is a parable about the diversity of audience interpretations in settings that lack direct interaction. It examines the results when sender and receiver, sower and eventual harvest, are loosely coupled. In contrast to the *Phaedrus*, which at key points is nervous about the folly of scattered seeds and the dangers of promiscuous couplings, the parable of the sower celebrates broadcasting as an equitable mode of communication that leaves the harvest of meaning to the will and capacity of the recipient. The hearer must complete the trajectory begun with the first casting. Though much is thrown, little is caught. And the failure of germination is not necessarily something to lament. Like the second half of the *Phaedrus*, the parable of the sower sorts types of souls (soils) in public address (though not with any programmatic purpose).

The parable of the sower, again, exemplifies the operation of all parables; it is a kind of metaparable. Parables are marked by uniformity in transmission and diversity in reception. Even "parable," from the Greek *paraballein* (meaning "to cast beyond, to place side by side"), suggests casting seeds onto soils or words onto souls. The Greek term *parabolē* can also mean a comparison or an enigma; it is closely related to "problem," both words suggesting something that calls for interpretation.[35] The meaning of the parable is quite literally the audience's problem. In other words, when the distance between speaker and listener is great, the audience bears the interpretive burden. Those who have ears to hear, let them hear! It becomes the hearer's responsibility to close the loop without the aid of the speaker. The point of such "indirect communication," said Kierkegaard, "lies in making the recipient self-active."[36] Or as Stuart Hall writes of television, the moments of encoding and decoding (production and consumption, roughly) are relatively autonomous, allowing audiences to find meanings wildly divergent from those intended by the producers.[37] But this gap between encoding and decoding, I suggest, may well be the mark of all forms of communication. It often takes a new medium and its accompanying disruptions to reveal the gaps that were already implicitly there.

The Gospels have it that the actual audience of this parable was largely mystified, being perhaps stony soil. Later the disciples (and by implication the readers of the Gospel narrative) get the inside scoop in a private audience with Jesus: the sower is not just a mad farmer but is one who spreads "the word of the kingdom." The strategy of speaking in parables turns out to be a cloaking device, a means to keep people

35. In the Septuagint, *parabolē* translates the Hebrew *mashal*, which means both a genre of Judaic teaching (an illustrative anecdote) and something puzzling or astonishing; see, e.g., Deut. 28:37.
36. Søren Kierkegaard, *Practice in Christianity*, ed. Howard V. Hong and Edna H. Hong (1848; Princeton: Princeton University Press, 1991), 125.
37. Stuart Hall, "Encoding/Decoding" (1974), in *Culture, Media, Language: Working Papers in Cultural Studies, 1972–1979*, ed. Stuart Hall et al. (London: Hutchinson, 1980), 129.

from understanding the doctrine.[38] The signal was open to all, but only some perceived the sign. For Socrates the virtue of the living, spoken word is that it is always accompanied with directions for use offered by a guiding father or teacher. In contrast, the sower sends messages whose interpretive cues are hidden or missing, to be provided by those who have ears to hear. The sower engages in a purely one-way act: no cultivation of the fledgling plants occurs, no give-and-take, no instruction as to intended meaning.

Plato's version of Socrates privileges a private and esoteric mode of communication. In the intimate setting of dialectic the receiver is carefully selected by the speaker in advance and carefully brought to understand. Socrates of course will debate all comers in the public spaces of Athens, but he refuses to scatter his doctrinal seeds except for amusement; more to the point, only an elite few were admitted to Plato's academy. Jesus, in contrast, performs a radically public, exoteric mode of dispersing meanings—even though the hearers often fail to catch the hint—in which the audience sorts out the significance for itself (save on those occasions when he decloaks parables for his inner circle). The synoptic Gospels repeatedly undercut reciprocal and hermetic relations in favor of relations that are asymmetrical and public. Though the dream of mutuality has an intense hold on the ways we imagine communication from Plato on, several elements in the Christian tradition offer dissemination as a mode of communicative conduct equal or superior in excellence to dialogue.

The suspension of reciprocity is a point rigorously pursued in some other parables in the synoptic Gospels (there are no parables in the Gospel of John). In Matthew's parable of the laborers, for instance, some workers are hired early in the day to toil all day in the sun for one denarius, a standard day's pay. Others are later hired to work part of the day, and others work only the final hour, but all receive the same payment—one denarius.[39] When those who labored all day complain about the injustice of compensation, the master reminds them that they got what they had contracted for, so what business was it of theirs that he paid others the same amount for less work? This parable portrays a uniform response to a diverse event; the parable of the sower portrays diverse responses to a uniform event. In each case the dispenser of the goods (seeds or payment) is invariant and explicitly insensitive to individual differences—much like Socrates' description of the written word,

---

38. Mark 4:11–12; cf. Luke 8:10.
39. Matt. 20:1–16.

which just keeps signaling the same thing regardless of what inquiry is made of it. There is no proportional adjustment. The impersonality of writing can thus in some cases model just treatment of one's fellows. Justice, in some cases, means treating people by the book. There is something both democratic and frightening about such apparent indifference to merit.

The suspension of fair exchange not only does apparent violence to individual differences but can also occur in the name of care for the individual. In all three parables in Luke 15 about lost objects (the lost coin, sheep, and son), the cycle of quid pro quo is derailed. Each parable is a meditation on the paradox that in love the particular is esteemed more highly than the universal.[40] The first two pair female and male protagonists. A woman, who has lost one of ten coins, sweeps the house till she finds it and then celebrates with her friends. Similarly, a shepherd leaves his flock of ninety and nine to hunt for a lost sheep and also rejoices when he finds it. These are homely tales of ordinary human behavior, but the insight consists in the way everyday action is moved by something more or less than the rationality and reciprocity of exchange. What cost-benefit analysis would predict that someone would take greater joy in one coin than in nine? What business strategy would have a shepherd abandon ninety-nine sheep for one? The passions operate according to strange arithmetic.

It is no less strange for a father to rejoice in his errant son and to ignore the dutiful one, as occurs in the parable of the prodigal son. The forgiving father showers gifts on the returning wastrel—a ring, a robe, sandals, a party and fatted calf, and an embrace. Though the prodigal son plans to confess his wrongs to his father and offer to work only as a servant, he never has a chance. He is interrupted before he can begin by a father who is deaf to all explanations. By the standards of reciprocity and the norm of attentive listening the father's refusal to listen is wrong, just as Socrates reproaches the written word for refusing to engage in dialogue or as the workers reproach the master for insensitivity to the varying amounts of work done by individual laborers. But the father's deafness cannot be a failing in the world of the parable. The father is so taken with joy that nothing can stop the celebration. He is indifferent to whatever explanation his son may have. His forgiveness sweeps even the faintest notion of confessional dialogue out of the picture. If there is any proportionality in the parable, it is that the father is

40. Søren Kierkegaard [Johannes de Silentio], *Fear and Trembling*, trans. Alastair Hannay (London: Penguin, 1985).

as prodigal in his gifts as his younger son was in his sins. The welcome home celebration is an act of sheer expenditure, not of reciprocity.

Of course the older brother, whom the father fails even to inform about the party and who overhears the music and reveling, is outraged at the unfairness of such a welcome. He, who has slaved faithfully for years in his father's service, never once received such treatment. His is the cry of reciprocity: his rationality is based on merit and fair pay, not on extravagance. "But when this son of yours came, who has devoured your living with harlots, you killed for him the fatted calf!"[41] This is the eternal complaint of economics against love. Though the older brother is quite a different figure from Lysias, both are worried about the mania that overtakes those who love. According to Luke 15, part of what it means to be a father, shepherd, or householder is to know when to go beyond rationality, reciprocity, or fairness—to know, in short, when love triumphs over justice. As with the *Phaedrus,* the frenzy of love has its place.

These are messy doctrines, and doctrines about messes. Socrates disdains waste (specifically, wasted *spermata*); Jesus celebrates it. The practice of the sower is wasteful. He lets the seeds fall where they may, not knowing in advance who will be receptive ground, leaving the crucial matter of choice and interpretation to the hearer, not the master. The prodigal is the wasteful son, though the tale is about an apparently wasteful father as well. In a larger sense, the whole narrative of redemption of the Christian Gospels centers on a wasteful act. The son of God dies for every living creature, most of whom will not accept, appreciate, or even know of the sacrifice. As a means of spreading seeds widely, dissemination is excellent, but it is not an efficient means of securing a good harvest. Indeed, godlike love—known as *agapē* in the New Testament—is often figured as broadcasting. "Love your enemies, bless them that curse you . . . that ye may be the children of your Father which is in heaven: for he maketh his sun to rise on the evil and the good, and sendeth rain on the just and on the unjust."[42] In this well-known passage from the Sermon on the Mount Jesus invites his hearers to transcend the intense but limited affections of family and friends for a love as indiscriminate as rainfall, one that embraces all humanity alike, including one's enemies. The Epistle of Peter likewise proclaims that God is "no respecter of persons." A more recent translation reads, "God has no favorites," but more literally, it means that God does not take people

41. Luke 15:30 RSV. Note the elder brother's renunciation of kinship: "this son of yours."
42. Matt. 5:44–45 KJV.

by their faces.[43] Love is supposed to be universal and indifferent to personalities. Scattering and impersonality can be good things. *Agapē*—or Christian love—is supposed to be mass communicated.[44]

Plato's celebration of reciprocity marks out one recurring option in our deliberations about the justice of varying modes of communication. But the celebration of dialogue also risks missing the defects in the notion of reciprocity. One-way communication is not necessarily bad. Reciprocity can be violent as well as fair. War and vengeance obey a logic of strict reciprocity as much as do conversation and trade. Justice demands an eye for an eye and a tooth for a tooth. Its underlying logic says, one turn deserves another. This crime, we say, warrants that punishment; this commodity, that price. If nothing but reciprocity governed social relations, life would be a monotonous round of quid pro quo. Social life would be a cycle of payment, rather than of gifts. Without reciprocity life would be grossly unfair. With only reciprocity, it would be desolate. If no question could be left unanswered and every question was posed with the demand for a response, what boredom and tyranny would result. A just community rests at once on the rationality of tit for tat and on its suspension. Reciprocity, crucial as it is, needs other principles: hospitality, gift giving, forgiveness, and love. To live among others is necessarily to incur obligations; to be mortal is to be incapable of paying them all back.

Even the Golden Rule is not about returning favors, but about the radical otherness of selves. George Bernard Shaw tried to undermine the Golden Rule: "Do not do unto others as you would that they should do unto you. Their tastes may not be the same."[45] Shaw's mischievous variant still captures a key part of the maxim. Especially if paired with the injunction to turn the other cheek, the point of the Golden Rule is to treat the other as a self. The command is not to react to the other's provocation, but to treat people invariantly whatever their deeds and deservingness. Whether kissed or slapped, one is supposed to remain the same way, like Socrates' written word, as invariant as a sundial. This is the dead end of quid pro quo. This doctrine has a superficial resemblance to Stoicism's ethic of unresponsiveness, but there is no Stoic *apathy* or tranquillity in the Golden Rule. Instead there is active care or, to

43. Acts 10:34; cf. Rom. 2:11, Eph. 6:9. The word is *prosōpolēmptēs*. Cf. Lev. 19:15.

44. A 1920s Louisville church, impressed by radio, posted a sign, God Is Always Broadcasting: Erik Barnouw, *A Tower in Babel: A History of Broadcasting in the United States to 1933* (New York: Oxford University Press, 1966), 104.

45. George Bernard Shaw, "Maxims for Revolutionists," from *The Revolutionist's Handbook*, in *Four Plays by Bernard Shaw* (New York: Washington Square Press, 1965), 483.

speak with Kierkegaard, anxiety. The Christian is supposed to be indifferent to both the consequences of action and the recipient's merit, but not to the other as an irreplaceable creature. The Stoic maintains equanimity via psychic withdrawal; the Christian is called to impartial kindness combined with intense psychic engagement. The Gandhian ethic of passive resistance likewise teaches abstention from reaction. To say, then, that modes of communication that involve a one-way dispersion are necessarily flawed or domineering is to miss one of the most obvious facts of ethical experience: the majesty in many cases of nonresponsiveness.

Moreover, not only is blindness to the personal uniqueness of the other a feature of justice, love is blind as well. Justice involves not only impartial treatment but also a profound sensitivity to the individual case—giving each his or her due. Love likewise is not only individuated care but also undeviating constancy, "an ever-fixed mark."[46] Just as the sower represents resources bestowed on all alike, the New Testament also speaks of a minutely particular sort of love that numbers the hairs on the head of the beloved (Matt. 10:29–31); in Adorno's words, "Love uncompromisingly betrays the general to the particular in which alone justice is done to the former."[47] Love, like justice, is multidimensional, both general and personal, uniform and differentiated, diffuse and focused. There is an aspect of both justice and love that is invariant and uniform and an aspect that is personal and particular. Justice that is not loving is not just; love that is not just is not loving. Just so, dissemination without dialogue can become stray scatter, and dialogue without dissemination can be interminable tyranny. The motto of communication theory ought to be: Dialogue with the self, dissemination with the other. This is another way of stating the ethical maxim: Treat yourself like an other and the other like a self.

The value of one-way dissemination can be seen in the case of gift giving. As one of the *logia* of Jesus has it, it is more blessed to give than to receive.[48] The giving end has precedence over the receiving end. Not so curiously, this saying is also directly relevant to the economics of communication. It is more profitable to purvey advertising than to receive it; teachers are paid to teach, but students are rarely paid to learn; one exerts more cultural capital in directing a film than in viewing one. Messages are almost always worth more in dissemination than in recep-

46. William Shakespeare, sonnet 116, line 5.
47. Theodor W. Adorno, *Minima Moralia: Reflections from Damaged Life,* trans. E. F. N. Jephcott (1944–51; London: Verso, 1974), 164.
48. Acts 20:35.

tion. Giving can be a form of power, a way to impose obligations. We do not know what kinds of obligations the prodigal son incurred in the great homecoming feast, but that may have been the father's precise point: to impose the privileges and obligations of a son, not a servant. Indeed, a gift always hovers somewhere between unprovoked generosity (one-way) and the call for a later return gift (reciprocal).

As Pierre Bourdieu argues, exchange relations are governed by two dimensions: difference in the object and deferral in time.[49] If identical objects are exchanged but the transfer is deferred in time, we speak of a loan; if the objects are different and the exchange is simultaneous, it is a trade; and if identical objects are simultaneously exchanged, it is in effect a refusal. A gift must play strategically within the horizons of difference and deferral: it must be different enough in kind and asynchronous enough in time to seem a spontaneous act of goodwill rather than a payment. Bourdieu's great insight is to go beyond the unmasking that a structuralist analysis would perform—showing the participants in gift circuits as simply deceiving themselves about the reciprocity of their actions. In the temporal experience of practice as opposed to the spatial logic of structure, mystification is a possibility. The participant sees a series of unilateral acts, and the observer sees people deluding themselves about a circular exchange system. Misrecognition of the ultimate reciprocity of gift cycles, argues Bourdieu, is not an error but a socially productive strategy that sustains rich networks of mutual obligation. To give or to receive is to disavow obligations that everyone knows—but everyone denies—eventually will have to be met. All gifts come with strings attached, but acknowledgment of that fact is banned. Such failure to recognize allows suspension in the webs of credit and debt. Collective looking away from the mechanism of reciprocity allows something like a higher reciprocity to occur in the long haul. The gift enables a moral economy of loops, suspensions, and deferments, interactions that can be strung out over long expanses of time. It is certainly an economy, but one that plays by rules other than strict reciprocity.

If every social act were moved by indebtedness, we would be sluggish actors indeed. Love and prostitution, gift and payment would be indistinguishable. Lysias, with his call to do kindness only to those able to return it, would prevail.[50] Gifts can both arrest and accelerate the cyclical motion of tit for tat. "Overmuch eagerness to discharge one's obligations," as Bourdieu quotes La Rochefoucauld, "is a sign of ingratitude."

49. Pierre Bourdieu, *Outline of a Theory of Practice*, trans. Richard Nice (Cambridge: Cambridge University Press, 1977). I am grateful to Michael K. Sáenz for advice on Bourdieu.

50. *Phaedrus*, 233e–234a.

The Latin proverb captures the converse, *Bis das si cito das:* You give twice if you give quickly. The giver is not supposed to keep score or respond directly at all. "Don't mention it," we say when thanked. The one-way character of the gift is not a deficiency but a strength. A system of rotating potlatches—celebratory feasts given publicly to the community—is as viable a way of organizing social life as is direct tit for tat. The horrors of broken dialogue can also be the blessings of just treatment. In some settings we would like to be treated as unique individuals (with family or friends); in others we want to be treated exactly the same as any other human (in court or the market). One's personal uniqueness can be a hindrance to justice and the basis of love. A life without individuated interaction (dialogue) would lack love; one without generalized access (dissemination) would lack justice.

Taking gifts as our analogy for communication shows that something more than reciprocity must prevail. Those strange and distended forms of dialogue that happen when people correspond over great distances of time or space are not just uncanny and bizarre, as many in the nineteenth century thought, recently confronting the lightning lines of the telegraph or the death-defying tracings of the photograph, but are the shapes in which we live and move among other people all the time. Clearly there is nothing ethically deficient about broadcasting as a one-way flow. Nor are the gaps between sender and receiver always chasms to be bridged; they are sometimes vistas to be appreciated or distances to be respected. The impossibility of connection, so lamented of late, may be a central and salutary feature of the human lot. The dream of communication has too little respect for personal inaccessibility. Impersonality can be a protective wall for the private heart. To "fix" the gaps with "better" communication might be to drain solidarity and love of all their juice.

It is tempting, given compelling studies of the contrast of eros and *agapē*, to overestimate the differences between Socrates and Jesus.[51] Likewise, the Platonic and Christian traditions have known a long confluence. Both Socrates and Jesus want to transcend a narrow rationality—Socrates in the name of a higher mutuality, Jesus in the name of a higher scattering. Both see love as a kind of blessed madness. Platonic eros,

---

51. Anders Nygren, *Agape and Eros: A Study of the Christian Idea of Love,* trans. A. G. Hebert, 2 vols. (New York: Macmillan, 1938–41); Denis de Rougemont, *Love in the Western World,* trans. Montgomery Belgion, rev. ed. (New York: Pantheon, 1956).

after all, involves the soul intensely (it is the soul that sprouts wings), just as Christian love for the neighbor makes care for his or her body essential. The delirious exuberance of eros—sheer delight in the other without regard for compensation or return—is, as a long line of Christian mystics have seen, an instructive model for the unconditional love of God and neighbor, oblivious to any eventual payback.[52] Likewise, Socrates rejects any notion of love, such as that espoused by Lysias, that shirks the welfare of the beloved. Though it is easy at first glance to say that eros involves sexual passion for the body as *agapē* involves spiritual care for the soul, closer inspection melts down the contrasts between the concepts.

There is, however, a final important difference. Socrates does not ultimately countenance love for the imperfect or the particular. At the end of his speech in the *Symposium*, Socrates argues that truly philosophical love moderates the "violent love of the one" by raising us on the ladder of love to an impersonal love of beauty in general. "Personal beauty is but a trifle." Philosophy provides "the science of beauty everywhere."[53] The mortal, singular other is ultimately an unworthy object of love, a stance that harbors a frightening chilliness for which Alcibiades bitterly reproaches him later in the *Symposium*.[54] Love that cannot be generalized or universalized is, for Socrates, not love at all. He could not agree with Kierkegaard that in love the particular is higher than the universal.

The parables invite an embrace of the frail stuff we are made of, not a flight from it. Platonic eros is attracted by beauty; love in the synoptic Gospels is attracted by need, even, in the case of the parable of the good Samaritan, by disgust or impurity, for the wounded man lying in the road is portrayed as looking like a corpse.[55] Socrates imagines the lover as being drawn by the most eternal and splendid portion of the beloved; the Gospels point to the spell cast on the lover by the most fragile and imperfect portion. The fundamental question is whether the epitome of love should be the love that occurs between equals who are present to each other in body and soul or the love that leaps across the chasms. If the former, then communication will be conceived of as a flight toward unity; if the latter, it will be conceived of as making do with the frag-

52. Catherine Osborne, *Eros Unveiled: Plato and the God of Love* (Oxford: Clarendon Press, 1994), chap. 4.

53. Plato, *Symposium*, in *The Works of Plato*, trans. Benjamin Jowett (New York: Modern Library, 1956), 377–78.

54. Martha Craven Nussbaum, "Socrates, Ironist and Moral Philosopher," *New Republic* 205 (16–23 September 1991): 34–40.

55. Julia Kristeva, *Powers of Horror: An Essay on Abjection*, trans. Leon S. Roudiez (New York: Columbia University Press, 1982), treats the centrality of abjection to Christianity.

ments we find in ourselves and others. The Gospels know a kind of individuality strange to the classical Greeks: one marked by agony and duress.

The *Phaedrus* and the *Symposium* figure love as the yearning for oneness; the synoptic Gospels as compassion for otherness. The one favors symmetry, circles, and reciprocity; the other, difference, ellipses, and suspension. Socrates exalts the soul's rapturous flight toward the heavens, tickled by beauty and trailing clouds of glory; the Gospels enjoin a descent into the pains and wounds of the other. "Socrates" wants to admit no impediments to the marriage of true minds; the parables teach that the impediments are precisely what give us reason to love. Broadly speaking, Christianity calls for a love based not in comradeship (as in Aristotle's notion of *philia*), the desire for beauty (eros), or the "natural" ties of the clan or city, but in the recognition of the kinship of all of God's creatures. Socrates' idea of love includes the "type of soul" of the beloved or of the audience of speeches but has little notion of the uniqueness of each soul in itself. The beloved becomes a substitute for the far vaster ocean of celestial beauty. The open casting of the sower results in the most individualized and idiosyncratic harvests possible, each recipient hearing as he or she will. Platonic eros passes through the particular to arrive at the general; Christian *agapē* passes through the general to arrive at the particular. Does love arise from the transcendence of the flesh or from its touch? Should we think of communication as perfect contact or as patience amid the imperfections? The contrast of dialogue and dissemination boils down to the mercy we can muster for human folly.

In sum, though reciprocity is a moral ideal, it is an insufficient one. The Christian doctrine of communication is a doctrine of broadcasting, of single turns, expended without the expectation that one good turn deserves another. Love is rare that occurs within a relationship of perfect equality. Parents do not love their children because their children reciprocate equivalently. The Gospels celebrate gifts given without care for reimbursement and depict *agapē* as occurring in relationships of impossible recompense. The Samaritan and the wounded man, Christ and the leper, God and humanity—the members of each pair are radically asymmetrical. The injunction in the Sermon on the Mount to give alms in secret aims to keep good works from becoming a public opinion racket. One is not supposed to anticipate the response, only to act. Take no thought, God loves a cheerful giver: such maxims are meant to postpone deliberation on consequences indefinitely and to keep exchange logic at bay. Caring for animals, children, or the planet, for example, does not depend on the capacity to communicate on an even footing. Infants, though quite incapable of direct communication, are invariably radiant to their parents and others; the avidity with which they receive affection helps account for their remarkable magnetism.

There is, in sum, no indignity or paradox in one-way communication. The marriage of true minds via dialogue is not the only option; in fact, lofty expectations about communication may blind us to the more subtle splendors of dissemination or suspended dialogue. Dialogue still reigns supreme in the imagination of many as to what good communication might be, but dissemination presents a saner choice for our fundamental term. Dissemination is far friendlier to the weirdly diverse practices we signifying animals engage in and to our bumbling attempts to meet others with some fairness and kindness. Open scatter is more fundamental than coupled sharing; it is the stuff from which, on rare, splendid occasions, dialogue may arise. Dissemination is not wreckage; it is our lot.

TWO

History of an Error: The Spiritualist Tradition

Though "communication" acquired the sense of immaterial contact between distinct souls only late in the nineteenth century, its intellectual architecture and imagery were long in the making. In this chapter I explore three broad moments in which the vision of soul-to-soul converse was articulated: early Christianity, especially the writings of Saint Augustine; British empiricism, especially the writings of John Locke; and the varieties of nineteenth-century spiritualism from mesmerism through psychical research. Dominant strains within Christianity establish spirit-to-spirit linkage as a normative vision of how intercourse ought to work; Locke gives the first sustained philosophical use of the term "communication" as a central principle of speech and language; and nineteenth-century spiritualism bequeaths both a vocabulary (medium, channel, and communication) and a repertoire of images (hypnosis, community of sensation, or the telepathic ties of distant lovers) to thinking about what "communication" might be. Though it is a stretch to speak of these diverse intellectual movements and moods as a coherent tradition in any strong sense, they represent a ghostly set of resources that often appear when we take the word "communication" in our mouth. Many other sources could be invoked but are not; those who have ears to hear will hear.

Augustine and Locke both provide articulate defenses (but with very different purposes) of ideas foundational to the modern notion of communication: the interiority of the self and the sign as an empty vessel to be filled with ideational content. In its everyday usage, "communication" rests squarely on such conceptions: Each of us has a treasure chest of thoughts and wishes uniquely our own. Our interiors are private, goes the tale, and trapped inside by the privacy of our senses and the individuality of our minds. Our experience of pain, color, sweetness, or joy is uniquely our own and inaccessible to anyone else, as are our innermost thoughts and dreams. Language and signs are crude carriers for the inner life. Words are at best conventions; they refer to meanings inside people's minds and to objects in the world. When we express ourselves, we trust private self-stuff to public symbol proxies. Other people catch only the proxies, not the original fullness we had when we uttered our innards. Every utterance is thus a fall or at least a transition into a crossroads of sign traffic that is subject to collisions and bottlenecks; all communication, whether face-to-face or distant, becomes a problem of mediation. If only the signifying vehicles would vanish so that we could see into each other's hearts and minds, genuine communication would be possible. If only we were angels, with transparent bodies and transparent thoughts, goes the plaint.

Though this description is slanted in the direction of romantic pathos, such ideas are remarkably deep rooted—in intellectual history (which Augustine structured in an important way) and in the structure of the English language (of which John Locke was one important architect).[1] The heart of the spiritualist tradition, as I will call it, taking the nineteenth-century movement as part for the whole, is the proposition that communication happens best when bodies and language are transcended in favor of more ethereal modes of thought transference. Talk may happen, but without a meeting of interiors, it is little more than intergroup grooming and stroking. Meaning is separable from media, content from form. Signs, like bodies, are the containers of spirit. The task of communication is to move beyond, behind, or above sign-bodies to the immediate purity of meaning-minds. Spiritual content should be poured from one mind to another. It not only is possible to achieve an identity in spirit between individual minds, it is imperative.

As we saw in the introduction, there are a variety of theoretical traditions that do not hold to such views or embrace them with such pathos. Yet Augustine and Locke do hold such views, with key qualifications and refinements, as do a host of lesser figures. Ultimately, their vision

---

1. Michael J. Reddy, "The Conduit Metaphor," in *Metaphor and Thought,* ed. Andrew Ortony (Cambridge: Cambridge University Press, 1979), 284–324.

of communication rests on a vision of the self as an eternal, self-identical soul whose nature is not affected by its embodiment. The soul is self-existent and detachable—something that allows for its immortality and freedom from earthly soilage. Communication involves establishing some identity between two souls. In contrast, later in this book I will argue, following Hegel, that identity is only the momentary containment of difference. In the formula of Charles Taylor, "Identity is the identity of identity and non-identity."[2] This means that, at best, communication is a dance of differences, not a junction of spirits. The problem of communication, as I argue in chapter 3, ceases to be one of polishing the intellectual instruments so that they more accurately transport spiritual or mental content and becomes one of establishing lived conditions of partaking and expression that are just and loving. Communication becomes a political problem of access and opportunity, not a psychological or semantic one of purifying the media.

The spiritualist view of communication oscillates between the dream of shared interiorities and the hassle of imperfect media. The middle ground of pragmatic making-do is rarely noted. Media, like bodies, become pipes that are interesting only in their tendency to become clogged. But media are not mere "channels." Media matter to practices of communication because embodiment matters. The body is our existence, not our container. To anticipate my conclusions, the body is not a vehicle to be cast off, it is in part the homeland to which we are traveling. Any adequate account of the social life of word and gesture—of "communication" in the broadest sense—needs to face the splendid and flawed material by which we make common cause with each other. That any achievement of communion consists in a concert of differences is a blessing rather than a curse.

My aim in this chapter is not to write off a long record of human yearning as merely misguided. The quest for mystic experience and the romantic yearning for fusion with one's other half, ranging from Aristophanes' hilarious speech in Plato's *Symposium* through mystical visions of Christ as the bridegroom of the soul to recent hopes for full couplings across the distances of cyberspace, express precious longings that perhaps ought not to be shouted from the rooftops and that certainly ought not to count as routine models of what we hope for from each other. The notion that two souls could blend "into the yolk and white of the one shell," as Yeats put it, makes for gorgeous poetry. But the demand that our word work and wordplay achieve such exalted status

2. Charles Taylor, *Hegel and Modern Society* (New York: Cambridge University Press, 1979).

is dangerous if it invites despair at the impossibility of communication when fruitful cooperation is abundantly available. Further, the notion that communication mingles souls makes it difficult to distinguish between refusing to communicate and asserting one's dignity, for who but a bad person (in this vision) could renounce the call to engage in a dialogue? The dream of consubstantiality in spirit directly leads both to the nightmare of communication breakdown and to disdain for those who opt out of the game of interpersonal mimesis. We need ways to respect the limits of each other's souls and of the demands we can place on each other rather than yearning for bridges and lamenting walls.

Christian Sources

Although, as I argued in chapter 1, some strains in the Christian tradition emphasize imperfection and asymmetry as conditions of compassion, the mainstream of doctrine solidifying in later antiquity calls for those who love to be "in" each other in a decidedly unphysical way. The Gospel of John is perhaps the first Christian source for the characteristically double mixture of tragicomic breakdown and soulful unity that still informs communication theory. John, compared with the synoptic Gospels, is rich in face-to-face dialogue, and much of it consists of more or less spectacular misfires: the woman at the well, mistaking Jesus' teaching about living water, asks for water that will never run out; Nicodemus, puzzled at being told he has to reenter the womb, fails to understand the command to be born anew; the disciples are as dopey in their inability to "get it" as the tendentiously portrayed Pharisees are willful in their misunderstanding. The Gospel of John is structured in many ways by dialogic mishaps. The hearers of Jesus consistently mistake the body of the metaphor for the spirit (to use John's language). And often, just when the dialogue has collapsed, there comes the moment of recognition. Something larger breaks through. John is thus, to be sure, no booster of dialogism—the faith that conversation leads to mutual clarification. The book shows how often dialogue is motivated by misunderstanding in the first place. When higher powers burst onto the scene—the wind, the light, the other world—dialogue vanishes into something else: prayer, loss, bafflement, faith.

John paints on a cosmic canvas. The whole book is about the revelation of light and resistance to it.[3] Conversational collisions are everyday

---

3. For the argument that the medium *and* message of John are revelation, see John Ashton, *Understanding the Fourth Gospel* (Oxford: Clarendon Press, 1991), chap. 14.

mirrors of the larger battle between light and darkness. As the call finds no response, so the light is often ignored. The witness of truth is taken as a scandal. At the end of Jesus' long and highly metaphorical bread of life sermon, which climaxes in the shocking command to eat his flesh and drink his blood, he says: "It is the Spirit that quickeneth; the flesh profiteth nothing: the words that I speak unto you, they are spirit, and they are life."[4] The priority of the spirit over the flesh is here not only a metaphysical and moral admonition, but an interpretive principle that resonates in later Christian hermeneutics.[5] Right understanding, for the Gospel of John, comes from catching the tenor without tripping on the vehicle. We are to dwell in the metaphor's meaning, not its mechanics— to discover the *logos* within the flesh. But such apprehension is hidden from most.

The fourth Gospel dramatizes the antinomy of transparency and obstruction in communication. Perhaps most intensely, in the farewell speech of chapters 14–17, especially in the climactic intercessory prayer of chapter 17, Jesus is portrayed as advocating shared being on a spiritual plane as the highest state his disciples can attain with each other, him, and the Father, perhaps almost as if in compensation for the dialogue follies in the rest of the book. The Gospel of John makes frequent use of the grammatical case called "the ontological dative," a form that makes it possible to speak of one person's being "in" another, as God is in Christ, or Christ is in his disciples. The ontological dative opens up thinking about how persons can share spiritual substance, something important in the theology of the Trinity, as well as angelology and communication theory. The Gospel of John does not, of course, offer an account of communication as the symbolic modes of connections among minds. It does provide both a vision of consubstantiality that is attained only in spirit and a sharp sense for all the obstacles to seeing. John gives us the combination of blocked understandings and wished-for unions characteristic of "communication" as a concept.

AUGUSTINE: THE SPIRIT OVER THE LETTER Augustine is in many ways a fountainhead of the concept of communication and a key figure in the history of linguistic theory. Tzvetan Todorov regards him as the key figure in semiotic theory between Plato and Saussure.[6] Whatever the origi-

---

4. John 6:63 KJV.

5. For example, Augustine, *The City of God,* Great Books of the Western World, ed. Robert Maynard Hutchins, vol. 18 (Chicago: Encyclopaedia Britannica, 1952), 313 (10.24).

6. Tzvetan Todorov, *Theories of the Symbol,* trans. Catherine Porter (Ithaca: Cornell University Press, 1982), 15; Giovanni Manetti, *Theories of the Sign in Classical Antiquity,* trans. Christine Richard-

nality of his thinking on language and signs, no one can dispute its thoroughness or its subsequent influence. As the intellectual architect of Latin Christianity, Augustine (354–430) exerted a massive influence on European life from the fifth century through the Renaissance and, via his influence on Luther and the Puritans, on modern intellectual life as well.[7] The literary genre he made famous in the *Confessions* has never been more alive. This formidable man may not have used the word "communication" as we do, but he certainly set up conditions for its flourishing. Forging neo-Platonist currents and Christian doctrine, Augustine saw the soul as immaterial and developed the full armor of oppositions that communication is still designed to overcome and reproduce, such as soul and body, intellect and sense, eternity and time, and inside and outside. Augustine helped build both the interior self and the dream of overcoming it in communication.[8] If communication is what makes the privacy of the self accessible to others, the concept presupposes—even needs—the principle of interiority.[9]

Augustine's theory of the sign is elaborated in many works, but his early dialogue *De Magistro* (On the teacher) articulates many of his key positions, but with few of the larger theological ramifications that come later. A sign is a marker of interior and exterior realities. It points to and shows things that antedate it, but it has no legitimate role as an agent of imagination or invention. "Words possess only sufficient efficacy to remind us in order that we may see things, but not to exhibit the things that we may know them." A teacher may use signs to draw the learner's attention to certain aspects of a topic, but ultimately there "is nothing which is learned by means of signs." Nothing can be ultimately learned from a teacher in any case: instruction comes not from words "but by means of the things themselves which God reveals within the soul." The things themselves are all but infinitely superior to words. In sum, "we should not attribute to words more than is proper." Words are like cue cards, pointers to things mental and material, but their value lies outside them.[10] Augustine is here quite far from Saussure (for whom words acquire significance in their mutual semiotic relationships) or

---

son (Bloomington: Indiana University Press, 1993), 157; Åke Bergvall, "The Theology of the Sign: St. Augustine and Spenser's Legend of Holiness," *Studies in English Literature* 33 (1993): 22–42, at 24.

7. For instance, Schelling, Kierkegaard, Freud, Heidegger, and Wittgenstein.

8. Charles Taylor, *Sources of the Self: The Making of the Modern Identity* (Cambridge: Harvard University Press, 1989), chap. 7.

9. See Briankle G. Chang, *Deconstructing Communication: Representation, Subject, and Economies of Exchange* (Minneapolis: University of Minnesota Press, 1996), chap. 2.

10. St. Augustine, *De Magistro*, trans. George G. Leckie (New York: Appleton-Century, 1938), 46, 43, 50, 55 (from chaps. 10, 11, 12, 14).

Wittgenstein (for whom words behave in language games, interwoven with concrete forms of life).

For Augustine, the sign is a passive vessel that suppresses itself for the sake of what it carries. In one sense, Augustine may be the inventor of the concept of "medium."[11] Communication happens both because of and in spite of the medium, a term he uses in a broad sense to refer alike to the body, a means to an end, and a means of conveyance. Means are to be used (*uti*), and ends are to be enjoyed (*frui*). Throughout *De Doctrina Christiana* Augustine argues for the legitimacy of the sign as an interpretive help as long as it does not usurp the all-important spirit it is supposed to point to. Scripture can be read with any aid available— including knowledge of Hebrew or Greek or the pagan arts of grammar, rhetoric, history, science, and philosophy—so long as one does not conflate the aid with the end. The hermeneutic "as" is fine, substituting one thing for another, so long as we arrive at the underlying meaning and kick away the ladder once we get there. Augustine wants interpreters not to get caught in technical difficulties or interference in transmission. Such is servitude to the letter rather than liberty in the spirit.

Augustine's examples of means are often in fact what we would call media of transport and communication (the same word, after all, is used for both in Latin). His metaphors of traveling in fact capture much about both his view of interpretation and of the human sojourn more generally. Our self-love, he writes, we ought to treat "not with such love and delight as if it were a good to rest in, but with a transient feeling rather, such as we have toward the road, or carriages, or other things that are merely means."[12] Media are not to be loved, only to be used. The danger for us pilgrims is in confusing things to use and to enjoy: "The beauty of the country through which we pass, and the very pleasure of the motion, charm our hearts, and turning these things which we ought to use into objects of enjoyment, we become unwilling to hasten the end of our journey; and becoming engrossed in factitious delight, our thoughts are diverted from that home whose delights would make us truly happy. Such is a picture of our condition in this life of mortality."[13] Such is also a picture of the plight that awaits those who linger too long in the letter.

11. See Paul A. Soukup, "Thinking, Talking, and Trinitarian Theology: From Augustine to Aquinas on Communication," paper presented at seventy-second annual conference of the Speech Communication Association, Chicago, 1986.

12. Augustine, *On Christian Doctrine*, Great Books of the Western World, ed. Robert Maynard Hutchins, vol. 18 (Chicago: Encyclopaedia Britannica, 1952), 634 (1.35).

13. Augustine, *On Christian Doctrine*, 625 (1.4).

Augustine uses the contrast of flesh and spirit to explain signs. The sound of a word is material; the significance of a word is mental. Like human beings, the word is split into a body (sound) and spirit (meaning). To explain the word, Augustine often resorts to the Word, the *logos* of the Gospel of John, "the Word made flesh," the second member of the Trinity; it is remarkable how consistently discussions of the work of language accompany his discussions of the Incarnation. Just as the "incarnate Word" took a body of clay to be sensible to a fallen humanity, so our inner thoughts must assume the acoustic tabernacles of articulate speech in order to be sensible to other people. In both cases embodiment serves as a means of communication or manifestation.

Just as when we speak, in order that what we have in our minds may enter through the ear into the mind of the hearer, the word which we have in our hearts becomes an outward sound and is called speech; and yet our thought does not lose itself in the sound, but remains complete in itself, and takes the form of speech without being modified in its own nature by the change: so the Divine Word, though suffering no change in nature, yet became flesh, that He might dwell among us.[14]

This remarkable analogy speaks volumes. Neither the thought nor the Word loses itself in its descent into sensible form. The nature remains constant in a new carrier. Embodiment is at best an expedient of exhibition, not of ontological importance. This is the program of communication as the meeting of two inner ideas, unperturbed by their materialities. The content remains identical across all its embodiments.

Indeed, the inner word in the human heart has little to do with body, culture, or history. It is not Latin, Greek, or Hebrew but only employs such perceptible carriers. In a meditation in the *City of God* on the tower of Babel and the angels, the two great archetypes of failed and perfect communication in the Western tradition, Augustine argues that divine speech needs no such carriage. God speaks to the angels "in an ineffable manner of His own . . . [which] has no noisy and passing sound," since God can evoke the inner word immediately, without recourse to mediation. In contrast, when God speaks to us he must adapt to the grossness of our instruments. Sensible signifiers are concessions to our carnal state. If we are especially open, however, God's words can circumvent the mediation of physical signs and be perceived (not heard) within. Generally, however, humans grasp each other's thoughts only via acoustic or visual means. "For either the unchangeable Truth speaks directly

14. Augustine, *On Christian Doctrine*, 627 (1.13).

to the mind of the rational creature in some indescribable way, or speaks through the changeable creature, either presenting spiritual images to our spirit, or bodily voices to our bodily sense."[15] Augustine leaves no doubt that the indescribable speaking of truth to spirit is preferred over the audiovisual stimulation of bodily sense.

For Augustine, the appearance of God to humans is essentially a media problem. For how could God, he asks, "appear" to the patriarchs and prophets when God has no appearance or physical form? If God appeared to appear, he was resorting to deception, donning a disguise to meet the crudity of human sense organs. Theophany is either deception (of humans) or debasement (of God). Augustine's notion of communication solves the riddle: "For as the sound which communicates the thought conceived in the silence of the mind is not the thought itself, so the form by which God, invisible in his own nature, became visible, was not God himself." Both God's appearance and the movement of words between people involve what we might call the principle of bodily indifference. "Nevertheless it is He Himself who was seen under that form, as that thought itself is heard in the sound of the voice; and the patriarchs recognized that, though the bodily form was not God, they saw the invisible God."[16] To borrow a Johannine distinction, God was in the appearance, but not of the appearance. In the interior lies the truth.

God in Augustine's account is thus willing to stage a tête-à-tête for a human audience, putting on a ventriloquist show of sorts for human consumption—even, as Augustine says, making his voice obey the laws of resonance in real space. "For God speaks with a man not by means of some audible creature dinning in his ears, so that atmospheric vibrations connect Him that makes with him that hears the sound." Though humans may experience such vibrations, they are not direct tokens of God's presence. Such contact is not possible between mortals and eternal beings, since "it is by means of a semblance of a body that He speaks, and with the appearance of a real interval of space."[17] Communications from God are effects designed for the capacities of human senses. Since God is supposedly nowhere and no-when, he must create effects of presence for his children. Augustine's account of divine communication with mortals foreshadows modern communications and the problem of how to conjure the credible presence of an absent body for an audience remote in time, space, or degree.

15. Augustine, *City of God,* 426 (16.6).
16. Augustine, *City of God,* 307 (10.13).
17. Augustine, *City of God,* 323 (11.2).

In sum, for Augustine the word is a marker that points to external and internal realities. It has the crucial job of revealing interiors, the world of thought and spirit. Just as we humans are encased in flesh, words are as well. God and angels may occasionally circumvent our bodies but in general must condescend to them. For him, to bypass language is to foretaste redemption from our bodies and to emulate the angels, who dispense with outer signs and traffic solely in inner meanings. Communication without words is, in his view, a legitimate aspiration for humans, an ideal that might help us rise out of the Babel of the earthly city. When "we hear with the inner ear some part of the speech of God, we approximate to the angels."[18] Or as R. A. Markus writes, "For Augustine semantic activity—understanding and communicating through language—was the index of the human need for transcendence in the most general terms: for union with other minds in the very act of understanding a shared world."[19] Nothing less than spiritual liberation is at stake in our relation to the sign: "And nothing is more fittingly called the death of the soul than when that in it which raises it above the brutes, the intelligence namely, is put in subjection to the flesh by a blind adherence to the letter. . . . it is surely a miserable slavery of the soul to take signs for things, and to be unable to lift the eye of the mind above what is corporeal and created, that it may drink in eternal light."[20] Our struggle with communication is an index of our fallenness, one portion of our lot as immersed in a world of lights and colors trying to find our way back to God. Augustine exhorts us to overcome our deficiencies—our opaque flesh and obstreperous wills—and become like angels whose relationships with others are unlimited by the barriers of skin and skull.

Augustine's theology of the incarnate Word, metaphysics of flesh and spirit, and psychology of inner and outer, all sustain his vision of communication as coordinated interiorities. His sense that the human lot is to be moved by desire, often for the wrong things, resonates with the vision of eros from Plato to Freud. Even language for Augustine is moved by passion. Though I have barely sounded the subtleties of his thought, it should be clear enough why Augustine is such a ready target for recent critics. His theory of language was an explicit foil in Wittgenstein's *Philosophical Investigations,* since Augustine (in Wittgenstein's version) ar-

18. Augustine, *City of God,* 426 (16.6).
19. R. A. Markus, "Signs, Communication, and Communities in Augustine's *De Doctrina Christiana,*" in *De Doctrina Christiana: A Classic of Western Culture,* ed. Duane W. H. Arnold and Pamela Bright (Notre Dame: University of Notre Dame Press, 1995), 100.
20. Augustine, *On Christian Doctrine,* 660 (3.5).

gues that the meaning of words consists in their reference to things rather than springing from their place in ecosystems of lived practices.[21] Though Derrida has spent more effort tracking ontotheological clues in Rousseau, Hegel, or Heidegger, could there be a better example of a "logocentrist," a devotee of the transcendental signified, an ontotheologian, than Augustine?[22] He ranks writing below speech, exemplifying the grammatological regime that Derrida has taken such pains to dismantle: "But whereas we exhibit . . . bodily signs either to ears or eyes of persons present to whom we speak, letters have been invented that we might be able to converse also with the absent; but these are signs of words, as words themselves are signs in our conversations of those things which we think."[23] It does not take much squinting, here or elsewhere, to see Augustine as a proponent of the metaphysics of presence.[24]

Augustine's theory of communication, as well as Christian hermeneutics more generally, has still greater political and ethical stakes. Derrida's larger aim may be not only to redeem writing from its subservience to speech, but to rescue the people of the book from their oppression by a hermeneutics that equates liberty with the spirit and bondage with the letter, a hermeneutics that Augustine upholds.[25] He singles out the Jews as the people most captive to the letter. The Gentiles take literal truths figuratively, he argues, as the Jews take figurative truths literally.[26] Either is a grave spiritual error (though he thinks the Jews have it more right than the Gentiles, since their service to the letter is at least motivated by devotion to God). Modes of interpretation, again, are not just spectacles through which to view the world; they are symptoms of one's spiritual condition. Augustine agrees on both moral and interpretive grounds with Paul's formula: "The letter killeth, but the spirit giveth life."[27]

Recent critiques of communication as spirit-to-spirit concourse, then, are often motivated not only by a sense of the descriptive inadequacy of that vision, but by its felt legacy of persecution, its long entanglement with a policy that denigrates the letter. As Susan Handelman argues,

21. Ludwig Wittgenstein, *Philosophical Investigations,* trans. G. E. M. Anscombe (Oxford: Basil Blackwell, 1953), secs. 1–4.
22. Susan Handelman, *The Slayers of Moses: The Emergence of Rabbinic Interpretation in Modern Literary Theory* (Albany: SUNY Press, 1982), 118; see 107–20.
23. Augustine, *On the Trinity,* trans. Arthur West Hadden, in *The Works of Aurelius Augustine,* ed. Marcus Dods (Edinburgh: Clark, 1873), 7:399 (15.10.19).
24. Jacques Derrida, *De la grammatologie* (Paris: Minuit, 1967).
25. Allan Megill, *Prophets of Extremity: Nietzsche, Heidegger, Foucault, Derrida* (Berkeley: University of California Press, 1985), chap. 8.
26. See *De Doctrina Cristiana,* book 3.
27. 2 Cor. 3:6 KJV.

such thinkers as Freud, Harold Bloom, Jacques Lacan, Gershom Scholem, and Jacques Derrida all stem from a heretical tradition of rabbinical interpretation that has long resisted the Christian privilege of the spirit over the letter as a regime in which difference is outlawed.[28] The resistance to communication as spiritual transportation has a moral and political motive: the defense of difference over—or within—identity. Derrida and his compatriots invoke a world in which texts do not have outsides, interiority is a feature not of psychology but of discourse, and strange exchanges take place between the living and the dead. John and Augustine are both advocates of interiority whose texts are laced with anti-Semitism in intricate ways, and this fact will have to inform any responsible reading of their calls for oneness in soul or transparency in interpretation.[29] For my part, I do not take the sublimities of Christian-romantic hermeneutics as a *simple* product of sublimation or the yearning for spiritual unity as *reducible* to hatred of the world. The Christian tradition, if one can speak of such, invites us not to abandon the possibility of a community unsullied by scapegoating. Its utopia is a solidarity in which no Other is expelled. The Jewish tradition, in counterpoint, reminds us of the otherness that crops up everywhere, even—or most especially—where we wish it absent in our communions with other texts like ourselves. The one tradition brings the tidings that the reconciliation has taken place; the other reminds us that it hasn't happened yet. Suspended between the hope of an atonement that enables solidarity with all creatures and the keen awareness of its recurrent absence may be the place to abide. (This may be, by the way, the neighborhood of the Gospel of John.)

ANGELS: THE PRINCIPLE OF BODILY INDIFFERENCE Speculation about the angels has been one dominant form of considering communication in the history of European thought.[30] Since they have no carnal bodies, they are quite capable of fusing together in the bliss of pure intelligence. Though traditions of angelology are diverse, both orthodox and esoteric, ranging across such traditions as Christian Gnosticism, Sufism, and Kabbalah, angels present a model for communication as it should be. They provide us a lasting vision of the ideal speech situation, one

---

28. Handelman, *Slayers of Moses.*

29. Daniel Boyarin's treatment of the intertwined universalism and racism of Paul's thinking is a model of how to confront such intricacy: *A Radical Jew: Paul and the Politics of Identity* (Berkeley: University of California Press, 1994).

30. See Stuart Schneiderman's neglected but brilliantly deadpan book, *An Angel Passes: How the Sexes Became Undivided* (New York: New York University Press, 1988).

without distortion or interference. Angels—a term that comes from the Greek *angelos,* messenger—are unhindered by distance, are exempt from the supposed limitations of embodiment, and effortlessly couple the psychical and the physical, the signified and the signifier, the divine and the human. They are pure bodies of meaning.

The angels are highly relevant, not just forgotten creatures from the childhood of the race. It is a cliché to disparage medieval Scholasticism for calculating how many angels could dance on the head of a pin, but this question is of some moment for communication theory, since it concerns the physical basis of significant differences. Is the sign material? Is information? What is the physical status of a just noticeable difference? Does the carrier of the message occupy space or not? Is the "spirit" of meaning separable from the "flesh" of the sign? With a little transposition, the question of the capacity of the angels' dance hall takes us to the heart of semiotic theory, the coupling of signifier and signified. If an infinity of angels can dance on the head of a pin, then angelic bodies and souls are consubstantial in a way that Plato's lovers could only dream of. Unrestricted communication would then be possible. If the head of the pin gets at all crowded, however, clearly angelic bodies occupy space, however infinitesimal. A principle of finitude arises. Invitations to the ball must then be restricted. If the floor space is in fact scarce, things intellectual do indeed have a corporeal correlate— thoughts might have weight and extension—which troubles the dream of communication, reminding us again of the body and the letter.

Ghosts and angels haunt modern media, with their common ability to spirit voice, image, and word across vast distances without death or decay. The logo of Deutsche Grammophon was long an angel with a stylus inscribing sound directly onto the phonograph disk; AT&T bragged of the speed and extent of its system with images of cherubically plump angels adorning the telephone wires.[31] Angels carry dispatches that are never lost or misdelivered or garbled in transit, at least not by the good angels. Though angels have been a chief target of enlightened mockery—Hobbes, Voltaire, Gibbon, and Freud all made both sport and theory from them—they preside over some of the high points of Western literature (Dante's *Paradiso,* Milton's *Paradise Lost,* Goethe's *Faust*) and hover over modernist literature and art (Rilke, Klee, Chagall, Benjamin, Wallace Stevens) and over more recent works (Rushdie's *Satanic Verses,* Wenders's *Wings of Desire,* Kushner's *Angels in America*). Im-

31. *The Magic of Communication: A Tell-You-How Story* (N.p.: AT&T Information Department, 1932).

ages of childhood purity, feminine long-suffering, ethnicity, and cyber-space all borrow from the mother lode of angelology. Above all, the angels embody our worries about communication, forming the horizon of our upward possibility. Since Augustine at least, angels have been the epitome of perfect communication, a model of how we would talk if we had no obstructions. Even since the earliest dreams in the seventeenth century of instantaneous long-distance communication among humans, angelic swiftness has been the standard against which human capacities were measured. The angels are our communicative betters.

As Stuart Schneiderman suggests, angelology can be read as semiotics by other means. The bodies of angels and their couplings are allegories of signs and their syntax. But in the dominant Thomistic tradition, angels stand for communication as if bodies did not matter. Mortimer Adler, a leading student of the angels, suggests that one lesson the angels teach us is what love would be in a world without sex or gender.[32] Adler takes the adoration of universals stripped of any personal content as love in its most noble form. But his angels lack the organs of eros. Even more fatally, they lack the bodies whose vulnerability might stir a fellow creature's bowels of mercy. It's unclear how real either eros or *agapē* could be to them. Adler's gutless angels exemplify the aridness of much hankering after "communication" that persists to this day. There are of course countertraditions of fallen or meddling angels, some of them quite naughty, making all kinds of mischief, sexual and otherwise, with mortals, gods, and creation itself.

Saint Thomas Aquinas, the Doctor Angelicus and Adler's inspiration, is a high point in Scholastic angelology and offers a beautiful example of the dream of communication. He is more explicit than Augustine on how the speech of angels, who themselves are hierarchically arranged into angel species or "choirs," works. The need to communicate, Aquinas argues, is not only a product of the deficiencies of earthly knowledge and vision. Since diverse orders of angels each enjoy a varying degree of knowledge of God and his works, a motive for talk remains among them.[33] Like Augustine and Plato, Aquinas contrasts inner and outer speech. Inner speech among mortals can be cloaked by two things: by the density of our bodies and by our wills. This cloaking can be either devious or proper depending on the situation. Since his angels have no fleshly bodies, nothing to hide, and no reason to conceal anything, the external speech of the voice "does not befit an angel, but only interior

---

32. Mortimer Jerome Adler, *The Angels and Us* (New York: Macmillan, 1982).
33. Thomas Aquinas, *Summa Theologica*. Great Books of the Western World, ed. Robert Maynard Hutchins, vol. 19 (Chicago: Encyclopaedia Britannica, 1952), 546.

speech belongs to him." Since the purpose of mortal speech is to manifest what is hidden, what use would speech be among such lucidly intelligible beings? Angels speak by directing their "concept" or mind "in
such a way that it becomes known to the other." Aquinas's vision of
angelic contact is similar to what psychical research called "thought-
transference" or telepathy. The speech of angels "is interior, but perceived, nevertheless, by another."[34] The interiority of one angel is transmitted to an other without loss or remainder. Since angels, as pure form,
lack material bodies, "neither difference of time nor local distance has
any influence whatsoever." Angels commune through a noiseless rustle
of intelligence without the ministry of language or matter. In just this
way, Aquinas adds, human minds, after the Resurrection, will no longer
be hidden from each other, to the delight of the righteous and the horror of the wicked. For Aquinas, angels understand others in an instantaneous unfurling of interiorities. The self and the other would both be
transparent to behold.

The angels, in sum, are supposed to show us the way out of the fly-
bottle of our ineluctable privacy. They, of all beings, know no communication breakdown, for they are not encased within a shell of flesh or
subject to an obstreperous will. Their selfhood is both individual and
collective. Since their bodies have no matter, which is the principle of
individuation, they are simultaneously themselves and their entire species.[35] Compared with such "connaturality" (a Thomistic term that gives
us the French verb for being acquainted with, *connaître*), our lowly attempts at "communication" appear woefully deficient!

From Matter to Mind: "Communication" in the Seventeenth Century

The angelology of Augustine, Aquinas, and others gives us the intellectual basis for the dream of shared interiors in communication. But their
language was Latin, and the term *communicatio* itself did not have a
privileged role in such discussions. *Communicare* in Latin meant to share
or make common and had no special reference to sharing thoughts.[36] It
is largely in the seventeenth century that the new sense of "communication" first begins to emerge in modern English, and we can see the development of the concept by briefly examining such central figures of
British science in the seventeenth century as Bacon, Glanvill, Wilkins,

34. Thomas Aquinas, *Summa Theologica*, 549–51.
35. Frederick Copleston, *A History of Philosophy* (1948; Garden City, N.Y.: Image Books, 1985),
2:330–31.
36. *Oxford Latin Dictionary* (Oxford: Clarendon Press, 1968), 369.

and Newton. The concept of communication as we know it originates from an application of physical processes such as magnetism, convection, and gravitation to occurrences between minds. In the seventeenth century the term was consistently used to refer to what the Scholastics called *actio in distans*—action at a distance. Since at least the Scholastics, action at a distance has been a problem in natural philosophy: How can one body influence another without palpably touching it?[37] It is speculations about such action, including between minds—what Francis Bacon called "the transmission of immateriate virtues"—that sets "communication" on its modern course. Ideal relations between souls have long been understood as a question of action at a distance—Plato's lovers who do not touch or Aquinas's angels for whom no distance matters—and this notion gets recapitulated in the quasi-physical dreams of communication by scientists in the seventeenth century and spiritualists in the nineteenth.

The semantic history of "communication" owes much to psychophysical speculations. Francis Bacon, for instance, the founding spokesman for modern science, thought it "agreeable to reason, that there are at the least some light effluxions from spirit to spirit, when men are in presence one with another, as well as from body to body."[38] His list of "operations by transmission" that "work at a distance, and not at touch" includes light, sound, heat, gravity (pre-Newtonian), and magnetism; odors, infections, and "the affections"; and sympathetic transmission, as between amulets and actions, or a sword and the wounds it caused, however distant the victim. This uneasy mix for later thinkers does not respect the interdependent separation of nature and society in what Bruno Latour calls the "modern constitution."[39]

Bacon's inclusion of psychological phenomena among remote processes, not unlike the approach of his later heirs in psychical research, is echoed by his disciple Sir Joseph Glanvill, who used the phenomenon of sympathetic vibration in acoustics to explain how one mind may "bind" (secretly control) another. Imagination consisted of cerebral motions that agitated the "Aether" and propagated through this "liquid medium" to other minds, just as plucking a lute's string "causeth a proportionable motion in the sympathizing consort, which is distant from

37. Mary B. Hesse, *Forces and Fields: The Concept of Action at a Distance in the History of Physics* (Westport, Conn.: Greenwood, 1970).

38. Francis Bacon, *Sylva Sylvarum, or A Natural History* (1605), in *The Works of Francis Bacon*, ed. Basil Montagu (Philadelphia: Carey and Hart, 1848), 2:129.

39. Bruno Latour, *We Have Never Been Modern*, trans. Catherine Porter (Cambridge: Harvard University Press, 1993).

it and not sensibly touched." Such vibration at a distance also explained, Glanvill added, how "Angels inject thoughts into our minds, and know our cogitations."[40] Imaginative empathy or acoustic action: the notion of sympathy has inhabited moral and physical universes since Pythagoras. Here with the fusion of mental and material processes occurring through a subtle ether, Glanvill articulates the framework within which communication would be thought about for well over two centuries.[41]

Angelic alacrity also inspired a striking seventeenth-century anticipation of telecommunications. Bishop John Wilkins, like Glanvill both a Baconian and a founder of the Royal Society, wrote a book in 1641 called *Mercury, or The Secret and Swift Messenger, Shewing How a Man May with Privacy and Speed Communicate His Thoughts to a Friend at Any Distance,* whose title expresses the enduring ambitions of privacy and speed in long-distance communication. Angels, he argues (like Aquinas), discourse *per insinuationem specierum*—by "an unveiling of their own Natures in the knowledge of such Particulars as they would discover to another." Humans, having "Organical Bodies," however, "cannot communicate their thoughts [in] so easie and immediate a way. And therefore have need of some Corporeal Instruments, both for the Receiving and Conveying of Knowledge."[42] Our instruments—ear, eye, tongue, and feet—are tortoiselike compared with those of the angels, whose speed matches that of the "Primum Mobile," the outermost sphere of the Ptolemaic universe. Our bodies, then, are multiply handicapped. Wilkins's proposed compensation for our handicaps was a binary coding of the alphabet in visible or audible media, such as trumpets, bells, cannons, drums, flame, or smoke. Unlike the nineteenth century, Wilkins had no idea of physical means such as the telegraph to send signals themselves; he relied on the eyes and ears, these being the only senses that "are of quick Perception, when their objects are remote."[43] The distances Wilkins could cover are limited by the acuity of the eyes and ears and the curvature of the earth. He did not yet know the quicksilver status of the electrical signal.

Newtonian physics, the capital fact of science and philosophy in

40. Joseph Glanvill, *The Vanity of Dogmatizing* (New York: Columbia University Press, 1931), 199–200.

41. On Renaissance notions of natural sympathy, see Michel Foucault, *The Order of Things* (New York: Pantheon, 1970), 17–44, and François Jacob, *The Logic of Life: A History of Heredity,* trans. Betty E. Spillman (New York: Pantheon, 1974), 20–32.

42. John Wilkins, *Mercury, or The Secret and Swift Messenger: Shewing How a Man May with Privacy and Speed Communicate His Thoughts to a Friend at a Distance,* 3d ed. (1641; London, 1707), 1–2.

43. Wilkins, *Mercury,* 69.

eighteenth-century Europe, gave new energy to speculation about action at a distance and hence boosted the fortunes of communication as
well. Newton's description in his 1687 *Principia* of universal gravitation
and its operation was first and foremost an account of action at a distance. Like magnetism, light, and heat, he thought gravity traveled via
an "imponderable" or insensible fluid. The word Newton used for this
fluid, in both his English and Latin writings, was "medium."[44] Newton
called this "universal and subtle" medium the *sensorium dei* (sensorium
of God). He saw the cosmos as bathed in a cosmic intelligence communicating at a distance through a marvelous, intangible essence. This
force or intelligence prevented us from flying off into space and kept
the moon in orbit and the tides ebbing and flowing. Like his late
nineteenth-century British successors in physics, Newton took this medium not simply as a sterile physical fact but as full of spiritual suggestion. In Newton "communication" and "medium" have much of their
modern senses without their modern spheres of use. One means the
transmission of immaterial forces or entities at a distance, the other the
mechanism or vehicle of such transmission.

Bacon, Glanvill, Wilkins, Newton—these are not crackpots, but the
cream of English science in the seventeenth century and founders of
modern scientific culture. Their interest in angels and the ether, and
in natural and cultural communicative action at a distance, was not
retrograde but transitional. These examples show that "communication" mainly referred to physical processes of transmission and metaphysical processes of consubstantiation, the boundary between subject
and object being quite ragged. Tangibles such as robes, fortunes, plants,
and commodities and intangibles such as light, heat, blessings, praise,
secrets, vices, thoughts, and ideas could all be "communicated."[45] In the
process of remaking Scholastic categories into scientific ones, "communication" took a new turn.

JOHN LOCKE: PRIVATE PROPERTIES OF MEANING   John Locke was perhaps
most decisive in nudging the term's orbit from matter to mind. As a
major shaper of the culture and politics of individualism and much else
in the English-speaking world, it is significant that he should be the
author, in some sense, of communication as we know it. Locke's use of
"communication" to describe the sharing of ideas between people was

44. Leo Spitzer, "Milieu and Ambiance," in *Essays in Historical Semantics* (New York: S. F. Vanni,
1948), 179–225.
45. *Oxford English Dictionary,* s. v. "communicate."

something of an innovation. Though similar usages in English are found before Locke, both Dr. Johnson's *Dictionary of the English Language* (1755) and the *Oxford English Dictionary* make Locke the fountainhead of this sense. Even so, Locke's prose mingles old senses of the term with innovative ones. He speaks not only of people communicating ideas to each other, but of God communicating perfections to his angels and of the spirit communicating (interacting) with the body. Though he was influential on a certain strand of rhetorical theory and practice, Locke understood communication not as a kind of speech, rhetoric, or discourse, but as their ideal end result. Locke launched this term on its long drift from physical to mental sharing. Whereas for Augustine the obstacle was often the body, for Locke language itself can prevent ideas from flowing between minds with all the ease with which a lodestone "communicates" with a piece of iron. Locke's claim that words must be "serviceable to the end of Communication . . . which is the end of Discourse and Language" (*Essay,* 3.9.6) invents a new word about words: "communication."[46]

In his vision of the "end" of discourse and language, as well as their contrast between the inner thought and the outer word, Locke resembles Augustine. (In their vision of the human estate, there are continuities as well: "We are all men, liable to errors, and infected with them": *Essay,* "Preface").[47] But their overall projects are very different. Augustine thinks of signs as bodies; Locke thinks of them as property. The former offers an incarnational theology of the sign, the latter an individualist politics. Locke treats the meanings of words as a sort of private property in the individual's interior. Indeed, his individualism extends from his political theories, as found in his *Second Treatise of Government,* to his psychological and linguistic theories, as found in his *Essay concerning Human Understanding.* Both inform his account of communication. The individual (and not society, language, or tradition) is the master of meaning, which makes common understanding between individuals both desperately urgent and highly problematic. Locke helps supply the social and intellectual conditions that make "commu-

46. I will cite the *Essay concerning Human Understanding* parenthetically in the text by section number or page. I have used the edition by Peter H. Nidditch (1690; Oxford: Oxford University Press, 1975).

47. W. M. Spellman, *John Locke and the Problem of Depravity* (Oxford: Clarendon Press, 1988), argues against the prevalent interpretation of Locke by eighteenth-century thinkers—for example, Condillac, Helvetius, Richardson (*Pamela*), and Chesterfield—who considered him the theorist of human nature as a tabula rasa (a term not found in the *Essay* but present in the writings on education). They slighted the qualifications in Locke. Spellman argues that Locke did play an important role in moderating the view of depravity in education, without ever abandoning the conviction of our natural infection with error.

nication" both necessary and impossible, though it took two centuries after Locke for such longings and anxieties to reach their fever pitch. Like Descartes, Locke is a chief agent in the subjectification of the world.[48]

Locke's notion of communication rests on his understandings of mind and of language. First, his psychology allows him to justify individual autonomy in meaning making that is analogous to such autonomy in propertyholding. Central to Locke's account of the human understanding is the "'idea' idea" based on Descartes's view that we have no direct access to the real world.[49] We never see clouds, feel tables, or smell roses; our eyes, fingers, or noses bring us "ideas" from those entities. The internal chain of ideas is supplied by what Descartes calls "the intermediary of the senses." An idea, according to Locke, is an "immediate object of the Mind, which it perceives and has before it distinct from the sound it uses as a sign" (*Essay,* "Epistle to the Reader," p. 14). Though "idea" is a word put to a bewildering variety of uses by Locke (as his critics have long noted), it constitutes the basic currency of his epistemology. "Simple ideas" are the raw material of all knowledge, and all genuine knowledge can be ultimately traced to simple ideas. He denies innate ideas—nothing is in the mind that was not first in the senses. A simple idea is an immediate datum of sense that cannot be defined. For Locke, these most basic components of human understanding are neither social nor linguistic. No one else can give you the experience of "sweetness" or "red" or explain what it is. You must simply taste or see for yourself. The basing of knowledge in sensation makes the sharing of knowledge radically problematic. The stuff of knowledge is conceived as something isolated and off-limits to others, confined to our private perceptual apparatus.

It is not unfair to find a political motive in Locke's location of epistemological authority in the individual's senses. Knowledge can serve as the basis of liberation: individuals see things as they are for themselves, not as they are painted by church, Crown, or custom (see *Essay,* 4.3.20). His examples—the flavor of a pineapple, the color red, the malleability of gold—are kinds of experiences that seem, on the one hand, obviously

48. Hannah Arendt, *The Human Condition* (Chicago: University of Chicago Press, 1958).
49. On the philosophical fortunes of the word "idea," see Godfrey Vesey, "Foreword: A History of 'Ideas,'" in *Idealism Past and Present,* ed. Godfrey Vesey (Cambridge: Cambridge University Press, 1982), 1–18. On the "'idea' idea," see Ian Hacking, *Why Does Language Matter to Philosophy?* (Cambridge: Cambridge University Press, 1975), 15–53, 163–70; Richard Rorty, *Philosophy and the Mirror of Nature* (Princeton: Princeton University Press, 1979), 48–50, 192ff.

common yet also strangely incommunicable. I can never know for sure whether what I call "green" or "sweet" has the same experiential correlate for you. Since reference to experience is the ground of all significance, verification that real contact has occurred between distinct individual minds in Locke's scheme is an ever-receding horizon. Locke at once gives individuals resources to defy tradition and inaugurates the potential for radical disconnection in meanings. For Locke "meanings are in people," not in culture. Language is decidedly not a source of knowledge, a shaper of thinking, or a part of the essence of human being. It is "the great Instrument, and common Tye of Society" that God gave to humans, so they could be sociable creatures (*Essay*, 3.1.1). Book 3 of the *Essay*, "Of Words or Language in General," turns out even to be something of a change in plan, since Locke began his work thinking that little attention to language would be needed in a work on the understanding!

Like Augustine, Aquinas, and many thinkers of the seventeenth century, Locke conceives of two sorts of "discourse": the internal stream of ideas that derives from sensation and reflection, and the public or external use of language (what we call "discourse" today). As Locke's contemporary and fellow Royal Society member John Wallis said in 1687, "In our English language we say Discourse at one time in relation to the internal reckoning of the mind, and at another time concerning external colloquy."[50] Words are "external or sensible signs" of ideas or "internal conceptions." As in Augustine, the inner word (for Locke, the *idea*) is authoritative. Signs without support from ideas are "Sounds without Signification" (*Essay*, 3.2.2). Locke often figures words as a currency that is secured only by the cash of ideas on deposit in people's minds. If words circulate without the backing of ideas (as, to Locke's chagrin, he thought they did), they are counterfeit agents of trickery and confusion (examples of Locke's monetary metaphors for language can be found in *Essay*, 3.8.2, 3.10.2–5, 3.11.11).[51]

Language makes the inner life of ideas—the savor of pineapples, the varieties of colors, the feel of substances—publicly accessible. Just as Augustine thought the Word's becoming flesh had no effect on its na-

---

50. Quoted in Wilbur Samuel Howell, *Eighteenth-Century British Logic and Rhetoric* (Princeton: Princeton University Press, 1971), 32.

51. No other "substance" is invoked in the *Essay* as often as gold. On Locke and coinage, see Joyce Appleby, "Locke, Liberalism, and the Natural Law of Money," *Past and Present* 71 (May 1976): 43–69; Marcelo Dascal, "Language and Money: A Simile and Its Meaning in Seventeenth Century Philosophy of Language," *Studia Leibnitiana*, 8, 2 (1976): 187–218.

ture, so Locke thinks the expression of thoughts, ideally, should be unaffected by language:

> Man, though he have great Variety of Thoughts, and such, from which others, as well as himself, might receive Profit and Delight; yet they are all within his own Breast, invisible, and hidden from others, nor can of themselves be made to appear. The Comfort and Advantage of Society, not being to be had without Communication of Thoughts, it was necessary, that Man should find out some external sensible Signs, whereby those invisible Ideas, which his thoughts are made up of, might be made known to others. (*Essay,* 3.2.1)

Locke engages in the solipsistic fantasy beloved in British thought, Robinson Crusoe's having to reinvent civilization solo, and here too it serves to reinforce an individualist politics. People are not born into language in this scenario: they have to invent it. The meaning of words comes not from words' placement in a total system of signs (as for Saussure), nor from their reference to objects (as for Wittgenstein's version of Augustine), but from their reference to ideas in minds. "Words in their primary or immediate Signification, stand for nothing, but the Ideas in the Mind of him that uses them" (*Essay,* 3.2.2). Language is not an art of seduction (as for Rousseau), the way we articulate our being in the world (Heidegger), or a mode of performing actions (Austin), but a means of transporting ideas. Locke emphasizes the cognitive over the poetic or phatic functions of language.[52] Successful transmission is his criterion. "When a Man speaks to another, it is, that he might be understood; and the end of Speech is, that those Sounds, as Marks, may make known his *Ideas* to the Hearer" (*Essay,* 3.2.2). This vision of the word as a receptacle of meaning, as the body is a receptacle of the soul, makes communication into a problem of transporting mental cargo. Indeed, Locke calls language "the great Conduit" (*Essay,* 3.11.5).[53]

Communication breakdown looms in Locke's scenario. The particulars of the linkage between sound as marks and ideas is up the individual. Words are "voluntary Signs" (*Essay,* 3.2.2) and acquire their meanings from the consent of their users, since "every Man has so inviolable a Liberty, to make Words stand for what Ideas he pleases, that no one hath the Power to make others have the same Ideas in their Minds, that he has, when they use the same Words, that he does" (*Essay,* 3.3.8).

---

52. Roman Jakobson, "Closing Statement: Linguistics and Poetics," in *Style in Language,* ed. Thomas A. Sebeok (Cambridge: MIT Press, 1960), 350–77.

53. Paul de Man makes great sport of the plumbing imagery of book 3 of the *Essay* in "The Epistemology of Metaphor," *Critical Inquiry* 5 (1978): 13–30; see also Reddy, "Conduit Metaphor."

Locke is a conventionalist in his semantics.[54] The link of word and idea, for Locke, is a social contract held up by the collective agreement of individuals. If words were naturally connected to ideas, he reasons, all the world would speak one tongue. Anyone may thus withdraw from language any time, though the practicalities of daily intercourse exact the "tacit consent" of almost everybody to language as presently constituted (*Essay*, 3.3.8). The liberty of individuals in meaning making makes the conveyance of thoughts dubious. The inviolable semantic liberty of the individual protects individuals from the illegitimate control of other wills but also means we can never be sure when we have shared thoughts as opposed to merely filling the air with sounds. The individual, for Locke, is lord of the signifier.

Communication becomes a rather paradoxical concept. On the one hand, Locke calls for freedom to combine words and ideas; on the other, he hopes for exact correspondence. "To make words serviceable to the end of Communication, it is necessary . . . that they excite, in the Hearer, exactly the same Idea, they stand for in the Mind of the Speaker. Without this, Men fill one another's Heads with noise and sounds; but convey not thereby their Thoughts, and lay not before one another their Ideas, which is the end of Discourse and Language" (*Essay*, 3.9.6). Locke places the word "communication" squarely in the intellectual problematic of privacy of the *cogito*, the thinking self. Why should one person acknowledge the meanings that another annexes to signs? If each individual is a legislator of signs, what is to keep society from becoming a collection of monads, shut up in the solitude of their private coding schemes? Individual liberty (in which people are sovereign over their own private consciousness) sits uneasily with "communication" (in which mental contents are seemingly replicated). Locke's principles set up an antinomy: the dream of communication as replication of ideas and the sovereignty of the individual over his or her own consciousness.

The philosophical antinomy reflects a material one. Locke's politics and semantics intertwine. Both defend the individual as an owner of private property, whether the private property of consciousness ("ideas") or real property ("life, liberty, and estate"). Both base that claim on the privacy of the individual body. Locke must find ways to move between what is common (and owned by all) and private (and owned by one or few). In his account of language, Locke expresses his cardinal semiotic principle (the conventionality of meaning) in terms of

54. Hans Aarsleff, *From Locke to Saussure: Essays on the Study of Language and Intellectual History* (Minneapolis: University of Minnesota Press, 1982).

his cardinal political principle (the inviolable liberty of the individual). Locke's theory of property is found in his *Second Treatise of Government,* published anonymously the same year as the *Essay* (1690). A chief task of the work is to account for the origin of private property and to legitimize what Locke calls "civil society." In the *First Treatise,* Locke worked to discredit the notion, which was used to legitimate hereditary monarchy, that God gave Adam and his royal lineage exclusive rights to dominion over the earth in a line of unbroken patriarchy (the divine right of kings). In the *Second Treatise* he tries to show how differences in possessions originated, even though God initially gave the world to all "men" (not women) as a common inheritance.[55] In the beginning, Locke hypothesizes, everything in the world was held in common by everyone. Since the world's materials are the spontaneous productions of nature, "the common Mother of us all," no one had an exclusive right to any of those materials. Yet this primordial state of commonness could not have lasted long, since as soon as people act in and upon the world, they "mix" their labor with materials. Labor is not common property, but private to each: "Though the Earth and all inferior Creatures be common to all Men, yet every Man has a *Property* in his own *Person;* this no Body has any Right to but himself. The *Labour* of his Body and the *Work* of his Hands we may say are properly his."[56] We have liberty to use our lives to build up our estate. By mixing labor with the common world of nature, various people may fence in part of it. Labor, Locke argues, provides nearly the complete value of all products. The original right of ownership over one's own labor becomes transferred to the materials in which that labor is invested. Labor, one might say, involves the transfer of properties in the double sense of personal characteristics and real estate. (I return to the problematic place of money in Locke's thinking in chapter 3.)

The distinction between common (or public) and private underlies Locke's thinking about both property and communication. The problem for his theory of property is how to get from an Edenic community in the state of nature to the privacy of property in civil society. He takes the common as a drowsy state of primitive quiescence, modeled partly on what he had read of native peoples of the Americas. The private, in contrast, arises whenever people employ their faculties in reworking the world. The common is a given, the private is an achievement. Privacy

55. Carole Pateman, "The Fraternal Social Contract," in *The Disorder of Women: Democracy, Feminism, and Political Theory* (Stanford: Stanford University Press, 1989), 33–57.

56. John Locke, *Two Treatises of Government,* ed. Peter Laslett (Cambridge: Cambridge University Press, 1988), sec. 27; emphasis in original.

needs protection while commonness can be taken for granted. (This weighting of public and private decisively marks Locke's difference from later critics of individualism such as Tocqueville, who wants to protect the public realm against the retreat into privacy.) The problem for Locke's account of language is the inverse of his account of property: how private owners of experiences of the world can ally themselves in a common world of understanding. To communicate is to make common. Sensation is analogous to labor: as people sense the world, they gather pieces of it unto themselves. Since Locke made the privatizing labor of the individual so fundamental, he is left with the task of explaining how different people can have understandings in common.

Locke's accounts of property and communication, then, are twins. For property he must explain how to get from the common to the private (in matter); for communication he must explain how to get from the private back to the common (in mind). Locke's theory of language, and especially his innovative use of "communication," I take as attempts to plug a hole in a theory that insufficiently explained how a society of free individuals could hang together. Locke wanted to posit common meaning as not existing and then ask how it came to exist. Rather than taking the origin of individual minds as the problem, he made public meaning appear flimsy and improbable. But Locke was engaged in a political struggle and had to posit the individual as primary. "Communication" showed one way that individuals could coexist without compromising their sovereignty. Almost like angels, they would share thoughts.

To be fair, however, one of Locke's virtues is that he did not hold up the angels as a model: he allowed for the possibility of pragmatic making-do in words. A difference between Locke and earlier and later dreamers of communication is that though he made the conveyance of thoughts his norm of productive language use ("To make words serviceable to the end of Communication, it is necessary . . . that they excite, in the Hearer, exactly the same *Idea,* they stand for in the Mind of the Speaker" [*Essay,* 3.9.6]), he did not think we could ever communicate like the angels. Spirits, he wrote, have "a perfecter way of communicating their Thoughts, than we have, who are fain to make use of corporeal Signs. . . . But of immediate Communication, having no Experiment in our selves, and consequently no Notion of it at all, we have no *Idea* how Spirits, which use not Words, can with quickness; or much less, how Spirits that have no Bodies can be Masters of their own Thoughts, and communicate or conceal them at Pleasure, though we cannot but necessarily suppose they have such a Power" (*Essay,* 2.23.36). Locke was dancing at the edge of his epistemology, exploring something he had no sensory experience of. That, of course, is part of the point: angels, seraphim, and the divine evade our understanding. (The question how angels could have private thoughts without bodies in which to contain them is a good example of Locke's principle that embodiment is the source of private property and the container of interiority.) Likewise, Locke admitted of varying degrees of exactness in the conveyance of ideas, distinguishing "civil" and "philosophical" communication (*Essay*, 3.9.3). The former allows customarily loose ties between words and ideas while the latter, fit for scientific investigation, demands far greater exactness.

Locke's use of the term "communication" combines an Augustinian semiotic of inner and outer, a political program of individual liberty, and a scientific imagination of clean processes of transmission. He saw communication as a norm of thought conveyance, something his own principles did not allow. If he did not unfold all the consequences of the antinomies of communication—the possibility of shared minds and the horror of solipsism—he set later meditation on "communication" in that direction. Locke's legacy lives when we bemoan the inadequacy of words for catching our inner feelings, fear the tyrannical power of words, or praise scientific method as a way to ensure reasonable human intercourse. Locke teaches us to see meaning as dwelling in the individual, out of a fear for the political consequences. If individuals do not control meaning, or it is situated somewhere besides people's private experiences, Locke's heirs fear that tyranny is hovering nearby. Only bad people think of meanings as existing outside of mind, for any other location is an affront to the dignity of the individual. Words—divorced from social relations—get demoted, at worst, into agents of violent imposition on our own unique experiences or, at best, clumsy tools of making sense of ourselves. The notion of private property in mind makes communication both necessary and impossible.

For Locke's heirs, communication is both doomed to failure and blessedly wordless.[57] Locke's commitment to the individual as sovereign in both meaning and property sets up the subsequent hopes and dangers of communication. Even if not always the exact source, Locke's thought is exemplary of many of the commitments that trail that concept. To define the social life of language as communication makes the individual the lord of the signifier but obscures, even demonizes, any

---

57. Adam Smith, who clearly takes much from Locke's psychology, does not believe in any such thing as soul sharing. In this respect Smith stands in the wise lineage of those who deny direct communication. See John Durham Peters, "Publicity and Pain: Self-Abstraction in Adam Smith's *Theory of Moral Sentiments*," *Public Culture* 7 (1995): 657–75.

conception of public meaning. The ancestral commitment to the sovereignty of the individual governs much of communication and its confusions. Whenever we set out to think or discourse seriously about communication, we almost always find ourselves enacting a philosophical and political drama first written by John Locke.

Nineteenth-Century Spiritualism

John Locke was no romantic. His was a clean and well-ordered universe of sensations and particles. Madness, the occult, longing for distant love, haunting by the dead—such hardly registered for him. But for the long nineteenth century, running from the French Revolution to World War I, dominant discourses of communication were enveloped in a romantic mist. Solipsism and identity of consciousness were only two extremes in Locke's vision of language as working well enough, most of the time, at least for everyday purposes. But by the nineteenth century the agony of solitude and the yearning for unity were far more intense. As it was put by William Blake, who, representative of the romantics, early expressed "Contempt & Abhorrence" for Locke, "What is now proved was once only imagined." The mingling of physical and psychical universes proliferated, as did a wish to be like the angels—or with the dead.

DR. MESMER AND HIS FLUIDS The practice of mesmerism and its many offshoots exerted a large but subterranean influence on literature and thought in the nineteenth century. Mesmerism played out some of the cultural consequences of Locke's semantic individualism. The state of being in mesmeric unity with another could be not only a vision of mental harmony but also a nightmare of loss of self to another's will. Mesmerism, with its scary and blissful violation of the self, fascinated and horrified a wide range of French, German, British, and American writers, including Balzac, Guy de Maupassant, J. G. Fichte, E. T. A. Hoffmann, Edgar Allan Poe, Nathaniel Hawthorne, Elizabeth Barrett Browning, Robert Louis Stevenson, and George du Maurier. A mesmerized character in a Guy de Maupassant story laments: "Someone possesses my soul and governs it. Someone directs all my actions, all my movements, all my thoughts. I myself am nothing but a terrified, enslaved spectator of the things I am accomplishing."[58] Du Maurier's *Trilby*

58. Quoted in Henri F. Ellenberger, *The Discovery of the Unconscious: The History and Evolution of Dynamic Psychiatry* (New York: Basic Books, 1970), 165; for mesmerism's literary influences, see Robert Darnton, *Mesmerism and the End of the Enlightenment in France* (Cambridge: Harvard University Press, 1967), chap. 5, and Ellenberger, *Discovery of the Unconscious,* 158–70.

(1894), the best-selling novel of the 1890s and perhaps of the entire century, concerns how the mysterious Svengali hypnotizes the tone-deaf Englishwoman Trilby into becoming a virtuoso singer, at a severe price to her body and soul. Our enduring images of subjection and seduction are stamped by mesmerism, but the antinomies—the self as sovereignly shut or dangerously open—were set up by Locke. Mesmerism showed that romantic spiritual intercourse could be double-edged, spelling both the bliss of romance and the horror of soul trespassing.

It is easy to forget that mesmerism refers to a historical figure, Franz Anton Mesmer (1734–1815), who considered himself the Newton of the human soul. The words "mesmerism" and "mesmerize" rarely make us think of Dr. Mesmer but rather recall hypnotism, a phenomenon not named until the 1840s. Mesmer belonged to an age when men lent their names to electrical processes (Volta, Galvani, Gauss, Watt, Ohm, Ampère). "Animal magnetism"—his name for his discovery—he took as the key to attraction both physical (gravity) and social (love). (The notion of a cosmic magnetism encompassing both heavenly and earthly bodies has older roots in German thought, in Paracelsus and Athanasius Kircher.)[59] First in a succession of Viennese physicians who claimed to possess the secret of the soul, Mesmer was a quirky *Aufklärer,* a freemason, and a grandiose if sincere quack. Holding forth with style and success among the upper classes of prerevolutionary Paris from 1778 to 1785, Mesmer taught that a universally diffused "fluid" held the key to sickness and health. The fluid coursed from person to person and from humans to cosmos, acting, like magnetism, at a distance. (The term "animal magnetism" was meant to contrast with physical magnetism, "animal" deriving from Latin *animus* or spirit.) In the late eighteenth century, fluids were at the cutting edge of science, showing up, for example, in Lavoisier, the architect of modern chemistry. As Robert Darnton puns, "There were enough fluids, sponsored by enough philosophers, to make any eighteenth-century reader's head swim."[60] Mesmer and his disciples considered themselves neither occultists nor a circus sideshow but the latest stride of the march of reason. They were offering a unified field theory of the material and moral forces. As gravitation held the planets in orbit, so animal magnetism kept souls in love and health and communication.

Mesmer's healing practice used animal magnetism to treat patients, largely aristocratic women, usually afflicted with what a later generation would call neurosis. Often remarkable "healings" occurred, in which

---

59. Michael Neumann, *Unterwegs zu den Inseln des Scheins: Kunstbegriff and literarische Form in der Romantik von Novalis bis Nietzsche* (Frankfurt: Vittorio Klostermann, 1991), 456–59.

60. Darnton, *Mesmerism,* 11.

Mesmer saw a fact of nature, not mind; of physics, not psychology. Mesmer was a Columbus: he discovered a new world (the continent of the unconscious and the peninsulas of neurosis and hypnosis) yet remained mistaken about its identity to his dying day.[61] The techniques of mesmeric healing seem almost like a parody of romantic seduction—in part because mesmerism supplies romanticism with much of its imagery of love and possession. When a magnetizer threw a patient into a "crisis" (hysterics or seizures), for instance, that occurred because of his ability to concentrate the flow of animal magnetism through his eyes and hands. The generic "he" is apt since, as in psychoanalysis (or *Trilby*), the social constellation of mesmerism typically involved a male practitioner and a female patient—something that did nothing to counteract anxieties, sexual and otherwise, about mesmerism's padded rooms and occult physical attractions.[62] Indeed, in a cause célèbre, Mesmer was accused of raping the blind composer Maria Theresia von Paradies, whom he also briefly "healed" from blindness. Treatments included a variety of props, such as magnets, vials of magnetized fluids, and magic wands, as well as massage and music. Sickness resulted from "obstacles" blocking the fluid's flow through the body. Mesmer would run his fingers all over the patient's body in search of the "poles" of the body's magnetic fields or "make passes" over the body with magnetized objects, a practice that may be the origin of the phrase "to make a pass," an expression that, like much else, migrated from mesmerism to romanticism and romance.

Animal magnetism created an arresting image of the total fusion of two or more souls that would, in conjunction with romantic and occult currents, reverberate through European and American literature in the nineteenth century. The mesmeric condition of being *en rapport* or, as it was often translated, "in communication" was another term borrowed from electricity.[63] Late eighteenth-century experiments had shown that human bodies could conduct electricity. A popular pastime in places such as London and Paris was for a group of people to link hands to serve as a channel of electrical impulses. If the chain broke, no "communication" of electricity took place. For transmission to occur, people had to be *en rapport* or in contact.[64] Mesmer seems to have appropriated the

61. Ellenberger, *Discovery of the Unconscious*, 57.

62. Donald R. Hoffeld, "Mesmer's Failure: Sex, Politics, Personality, and the Zeitgeist," *Journal of the History of the Behavioral Sciences* 16 (1980): 377–86.

63. Parley Parker Pratt, an important early Mormon theologian, wrote in his treatise *Key to the Science of Theology* (1855; Salt Lake City: Deseret Book, 1966), 106: "Two beings, or two millions—any number thus placed 'in communication'—all possess one mind." Pratt explicitly called this "a modern magnetic term," suggesting he saw "in communication" as a borrowing from mesmerism.

64. Ellenberger, *Discovery of the Unconscious*, 152.

notion of electrical communication for one of his treatments. Patients would gather around a *baquet*, a sort of tub that he invented, each touching an iron frame that was supposed to concentrate the collective animal magnetism of the patients' bodies. The patients would feel the fluid coursing through them and would often undergo "crises" in order. Soon electrical communion no longer needed the *baquet*, only the gaze of the mesmerist, acting at a distance. Two souls *en rapport* could share every thought and feeling. Some mesmerists argued that "community of sensation" (as it later became known in parapsychology) took place even though the people were separated by hundreds of miles.[65] Here again is a transfer from the flight of electricity to the juncture of minds.

A rift quickly arose in animal magnetism's purported dominion over subject and object alike. As early as 1785, a schism appeared between fluidists (who held fast to the notion of an imponderable fluid) and animists (who believed mesmerism's effects were due to social and psychological factors, specifically the power of the mesmerist's will; these are the ancestors of hypnotism). Mesmer himself was discredited by a scientific commission in 1784 that included Antoine-Laurent Lavoisier, Joseph-Ignace Guillotin, and Benjamin Franklin, which declared the effects of animal magnetism due solely to imagination and not to physics (much more in line with the modern constitution than was Francis Bacon!). Mesmer spent the rest of his life in obscurity.

A third branch of animal magnetism was the most short lived of all. Some saw the description of how people can be put *en rapport* as the natural fulfillment of Jean-Jacques Rousseau's politics of pity. Nicolas Bergasse, one of Mesmer's most influential disciples and a key player in the French Revolution, developed the branch of mesmerism later dubbed political mesmerism.[66] Mesmerism fit the nascent democratic sentiments of its age, showing how each person possessed a power given by nature that could not be removed by despotism or tyranny.[67] Bergasse saw mesmerism as a way to correct deficiencies in Rousseau's philosophy. Rousseau, like Adam Smith, had made the ability to put oneself in another's place a cornerstone of manners and morals but, according to Bergasse, had left the mechanism unclear. Bergasse did not want to stop at understanding the other; he wanted a sure means of contact. Mesmer-

65. Charles Ferson Durant, *Exposition, or A New Theory of Animal Magnetism* (1837; New York: Da Capo Press, 1982). Durant adds a Lockean/corpuscularian touch: "The magnetic fluid is composed of globular molecules which touch each other, and form strings or magnetic cords from one brain to the other" (79).

66. Vincent Buranelli, *The Wizard from Vienna: Franz Anton Mesmer* (New York: Coward, McCann, and Geoghegan, 1975), 205.

67. Darnton, *Mesmerism*, chaps. 3–4.

ism for Bergasse realized Rousseau's politics of compassion by showing that our spiritual fellowship with one another involved a physical transfer of magnetic forces, not just an act of imagination.[68] Such fellowship involved real community of sensation, not one-way efforts at empathy.

J. G. Fichte, the founder of German idealism, called animal magnetism "the physicalization of idealism."[69] Animal magnetism and its fellows were clearly a kind of "idealism for the people." They brought spirit, soul, and the annihilation of time and space into people's living rooms and meeting halls. Here idealism was free of the rigors of negation; it existed as a substance. For instance, in Hawthorne's *Blithedale Romance* (1852) a quack "professor" expounds what is evidently some sort of mesmerism in a village hall. The narrator remarks of the lecture that it "was eloquent, ingenious, plausible, with a delusive show of spirituality, yet really imbued throughout with a cold and dead materialism . . . [it would not] have surprised me, had he pretended to hold up a portion of his universally pervasive fluid, as he affirmed it to be, in a glass phial."[70] Little wonder Emerson objected to mesmerism.[71] His Oversoul was decidedly not the kind of thing that lent itself to bottling. But for every Emerson with his high standards, there was a village hall full of curious folk eager to be entertained.

Notions of mesmeric control, transmitted via hypnotism into crowd psychology, also appear in visions of mass communication and of mass communication gone bad in the twentieth century.[72] As an active political force in the French Revolution, mesmerism had a short life; but as a fund of images for the redemptive and diabolical features of mass communication it lives on, thanks to its influence on crowd psychology, mediated by hypnotism.[73] By showing the vulnerability of the Lockean citadel of the consenting self, hypnotism became a chief metaphor for describing the spell that dictators and admen cast on their audiences

68. Darnton, *Mesmerism*, 118–19.

69. Günter Schulte, "Übersinnliche Erfahrung als transzendental-philosophisches Problem: Zu Fichtes 'Tagebuch über den animalischen Magnetismus' von 1813," in *Der Transzendentale Gedanke*, ed. Klaus Hammacher (Hamburg: Meiner, 1981), 278–87.

70. Nathaniel Hawthorne, *The Blithedale Romance* (1852; New York: Bantam Books, 1986), 180.

71. Ralph Waldo Emerson, "Demonology" (1839), in *The Early Lectures of Ralph Waldo Emerson*, ed. Robert E. Spiller and Wallace E. Williams (Cambridge: Harvard University Press, 1972), 3:151–71.

72. Cf. John Durham Peters, "Satan and Savior: Mass Communication in Progressive Thought," *Critical Studies in Mass Communication* 6, 3 (1989): 247–63.

73. Serge Moscovici, *L'âge des foules: Un traité historique de psychologie des masses* (Paris: Fayard, 1981), shows repeatedly the strong input of notions of hypnotism on his triad of crowd theorists, Gustave Le Bon, Gabriel de Tarde, and Sigmund Freud. See also Susanna Barrows, *Distorting Mirrors: Visions of the Crowd in Late Nineteenth-Century France* (New Haven: Yale University Press, 1981), and Jonathan Miller, "Crowds and Power: Some English Ideas on the Status of Primitive Personality," *International Review of Psychoanalysis* 10 (1983): 253–64.

via radio, film, and television. Mesmerism's afterlife helped shape the understanding of mass media in the twentieth century as agents of mass control and persuasion that somehow, via their repetition, ubiquity, or subliminally iniquitous techniques, bypassed the vigilant conscience of citizens and directly accessed the archaic phobias (or ignorance and sloth) of the beast within.

SPIRITUALIST MEDIUMS AND MEDIA   Mesmer was too early to see how the electrical telegraph could put people *en rapport*. But the popular reception of both the telegraph and the wireless telegraph or radio shows the persistence of the dream that electricity can mingle souls. When Samuel F. B. Morse appealed to the United States Congress in 1842 for funding to build a telegraph line from Washington to Baltimore, so preposterous did the proposal sound to one fine congressman from Tennessee that he mockingly proposed half of the funds be spent on research in mesmerism. He evidently found it easy to lump animal magnetism and electromagnetism together.[74] (Morse did get the money—$30,000.) Both mesmerism and telegraphy draw on a common cultural project: electrical connection between distant individuals. The telegraph both stimulated and drew on older discourses about immaterial action at a distance. The so-called lightning lines introduced the problem that James Carey, following Norbert Wiener, calls "the economy of the signal": the movement not of cargoes but of informational differences with no clear physical status.[75] The problem of how many angels can dance on the head of a pin is the problem of the electrical signal—so intangible and yet so dependent on a continuum of interconnecting wires. To many, the electrical telegraph seemed the latest in a long tradition of angels and divinities spiriting intelligence across vast distances.[76] It only needed the ministry of a telegraphist to interpret and transcribe the code.

That the telegraph opened access to the spirit world is not a fanciful metaphor I am imposing retroactively; the spiritualist haunting of the new medium decisively shaped the popular reception of the technology. Spiritualism, the art of communication with the dead, explicitly modeled itself on the telegraph's ability to receive remote messages. Though the ambition of forging contact with the dead via mediums is ancient

74. Ann Braude, *Radical Spirits: Spiritualism and Women's Rights in Nineteenth-Century America* (Boston: Beacon Press, 1989), 4–5.

75. James W. Carey, *Communication as Culture* (Boston: Unwin Hyman, 1989), chap. 8.

76. I am referring to the electrical telegraph; visual mechanical telegraphs were first used in the late eighteenth century. See Geoffrey Wilson, *The Old Telegraphs* (London: Phillimore, 1976).

and widespread, spiritualism's birth as an organized practice dates to 1848, four years after the successful telegraphic link of Baltimore and Washington. Spiritualism's inventors were the sisters Kate and Margaret Fox of Hydesville, New York, a town squarely in the "burned-over district" of New York State—a region that gave birth to Mormonism, Seventh-Day Adventism, the feminist movement, Kodak, and Xerox. (Rochester is the home of machines for making duplicates: spiritualism, photography, and photocopying.)[77] The sisters discovered "rapping" sounds in their house, caused, they declared, by a departed spirit that had been murdered there years before.[78] From the beginning debunkers claimed the raps were produced by the sisters themselves, since they were never heard apart from the sisters' presence. In 1889 one of the women confessed to making the sounds by subtly cracking her toe joints, a confession that true believers have regarded as tarnished by compulsion or senility.

The sisters understood the raps as a telegraphic cipher attempting to bridge the chasm between the living and the dead. At first the spirits responded only to yes/no questions (the economy of the signal again). Later the sisters helped move the spirits out of the digital domain by serially reciting the alphabet. When the correct letter was reached, the spirit would rap three times, allowing the laborious spelling out of words and sentences, a technique that would become the principle of the Ouija board.[79] "This method of rapping to the alphabet so resembled the telegraph that the term 'spiritual telegraph' was applied to it almost from the first."[80] (The *Spiritual Telegraph* was also the name of a leading New York City spiritualist weekly in the 1850s.) While they were touring England in 1852, a newspaper account described the Fox sisters as using a "systematic mode of telegraphy."[81] Such cross-fertilization between spiritual and technical realms is decisive in the making of the modern vocabulary and vision of communication and continues in the direction begun by Locke and Mesmer. The reception of distant messages made Kate and Margaret Fox telegraphists of the spirit world. Even more crucial is the element of structural doubt built into the communications

77. Tom Gunning, "Phantom Images and Modern Manifestations: Spirit Photography, Magic Theater, Trick Films, and Photography's Uncanny," in *Fugitive Images: From Photography to Video*, ed. Patrice Petro (Bloomington: Indiana University Press, 1995), 42–71.

78. "Spirits and Spirit-Rapping," *Westminster Review* 69 (1858): 29–66; see 35–36.

79. Burton Gates Brown, "Spiritualism in Nineteenth Century America" (Ph.D. diss., Boston University, 1972), chap. 2. The term "ouija" is a compound of the words for "yes" in French and German.

80. Brown, "Spiritualism in Nineteenth Century America," 44.

81. John Morley, *Death, Heaven, and the Victorians* (Pittsburgh: University of Pittsburgh Press, 1971), 105.

they claimed to receive. Though debunkers abounded, the sisters always skillfully managed to keep open-ended the question of the authenticity of their contact with the other side. The improbability of communication (in this case, with the dead) whetted the appetite for it.

An epidemic of raps blazed through the land and across the sea, and by 1850 the professional medium had been born and spiritualist circles were established in New York, Philadelphia, Boston, and Providence. The Fox sisters were hired by P. T. Barnum and became celebrities in the Anglo-American world. One of the reasons for the success of spiritualism as a popular movement in the 1850s and after was that it was good theater, as we have already seen in Hawthorne's *Blithedale Romance*. It provided bread and circuses to the spiritually hungry and bored, to those who suffered from the religious crises and disruptions of nineteenth-century America, England, and elsewhere. Moreover, it offered Americans a religious vision quite free of the old Calvinist rigor and negativity.[82] It showed a way to communicate with the spiritual realm without steep demands on personal righteousness; the other side could readily appear.

The movement, with its individualist emphasis on the capacity of anyone—including or especially women—to become a medium of spiritual life, was tied to reform efforts such as abolition, temperance, and women's rights. Indeed, spiritualism was born in the same year and region that Elizabeth Cady Stanton and Lucretia Mott launched modern feminism at the Seneca Falls Convention in 1848, and the Fox sisters were first received in radical abolitionist circles. Ann Braude argues that spiritualism offered women a means to rework gender stereotypes—specifically, women as sensitive, passive recipients of spiritual things—in ways that gave them the power to speak and act in public, at least until the 1870s, when the cultural prestige of mediumship, along with so much else, began to be redefined as unrespectably outré in a more repressive climate.[83] In Victorian culture, spirituality at least was one arena open to feminine virtuosity. The history of communication via mediums, unlike that via media, has been dominated by women. The term "medium" described both the telegraph (which communicated across distances) and the human channeler (who communicated across the gap between living and dead). Both sorts of mediums required exquisite sensitivity to remote impressions of an ethereal sort.

By the mid-1850s, the spirits no longer limited themselves to raps.

82. R. Laurence Moore, *In Search of White Crows: Spiritualism, Parapsychology, and American Culture* (New York: Oxford University Press, 1977).
83. Braude, *Radical Spirits*, chap 7.

Mediums employed a diversity of media for spanning the chasm, including table turning, writing, speaking, drawing, singing, dancing, the displacement of animate and inanimate objects, and musical instruments, especially guitars.[84] The typical genre for spiritualism was of course the séance (from the French word for sitting or session), at which people would call up departed spirits via a "medium" or "sensitive," often on behalf of a grieving family member. Mary Todd Lincoln, for example, invited a medium to the White House to make contact with her dead child (she was also portrayed in a ghost photograph with an image of her dead husband hovering benevolently behind her). Spiritualism was one clear manifestation of the Victorian cult of the dead. The spiritualist séance offered a variety of religious experience that was potentially subject to empirical investigation and free of the terror of hell or damnation. As Peter Washington notes, "The seance offers a new version of holy communion, in which faith is replaced by evidence, blood and wine by manifested spirits."[85] Access to the hidden things of the spirit depended not on one's righteousness but on having the right medium, and the revelations that came were grasped not by faith, but through the senses. And what the spirits revealed was not always so lofty. As Henry David Thoreau quipped (ever ready to take Yankee shrewdness to comic excess), if the spirit rappers gave a reliable picture of eternity, he'd gladly trade in his prospects of immortality for a glass of cold beer.[86] The necrophilic romanticism of a Poe was rarely in evidence; more frequent were comforting doggerel and slangy converse with departed heroes.

As with the telegraph, so with the camera. Spirit photography was a practice that evolved in a variety of forms and styles. Daguerreotypy, as is well known, was widely seen as haunted or as usurping God's place. Thanks to the length of sitting times, up to twenty to thirty seconds, daguerreotype portraiture often registered blurred and hence ghostly images of the sitters. Children, even less likely to sit still and unable to employ a brace for sitting, were often photographed asleep, a practice that was unnervingly close to the daguerreotype portrait as a memento of the deceased for mourning.[87] In its beginnings spirit photography developed from portraiture and typically involved a double or multiple

---

84. "Spirits and Spirit-Rapping," 39–45.
85. Peter Washington, *Madame Blavatsky's Baboon* (New York: Shocken, 1995), 10.
86. John B. Wilson, "Emerson and the 'Rochester Rappings,'" *New England Quarterly* 41 (June 1968): 248–58.
87. Cathy N. Davidson, "Photographs of the Dead: Sherman, Daguerre, Hawthorne," *South Atlantic Quarterly* 89 (1990): 667–701.

exposure so that a sitter could be photographed surrounded or sometimes embraced by spirits (cinematically called "extras") supposedly invisible to the eye but not the camera. Spirit photography served the
multiple functions of documentation (of the objective existence of spirits), comfort (the care of the dead), and entertainment (as part of nineteenth-century visual amusements).

After the Civil war, spiritualist practices became even more visually
oriented, with the rise of materializing mediums, who would reveal images, claim to take photographs during a sitting, or produce floating
musical instruments, hands, feet, or even entire spirits, such as the "Katie King" manifested by Florence Cook and photographed by William
Crookes in 1874. Mediums, like media, moved into a more complicated
apparatus: the cabinet, a kind of closet in which the spirits were capable
of far more boisterous antics, including raucous musical noises, harassment of the spectator in the cabinet, and most important, physical materialization. Tom Gunning has noted the remarkable ways such cabinet
séances serve as an allegory of late nineteenth-century image practices.[88]
Mediums would change their dress and walk among the sitters in the
guise of a departed spirit, touching and sometimes kissing them, offering them the incontrovertible token of presence, the flesh itself.

The strangest materialization of all was so-called ectoplasm, apparently a direct emanation of the medium's body. Here mediums outstrip
media by producing not only visual and acoustic ghosts of people, but the
body itself. Ectoplasm, the "delicacy of the spirit world in the nineteenth
century," was a "white, viscous substance, with an ozone-like smell," that
could also occasionally appear in "grey, black, or even flesh colour."[89]
The physiological explicitness of ectoplasm goes beyond the late nineteenth-century triad of phonograph, film, and typewriter (Kittler) toward a kind of nonvirtual reality in which the flesh itself, and not only
the eyes, ears, and sensory system, could be replicated over distance. The
French medium who called herself Eva Carrière and is known in the an-
nals of psychical research as Eva C exuded the stuff from the mouth, the
nipples, the navel, and the vagina. Other mediums used other orifices,
including the nostrils, and produced it in solid or vaporous condition.
One writer suggested that ectoplasm is "a physical duplication of the

---

88. Gunning, "Phantom Images and Modern Manifestations." This fine work has shaped my
treatment.

89. Christine Bergé, *La voix des esprits: Ethnologie du spiritisme* (Paris: Métailié, 1990), 91; Fred
Gettings, *Ghosts in Photographs: The Extraordinary Story of Spirit Photography* (New York: Harmony
Books, 1978), 115.

medium"—another phantasmic doppelgänger.[90] The Munich physician Baron von Schrenck Notzing, who studied, collaborated, and colluded (with what degree of awareness is unclear) with Ms. C in the late naughts and early 1910s, described some of her carnal manifestations in his massive tome *Phenomena of Materialisation:* whitish threads, clouds and mists, hands, fingers, heads, limbs, pseudopods, white fleshly masses in various states of development, and "fragments of animal and human limbs." His book is creepy, almost pornographic, as the good doctor relates with supposed medical passivity his all too thorough inspections of Ms. C's bare body before and after sittings (so as to prevent any use of props). He also provides over 225 photographs, including a small piece of human skin he captured in a petri dish during one sitting.[91]

In spiritualist materialization, including the marvelous coinage "teleplasm" (flesh at a distance), it is as if the communication apparatus— quite literally the medium—had the power not only to make visual, auditory, or verbal replicas, but to transport or "energize" (as they say on *Star Trek*) the carnal share of the human form. Materialization is quite literally the attempt to recreate the flesh in a telecommunications medium. The reproduction of new living bodies is of course a female province, and I know of no male materializing mediums. Ectoplasm is an outrageous parody of the Eucharist (fragments of a body as proof of unseen powers) and of birth (Eva Carrière, the career Eve, posing as the mother of all living).[92] Ectoplasm is perhaps the most desperate version of the fateful aspiration that Kafka found in the invention of the railroad, automobile, and airplane: to transport distant souls not in spirit but in the flesh. Whatever its meaning, ectoplasm expresses, in the most extravagant way possible, the attempt within the developing media culture of the late nineteenth and early twentieth centuries to provide an undeniable presence that would quench gnawing doubts about simulation, fakery, and breakdown in communication (see chapter 5).

90. Gustave Geley, *Clairvoyance and Materialisation: A Record of Experiments*, trans. Stanley De Brath (London: T. Fisher Unwin, 1927), 176. Morley, *Death, Heaven, and the Victorians*, 109, notes a catalog of items for professional mediums called *Gambols with the Ghosts* from Sylvestre and Company, established 1872, including "Luminous Materializing Hands and Faces" and "Luminous Materialistic Ghosts and Forms." I have been unable to discover if this company also stocked ectoplasm.

91. Albert von Schrenck Notzing, *Phenomena of Materialisation: A Contribution to the Investigation of Mediumistic Teleplastics*, trans. E. E. Fournier d'Albe (London: Kegan Paul, Trench, Trubner, 1923), 15, 75–76, and fig. 16.

92. The materializations of the 1870s also marked a new passivity for the medium; previously an active participant, now mediums often were tied down, immobile, and under the care of male impresarios, which may echo the condition of childbearing women as well: see Braude, *Radical Spirits*, 176–77.

Spiritualism was one of the chief sites at which the cultural and metaphysical implications of new forms of communication were worked out, as I have suggested, and it is also the source for much of our vocabulary today (medium, channel, and communication). Mediums, thanks to such abilities as clairvoyance and clairaudience, resembled media, with their ability to transport sights and sounds from afar. As a cultural phenomenon, spiritualism ranged from the circus antics of charlatans to sincere inquiries into the possibility of contact with the other side by figures such as Robert Owen, the father of English socialism, Alfred Russel Wallace, codiscoverer with Darwin of the theory of evolution, Sir William Crookes, Sir Oliver Lodge, and much later, Sir Arthur Conan Doyle. In spiritualism, "communication" was a concept that straddled the line between physical transmissions (the telegraph) and spiritual ones (messages from the other side). The spiritualist imagery of media is still with us today.[93]

Still highly attuned to the spirits conjured by media, spiritualists today use audiovisual media as means of receiving messages from the dead. There are strong but small spiritualist traditions and movements in Europe, North America, and Latin America. Ethnographies of spiritualists show their ongoing engagement with questions of communication and mediation. One study of a group of Welsh spiritualists describes their preoccupations significantly as "the privacy of pain, their experience of isolation and their anxieties about communication."[94] A more recent study of French spiritualists features their creative engagement with audiovisual media as means of contact with the dead.[95] One recent American medium explains her preference for working with tape recorders: "With automatic writing, for instance, one never knows if it's our unconscious that is speaking or a spirit."[96] Machines offer a more objective way to register messages from the other side. Specifically, any source of white noise can both hide and reveal the whisperings of departed spirits. One tapes the noise, then sorts and sifts—at high speed, low speed, running forward and backward, in what must be a process of astronomical tedium—for utterances from the dead. The spirits seem to have trouble with grammar and syntax, but their fragmentary discourse

93. See the interesting exploration of contemporary developments in Sarah Waters, "Ghosting the Interface: Cyberspace and Spiritualism," *Science as Culture* 6, 3 (1997): 414–43.

94. Vieda Skultans, *Intimacy and Ritual: A Study of Spiritualism, Mediums, and Groups* (London: Routledge and Kegan Paul, 1974), 2.

95. Bergé, *Voix des esprits*. See also Hildegard Schäfer, *Stimmen aus einer anderen Welt: Chronik und Technik der Tonbandstimmenforschung* (Freiburg: Hermann Bauer, 1978).

96. Christine Bergé, "Machines à convertir: Les magnétophones transmettent la voix des morts," *Techniques et Culture* 17–18 (1991): 331–43.

style fits in the long tradition of telegraphic speech as well (earthly history, as usual, seems to shape the practices of the spirits). *Popular Electronics* in 1995 even ran an article on how to tape-record ghost voices, suitably deadpan in its treatment of their objective existence.[97] The spiritualist movement has always explored the troubles and utopias of communication across the gaps.

ETHER FROLICS: PSYCHICAL RESEARCH Spiritualism, again, offered a bridge between physics and metaphysics; Lodge and Crookes were both key agents in the development of radio, a technology whose spiritualist relevance escaped neither one. As Henry Adams observed, the greats of English science—Newton, Darwin, and Maxwell—had all "sailed gaily into the supersensual" at one point or another.[98] Such sailing was nowhere more evident than in the Society for Psychical Research (SPR), founded in London in 1882, and the American Society for Psychical Research, founded in Boston in 1884. A loose collection of spiritualist true believers, open-minded skeptics willing to put paranormal phenomena to a scientific test, and outright debunkers, the British Society counted among its ranks some of the leading scientists of its day. The British SPR had the twofold aim of fending off the anarchy of the pop spiritualism of the middle and lower classes and preserving a properly scientific hold on the supersensual universe, which could include the radiations of the ether as well as the emanations of mind. This tightrope walk is evident, for example, in the argument of Lord Kelvin, the doyen of late nineteenth-century physics, in favor of a sixth "magnetic sense" in addition to the usual five; still, in the best condescending style, Kelvin kept his distance from such "groveling superstitions" as mesmerism and spiritualism.[99] Many of the elite of British physics were also connected, by friendship, family, and inclination, with conservative politics and ethics. Eleanor Balfour Sidgwick, for instance, was a long-standing president of the SPR and sister to the Tory prime minister Arthur James Balfour. The vision of the universe as held together by a transcendent, invisible principle of order—the ether—certainly had its resonance with a conservative social outlook.[100]

97. Konstantinos, "Ghost Voices: Exploring the Mysteries of Electronic Voice Phenomena," *Popular Electronics* 12 (October 1995): 37–41.

98. Henry Adams, *The Education of Henry Adams* (1907; New York: Modern Library, 1931), 452.

99. James Coates, *Seeing the Invisible: Practical Studies in Psychometry, Thought Transference, Telepathy, and Allied Phenomena* (London: L. N. Fowler, 1909), 6–7.

100. Brian Wynne, "Natural Knowledge and Social Context: Cambridge Physicists and the Luminiferous Ether," in *Science in Context: Readings in the Sociology of Science*, ed. Barry Barnes and David Edge (Cambridge: MIT, 1982), 212–31.

The ether, a construct reminiscent of Newton's notion of a *sensorium dei*, was a breeding ground for speculations about the ultimate unity of the physical and psychical. As Frederic W. H. Myers, a classicist polymath, Platonist, and founder of the SPR, put it, "My ideal would be to attempt for the realm of mind what the spectroscope and law of gravitation have effected for the realm of matter."[101] Henry Adams, perhaps the most sensitive explorer of the cultural and philosophical implications of late nineteenth-century physics, called the ether an "undifferentiated substance supporting matter and mind alike."[102] In such formulations we see how the notion of communication, as in the seventeenth century, hovered between physical and psychical realms.

The ether was the mother of all media that allowed light, electricity, and magnetism to work at a distance. James Clerk Maxwell (1831–79), whose equations first unified electricity, magnetism, light, and heat and who thus is a key source for modern wireless communication as well as probably the greatest theoretical physicist between Newton and Einstein, waxed rhapsodic on the ether (even though, in contrast to many of his overinvested colleagues, he regarded the ether as conjectural at best):

The vast interplanetary and interstellar regions will no longer be regarded as waste places in the universe, which the Creator has not seen fit to fill with the symbols of the manifold order of His kingdom. We shall find them to be already full of this wonderful medium; so full, that no human power can remove it from the smallest portion of space, or produce the slightest flaw in its infinite continuity. It extends unbroken from star to star; and when a molecule of hydrogen vibrates in the dog-star, the medium receives the impulses of these vibrations.[103]

Maxwell continues in the tradition of Newton, reading the signs of divine order in the medium that undergirds the interplanetary and interstellar regions; but he also anticipates wireless telegraphy and its delicate receptivity to infinitely distant vibrations via this same wonderful me-

---

101. F. W. H. Myers, *Human Personality and Its Survival of Bodily Death,* ed. Susy Smith (1903; New Hyde Park, N.Y.: University Books, 1961), 208.

102. Henry Adams, "The Rule of Phase Applied to History," in *Degradation of the Democratic Dogma* (1909; New York: Macmillan, 1919), 275. On Adams as interpreter of physics, see Stephen G. Brush, *The Temperature of History: Phases of Science and Culture in the Nineteenth Century* (New York: Franklin, 1978).

103. James Clerk Maxwell, "On Action at a Distance," in *Scientific Papers,* ed. W. D. Niven (Cambridge: Cambridge University Press, 1890), 2:322. I thank Professor C. W. F. Everitt for guidance on Maxwell.

dium.[104] The universe seems to be in constant communication with it-self.[105]

As a scientific notion, the ether was cast into doubt by the Michelson-Morley experiments in 1881, which failed to find the hypothesized drag of the ether on the speed of light, and demolished by Einstein's special theory of relativity in 1905, but it survived into the mid-twentieth century as a figure of speech for "the airwaves." For instance, Lord Reith, founder of the BBC, wrote in 1924: "'Wireless' is manifestly dependent for its functioning upon the universal ether, a fascinating but illusive, and probably incomprehensible, medium."[106] With charming obfuscation, Reith is out of date on his physics but quite on the money regarding the spectral milieu that surrounded early discourse on the means of broadcasting. Obviously the term "wireless" boasts of action at a distance, and wireless communication was one technical crown on a century's work in physics, from Ørsted and Faraday to Maxwell and Hertz. Radio traveled through the recently analyzed electromagnetic spectrum. (The term "spectrum" had once simply meant ghost.) Wireless technology had everything that made the telegraph seem so miraculous (instantaneous electricity-borne intelligence) with the added plus that it needed no medium but the universal ether. We are at the heartland of the problem of communication: contact between people via an invisible or elusive material linkage. The radio reactivates the dreams of angels and of mesmerism without, as we will see in chapter 5, being able to satisfy them.

The prospect of radio in the 1890s, and its exploitation in the first two decades of the twentieth century, gave rise to a mass of "groveling superstitions" that could only have horrified Kelvin and his compatriots. X-rays, radioactivity, and radio, all discovered in the 1890s, excited a diverse class of writers, whose literary remains still occupy several feet of dusty shelf space in many university libraries. One gets a sense of this yeasty brew from the title of a 1913 book by one Horace C. Stanton: *Telepathy of the Celestial World: Psychic Phenomena Here but the Foreshadowings of Our Transcendent Faculties Hereafter; Evidences from Psychology and Scripture That the Celestials Can Instantaneously Communicate across*

104. On the metaphor of the etheric ocean in early radio, see Jeffrey Sconce, "The Voice from the Void: Wireless, Modernity, and the Distant Dead," *International Journal of Cultural Studies* 1 (1998): 213–35.

105. James Clerk Maxwell, "The Ether," in *Scientific Papers*, ed. W. D. Niven (Cambridge: Cambridge University Press, 1890).

106. J. C. W. Reith, "Broadcasting," *Quarterly Review* 242, 481 (1924): 398–414, at 398.

Distance Indefinitely Great. "Physics stark mad in metaphysics," as Henry Adams put it.[107]

Though one might be amused at extreme forms of the enthusiasm to connect mediumless communication to deep metaphysical interests, early radio history is inseparable from daring imaginings about the flight of souls, voices without bodies, and instantaneous presence at a distance. Dreams of bodiless contact were a crucial condition not only of popular discourse but of technical invention as well. Sir William Crookes, for instance, was equally a student of Faraday, expert on diamonds, spectroscopist, discoverer of the element thallium, inventor of the cathode-ray tube, spiritualist, and spirit photographer. His 1892 article "Some Possibilities of Electricity" was extremely influential on the first generation of radio inventors. "There is hardly any one figure important in the early days of radio who does not at some point in his memoirs or correspondence refer to the article of 1892 as having made a difference."[108] In this piece Crookes boldly explored the "possibilities of transmitting and receiving intelligence" via "telegraphy without wires."[109] Two friends "could thus communicate as long and as often as they pleased" via Morse code on mutually tuned sets. After Crookes's prophecy of something like ham radio, he proposed dispensing with the apparatus altogether. Perhaps "brain waves," he ventured, could travel from brain to brain. The notion of brain wave, incidentally, was invented in the 1880s in psychical research to describe possible telepathic transmissions between brains; the term did not take an electrophysiological meaning until the 1930s.[110] For Crookes, as for many others, the propagation of wireless signals and the sharing of thoughts were allied if not indistinguishable processes. Thought was not a sign expressed by a body but, as one psychical enthusiast put it, "a dynamic force or an X-form of energy."[111] The problem of "communication," in this view, was one not of love or justice, but of proper tuning or channeling. Thus communication theory continued to be heir to what Fichte had called the physicalization of idealism. All the real spiritual and material problems of meeting others in the world become subsumed by radio tuning.

Telepathy was radio's doppelgänger. In 1899 John Trowbridge, a Harvard physicist who also wrote a short biography of Morse, wrote, "Wire-

107. Adams, *Education,* 382.
108. Hugh G. J. Aitken, *Syntony and Spark: The Origins of Radio* (New York: Wiley, 1976), 114.
109. William Crookes, "Some Possibilities of Electricity," *Fortnightly Review* 51 (February 1892): 173–81, at 174.
110. *Oxford English Dictionary,* s. v. "brain-waves."
111. Coates, *Seeing the Invisible,* chap. 8.

less telegraphy is the nearest approach to telepathy that has been vouch-safed to our intelligence."[112] Not unlike Crookes's connection between brain waves and radio transmission, a psychical researcher hypothesized in 1907: "If a machine can produce etheric waves, capable of cognition and communication, the same possibility should exist within our-selves."[113] A 1913 letter to the editor of *Scientific American* argued in a similar way that once Marconi's discoveries were fully applied they would allow "communication . . . at will, at any time, between human beings separated by great distances" without any technical apparatus. Just as transmitter and receiver had to be mutually tuned, people would have to be "strongly bound together in unity of aim and thought" to dispense with the machine.[114] The editor's response drew the crucial dis-tinction: "The wireless telegraph does not transmit thought, but simply signals which can be translated into an intelligible communication. Te-lepathy, on the other hand, deals with the direct communication of thought."[115] The editor, bless his heart, recognized the inevitability of semiotic mediation.

Telepathy, in turn, was clearly modeled on the apparently medium-transcending capacities of the telegraph and perhaps also the telephone. Coined in 1882 by Frederic W. H. Myers, telepathy was defined as "the communication of impressions of any kind from one mind to another, independently of the recognized channels of sense."[116] In such a usage as this, "communication" teeters between a pure physics sense (trans-mission) and the ideal social sense (instant contact). The term "telepa-thy" was not originally supposed to be paranormal, in sharp contrast with its current status; it was rather an attempt on the part of psychical research to explain spiritualist phenomena scientifically.[117] Telepathy specifically was intended to explain a medium's sometimes remarkable access to private facts about the dead or living that she could not nor-mally have known. Myers suggested that the medium's access to per-sonal information derived not from supposed communion with the

112. John Trowbridge, "Wireless Telegraphy," *Popular Science Monthly* 56 (November 1899): 80.

113. Frederic Fletcher, *The Sixth Sense: Psychic Origin, Rationale, and Development* (London: Fowler, 1907), 8.

114. Scudday Richardson, "The Law of Magnetic Communications Between Human Beings," letter to the editor, *Scientific American* 109 (6 August 1913): 127.

115. *Scientific American* 109 (6 August 1913): 127. *Scientific American* published much in psychi-cal research. One later article explored the radio studio as a means of broadcast telepathy: J. Malcolm Bird, "Telepathy and Radio: Results of the *Scientific American* Test of Thought Transference from the Broadcasting Studio," *Scientific American* 130 (June 1924): 382, 433.

116. F. W. H. Myers in *Proceedings of the Society for Psychical Research* 1, 2 (1882): 147.

117. See Ian Hacking, "Telepathy: Origins of Randomization in Experimental Design," *Isis* 79 (September 1988): 427–51.

dead but from the unconscious minds of the sitters via some kind of quasi-physical process of thought transference. It is an open question whether Myers's attempt to simplify the account of mediumistic performance quite met Occam's razor—it did keep paranormal communication restricted to the living at least—but other coinages followed hard upon: "telesthesia" (1892), the sharing of feelings at a distance, and "telekinesis" (1890), the movement of objects through psychic powers. By the 1890s the notion of telepathy had spread throughout Anglo-American culture, a symptom of the ancient and modern longing to pass messages "through space, for great distances, from brain to brain in the entire absence of any known means of physical communication between two widely separated stations,"[118] as one author put it, writing not of telepathy, but of Marconi's wireless experiments. Wireless induction replaced the City of God as the way to commune like the angels.

I will bring this chapter to a close with two examples, early and late, of radio as a device for spiritual communication. Rudyard Kipling's 1902 story "Wireless" concerns a young pharmacist. Dying of consumption and in love with a woman named Fanny, he begins spontaneously to "compose" some of Keats's poetry. The similarities of biography evidently attune the pharmacist somehow to Keats's channel in the great world of *Geist;* the story makes it clear that the man had no previous knowledge of Keats or his poetry. Meanwhile, upstairs, an amateur wireless operator tries to make contact with other operators but can only overhear pieces of messages sent between ships in the English Channel. This primal scene of communication breakdown calls forth the lament, "It's quite pathetic. Have you ever seen a spiritualist seance? It reminds me of that sometimes—odds and ends of messages coming out of nowhere—a word here and there. No good at all."[119] The moral of the story: "There are many kinds of induction." Induction, of course, is a technical term for pulling signals out of the air; in this story the twist is that the poetic induction works better than the wireless. Unintelligible messages suspended in limbo and a "medium" sensitive to delicate vibrations from afar—these were known in spiritualism well before they were in radio. Both early radio and séances were quests for connection that just as often became excursions into the labyrinth of lost or cryptic messages. It is misguided to construct a history of radio in which the spiritualism is an excrescence; it was one key to the medium's very development.

118. James T. Knowles, "Wireless Telegraphy and 'Brain Waves,'" *Living Age* 222 (8 July 1899): 100–106, at 100.

119. Rudyard Kipling, "Wireless," *Scribners* 32 (August 1902): 129–43, at 143.

Upton Sinclair's book *Mental Radio* (1930) concerns his wife's ability to receive images at a distance. The medium of transmission was something like the ether of broadcasting. This book (Albert Einstein wrote an introduction for the German edition) contains 146 graphic reproductions, most of them paired drawings: the first is an original, drawn by Sinclair or others, and the second is Mary Craig Sinclair's rendition after she had concentrated on the original object (hidden within a box or stared at by a compatriot who was miles distant). The figures are offered as proof of the possibility of mental radio (or television, as we might prefer today). Sinclair not only dreams of communication as the mating of identicals, he tries to establish it with indisputable visual evidence.

Actually, of course, figures A and B rarely look alike to an uninitiated eye. Sinclair provides each image with captions and resorts to long and elaborate explanations about the context and the intentions of participants to reveal the commonality underneath the interference. Thus he reveals much about the labor of interpretation when evidence is scarce—a common situation in twentieth-century scenes of communication breakdown (chapter 6). The interpretive apparatus Sinclair deploys shows precisely what he argues against: that Craig Sinclair's images arise from a larger sign process rather than from immediate perception. His zest to establish identity only reveals the intractability of difference. Second, the method enjoys all but infinite degrees of freedom in interpretation. In his early 1880s experiments on telepathy, specifically on infinitesimally slight sensitivities in human perception, Charles Sanders Peirce invented the double-blind experiment so as to prevent the unwitting collaboration of the experimenter's will.[120] Sinclair, in contrast, takes no care to factor out his own interpretive desire. Sinclair's readings are constant testimonies to semiotic plenitude, to the fact that any juxtaposition can yield a connection. It would be better, to my mind, if Sinclair recognized his own and his wife's role as active agents of surrealistic construction. The drama would then lie less in mental radio than in the creative labor by which some kind of bridge was hung across the gaps. Sinclair thinks communication amazing only when it transcends normal channels.

In one particularly choice episode, Craig Sinclair drew concentric circles around a black dot with an ink smear in the lower right quadrant. This she took as a foreboding of a hemorrhage in her tubercular brother. A few days later when the brother visited, the Sinclairs discovered that he indeed had—a hemorrhoid. Concluded Sinclair: "I do not see how

120. Hacking, "Telepathy."

there could possibly be more conclusive evidence of telepathic influence."[121] If the slide from the mortal danger of a hemorrhage to the bathetic irritation of a hemorrhoid is evidence of paranormal perception, it is enough to make one, with Thoreau, trade in the dream of communication for a cold one. Radiolike clairvoyance turns out to be as subject to the insistence of the letter as any other form of human discourse; the link lies much more in the root *hemorrh*-than in any clairvoyance. Sinclair has inadvertently discovered the insuperability of interpretation, the subtle determination of sense by context, and the lack of anything more certain than faith for verifying the inner states of others. As in Locke, the desire to found an economy of knowing on sensation that is superior to speech only brings him back to signs in their stubbornness. By trying to circumvent them, Sinclair only faces more directly the difficulty of persuasion and belief—the old hard facts on which the dream of communication has continually foundered. The repressed—the necessity of interpretation and the ineradicable distinctness of souls—has returned.

In sum, a long string of notions, all of them dispensing with mediation and interpretation, invest the modern notion of communication: the spirit trumping the letter; the immediate communion of angels; the "communication" of ideas via the medium of sensible signs; the mind-binding power of animal magnetism; the lightning flashes of spiritual telegraphy; and the wireless rays of radio and brain wave ethers. As a term that long signified physical or metaphysical action at a distance, "communication" came, especially with the telegraph's harnessing of electricity for messages between people, to represent a state of shared understanding and instantaneous sympathy between people that could be achieved without reliance on the grosser vehicles of word or speech. The catch was that such communication, even with telegraphy and telepathy, was rarely complete or free of obstacles. The dream was only one side of the new world of electrical media; the other side was an array of such real mishaps as missent notices, dead letters, downed wires, and interpretively obscure messages. As we will see, the dream of communication only upped the longing for an escape from the morally intractable condition of plurality, that is, of life among other creatures whose perspectives are both hidden from us and never exactly our own.[122]

121. Upton Sinclair, *Mental Radio* (Pasadena, Calif.: Station A, 1930), 63. See figure 19a. This same publisher printed Sinclair's pamphlet in his 1934 bid for governor of California. See also Walter Franklin Prince, "Mrs. Sinclair's 'Mental Radio,'" *Scientific American* 146 (March 1932): 135–38.
122. The notion of plurality I take from Arendt, *Human Condition*, 7–8 and passim.

THREE

Toward a More Robust
Vision of Spirit: Hegel, Marx,
and Kierkegaard

Like the spiritualist tradition, G. W. F. Hegel puts Spirit at
the center of communication; unlike it, Spirit (*Geist*) is always embodied and tragically conflicted. Hegel and his
renegade disciples Karl Marx and Søren Kierkegaard sub-
scribe to principles that are contrapuntal to the spiritualist
tradition: the irreducibility of embodiment, the doubleness
of the self, and the publicness of meaning. They are interested in the objective conditions that make the self possible in the first place and are much more attuned to pathology, power, and distortion in intersubjective relations
than are the spiritualists. Their analysis of the conditions
of possibility of communication is far deeper than most
later thinking on that topic. Though Kierkegaard is the
only one to write extensively about communication per
se, all three—despite their large and crucial differences—
offer visions of self, sign, and world that allow for a profound rethinking of what communication might mean
today.

Hegel on Recognition

Hegel, like his rebellious intellectual offspring Marx and
Kierkegaard, took eros as the principle that held the universe together in an all-embracing totality. This is not to

109

make Hegel into a romantic, for no one hated romantic *Schwärmerei* (gushing) more than he. He thought the attempt by his erstwhile colleague F. W. J. Schelling to make people at home in the world via the archromantic project of an aestheticized world fell short of a fully rigorous account of the problems that had to be faced to achieve a genuine at-one-ment. Still, the quest for a reconciliation of subject and object is the prime mover of Hegel's mature system—especially his philosophy of nature and of spirit—as it was throughout his intellectual development. I do not consider it unfair to think of this as, at least in part, an erotic principle owing something to the *Phaedrus* and the *Symposium*, two key influences on Hegel. To put words in his mouth, the aim of his entire system is communication: not in the sense of shared information, but in the richer sense as the process whereby a free human world is built collectively.

Hegel interpretation is a vexed business. The same thinker who inspired the young Marx and Dewey with his dynamism has been seen by others as an overweening systematizer, the theorist of the all-devouring bourgeois ego. Marx mocked Hegel for walking about on his head; Kierkegaard made fun of contemporary Danish Hegelians for having huge heads that were threatening to become disconnected from their bodies. Today both liberals and postmodernists find something to oppose in Hegel. As Charles Taylor notes, Hegel suffers from too much originality. In Hegel, various readers have found sources for Marxism, existentialism, atheism, Christian theism, the Victorian family, fascism, and poststructuralism. Part of the conflict of interpretations springs from the diverse points of textual entry into his work. As Vittorio Hösle argues, Hegel is a watershed between the philosophy of subjectivity (from Descartes to Fichte) and the post-Hegelian focus on intersubjectivity. Hence it is difficult to know whether to read him as the last great thinker of the *cogito* or the first thinker of "the other." Hösle's thesis is that a fault line runs in Hegel's system between the *Logic*, which culminates in absolute subjectivity, and his "Realphilosophie" (philosophy of nature and spirit), which is motivated by insights into intersubjectivity, however unevenly they are integrated into the system as a whole. A price Hegel paid for his ultimate systematic coherence, argues Hösle, was the suppression of intersubjectivity; hence the *Phenomenology* is far richer than the *Encyclopaedia* on this topic.[1] Here I focus on the *Phenomenology*, ac-

---

1. Vittorio Hösle, *Hegels System: Der Idealismus der Subjektivität und das Problem der Intersubjektivität*, 2 vols. (Hamburg: Felix Meiner, 1987). See, e.g., 2:385, 407.

knowledging that a full treatment of sources for a Hegelian theory of communication would have to range much further.[2]

The *Phenomenology,* an "unusual, early work" as Hegel called it late in life, suggests several doctrines fruitful for rethinking the dominant, spiritualist model of communication as shared consciousness. First, there is no content separate from form. Hegel would eschew the principle of bodily indifference so central to angelology. His philosophical method is a kind of incarnational analysis. "Phenomenology" is the logic of appearances, "the science of appearing knowledge."[3] Hegel does not believe, at least in the *Phenomenology,* that a philosophical doctrine can be understood apart from its embedment in the spiritual and material conditions of its time. One must tread an experiential path to the doctrine, almost viscerally appreciating the conditions and horizons within which it came to be. Philosophy is a relentlessly historical inquiry for which circumstantial details can never be merely accidents. Unlike Augustine, who sees our conveyances through the world as mere extras to be ignored where possible, Hegel cannot separate means from ends. The path of knowledge must be traversed in its full length. To take shortcuts is to miss the wisdom. The summit is found not in the extinction of all appearances, as some versions of Plato might hold, but in the manifold unity of appearance and essence, what Hegel calls a "gallery of images."[4] For Hegel there is, to use the language of twentieth-century postwar communication theory, no message apart from a channel. In short, for Hegel Spirit never exists without a body.[5] This claim has massive implications for how the Hegelian aftermath would consider communication.

Second, communication is a problem of the object as much as the subject. The task is not to fuse one subject with another, but to form a set of historical relations in which subjects are objectively possible. As Charles Taylor puts it, in Hegel's ontology "the lowliest form of being must be understood as an imperfect proto-form of the highest, which is

2. I have attempted a somewhat fuller reading in John Durham Peters, "The Root of Humanity: Hegel on Communication and Language," in *Figuring the Self: Subject, Individual, and Spirit in German Idealism,* ed. David E. Klemm and Günter Zöller (Albany: SUNY Press, 1997), 227–44.

3. G. W. F. Hegel, *Phänomenologie des Geistes* (1807; Hamburg: Meiner, 1952), hereafter referred to as *PhG* with reference first to page number and then to paragraph number. English translations I take from *Hegel's Phenomenology of Spirit,* trans. A. V. Miller (New York: Oxford University Press, 1977).

4. *PhG,* 563, par. 808.

5. Despite the meager room Hegel's completed system left for most traditional Christian beliefs and practices, Christian and trinitarian categories undeniably shape his system. Throughout, I use "Spirit" with a capital *S* for *Geist* (following A. V. Miller).

subject."⁶ Nature and history are pregnant with the embryos of subjec-tivity. The task of Spirit is to play midwife and raise them to maturity. The potential subject, which exists only *an sich*—in itself or implicitly—must become actual—*für sich*—for itself or explicitly. These embryos are often unrecognizable and are mistaken as only matter, not spirit. Subjec-tivity, much of the time in the *Phenomenology of Spirit,* is mired in objec-tivity. This stone, that tree, these hieroglyphics, all the unwritten books only dreamed of, this child, that slave—all of them need to be known from the inside out, for themselves. Each is implicitly part of the mean-ing of the universe and needs a chance to take part. Genuine knowledge must appreciate the jagged singularities of things and their part in the larger symphony. This revelation of interiority, this coming to be of Spirit, is a kind of interpretation that is also an objective appearance in the world.

Hence "communication" will always be more than the shuttling of mind-stuff. It is the founding of a world. For Hegel communication is not a psychological task of putting two minds *en rapport* but a political and historical problem of establishing conditions under which the mu-tual recognition of self-conscious individuals is possible. The issue is to reconcile subjects with their embodied relation to the world, with themselves, and with each other. Again the problem is, broadly speak-ing, an erotic one. The question of mutual recognition in such a way that individual differences are at once overcome and cherished is a leit-motiv of Hegel's thought, especially up to the *Phenomenology.* What Soc-rates in the *Phaedrus* hopes that philosophical lovers will seek is also, in a way, the chief principle of Hegel's metaphysics: "the union of union and non-union."⁷

Because subjectivity without objectivity is only a dream or a vapor, the self can never be self-sufficient, lord of the signifier or of anything else. To make a premature attempt at lordship is only to isolate and destabilize the self. The *Phenomenology's* famous master-slave drama, often seen in the twentieth century as a master key to the whole sys-tem, makes the point that there is no self without an other. As Hegel puts it, "*Self-consciousness achieves its satisfaction only in another self-consciousness.*"⁸ Like a long line of nineteenth-century authors inter-ested in doubles—the German romantics, Hoffmann, Poe, Baudelaire,

6. Charles Taylor, *Hegel* (Cambridge: Cambridge University Press, 1975), 235.
7. G. W. F. Hegel, "Fragment of a System" (1800), in *Early Theological Writings,* trans. T. M. Knox (Philadelphia: University of Pennsylvania Press, 1988), 312.
8. *PhG,* 139, par. 175; emphasis in original.

Dostoyevsky, and Freud—Hegel considers the self like a Möbius strip: a unity of two sides. But he is less interested in the exquisite pathologies exemplified by doppelgängers than in a rational reconciliation of selves and others in the world. The attempt to attain self-certainty outside historical relations with others is folly. In the rendezvous of two selves, we first encounter the concept of Spirit or *Geist*, which Hegel defines as the experience of the simultaneous diversity and unity of self-consciousnesses, an "I that is We and We that is I."[9] As Robert R. Williams writes, "This situation of reciprocal recognition is one of communicative freedom, which Hegel describes as being at home with self in another."[10] Unlike Fichte and Schelling, who earlier used the formula "I = I" to express the starting point of their systems, Hegel insists on the experience of Spirit within a community: "I = We."[11] It is fair, given the subsequent tradition, to see this as Hegel's answer to the question of what communication is. The ambiguity here is this: Do the I's dissolve themselves into the great We, or is it a harmony within diversity? Given Hegel's principle that the individuality of a moment is dialectically preserved rather than eradicated, I vote with the latter, acknowledging that others have good grounds for less charitable readings of Hegel.

Hegel attacks a core assumption of Lockean and commonsense notions of communication. For Hegel the self has no "inside"—its self-discovery goes on in the daylight of common life in the company of others. To argue that you cannot know what I really think or feel "inside" is an affront to the imperative of communication:

Since the man of common sense makes his appeal to feeling, to an oracle within his breast, he is finished and done with anyone who does not agree; he only has to explain that he has nothing more to say to anyone who does not find and feel the same in himself. In other words, he tramples underfoot the root of humanity [*Humanität*]. For it is the nature of humanity to press onward to agreement with others; human nature only really exists in an achieved community [*Gemeinsamkeit*] of consciousness. The anti-human, the animalistic, consists in remaining standing within feeling, and being able to communicate [*sich mitteilen*] only at that level.[12]

9. *PhG*, 140, par. 177. Robert R. Williams, "Hegel's Concept of *Geist*," in *Hegel's Philosophy of Spirit*, ed. Peter G. Stillman (Albany: SUNY Press, 1987), 1–20, outlines three competing models of *Geist* in Hegel scholarship: Spirit as a transcendental ego redivivum; as humanity itself; and as social or intersubjective. Both Williams and I favor the third reading.
10. Robert R. Williams, *Recognition: Fichte and Hegel on the Other* (Albany: SUNY Press, 1992), 149.
11. Cf. *PhG*, 257–58, par. 351, and *PhG*, 471, par. 671.
12. *PhG*, 56, par. 69.

In this Habermasian passage (every author, as Borges notes, invents his or her precursors), Hegel posits an anthropological urge to reach consensus. The process of recognition, in contrast to this inner oracle, suggests that the self's outside is just as hidden from itself as its inside is from others. For Hegel interiority and exteriority are temporal rather than spatial: one's subjectivity is *an sich* or "implicit" when one has *not yet* achieved recognition by another. Furthermore, no one really has an oracle in his or her breast, since, for Hegel, the self has no immediate relation with itself. You may not know the details of what remains unexpressed in my inwardness, but I have a similar lack of awareness about how I look to you or what my outwardness is like. I do not know in detail how I appear in public, how others take me, how my actions resound in the world, even what my quirks and mannerisms are.[13] My self, so plainly revealed to others, is largely opaque to me. My private self is obscure to you, but my public self is obscure to me. You surely have a better sense of me in many respects than I do. My private self, therefore, is also obscure to me, since it is made out of public materials. I have to rely on others for self-knowledge: I have no secret passageway to the holy of holies.

The self thus stands in the same position with regard to itself as to others. In Rimbaud's line, "Je est un autre." To use Kierkegaard's language (intended as a parody of Hegel), the self is a relation that relates itself to another. The American pragmatists took the insight in a productively social direction. As Charles Sanders Peirce says, "The recognition by one person of another's personality takes place by means to some extent identical with the means by which he is conscious of his own personality."[14] Josiah Royce makes a similar point: "One discovers one's own mind through a process of inference analogous to the very modes of inference which guide us in a social effort to interpret our neighbors' minds. . . . Although you are indeed placed in the 'interior' of yourself, you can never so far retire into your own inmost recesses of intuition as merely to find the true self presented to an inner sense."[15] For Hegel, likewise, the self has no privileged access to itself: it only finds itself post facto or in another self, who has recognized it as a self. Self and other

13. Walter Benjamin, *Illuminations*, trans. Harry Zohn, ed. Hannah Arendt (New York: Schocken, 1968), 137, notes the uniquely modern self-alienation of seeing oneself on screen or hearing one's recorded voice. Mirrors are more ancient.

14. Charles Sanders Peirce, "The Law of Mind," *Monist* 2, 4 (July 1892): 558.

15. Josiah Royce, *The Problem of Christianity* (New York: Macmillan, 1913), 2:138–39. Royce here seems to be commenting on Peirce, "Some Consequences of Four Incapacities," in *Philosophical Writings of Peirce*, ed. Justus Buchler (New York: Dover, 1955), 228–50.

intuit themselves in the same objective, public stuff—in *Geist,* which consists precisely in this in-betweenness.[16]

Here is no problem of a preexisting self trying to "annex," as Locke put it, words to its private ideas so that it may communicate with another. Rather, the very ground of its existence as a human being depends on the other's recognition. Augustine would agree with Hegel, at least in this, that modes of interpretation are not just ways of seeing but constitute one's place in the universe. Recognition enables humanity. Self-consciousness exists only as it is recognized.[17] The internal loop of self-recognition must pass through the external loop of being recognized by another self-consciousness, a *semblable.* Leo Rauch suggests the Berkeleyesque phrase for Hegel: *esse est agnosci,* to be is to be recognized.[18]

Finally, Hegel's conception of *Geist* locates meaning as public rather than private. To think of self-consciousness as existing, quite literally beside itself, in outer, material forms, opens the door to the rest of the *Phenomenology*—a "gallery of images" of distorted forms of intersubjectivity, ranging from the grotesque to the sublime, from the violence of battle to the ecstasy of the community work of art. Locating self and self-consciousness, like Spirit or *Geist,* in the precarious world of material things and mortal others is risky. But as Hegel insists, Spirit is rarely realized without tragedy.[19] That the Incarnation led to the Crucifixion, a fact that is rarely far from Hegel's thinking, is the highest expression of the glorious catastrophe of embodied *Geist.*[20] In his early Frankfurt writings on love, Hegel argued that love destroys all positivity, that is, anything contingent—especially the body. Love, faith, and hope were conceived as utterly worldless, states of spirit without any impress on objects. But from his Jena period on he argues that real love must include all the parts of the lovers, private and public, just as faith must involve real knowledge and hope must be based on conditions of ethical

16. Josiah Royce, *The Spirit of Modern Philosophy: An Essay in the Form of Lectures* (1892; New York: Dover, 1983), 208–9, n. 2, underscores this point by translating Hegel's *Allgemeinheit,* used in section 436 of the Berlin *Encyclopaedia,* where the self-consciousnesses affirmatively recognize each other as recognizing, by *publicity.*

17. *PhG,* 141, par. 178.

18. Leo Rauch, "Introduction: On Hegel's Concept of Spirit," in *Hegel and the Human Spirit: A Translation of the Jena Lectures on the Philosophy of Spirit (1805–6) with Commentary,* ed. and trans. Leo Rauch (Detroit: Wayne State University Press, 1983), 33.

19. See Williams's excellent discussion in *Recognition,* chaps. 9 and 10.

20. See, for example, G. W. F. Hegel, *Lectures on the Philosophy of Religion: The Lectures of 1827,* ed. Peter C. Hodgson (Berkeley: University of California Press, 1988), 465–68.

life. "For love is a distinguishing of two, who nevertheless are absolutely not distinguished for each other."[21]

Since there is no meaningful subjectivity that is not reconciled with its objective conditions, *Geist* or Spirit has both a material and a spiritual form. But there is nothing ghostly about *Geist.* Hegel clearly places it in cultural forms. The higher accomplishments of Spirit—law, the state, art, poetry, religion, and philosophy—do exist in material form (in texts, cities, communities, stone, paint, language, etc.). But they do not exist *as* Spirit without being recognized as having a significance that transcends their embodiment. Recognition always involves interpretation. An animal might see a sculpture, say, as a piece of stone useful for shelter or other purposes but could not recognize it as "sculpture," as an object enjoying a standing and meaning not exhausted by its animal uses and as belonging to a given community or given moment in the history of the human species. To recognize it as a work of art or human expression is to be a member of a world in which the sculpture has meaning and to be capable of practices of intelligent participation.

Geist, then, consists both in the material inscriptions of culture and in the embodied community of interpreters. Works of art or philosophy have a subjective, inward dimension just as human interpreters have an objective one. There is *Geist* in the *Mona Lisa* that is entirely autonomous from any viewer's perception of that painting. The painting is more than the sum of what it is in the eyes of its beholders, and it holds an objective intelligence that can never be reduced to the aggregated individual mental experiences of its viewers, as the Lockean, psychological tradition might have it. If the whole human species somehow became extinct but the *Mona Lisa* survived, it would be unrecognizable as a human thing and might seem to the surviving animals as interestingly patterned matter at best. It would be in the same position as the slave, its voice inward and mute, without audience, recognition, or community of interpretation. Its humanity would be rootless; but it would still have something to say even if no one was there to hear it. Whereas Locke asserts that meanings are in people, Hegel argues the worldliness, the objectivity, of meanings. Hegel is quite willing to see a painting and a human equally possessing subjectivity. Lack of recognition would be fatal to the human status of both.

In arguing that artifacts as well as organisms can be bearers of intelligence, Hegel offers an account of communication apt for an age of transformed conditions of human contact. Meaning, for Hegel, can

21. Hegel, *Lectures on the Philosophy of Religion,* 418.

dwell in things as well as people, in matter as well as minds. The nineteenth century would become increasingly familiar with expressions of the human spirit separated in time and space from the bodies of their makers—photographic images, telegraph signals, voices from the phonograph, telephone, and wireless, and moving images. To be sure, Hegel thought of writing as the medium that includes all other media, since he died too soon to see media that actually capture temporal sequences of sensory stimuli.[22] For those nourished by the Lockean principle that meanings subsist solely in the private individual, the Hegelian notion of *Geist* has long seemed ghostly or even ghastly. That works of Spirit speak from the dead and do so invariantly is not a source of horror, as for Socrates, but the basis of cultural continuity. Disembodied intelligence might seem uncannily spectral, but without some kind of intelligence that transcends the body, the dream of communication, after all, would be vain. Why should we be shocked to confront intelligence that does not have a human shape? Socrates found handwriting a ghostly, erotic stand-in for the author, but might not this concern be relevant for all signifying emanations from other people, whether voice, touch, or gesture? The excesses of spiritualism and psychical research—producing ghosts in order to explain what is better understood as *Geist,* the patterned material records of human self-expression—are an attempt to avoid facing the inhuman shapes that we, like other creatures, necessarily assume.

To take just one example, consider Sir Oliver Lodge's spiritualist account in *Raymond* (1916) of an old problem in the philosophy of art: the relation between artist and audience. Lodge is not willing to admit that there is intelligence in Beethoven's scores or Rembrandt's paintings per se. Rather, without an originating mind behind them, he argues, music and painting would be only daubs of color or acoustic disturbances. "Deposits in matter" alone, he insists, cannot carry any "emotional influence." Emotion does not lie in the works as such; the colors and sounds serve as channels for a near telepathic hold that the late spirits of Beethoven or Rembrandt still exert over their audiences. He thus evades the more truly ghostly prospect that sonic events and oils could be profoundly meaningful without any superintending mind. He will not grant the autonomy of the text. To keep all meaning anchored in mind, he literally has to conjure spirits to account for the effects of art. Telepathy becomes the general model of communication. "Matter

22. Friedrich A. Kittler, *Grammophon, Film, Typewriter* (Berlin: Brinkmann und Bose, 1986), 58–59.

is an indirect medium of communication between mind and mind. That direct telepathic intercourse should be able to occur between mind and mind, without all this intermediate physical mechanism, is therefore not really surprising."[23] Like Locke and unlike Hegel, Lodge has no notion of an intelligence that is inscribed somewhere outside the human mind, in material configurations such as texts, sculpture, architecture, or collective forms of life. Hegel's *Geist* is patterned matter interpreting itself historically, but for Lodge communication happens in spite of matter. Lodge does matter dirt, missing the glorious forms of lovable intelligence it can assume. He will not see the intelligence that has no organic life cycle.

Rather than making telepathy the explanation for how texts and readers interact—which involves importing a ghost into each end of the transaction—I would rather make the interaction of text and reader the model of communication in general. To live is to leave traces. To speak to another is to produce signs that are independent of one's soul and are interpreted without one's control.

Hegel invites us to see subjects as intertwined with objects, selves as intertwined with others, and meaning as public rather than psychological. In contrast to the intense faith in Anglo-American culture that only bad people or fascists believe in the objectivity of spirit, Hegel's notion of *Geist* actually provides a more sensible account of how people build common worlds of culture and how they might "communicate" in any sense. He insists on the intelligibility of inhuman forms in the species or larger community, including the living and the dead. Hegel is not calling for an annihilation of individuality; he is showing how it can flourish. *Geist* is found precisely in the commerce of the "I" and the "We," in the communicative practices of a community (leaving this much abused term open for now). Spirit is fundamentally a matter of what Josiah Royce called "interpretation," the signifying life of a body of people. The problem of communication for Hegel is not so much to make contact between individuals as it is to establish a vibrant set of social relations in which common worlds can be made. In contrast to the angelological tradition and its allies within the liberal family of Locke, Hegel sees communication not as a kind of thought transport but as a dangerous, sometimes tragic effort to organize lived conditions so that mutual recognition can be accorded to all. In particular, Hegel's

23. Oliver Lodge, *Raymond, or Life and Death, with Examples of the Evidence of Survival of Memory and Affection after Death* (New York: Doran, 1916), 339. All quotations are from this page. On 340 he argues that there is an evolutionary advantage for the lack of extrasensory communication: we can protect ourselves from the onslaughts of other minds by simply moving out of range.

insistence on the eccentricity of the self to itself and the objectivity of spirit can help cut through bad thinking about communication in our age.

Marx (versus Locke) on Money

Like Hegel's *Phenomenology of Spirit,* Marx's opus can be read as a theory of mediation and a critical account of the distorted expressions that subjectivity can take. A vision of communication lies at the core of his work, especially as an implicit diagnostic category for capitalism's pathologies. Like Hegel, whose "grotesque craggy melody" did not initially appeal to him, Marx does not conceive of communication as the touching of souls; with an explicitly antitheological definition of *Geist* as human rather than inhuman or superhuman, Marx—most explicitly in his early writings (on which I will focus here)—is the analyst of unhappy relations between subject and object. But he also holds to the ecstatic vision of "the reconciling yes!" that Hegel, and before him Plato's Socrates, articulates: the full matching of individualities in love—or, as Marx extended it, in labor.[24] As with Hegel, Marx takes Locke's notion of idea matching between private minds as rarefied. Individuality is the result of a collective human life, not the starting point. Marx's analysis of the topsy-turvy worlds of money and the commodity foreshadow much later thought about the uncanniness of mediated communication, with their power to give voice to alien beings. His horror at disembodied intelligence and animated bodies without souls is one response to the inhuman ways of embodying human personality in modernity. Marx's analysis provides us with much of the deep structure of modern media analysis, as it deals, essentially, with the enigmas of recording. Like the *Phaedrus,* Marx criticizes deathly and disseminative media.

Money, after all, is a kind of medium—and not only a medium of exchange, but a medium of representation as well.[25] Both Locke and Marx are anxiously fascinated by money's ability to embody and store value as well as other spiritual qualities, and a comparison of their views revisits the contrast between dissemination and dialogue. Before the audiovisual media of the nineteenth century, writing generally held a mo-

24. "Das versöhnende Ja" is a phrase from Hegel, *PhG,* 472, par. 671.
25. Georg Simmel, *Philosophie des Geldes* (Frankfurt: Suhrkamp, 1989); Marc Shell, *The Economy of Literature* (Baltimore: Johns Hopkins University Press, 1978); Jean-Joseph Goux, *Les monnayeurs du langage* (Paris: Galilée, 1984); Eugene Halton, *Meaning and Modernity: Social Theory in the Pragmatic Attitude* (Chicago: University of Chicago Press, 1986), chap. 10; Walter Benn Michaels, *The Gold Standard and the Logic of Naturalism: American Literature at the Turn of the Century* (Berkeley: University of California Press, 1987).

nopoly on the storage of intelligence as money did on the storage of abstract value. Socrates' worries about writing's curious powers of preserving and dispersing thought recur in Locke and Marx, who focus on money's strange power of storing value, but with different conclusions: Locke welcomes dissemination, Marx abhors it.

Locke's account of property, as we have seen, rests on the ability of human labor to imprint itself on matter. Property springs from the sovereignty of each individual over his (not her) own life and body: "Every Man has a *Property* in his own *Person;* this no Body has any Right to but himself."[26] Before money, property was defined by the criterion of finitude—how much one could work. Locke posits a proportionality between the labor one invests and the extent of one's possessions. Not quite Rousseau's noble savage, Locke's primitive laborer is figured as a Native American who via his labor encloses the common world given by God to all. Locke's state of nature is an idyll of reciprocity. Labor there is the equivalent to dialogue in the realm of objects: proportional, unique, personal.

The process of appropriation is naturally limited in scope. In response to the critique that "any one may *ingross* as much as he will," Locke answers decidedly, "Not so. The same Law of Nature, that does by this means give us Property, does also *bound* that *Property* too" (31). In the state of nature, waste sets the upper limit of accumulation. God has given us the world to enjoy, and any fruitless use of it is an infringement on the rights of others to live. "Nothing was made by God for Man to spoil or destroy" (31). As soon as we appropriate more than we can use, we surpass the bounds nature or God has placed on property. The natural checks against hoarding goods beyond their durability are the sheer irrationality of waste and the offense against one's neighbor. Most human necessities are "generally things of *short duration;* such as, if they are not consumed by use, will decay and perish of themselves" (46). The limit to just gain is determined by a commodity's ability to last without spoilage; it is not a matter of quantity, but of time. This is the law of propriety in the double sense of property and civility. Private property and human finitude are thus proportionate.

When money comes along, strange things start to happen. No longer is the transience of goods the natural upper limit to accumulation. Money abolishes the "rule of propriety" that limits accumulation. Precious metals can be stored without putrefaction. Locke's contrast is

26. John Locke, *Two Treatises of Government,* ed. Peter Laslett (1690; Cambridge: Cambridge University Press, 1988), sec. 27 in original. Parenthetical references are to sections of Locke's *Second Treatise;* emphasis, spelling, and capitalization follow the original.

clear: one kind of accumulation is wrong and wasteful, the king with his vast stores of rotting beef while the peasants starve, but "Gold and Silver . . . may be hoarded up without injury to any one, these Metalls not spoileing [*sic*] or decaying in the hands of the possessor" (50). Locke has found a storage medium subject to neither the corruptions of mortality nor the limits of the human body. More important, in contrast to Marx's insistence that all property is relational—that the beauty of the wealthy is paid for by the misery of the poor—Locke argues that money can be collected without any harm to one's neighbor. Because its value is "fantastical" (a term that Marx employs as well), Locke sees no intersubjective obligation in the accumulation of precious metals, unlike goods immediately useful for life.

When money arrives on the historical scene, a principle of leverage suspends the older interactionist model, and labor can be stored and disseminated beyond the bounds of the original scene. As in the *Phaedrus,* dialogic mutuality is here disrupted by a new technology insensitive to the older bounds, which imposes new bodily distortions and multiplications. The key issue at dispute between Locke and Marx— quite fateful for twentieth-century political and economic life—is whether the original dyad of subject and object remains the normative model or should be surpassed by something more extended and plural. In a great simplification, Locke sees the multiple and crisscrossing relationships enabled by money as a blessing, whereas Marx sees money as bringing a regime of incongruity, inversion, and exploitation. And yet Locke's state of nature and Marx's early dream of communist utopia both involve one-to-one interaction without amplification or distortion.

Since at least C. B. Macpherson, Locke has been sometimes viewed as an apologist for unlimited capitalist accumulation, and thus as a celebrant of money's ability to transcend labor as an engine of the economy.[27] But Locke's emphasis on the propriety of property and the sense of stewardship—the inherent responsibility to the object and to one's neighbor in any act of ownership—make him look as much like a medieval Christian as a protocapitalist. Property rests solely in the needs of human life, desires are balanced by a respect for the common world, and there is a just boundary to possessions. Property is more a matter of just care of the common stock than the accumulation of private commodities. Locke's world is not quite one of working-class misery or con-

27. C. B. Macpherson, *The Political Theory of Possessive Individualism: Hobbes to Locke* (Oxford: Clarendon Press, 1962).

spicuous consumption. The crux of the interpretive problem is Locke's reading of the effect of money's limitless power to disseminate and store value. For present purposes, it is enough to note how the appearance of money, a recording medium, turns dialogue into dissemination, just as the telephone, phonograph, and radio would all later play havoc with received ideas of conversation.

Marx deploys a very similar contrast between an original interaction of labor and matter and a mediated system no longer bounded by human requirements, but the interpretive question is less ambiguous. Marx sees money as mass communication, and he hates it. Although Locke's account of money has its occasional grotesque moment or image—rotting venison or spoiled apples—it cannot compare with Marx's analysis for exuberant imagery. Marx's task is to show, contra Locke and his intellectual descendants in classic political economy, how the accumulation of capital can be as unjust as the accumulation of perishables, and he does this by seeing capital as a vampirelike, blood-sucking operation by which the dead prey on the living. Marx unfurls all the key metaphors that have informed commentary on modern media: the living dead, idolatry, and the confusion of subject and object.

In Marx's 1844 manuscripts the products of labor, under a system of private property, confront the laborer as "something alien, as a power independent." We are already in the twilight zone: doppelgängers, confrontations with aliens, and objects that drain human powers dry, all the while claiming "to serve man."[28] Like Hegel, Marx is a critic of morbid and marginal forms of intersubjectivity. But Marx's laborer, unlike Hegel's slave, has no out, at least not through the process of work. The alien being facing the worker is a product of the self that it cannot recognize; moreover, the product consists of "labour which has been congealed in an object" (71).[29] "The worker puts his life into the object; but now his life no longer belongs to him but to the object . . . the life which he has conferred upon the object confronts him as something hostile and alien" (72). Labor rebounds back on the laborer "as an alien, divine or diabolical activity" (74). The worker has his or her best parts drained off by a greedy alien power. Here the self appears as an other, a prime condition of what Freud called the uncanny. This close encounter leaves no possibility of mutual recognition: no communication takes place between worker and object. Marx echoes the Hegelian master-slave story,

28. This vein of imagery famously continues in Marx's analysis of commodity fetishism in *Capital*.
29. Parenthetical references in what follows are to pages in the *Marx-Engels Reader*, ed. Robert Tucker (New York: Norton, 1975).

the primal scene of modern communication breakdown, in this dyad of worker and product.[30] In a Feuerbachian spirit, Marx hopes to unmask the alien other as just the estranged work of the self. The outer alien, Marx counsels, is nothing to fear. It is just a projection of internal dynamics, a nightmare that will fade when we awaken. Everywhere Marx wants to separate projections from authentic otherness and to diagnose incompletely realized subject-object junctions.

Marx's critical method consists in giving voice to the concealed human powers impressed onto inhuman materials. Private property is the "material, sensuous form" of estranged human labor. Whereas Locke sees private property as a clear and direct expression of personal labor power, Marx takes it to be a fundamentally distorting medium, one that inscribes the labors of our bodies and the works of our hands in damaged ways. Locke sees forms of intercourse that surpass the face to face as a basis of civil society, but Marx greets mass communication (any form of leverage) as corrupt, part of the *bellum omnium contra omnes* that reigns in civil society.

Marx states his guiding interpretive maxim in analyzing the plight of the worker: "All *objects* for him become the *objectification of himself*" (88). Every object is the result of objectification. (Like Hegel, the whole world for Marx is implicitly subject.) Every commodity in the Marxist optic is the scene of a displaced laboring body, a self squandering its powers on alien objects. But Marx does not lament the inevitable entanglement of the subject in the dumb object per se. He celebrates the labor process as the means to produce the world and the human being in concert. His complaint is that the object is alienated from the worker, not that subjectivity is necessarily spread across the field of its projects. Nineteenth-century culture is rife with those border zones between subject and object such as photographs, spirits, commodities, graveyards, phonographs, wax museums, telephones, and money, and one task of Marxism is to keep this border legal.

Marx's critique of money in the 1840s spells out principles for understanding the transgressive new powers of space binding and time binding that are occurring in his moment. Marx considers the "blow-up" powers of money just as fantastic as does Locke, but his evaluation of money's moral status is the opposite of Locke's. Money's crime is its distorting of the normative human relationship of person to person. Marx's vision of just exchange is a reciprocal one. "Assume *man* to be

---

30. As Marx wrote in the *Grundrisse*, "The presupposition of the master-servant relation is the appropriation of an alien will," *Marx-Engels Reader*, 266. This is also true, as we saw, of mesmerism.

man and his relationship to the world to be a human one: then you can exchange love only for love, trust for trust, etc." (105). The kinds of influences we would exert on each other in such an Arcadia of reciprocity would be commensurate with our personal abilities or arguments and not with externalities such as our power, status, or money. A key passage from Marx not only anticipates Jürgen Habermas's idyll of distortion-free communication but expresses the Platonic-Hegelian dream of authentic individual communion: "Every one of your relations to man and to nature must be a *specific expression,* corresponding to the object of your will, of your *real individual* life. If you love without evoking love in return—that is, if your loving as loving does not produce reciprocal love; if through a *living expression* as a loving person you do not make yourself a *loved person,* then your love is impotent—a misfortune" (105). Every human relationship must be a "specific expression" of one's unique personality. No Lysias, with his scheme of love indifferent to the individuality of the beloved, allowed here! Roles, shortcuts, mediations all fall short. Marx disdains the wastefulness of broadcasting. Two wills must choose each other. Marx, like Socrates, worries about the tragedy of one-way dispersion. The vision at the core of the *Phaedrus* of two souls turning toward each other in philosophical love returns as Marx's normative account of labor, life, and love. The sin of capitalism is to make unrequited love the norm.

And just as mass eros was one of the bad options presented in the *Phaedrus,* questions of erotic distortion are central to Marx's critique of money. "Money is the alienated ability of mankind" (104); as the gatekeeper between wish and reality, money casts an unsettling power over all human and natural relationships. As the mediator of social relations, it is a universal and therefore diabolical go-between. "Money is the pimp between man's need and the object, between his life and his means of life. But that which mediates my life for me, also mediates the existence of other people for me" (102). As in Lysias's scheme, money allows sexual traffic between individuals who care nothing for each other's individuality. Possessing money, "what I am and am capable of is by no means determined by my individuality. I am ugly, but I can buy for myself the most beautiful of women" (103). Marx's critique clarifies the norm that love should be a mutual affair between individuals attracted to each other, not to alien or external elements. Marx's metaphors—money as pimp, its possessor as the procurer of prostitutes—suggest a type of erotic coupling indifferent to personality (or what Socrates would call the soul). Prostitution is public, on display, of open dissemination. Like mass communication, it is open to all comers and need share little or no history with its audience. Money, Marx concludes, "is thus the general overturning of individualities . . . the confounding and compounding of all natural and human qualities" (105). It makes for a *verkehrte Welt* of topsy-turvy relationships, none of them a "specific expression" of one's "real, individual life."

Though Marx nowhere discusses "communication" in a sustained way, despite many suggestive remarks about *Verkehr* and *Mitteilung*, he offers a model of its just and unjust forms.[31] Just communication is personal and authentically mutual; unjust is corrupted by externalities and distorted by scale. Like Plato and Hegel, Marx calls for a personal meeting of two souls unimpaired by the distorting mechanisms of money, markets, or media. *Verkehr*—traffic or exchange—is the closest Marx gets to naming communication. Die Welt der Verkehr, for Marx, ist eine verkehrte Welt!

Marx calls for dialogic relations: private property is a vampire at the systemic level that sucks the blood of the living. With the same logic, media become agencies not only of alienation and cognitive fog (as in the standard Marxist critique) but of distortion and interruption of the face-to-face rendezvous—with nature, the product, the other, and the self—that full humanity requires. As in the *Phaedrus,* the Marxist dream of life, labor, and language conceived of as dialogue is lovely. However much Marx's stock might have dropped since 1989, the dream remains fundamental for assessing the distortions and oppressions of modern life. Though too wedded to the dyad, Marx sees the substance of our communication practices not only as the orchestration of our social worlds but as a criterion of the good society. (Habermas's valiant efforts to develop a systematic theory of communicative action, for instance, seek to reinvigorate the normative core of Marx's critique of communication.) Marxist thinking is a robust answer to the conceit prevalent today in therapeutic and technical discourses, that there is a fix for disturbances in communication without reorganizing the material and cultural structures of social life to allow access, safety, and liberty for all to speak. Marx's vision of communication serves as a salutary reminder that failures of communication often owe less to semantic mismatches than to unjust allocations of symbolic and material resources.

Though far superior to most thinking about communication in the past decades, Marx's vision is still insufficient. It admits into its realm only a small range of communicative practices—the dialogical ones—

31. See *Marx and Engels on the Means of Communication,* ed. Yves de la Haye (New York: International General, 1979). The bulk of this work concerns what we would today call transportation.

which are a poor guide for grappling with the extended strings of talk and interruption that inevitably occur on a large scale and in public life, and in daily life as well.[32] Nor has practical Marxist politics had a particularly distinguished record in offering a vision of public communication as anything more than the utopian dialogue of all with all or the manipulation of the many by the few in the name of class consciousness or propaganda. This is not, of course, to blame Marx for the sins of his supposed heirs, but Marx clearly did not value deliberation and speech as primary human activities that authentically define the human condition.[33] Marx, as Charles Taylor notes, "seemed to have been oblivious to the inescapable opacity and indirectness of communication and decision in large bodies of men."[34] Marx believed in the ultimate transparency of communication. Modes of human connection and communication that are distanciated, mediated, and layered were corruptions rather than necessary or even valuable.

In part Marx believed this because he saw the market (the *agora*), the primordial place of speech, as the source of irrationality and abuse.[35] In the *Grundrisse* he also treats the spell of the commodity as derived in part from the geographical displacement of the product from its place of origin.[36] The market's distortions of scale are a key part of its abusiveness. Loss of locality and disembodiment are real problems for him. Though some passages in Marx might suggest the neutrality of technology, there is still a deep tropism for the face-to-face as the site of truth and justice. Marx saw the haunting of communication by alien elements as a symptom of dominative social conditions. The alien was to be reintegrated and overcome, an accomplishment whose ultimate completion awaited revolution. To say that some parts of our lives were naturally mysterious was to capitulate to the powers that be. Mystery was always the fruit of mystification. Nature was always history in disguise. Marx found in the uncanny a token of pathology, and he sought a cure. He thought material reorganization sufficient to exorcise the demons. All problems of communication were ultimately resolvable.

As later parts of this book make clear, I do not believe that the ghosts

32. I argue this general point in John Durham Peters, "Public Journalism and Democratic Theory: Four Challenges," in *The Idea of Public Journalism*, ed. Theodore L. Glasser (New York: Guilford Press, forthcoming).

33. Hannah Arendt, *The Human Condition* (Chicago: University of Chicago Press, 1958), part 3.

34. Taylor, *Hegel*, 554.

35. Allan Megill, "Über die Grenzen einer gewissen Art von Sozialtheorie: Marx, der Rationalismus und der Markt," in *Republik und Bürgerrecht*, ed. Klaus Dicke and Klaus-Michael Kodalle (Weimar: Böhlau, 1998), 363–98.

36. James W. Carey, *Communication as Culture: Essays on Media and Society* (Boston: Unwin Hyman, 1989), chap. 8.

are escapable or that the animosities and animalities in communication can be expunged from the human estate. Some kinds of alienation are inescapable. In contrast to both Hegel and Kierkegaard, Marx lacks an adequate sense of the tragic. Rather than taking connection and disconnection with other creatures and ourselves as symptoms of our wretchedness, we can also find in them strange lessons of compassion.

Again, it is crucial to be clear. Criticizing Marx is a risky business, as Hannah Arendt noted, since you risk getting lumped together with those who have made a career of it, most of whom you agree with far less than Marx.[37] In exposing weaknesses of Marx's normatively dialogic vision of communication, I do not thereby mean to be composing an homage to reification, exonerating the broadcasting industries or praising those who spread doctrines or make policy unaccountably. In the ethical nervousness about criticizing dialogue, it becomes clear just how much rides on it as a principle of justice and authenticity. Dialogue *is* a principle both of connection and of responsibility: it can satisfy a need for belonging and offer a check on unreflective power. But in itself it is no more exempt from abuse and power than is dissemination. Not only psychoanalysts and feminists, but the mainstream of twentieth-century drama, poetry, and popular song have explored the agonistics and agony at the heart of the private sphere. The Marxist tradition risks writing off dissemination based on its one-way transmission alone, instead of acknowledging the varying relations of justice that might inform it. The task is to think about the justice of diverse kinds of communication free of prejudices about their scale or form. Indeed, part of Habermas's heresy within Marxist circles is to take seriously the liberal faith in dissemination, deliberation, and openness rather than seeing those as delusion and prostitution. I am taking a similar risk: to call for the legitimacy of mass communication, at least in principle.

Kierkegaard's Incognitos

The accidental is absolutely just as necessary as the necessary.
SØREN KIERKEGAARD, *EITHER/OR*, 1:234

Kierkegaard held to the inescapability of paradox. One key contrast between Marx and Kierkegaard is their stances on the elasticity of the individual body. For Kierkegaard, the individual is incommensurable with reality. The world and the subject are forever out of kilter, the void be-

---

37. Arendt, *Human Condition,* 79.

tween the two being a structural part of the human lot. For Marx, this analysis is acute enough as a description of a particular historical and class situation—the suspended existence of the bourgeois proprietor, who, like Hegel's master, is doomed to fade away.[38] But to argue an eternal split between self and world, in Marx's opinion, denies the full fertility of human capacities, which have the potential to remake everything once they are released from exploitative relations of private ownership and production. Kierkegaard, in contrast, thinks some measure of alienation is inevitable as long as we remain mortal beings who live in time. Marx imagines the possibility of ultimate reconciliation—material as opposed to theological, but with all the classic millennial overtones— here on earth, among people. This is Kierkegaard's sharpest disagreement with both Marx and Hegel. For him, no totality can assuage the jagged edge of finitude. If Kierkegaard slights questions of social relations and power, Marx slights questions of time and mortality. Marx faults Hegel for seeing the world upside down and thereby missing the real struggles outside philosophy; Kierkegaard faults Hegel for forgetting his head is connected to his body, that is, that Hegel is ultimately just one more individual doomed to die.

Kierkegaard rarely writes directly about the emerging world of media; dead by 1855, he got to see but little of the full strangeness of electrical communication. But like Marx, Kierkegaard is a keen observer of the topsy-turvy social relations of his time, the shifts in modes of seeing, hearing, and being that modern men and women must face.[39] He was a master telegraphist, to use one of his metaphors, of the unseen world. Though thinkers like Locke, Shaftesbury, Hume, Shelley, and Coleridge all used the word "communication" in various ways, and the idealist path of Fichte, Schelling, Hölderlin, and Hegel explored diverse escape routes from the terrifyingly incommunicable thing-in-itself, thus establishing the lasting philosophical framework for the problem of communication, Kierkegaard is perhaps the first to make communication (*Meddelelse*, the Danish cognate for the German *Mitteilung*) per se a philosophical problem.[40] Here communication is less a matter of better un-

38. T. W. Adorno, *Kierkegaard: Construction of the Aesthetic*, trans. Robert Hullot-Kentor (1933; Minneapolis: University of Minnesota Press, 1989), uses this analysis against Kierkegaard.

39. For one account of Kierkegaard as media theorist, see Douglas E. Johnson, "Kierkegaard's Optics" (manuscript, Department of Communication Studies, University of Iowa, 1995).

40. In a broad sense, communication is the theme of all his works. Key sites are Kierkegaard, *Practice in Christianity*, ed. and trans. Howard V. Hong and Edna H. Hong (1848; Princeton: Princeton University Press, 1991), 123–44, and Kierkegaard, *Concluding Unscientific Postscript to "Philosophical Fragments,"* ed. and trans. Howard V. Hong and Edna H. Hong (1846; Princeton: Princeton University Press, 1992), part 2, sec, 2, chap. 2. Helpful work includes Lars Bejerholm, *Meddelelsens Dialektik*

derstanding than of strategic misunderstanding. As he wrote in an un-sent letter to Regine Olsen, his jilted fiancée (and much of what he wrote was, in effect, an unsent letter to Regine): "I thank you for never having understood me, for I learned everything from it."[41] Like Heidegger, who took much from him, Kierkegaard saw communication as a mode of revealing and concealing, not of information exchange.

Many of Kierkegaard's pseudonymous narrators care little for being understood or accounting for themselves, quite like Herman Melville's Bartleby (chapter 4). Kierkegaard gives us a notion of communication that features not the union of hearts, but the impossibility of speech, the resistance to public opinion, the stuntsmanship of irony, and the higher law of inwardness. What Kierkegaard calls communication looks more like obfuscation or breakdown to those used to a technical or therapeutic understanding. In a time of oversupply, the task of communication is to make the elementals strange. "Because everyone knows the Christian truth," he wrote, "it has gradually become such a triviality that a primitive impression of it is acquired only with difficulty. When this is the case, the art of being able to *communicate* eventually becomes the art of being able to *take away* or trick something away from someone."[42] Kierkegaard saw himself as a religious trickster, breaking convention to recover a sense of the original. The quest for "a primitive impression" was communication sooner than a transfusion of two minds.

Kierkegaard was a master theorist and practitioner of irony. He viewed irony as a sort of spiritual midwifery. Socrates and Jesus are irony's two great practitioners; they stand at the center of his massive dissertation on the concept. The world is full of false bottoms that may drop out at any moment, and for Kierkegaard irony is the rhetorical stance that best suits this condition. Inasmuch as people are always unfolding themselves, communication will never be the transmission of pure thoughts but will be an allusive enterprise of hints and evasions. Kierkegaard is miles distant from the earnest, boring world of "communication" in late twentieth-century therapeutic culture. Take, for example, the epigraph to *Fear and Trembling,* a quotation in German from J. G. Hamann: "What Tarquinius Superbus spoke in his garden with the poppy blooms was understood by the son but not by the messenger."

_____
(Copenhagen: Munksgard, 1962), with an extensive English summary, and Peter Fenves, *Chatter: Language and History in Kierkegaard* (Stanford: Stanford University Press, 1993).

41. Georg Lukács, *Die Seele und die Formen* (Berlin: Egon Fleischl, 1911), 79.

42. Johannes Climacus, quoted in Howard V. Hong and Edna H. Hong, "Historical Introduction," in *Philosophical Fragments,* by Søren Kierkegaard (Princeton: Princeton University Press, 1985), xxi; emphasis in original.

Tarquinius's son, in the old Roman story, had gone to live among his father's enemies on the pretense that he had quarreled with his father. Tarquinius, not trusting the messenger with the message he was to carry, took him into his garden and lopped off the tops of the tallest poppies with his sword. He told him to repeat the gesture to Tarquinius's son, meaning that he should kill or banish the leading men of the city. Kierkegaard's epigraph, then, is a cryptic message about cryptic messages— and in a foreign language to boot. It is a guide to decoding the book, but also a warning that if you are not privy to the circuit of prearranged agreements, you may not know what is going on: you will see strange acts of decapitation, gestures of cutting off (as one cuts the knot of an engagement) that would otherwise seem fantastic and arbitrary. The epigraph serves not only as a Rosetta stone for deciphering the book but as an announcement of its themes: fathers, sons, swords, dissemblance, unspoken messages.

Fear and Trembling is offered to the market of public readers, but they are as the messenger, not the son. Like the parable of the sower, the book conceals a private message within a public dissemination. The readers in 1843 Copenhagen might think the book a dialectical lyric about Abraham and Isaac, but she who had ears to hear the hidden meaning of the text was Regine Olsen. Kierkegaard spent his literary career explaining the supremely overdetermined event in which he broke off the engagement with Regine, such that all readers of his pseudonymous works besides Regine are positioned as eavesdroppers. Like Luther, Kierkegaard believed that preaching often requires cloaking the kernel; general messages addressed to whom it may concern might conceal secret messages for those in the know.

Kierkegaard's theory of direct and indirect communication, most fully developed in *Practice in Christianity,* is based on an extreme sensitivity to what speech act theory would later call "performatives." Just as Augustine bases his semiotics on an understanding of the "incarnate Word," so Kierkegaard starts from Christ as the god-man. Christ can say to people in first-century Galilee, directly, "I am the son of God," but this in fact is indirect or apparently counterfactual communication, since the speaker of that utterance is palpably a man rather than a deity. The force of an utterance is inextricably tied to the ethos of its speaker, and Kierkegaard berates modern Christianity for its attempt to preserve the "message" of Christianity while forgetting the person of Christ, since in effect the medium is the message. This point breaks decisively with the spiritualist tradition's central principle, disembodied meaning-content. "A sign is something different from what it immediately is," says Kierkegaard, setting up a two-level scheme quite like Augustine's fleshly and spiritual sides of the word. Kierkegaard shares much with Augustine both theologically and semiotically, but whereas Augustine sees the embodied side of the Incarnation as a *vehicle* of the divine, Kierkegaard insists on the necessarily ill-coordinated and paradoxical character of the juxtaposition. Christ was not just a sign of the divine but a "sign of contradiction," a "secret agent" operating under an "incognito," inciting hearers to choose one way or another.[43]

A natural consequence of Kierkegaard's vision of the impossibility of direct communication is the critique of public life, clear in his review of *The Present Age* and in his notions of preaching. If the Sermon on the Mount exhorts people both to let their lights shine (Matthew 5) and conceal their good works (Matthew 6), it is clearly the latter strand that Kierkegaard follows. "In the Sermon on the Mount it is said, 'When thou fastest, anoint thine head and wash thy face, that thou be not seen of men to fast.' This passage bears direct witness to the truth that subjectivity is incommensurable with reality, yea, that it has leave to deceive." One consciously deceives others in fasting, appearing to be of good cheer, despite the hunger. One puts on appearances to avoid putting on appearances. Thus, while writing *Fear and Trembling* Kierkegaard "went about in the incognito of a flâneur," making an appearance at the theater every night for at least ten minutes to keep up his reputation as a party animal and to conceal that he was a penitent. "Repentance has a holiness that eclipses the aesthetic. It does not want to be seen, least of all by a spectator, and requires an altogether different kind of self-activity."[44] The concealment of one's purposes, though sometimes ethically indefensible, is also sometimes necessary to maintain purity of heart. Kierkegaard can be read as a Protestant iconoclast, a foe of the corruptions of visibility and publicity.[45] Disclosure is a trap.

Again, the mode of communication is inseparable from the "message." In one of those scenes of delicious comic absurdity at which he so excels, in the *Postscript* Kierkegaard imagines someone who set out to communicate that "truth is inwardness." This new convert would proclaim it at every opportunity and soon would have a small army of missionaries spreading the word. Soon "he had even gone so far as to obtain barkers, and a barker of inwardness is a creature worth seeing."

43. Kierkegaard, *Practice in Christianity,* 123–39.

44. Søren Kierkegaard [Johannes de Silentio], *Fear and Trembling,* trans. Alastair Hannay (London: Penguin, 1985), 121, 149.

45. John Durham Peters, "Beauty's Veils: The Ambivalent Iconoclasm of Kierkegaard and Benjamin," in *The Image in Dispute,* ed. Dudley Andrew (Austin: University of Texas Press, 1997), 9–32.

The attempt to propagate the insight shows that the insight was never possessed.[46] The publisher of inwardness finds himself caught in a performative contradition.

The argument that communication can be not the vehicle but the corrupter of authenticity is also central to *Fear and Trembling*. It was not by obedience to "the ethical" that Abraham became the "father of the faithful," but rather by its suspension. "The ethical" for Kierkegaard usually means something like the Kantian categorical imperative. For Kant the proof of right action comes in one's ability to generalize a given action, to say that it would be right for everyone to do it. Killing one's son does not, needless to say, rank very high on this scale. Abraham's righteousness, acclaimed by generations since, is a problem to be explained. What makes him different from either a would-be murderer or a tragic hero?

The key lies in Abraham's transcendence of the ethical. The universal (which guarantees right action) is both a comfort and a source of despair in its unrelenting command to cast off particularity. As in Adam Smith or Kant, universality is a disciplinary regime. Abraham acts without the comfort or the command of the universal: his is a completely private affair between him and God that cannot be mediated or converted into a spectacle of public heroics. Unlike tragic heroes such as Agamemnon, whose sacrifice of his daughter Iphigenia is recognized as just by his whole community, Abraham has no recourse to social recognition, no ultimate balm of ethics or metaphysics. All he has is faith. The tragic hero edits a public book; the knight of faith, a sealed book read only by God. Abraham's truth cannot come out. "The ethical, as such is the universal, again, as the universal it is the manifest, the revealed. The individual regarded as he is immediately, that is, as a physical and psychical being, is the hidden, the concealed." The ethical, in other words, is public, the individual private. Hegel, Kierkegaard complains, brings everything into the light, thereby annihilating the flora and fauna of the night. "The tragic hero renounces himself in order to express the universal, the knight of faith renounces the universal in order to become the individual."[47] The burden of the knight of faith is that he has only himself to rely on—the universal is a constant temptation, beckoning with its public commendation and ontological security. Like Nietzsche's *Übermensch* in many ways, Abraham is beyond good and evil.

46. Kierkegaard, *Concluding Unscientific Postscript*, 1:77.
47. Kierkegaard, *Fear and Trembling*, 91, 86.

Kantian ethics, unmodified, cannot grasp Abraham or God, as if any of us can. The point for Kierkegaard is the paradox, the distortion of our categories. The last thing he wants is to rationalize the story of Abraham and Isaac; rather, we must face it in its full horror. We ought not to cheapen it to an edifying story of unrelenting obedience but should be scared to death by a God whose commands transcend the security of our ways and reasons. Like Freud, Kierkegaard knows the healing process can be undermined if the pain is halted too soon. *Fear and Trembling* is quite clear that Abraham's suspension of the universal, of mediation, makes him speechless. He suffers from a God-induced aphasia, unable to disclose to Isaac, Sarah, or Eleazar what he is doing. He would like nothing more than for Isaac to understand that Abraham loves him but that he has to sacrifice him because of his love for God; but Isaac's misunderstanding is precisely part of the sacrifice. "O Lord in heaven, I thank thee," prays Abraham. "After all it is better for him to believe that I am a monster, rather than that he should lose faith in Thee."[48] Better that Isaac remain forever hurt by Abraham, that their relationship remain broken, than that Isaac know that God could command a father to murder a son.

There are, then, situations in which misunderstanding is inevitable. To try to communicate with Abraham is to make him less than Abraham. In a world of paradox, easy communication is necessarily false. Circumlocution and irony may be what save us. The way to salvation must be thorny. The notion of easy communication is, for Kierkegaard, a clearance sale in the realm of spirit, a lowering of the price of understanding. Right action, faith, other people—these things are a *skandalon,* a stumbling block, not something to be skirted without fear and trembling. (Not by accident does Kierkegaard invoke the Johannine and Pauline concept of *skandalon* here.) The conceit that communication necessarily improves relations or clarifies the underlying reasons of things is insufficiently acquainted with the night.

A similar argument against generality is made in the discussion of marriage by "Judge William" in part 2 of *Either/Or* (1843). The seducer keeps arguing that marriage is an unreasonable form of love. The judge responds that the husband, like Abraham, must refuse the universal. Though the institution itself may be universal, the particular choice of mate is highly partisan and selective. One person is to be privileged above all others on the face of the earth. Kant, like Kierkegaard a lifelong bachelor, thought marriage a concession to our animality. The injunc-

48. Kierkegaard, *Fear and Trembling,* 27.

tion "Tell the truth," Kant thought, applies to all rational beings (including angels and spirits), whereas "Do not commit adultery" applies only to creatures with sex organs. To a moral system like Kant's, which makes universalizability the test of the good, there is something absurd about wedded life: one cannot wish that all rational beings would marry one's spouse. Though Kantians will regard this point as a burlesque, suggesting that Kant would say rather that one could universally will that everyone be married, still it reveals the aporia of Kant's ethics when faced with the decision to choose one person, or one path, rather than another. *Either/Or* performs the oscillation between undecidables that such an ethics induces.

Kant's low estimate of the ethical value of embodiment meets a lively response in Kierkegaard. In love, as *Fear and Trembling* says, the particular is higher than the universal. The impossibility of public justification is not a defect but the essence of love: "The moment a lover can answer that objection [why he fell in love with one person among countless possibilities] he is *eo ipso* not a lover; and if a believer can answer that objection, he is *eo ipso* not a believer."[49] Love and faith alter their being when subject to mediation. Marriage is the giving of one's life to a distinct individual chosen from among one-half of the entire species. The generalization of marriage, in monogamous cultures, is either adultery or seduction. Kierkegaard sees the ways that the activity of communication reshapes the very things it carries. Media mean the multiplication of singular beings for the use of strangers. Kierkegaard knows that scale and circulation matter profoundly to the meaning of our messages and our couplings with others. His insistence on singularity rather than generality as the ruling principle of our relations with each other is a key insight at the dawn of the age of mechanical reproduction, when the images, voices, and words of beautiful and seductive others are proliferating at a rate unknown in previous human history. Amid a population explosion in the spirit world, Kierkegaard exhorts us to remember the limits and loveliness of the flesh. The criterion of truth may lie in what cannot be communicated. Nothing but the regime of falsity and chatter results when people try to fix communication breakdown, for such breakdown, Kierkegaard teaches, can be a well of revelation.

Marx regards the public sphere as a corrupt fantasyland concealing its status as war by other means, a *bellum omnium contra omnes*. Kierkegaard has an equally dour outlook: the public is a phantom, a panorama

---

49. Quotation from Kierkegaard's journals in Robert Bretall, "Introduction," in *A Kierkegaard Anthology* (Princeton: Princeton University Press, 1973), xxi.

of abstract infinity.[50] Participation in public occurs for Marx and Kierkegaard either by force or by subterfuge. But since, in the wake of Hegel, all communication is essentially public—interiority being achieved only via the recognition of the other—these thinkers make us face the clefts at the heart of what we too often want to dream of as the immediate sympathy of angels. Perhaps they do not show us the clearest way to build an inspired public realm, but they do expose the fantasy that all is well in dialogue. They are among the first thinkers to face modern communication in all its troubles. They register an almost anthropological shift in the modes of our existence in an age of time- and space-altering media.

50. Søren Kierkegaard, "The Present Age," in *A Kierkegaard Anthology* (Princeton: Princeton University Press, 1973), 260–69.

FOUR

Phantasms of the Living, Dialogues with the Dead

If the dull substance of my flesh were thought,
Injurious distance should not stop my way;
For then, despite of space, I would be brought,
From limits far remote, where thou dost stay.

WILLIAM SHAKESPEARE, SONNET 44

Recording and Transmission

Distance and death have always been the two great obstacles to love and the two great stimulants of desire. Great obstacles excite great passions; since eros, as Socrates argues in the *Symposium,* consists not in possession but in wanting, what could stimulate eros more than distance and especially death, itself the ultimate distance?[1] Eros seeks to span the miles, reach into the grave, and bridge all the chasms. It is the principle that seeks to transcend the limitations of our normal modes of contact with each other in word and in the flesh. New media, by smashing old barriers to intercourse, often enlarge eros's empire and distort its traditional shape, and hence they are often understood as sexy or perverse or both. In the *Phaedrus* Socrates saw written texts as an intellectual sperm bank that allowed conceptions to take place apart from paternity or person-to-person relationships. The Greeks took as natural

1. See Denis de Rougemont, *Love in the Western World,* rev. ed., trans. Montgomery Belgion (New York: Pantheon, 1956).

137

facts the limited range of the human voice and the weakness of memory. Memory and writing were the only record. Writing, by making possible remote control over other bodies and voices (of readers) and the preservation of thoughts (of the writer), made possible a new order of polygamous coupling among souls. The far could now speak to the near, and the dead could now speak to the living.

Something similar happened in the nineteenth century. Putting it too starkly, in the 1830s and 1840s the photograph overcame time and the telegraph overcame space. The formulation is too stark because the dreams of recording experience in something more substantial than human memory and of sending messages through the expanses are at least as old as writing and the angels; likewise, photography and telegraphy have their own long cultural and intellectual prehistories.[2] Still, the nineteenth century saw unprecedented transformations in the conditions of human contact, along two axes in particular: transmission and recording. The key changes are registered in the terms *tele-* and *-graphy,* so ubiquitous in subsequent media nomenclature. *Tele-* suggests a new scale of distances—telegraphy (word), telephony (sound), television (image), and telepathy (spirit); *-graphy* suggests new forms of inscription—telegraph (word), photograph (image), phonograph (sound), and electroencephalograph (brain waves). The nineteenth century saw a revolution in both space binding and time binding.[3] Space-binding media, such as paper or electricity, are portable and knit distinct points in space together over great distances. Time-binding media, such as statuary or architecture, are durable and "bind" distinct moments across great spans of time. Writing inscribed on stone is time binding; we can still read the Rosetta stone today. The telegraph, because its cargo is weightless and swift, is space binding.

The revolution in time binding meant that writing lost its monopoly as the chief record of human events and intelligence. Memory achieved a sort of jailbreak from the body and the (suddenly) sensorily challenged medium of writing. Mnemotechnics was an art no longer tied to the mortal individual; lost time could become captive; something besides writing could contribute to the historical record. Writing's handicaps— its blindness and deafness—were suddenly revealed. Scenes and, more

2. Peter Galassi, *Before Photography* (New York: Museum of Fine Art, 1981); Jonathan Crary, *Techniques of the Observer: On Vision and Modernity in the Nineteenth Century* (Cambridge: MIT Press, 1990); Nicholas J. Wade, ed., *Brewster and Wheatstone on Vision* (London: Academic Press, 1983); and Geoffrey Wilson, *The Old Telegraphs* (London: Phillimore, 1976).

3. Harold Adams Innis, *Empire and Communications* (Oxford: Clarendon Press, 1950).

important, events could now be caught without the intervention of word, pencil, or paintbrush, thanks to the camera. More strikingly yet, the epitome of transience—the flow of time itself—could now be transcribed in images and sounds by film or phonograph. By preserving people's apparitions in sight and sound, media of recording helped repopulate the spirit world. Every new medium is a machine for the production of ghosts. (Kafka knew this.) As Friedrich Kittler argues, "The spirit-world is as large as the storage and transmission possibilities of a civilization." The oldest available print of a printing press is a 1499 image showing skeletons cavorting about a press, pages in hand, doing a dance of the dead.[4] Spiritualists, as we have seen, did the *danse macabre* of the telegraph, celebrating the spirits conjured by electricity, the first of many in the nineteenth century to recognize that the realm of the immortals had expanded from the remembered dead to the recorded and transmitted dead.

The nineteenth-century revolution in space binding was marked by techniques of telecommunication. Simultaneity across distances—first in writing, then in speech, sound, and image—was made possible by the telegraph, telephone, radio, and facsimile. For the first time in human history, acuity of vision and hearing were no longer the limit to instantaneous remote contact; the only limits were the extent of the telegraph lines (and hence of capital). In principle the coefficient of friction for signals—but not bodies—was reduced to zero, even though access and cost kept the telegraph from being the utopia of universal contact that some early enthusiasts, excited about "the annihilation of time and space," dreamed of. As James W. Carey argues, the telegraph wrought the fateful separation of transportation and communication. Except for messages sent by line of sight or range of hearing, all sending had historically required some form of carriage by courier, boat, pigeon, or some other means.[5] The telegraph, in contrast, fits precisely into the lineage of Augustine, the angels, and Mesmer: communication without embodiment, contact achieved by the sharing of spiritual (electrical) fluids. The spookier consequence was, I will argue, that the human body retained its weight even amid new norms of spiritual communication inspired by the swiftness of electricity.

Contact between people at a distance has, to be sure, taken a variety of forms in the social history of our species, from diaspora and pilgrim-

4. Friedrich A. Kittler, *Grammophon, Film, Typewriter* (Berlin: Brinkmann und Bose, 1986), 24, 12.
5. James W. Carey, *Communication as Culture: Essays on Media and Society* (Boston: Unwin Hyman, 1989), chap. 8.

age to correspondence and statuary. The distantiation of sociability is by no means unique to the nineteenth and twentieth centuries.[6] What is new is a rash of incursions on the human incognito.[7] The capturing and dispersion of signals meant that the visual and auditory signs of human personality were no longer tightly tied to the presence of the person's body. To be sure, two and a half millennia of writing and four centuries of printing had made it possible for personal utterances—the seeds of thoughts, as Socrates would put it—to scatter abroad in space and time. Writing had been an expression of the unique "character" of each person, a term that shows the union of writing discipline and notions of personality. But the camera and cinema, telephone and phonograph, allowed for entirely new kinds of raids on and representations of the human form. The nuances of facial, vocal, and gestural expression could be immortalized in sound and image. A new realm of personal quirks and significances became available for storage and transmission, underscoring the truth of Kierkegaard's point that the accidental is as necessary as the necessary.[8]

Put slightly differently, the separation of communication from transportation meant the conjuring of a parallel universe in which personal replicas dwelled and abided by laws other than those that apply to us mortals. "Media always already yield ghost phenomena."[9] Though steam power made the transportation of people and cargo by rail and water much swifter, the body still could not keep up with its acoustic, graphic, and visual representations. Our bodies know fatigue and finitude, but our effigies, once recorded, can circulate through media systems indefinitely, across the wastes of space and time. Kafka saw that the effort to restore the peace of souls by bringing people together by train, car, and air was always outflanked by media that were more nutritious for the ghosts—the telegraph, telephone, and wireless—that all had as modus operandi the creation of doubles that sometimes work against us.

The humanoid replicas that served as proxies in distance communication were named well by Frederic Myers, a classicist polymath, coiner of the term "telepathy," and leader in the British Society for Psychical Research from its founding in 1882 till his death in 1903. He used the

6. The key works are Harold Adams Innis, *The Bias of Communication* (Toronto: University of Toronto Press, 1951), and Innis, *Empire and Communications*.

7. Walter Benjamin, "The Paris of the Second Empire in Baudelaire," in *Charles Baudelaire: A Lyric Poet in the Era of High Capitalism*, trans. Harry Zohn (London: NLB, 1973), 48.

8. Carlo Ginzburg, "Clues: Roots of an Evidential Paradigm," in *Myths, Emblems, Clues*, trans. John and Anne C. Tedeschi (London: Hutchinson Radius, 1990), 96–125, 200–214.

9. Kittler, *Grammophon, Film, Typewriter*, 22.

phrase "phantasms of the living" in 1886 for the apparitions proliferating in the spiritualist culture of his day. Writing within a decade of the introduction of the phonograph and the telephone, Myers wanted a term that would not imply an exclusively visual sense (as in "apparition"), whence his choice of "phantasm" over "phantom."[10] Phantasms of the living, he explained, could be voices, faces, or entire materializations of spectral bodies. What men and women in the late nineteenth century faced with alarm is something we have had over a century to get used to: a superabundance of phantasms of the living appearing in various media. The concern in psychical research—contact with spectral emanations of distant bodies, whether via writing, images, sounds, or even touch—is part of a larger effort in modernity to reorganize representations of the human body.[11] The joining of the phantasmatic body and voice of the actor was a long trend in the normalization of cinema.[12] Media both define and enlarge the spirit world, being populated by spectral beings who look or sound human but offer no personal presence and possess no flesh. Electronic media both supplement and transform the nineteenth-century culture of doppelgängers by duplicating and distributing indicia of human presence.[13] Fifty years after Myers, the psychologist Gordon Allport stated the phantasmatic fact of media well: the idea of "appearing in person," he wrote in 1937, "once seemed redundant, but it is less so now in the days of cinema and radio when partial appearance or appearance *not* in person is possible."[14]

The ability of persons to "appear" apart from the flesh was perhaps the most unnerving thing about the new audiovisual media. This created a dialectical crisis of representation. On the one hand, telephone managers, phonograph marketers, and radio spokespeople, among oth-

10. Frederic W. H. Myers, "Introduction," in *Phantasms of the Living*, by Edmund Gurney, Frederic W. H. Myers, and Frank Podmore, ed. Eleanor Mildred Balfour Sidgwick (1924; New York: Arno Press, 1975), ix. This is the book that Richard Burton has to shelve when he is working undercover at the library of the Society for Psychical Research in *The Spy Who Came in from the Cold* (1965).

11. Mark Bennion Sandberg, "Missing Persons: Spectacle and Narrative in Late Nineteenth-Century Scandinavia" (Ph.D. diss., University of California at Berkeley, 1991).

12. See Mary Ann Doane, "The Voice in the Cinema: The Articulation of Body and Space," in *Narrative, Apparatus, Ideology*, ed. Philip Rosen (New York: Columbia University Press, 1986), 335–48. But the problem of corporeal integration is general to a media culture rife with phantasms of the living.

13. Friedrich A. Kittler, "Romantik—Psychanalyse—Film: Eine Doppelgängergeschichte," in *Draculas Vermächtnis: Technische Schriften* (Leipzig: Reclam, 1993), 81–104; Tom Gunning, "Phantom Images and Modern Manifestations: Spirit Photography, Magic Theater, Trick Films, and Photography's Uncanny," in *Fugitive Images: From Photography to Video*, ed. Patrice Petro (Bloomington: Indiana University Press, 1995), 42–71.

14. Gordon W. Allport, *Personality: A Psychological Interpretation* (New York: Henry Holt, 1937), 37.

ers, sought to reassure their customers by reconnecting the mechanically reproduced representations to an originating body (via testimony and authentication). The effort to manifest the body within the mediating apparatus led to practices of sincerity in radio (chapter 5), and at their most extreme, the ectoplasms of materializing mediums. On the other hand, the sites where acoustic, optical, and verbal traces of the human could be registered started to multiply rapidly. Humans have long interacted symbiotically with their personal effects, but traces of subjectivity get even more scattered by these new media of dispersion and recording. As William James, much in tune with the new audiovisual order, argued, tracts within the material universe can serve as repositories of human personality, whether dead or alive. Media able to capture the flow of time, such as the phonograph and cinema, seemed to vaporize personages into sounds and images. To interact with another person could now mean to read media traces.

The phantasms of the living were always either disembodied or embodied in abnormal ways. Communication theory from Augustine to Locke had taken the body as a given and called for a more spiritual, less hindered means of connecting souls. The ability to engage in out-of-body communication is likewise the central theme of the intellectual reception of the telegraph, telephone, and radio—and of spiritualism. Spiritualism, and its later scientizing offshoot psychical research, is a chief vehicle for the formation of ideas about communication in the nineteenth and early twentieth centuries. The word, voice, or image of a person dead or distant channeling through a delicate medium: this is the project common to electronic media and spiritualist communication. Indeed, all mediated communication is in a sense communication with the dead, insofar as media can store "phantasms of the living" for playback after bodily death.

In sum, the new media of the nineteenth century gave new life to the older dream of angelic contact by claiming to burst the bonds of distance and death. As one 1896 phonograph enthusiast announced a trifle prematurely, "Death has lost some of its sting since we are able to forever retain the voices of the dead."[15] Such retention apparently allowed for revivication (resurrection?) at will.[16] But the price of such conjuring soon became evident: a world of doppelgängers that had no flesh. As soon as spirit-to-spirit contact became realized in new technologies,

15. "Voices of the Dead," *Phonoscope* 1 (1896): 1. Thanks to Mark Sandberg for providing a copy.
16. See W. Hartenau [Walter Rathenau], "Die Resurrection Co." (1898), trans. Louis Kaplan, *New German Critique* 62 (spring–summer 1994): 63–69.

mutual presence "in person" took on a new premium and a new deficiency. As we live through something of a digital revolution in our own time, revisiting old shocks can be highly illuminating. The urgent questions about communications today—the telescoping of space-time (e.g., the Internet) and the replication of human experience and identity (e.g., virtual reality)—were explored in analogous forms in the eras of the telegraph and photograph, the phonograph and telephone, the cinema and radio. In what follows I pursue the ways these media, in claiming to bring us closer, only made communication seem that much more impossible. Chapter 5 is devoted to the pathos of looking for signs of sure contact in transmission across media (and mediums). This chapter concerns dialogue with the dead, specifically the futility of the effort to commune spiritually with beings who can only be read hermeneutically. The next chapter concerns novel powers of transmission; this one, novel powers of recording. The distinction between transmission and recording, or the overcoming of distance and the overcoming of death, is largely a convenience of organization. To send a signal at a distance, it must be kept from dying along the way. Indeed, one motive for Edison's work on the phonograph was to make a better telegraph "repeater."[17] Once recorded, anything can be transmitted to new eyes and ears.[18] Socrates' concern about writing was precisely this: the inevitable promiscuity of any intelligence committed to permanence.

The experience of flight was central to the nineteenth-century conquest of distance. Both new means of transportation such as the railroad and new technologies of sensory amplification such as the camera, telegraph, and telephone were described as flying machines.[19] In 1859 Oliver Wendell Holmes Sr. famously characterized the sensation of the stereoscope as "a dream-like exaltation of the faculties, in which we seem to leave the body behind us and sail away into one strange scene after another, like disembodied spirits."[20] Just as a telegraph dispatch

17. Walter L. Welch and Leah Brodbeck Stenzel Burt, *From Tinfoil to Stereo: The Acoustic Years of the Recording Industry, 1877–1929* (Gainesville: University Press of Florida, 1994), chap. 1.

18. In "A Scandal in Bohemia," Sherlock Holmes helps the king of Bohemia cope with potential blackmail concerning a photograph of an early romance: Arthur Conan Doyle, *The Complete Sherlock Holmes* (New York: Doubleday, 1930), 1:161–75. See also Tom Gunning, "Tracing the Individual Body: Photography, Detectives, and Early Cinema," in *Cinema and the Invention of Modern Life*, ed. Leo Charney and Vanessa R. Schwartz (Berkeley: University of California Press, 1995), 15–45.

19. Paul Virilio, *War and Cinema: The Logistics of Perception*, trans. Patrick Camiller (London: Verso, 1989); Wolfgang Schivelbusch, *The Railway Journey: The Industrialization of Space and Time in the Nineteenth Century* (Berkeley: University of California Press, 1986), chap. 3.

20. Quoted in Sandberg, "Missing Persons," 15.

could leap from Washington to Baltimore in the twinkling of an eye, the stereoscope could crosscut from the immediate environment to far-off lands and ancient ruins (a favorite subject for stereoscopic images). Time travel was an equally remarkable achievement of nineteenth-century media. The stream of time could be bottled and stored for later use. The culture of historicism and lifelike representation (as found in the practice of taxidermy, for instance) all argued the possibility of transport across time (in the sense of either travel or rapture).[21] The light that shone on Nicéphore Niepce's courtyard in 1826, making the first photographic image, seems preserved in some sense for us to see today as well. Caruso's voice not only has dissipated into minute echoes traveling into deep space, it is available on record, tape, and compact disc. Phonography and film served not only as hearing and seeing aids, neurophysiological assist devices for the voice, ears, and eyes, but as new archives of consciousness. The sensuous, temporal impressions of events could be preserved in light and sound. Media of transmission allow crosscuts through space, but recording media allow jump cuts through time. The sentence of death for sound, image, and experience had been commuted. Speech and action could live beyond their human origins. In short, recording media made the afterlife of the dead possible in a new way. As *Scientific American* put it of the phonograph in 1877: "Speech has become, as it were, immortal."[22] That "as it were" is the dwelling place of the ghosts.

HAWTHORNE'S HAUNTED HOUSE   Nathaniel Hawthorne's *House of the Seven Gables* (1851) is a wonderful example of the metaphysical mischief unleashed by both photography and telegraphy.[23] Hawthorne wrote amid massive transformations in the capacities of data storage and transmission. The spirit world had opened a new frontier: communication at a distance and from the grave. The book is all about haunting. Hawthorne called it a "romance"; it is clearly a variant of the gothic genre, with its run-down mansion, ancestral guilt, and spookily paranormal powers. The Pyncheon family has dwelled in the house of the seven gables for over two centuries, and only four Pyncheons remain, haunted by the curse imposed by a seventeenth-century wizard, Matthew Maule, who had originally owned the property on which the

21. Stephen Bann, *The Clothing of Clio: A Study of the Representation of History in Nineteenth-Century Britain and France* (Cambridge: Cambridge University Press, 1984).
22. Welch and Burt, *From Tinfoil to Stereo*, 6.
23. See Cathy N. Davidson, "Photographs of the Dead: Sherman, Daguerre, Hawthorne," *South Atlantic Quarterly* 89 (1990): 667–701.

house was built. Colonel Thomas Pyncheon, the clan's founder, had loudly encouraged Maule's prosecution for witchcraft, since he had designs on Maule's property. Right before being hanged, Maule had cursed the Pyncheons. Subsequently the Pyncheons became masters of property, but the Maules had been rumored to possess quasi-magical powers, including influence on other people's dreams. The one family owned real estate, the other the unreal estate of image and memory. Hawthorne describes a mirror in the mansion that, thanks to "a sort of mesmeric process," was fabled to contain every image it had ever reflected. Thanks to their command over "the topsy-turvy commonwealth of sleep" and access to hidden interiors, the Maules inherit the key to this cameralike record of things past.[24] Like Hawthorne, they dwell in the ambiguous world of art.

All these themes appear in the character of Holgrave, a drifter, revolutionary, mesmerist, and daguerreotypist who comes to the mansion as a tenant and is climactically revealed to be the descendant of Matthew Maule. Holgrave, an aptly assumed name, is a dabbler in the spirit world who uses the truth of the sunlight to record the hidden truths of the visible world on his camera. "There is a wonderful insight," he says, "in heaven's broad and simple sunshine. While we give it credit for depicting the merest surface, it actually brings out the secret character with a truth that no painter would ever venture upon, even could he detect it."[25] His daguerreotype portraits reveal the true character of the face, showing that Judge Jaffrey Pyncheon, the smiling public man, has in fact the inherited scowl of his Puritan ancestor and that Clifford, the private recluse, has a beautiful smile. Despite his gift for revealing inner and outer surfaces, he does not dwell on the past or on property. He would agree with Marx's remark in the preface to *Capital,* volume 1 (1867): "We suffer not only from the living, but from the dead. *Le mort saisit le vif!"*

Holgrave is also, as it happens, a writer, and the appropriately numbered chapter 13 of the book offers one of his tales, intended for one of the magazines of the day, fictionalizing the sadistic mesmeric probing done by Matthew Maule of one Alice Pyncheon, a virginal young woman, in order to tap into the family secret. Holgrave's account unites optical technology, animal magnetism, and communication with the dead: "It appears to have been his object to convert the mind of Alice into a kind of telescopic medium through which Mr. Pyncheon and

24. Nathaniel Hawthorne, *The House of the Seven Gables* (1851; New York: Bantam, 1986), 13, 17.
25. Hawthorne, *House of the Seven Gables,* 68.

himself might obtain a glimpse into the spiritual world. He succeeded, accordingly, in holding an imperfect sort of intercourse, at one remove, with the departed personages in whose custody the so much valued secret had been carried beyond the precincts of earth."[26] Here mesmerism (binding another's mind) leads to spiritualism (contact with the dead). On tapping the secret, Maule refuses to share it and leaves the Pyncheons with the house, since it is too cursed to take. But Alice remains forever after under his spell, a degraded plaything of his whims. Wherever she happens to be, Maule can misogynistically command her emotions with a small gesture of his hand, making her laugh at funerals, weep at parties, and dance at inopportune moments. Here we see the dark side of soul binding, as we did in mesmerism before. In the story Alice eventually dies, much to Maule's chagrin, a victim in his class warfare on the Pyncheons.

As he reads this tale within a tale aloud to Phoebe Pyncheon, Holgrave mesmerizes her, thanks to his enthusiastic miming of the gestures used by the fictional/ancestral Maule. But despite the temptation and the evident enjoyment he derives from knowledge of his powers, Holgrave renounces the chance to dominate her, having "the high and rare quality of reverence for another's individuality."[27] Unlike Roger Chillingworth of *The Scarlet Letter*, who also toys with another's interiority, Holgrave here refuses to penetrate another's heart. Phoebe is clearly cast, like Alice, as particularly sensitive to magnetic and electrical sympathy. In this account of the scene of reading, Holgrave here chooses not to repeat the past but to turn it into literature—again, like Hawthorne. Like Emerson and Melville, Hawthorne takes soul-to-soul communication as a narrative we tell or a story we write, not as bodiless thoughts we send, though it clearly has dangerous powers of mind binding.

The book's vision of the telegraph has been relatively neglected compared with its treatment of photography. Clifford Pyncheon, a worldless aesthete wasting away under the pressure of accumulated ancestral guilt, finally escapes the house and flees by train. He rides in rapture and gushes to his rather more sober seatmate about the world's growing spirituality. Touching in quick succession such associated spiritual wonders of the age as mesmerism, rapping spirits, and electricity, Clifford turns to the telegraph lines that run parallel to the railway and declares: "An almost spiritual medium, like the electric telegraph, should be consecrated to high, deep, joyful, and holy missions. Lovers, day by day—

---

26. Hawthorne, *House of the Seven Gables,* 135.
27. Hawthorne, *House of the Seven Gables,* 162.

hour by hour, if so often moved to do it—might send their heart-throbs from Maine to Florida." Like Socrates telling of Diotima in the *Symposium,* Clifford imagines the telegraph as a means of a erotic junction between lovers. (His seatmate much more accurately notes that the telegraph's fate lies in the hands of politics and commerce.)

The "almost spiritual medium" enlarges not only the realm of amatory contact, but that of contact with the dead and the distant. Says Clifford, "When a good man has departed, his distant friend should be conscious of an electric thrill, as from the world of happy spirits, telling him—'Your dear friend is in bliss!' Or, to an absent husband, should come the tidings thus, 'An immortal being, of whom you are the father, has this moment come from God!'"[28] Clifford's "electric thrill" is found more in the line of telepathy than telegraphy; he sees none of the obstacles—the expense, need for coding, or enforced brevity—of telegraphic communication that would soon become clear to its more practiced users, such as newspaper correspondents and businessmen. Clifford states the enduring dream of communication at a distance as a bridge between distant lovers and a bringer of tidings of birth and death, the key portals between this world and the other side. The telegraph, like all other means of linking bodies at a distance, offered new potentials for making links between bodies and bodies (as in the case of lovers) or spirits and spirits (as in the case of the dead). Media—as things that come in between—are liminal objects par excellence, and they deal not only with information but with birth, sex, love, and death.

Hermeneutics as Communication with the Dead

The concept of communication was developed in a culture that routinely sought communication with the distant and the dead. What sex was to the Victorians, death is to us: the ultimate but inescapable taboo. We avert our eyes, fear dwelling on the corpse, sequester death in hospitals, and are easily persuaded by the hygienic rhetoric of cremation. We are miles apart from the nineteenth century's gloomy romanticism about death. We chuckle at Victorian primness, congratulating ourselves on our liberalism on topics sexual, but nothing is so veiled to us as death, so cloaked in euphemisms—or as pervasive in popular culture. Whatever the excesses of lamentation among the Victorians, nothing is so telling of our own times as our inability to mourn. We lack the cultural and religious practices that would protect us from being lonely

---

28. Hawthorne, *House of the Seven Gables,* 203.

psychological agents. Our perfunctory grief bespeaks a disturbance in that most crucial of all relationships, our relation to the dead. Perhaps in a time of video- and tape recording, photo albums and home movies, death seems less final.

The sensibility was different in Victoria's age. So were the conditions. Lewis Mumford suggests that the pervasive black clothing in the nineteenth century was an unwitting expression of a civilization in mourning.[29] The facts are well known: the population exploded, children died young, the laboring classes (which included children) toiled in sheer misery, and the middle classes lived in upholstered insecurity.[30] It was a rare house at any rung on the class ladder in which someone had not died. Corpses were relatively familiar if uncanny presences, not ghoulish objects to be hidden in hospitals. Mourning was central to culture and commerce. The paraphernalia of grief were aggressively marketed, especially to women, including such artifacts as mourning cards, *immortelles,* earthenware chimneypiece ornaments of famous criminals or murderers, sable furs, handkerchiefs embroidered with tears, "mutes" (professional mourners), curtains, jewelry, and lockets (with a daguerreotype or photograph or a lock of hair). Elaborate wreaths woven from the locks of the dead were a favorite parlor decoration. The color of one's clothing announced degrees of mourning: black, white, gray, and finally mauve. Queen Victoria, of course, led the way spectacularly, daily laying out Prince Albert's shaving kit for him until she died, decades after he did. The high point of Victorian poetry was characteristically a long lament for a lost comrade, Tennyson's *In Memoriam A. H. H.* Tennyson's soulmate died in 1833, but the poem was not completed until 1849. Tennyson spent sixteen years writing the elegy; no psychologically certified "stages of grief" for him! Victorian literature was filled with spirits returning from the dead; Dickens's Scrooge first thought Marley's ghost was "an ill-digested piece of cheese," but his materialistic suspicion of humbuggery would eventually bow to the incontrovertible proofs of the ghost's reality. Edgar Allan Poe is the archetypal romancer of the dead. Cemeteries were places of contemplation, pilgrimage, and picnics. "Nowhere is the strangeness of the period, with its obsessions about death,

29. Lewis Mumford, *Technics and Civilization* (New York: Harcourt, Brace, Jovanovich, 1934), 162.

30. James Stevens Curl, *The Victorian Celebration of Death* (London: David and Charles, 1972). See also John Morley, *Death, Heaven, and the Victorians* (Pittsburgh: University of Pittsburgh Press, 1971), and Michael Wheeler, *Death and the Future Life in Victorian Literature and Theology* (Cambridge: Cambridge University Press, 1990).

its high moral tone, and its sentimentality, better expressed than in the cemeteries."[31]

The two key existential facts about modern media are these: the ease with which the living may mingle with the communicable traces of the dead, and the difficulty of distinguishing communication at a distance from communication with the dead. The same phantasms of the living that are "communicated" to far-off destinations in telecommunications can be captured for playback in recording media. The key difference is that a dialogue can be conducted over distance, but a dialogue with the dead is quite another matter. As communicators the dead are a particularly enigmatic bunch. They tend not to respond to our entreaties. Their words are fixed and invariant. Like Socrates' description of writing, the dead repeat themselves, always signifying the same thing.[32] Certainly we can read the traces of the dead, but we cannot interact directly with them. Even in spiritualism, problems of linkage are enormous. As Eleanor Balfour Sidgwick noted in a 1924 retrospective of thirty-five years of psychical research on telepathy, "'Why,' say the critics, 'cannot the dead, if they communicate at all, say what they mean?'"[33] Our communication with the dead consists of dead letters, correspondence never delivered. The communicative stance to the dead can only be one of dissemination. The dead are tutors in the art of reading traces where dialogue is impossible. Communication with the dead is the paradigm case of hermeneutics: the art of interpretation where no return message can be received.[34]

Hermeneutics, the reading of texts that have drifted out of their original historical setting, is an old practice. It starts from a shattered communication situation in which writer and reader are in some way estranged from each other, by distance in time or culture. It begins precisely where the *Phaedrus* breaks off: with the weird couplings of mediated communication. One stream of hermeneutics, from Schleiermacher through Dilthey up to Gadamer, wants interpretation more or less to open up something more than texts, so that contact or at least conversation between the living and the dead can be attained. I follow

31. Curl, *Victorian Celebration of Death*, 179. On the American scene, see Garry Wills, *Lincoln at Gettysburg: The Words That Remade America* (New York: Simon and Schuster, 1992), and Ann Douglas, *The Feminization of American Culture* (New York: Knopf, 1977).

32. Plato, *Phaedrus*, 275d.

33. Eleanor Mildred Balfour Sidgwick, "On Hindrances and Complications in Telepathic Communication," in *Phantasms of the Living*, by Edmund Gurney, Frederic W. H. Myers, and Frank Podmore, ed. Eleanor Mildred Balfour Sidgwick (1924; New York: Arno Press, 1975), 432.

34. I thank Cătălin Mamali for this insight.

a more heretical tradition here, not in the mainstream of specifically hermeneutic thinking, that is more aware of the impossibilities than the bridges. Hegel, Marx, and Kierkegaard, despite their massive disagreements, all see relations with even the living as in some way hermeneutic, that is, as the interpretation of traces. No subject expresses itself except via the object.

Paul Ricoeur's argument that hermeneutics is about the distortion of dialogue also suggests a countervision quite immune to the pathos of communication breakdown. In fact, Ricoeur argues, almost all dialogue is always already broken down in the sense of being textual. Disturbance is what makes it dialogue in the first place. The need for talk arises from something problematic. Hence the features of textuality are not deviant but illustrate what is usually hidden in face-to-face communication. "The text is much more than a particular case of intersubjective communication: it is the paradigm of distanciation in communication. As such it displays a fundamental characteristic of the very historicity of human experience, namely that it is communication in and through distance." Once "inscribed," an utterance transcends its author's intent, original audience, and situation of enunciation. Such removal is not just an alienation; it is a just alienation. Inscription liberates meaning from the parochial and evanescent status of face-to-face speech: "*Verfremdung* [estrangement] is not only what understanding must overcome, but also what conditions it." In writing, the "narrowness of the dialogical relation explodes. Instead of being addressed just to you, the second person, discourse is revealed as discourse in the universality of its address. . . . It no longer has a visible auditor. An unknown, invisible reader has become the unprivileged addressee of the discourse."[35] Hermeneutics, once again, is the art of literary correspondence where no reply is possible. Since the text's intended audience is gone, it can be read only in conditions of eavesdropping. Hermeneutics involves the interpretation of stray texts. Though theorists of hermeneutics are rarely as explicit about the strangeness of the operation as we will find Kafka or even Emerson to be, the challenge is to stand in the place of those "invisible auditors"—in short, to "mate with the dead," as Nietzsche put it.

Thanks to mediation, we are surrounded with communication situations that are fundamentally interpretive rather than dialogic. Only the Lonelyhearts of the world expect a personal reply from the movie,

---

35. Paul Ricoeur, *Hermeneutics and the Human Sciences: Essays on Language, Action, and Interpretation*, trans. John B. Thompson (Cambridge: Cambridge University Press, 1981), 131, 140, 202–3.

phonograph record, or radio program. Or to be more precise, we are all Lonelyhearts inasmuch we "interact" with books, pets, infants, or distant correspondents. In each case, control over turn taking is restricted to one end of the transaction. A radio show broadcast at 2:00 A.M., an SOS in a bottle cast into the sea, a personal ad in the "agony columns" of the newspaper, or an inscription in an undeciphered script all speak, as it were, into the void, or at least to those who have ears to hear. They await completion of the loop. Herbert Menzel speaks of an "address gap" in such situations, a concept suggestively resonant with Ricoeur's notion of distanciation.³⁶ Hermeneutics and media face a common problem: the production and reception of texts within unforeseen horizons. The studio designing a television pilot, the merchant who has no way to know precisely who will hear the radio ad, the theologian reading Saint Paul, and the judge reading the United States Constitution all face the same interpretive dilemma: a gap between sending and receiving. The first two fret about how to get their "message" across the gap (rhetoric), and the latter two about how to read texts not addressed to them (hermeneutics), but all find themselves in a situation in which message making and message receiving have become distinct activities. As Stuart Hall puts it of television, though it is equally true of all hermeneutic situations, "There is no necessary correspondence between encoding and decoding."³⁷

Hall's "no necessary correspondence" reveals a poststructuralist sensibility about the contingency of articulations, but it is also a useful reminder of a more literal sort of correspondence: letter writing. When we are dealing with distanciated communication, there is no necessary correspondence—letters may cross in the mail, never arrive, or never be sent. Communication may be infinitely deferred. Pauses in conversation, often kept from growing too long in a face-to-face setting, can be dilated in correspondence; delays can stretch out indefinitely. With the dead, we may wait forever for a reply. But this does not stop our overtures. An unknown man leaves a bottle of cognac at Edgar Allan Poe's grave every year on the anniversary of his death; many leave flowers on the graves of their loved ones; a vault full of abandoned sundries has been collected from the United States Vietnam Veterans Memorial; and direct apostrophe of the deceased is a common practice in funeral ora-

---

36. Herbert Menzel, "Quasi-Mass Communication: A Neglected Area," *Public Opinion Quarterly* 35 (1971): 406–9.

37. Stuart Hall, "Encoding/Decoding," in *Culture, Media, Language: Working Papers in Cultural Studies, 1972–1979*, ed. Stuart Hall et al. (London: Hutchinson, 1980), 135.

tory.[38] As Samuel Johnson observed, "We profess to reverence the dead not for their sake, but for our own."[39] Communicating with the dead, along with sacrificing to the gods, may be the oldest sort of one-way offering. It occurs in situations in which dialogue is not possible or desirable. Gifts to the dead are the purest kind of dissemination; they involve some of the most splendid acts we can know and do.

In dialogue with the dead, infants, pets, or the distant, the speaker must hold up both ends of the conversation. The call must contain or anticipate the response. Our communication with the dead may never reach them, but such elliptical sending is as important as circular reciprocity. It would be foolish to disparage communications that never leave our own circle as only failures. Perhaps all dialogue involves each partner's enacting the response of the other. Dialogic ideology keeps us from seeing that expressive acts occurring over distances and without immediate assurance of reply can be desperate and daring acts of dignity. That I cannot engage in dialogue with Plato or the Beatles does not demean the contact I have with them. Such contact may be hermeneutic and aesthetic rather than personal or mutual. I may have to supply all the replies they might make to my queries—rather like the contact I have with the universe. Or with myself. In this respect Charles Horton Cooley was right to claim that our concourse with ghosts may be the most important kind we have (chapter 5).

EMERSON: THE PORCUPINE IMPOSSIBILITY OF CONTACT

In strict science, all persons underlie the same condition of an infinite remoteness.
RALPH WALDO EMERSON, "FRIENDSHIP"

Perhaps even as much as money, the archmedium may be the cemetery, the place where the bodies of the dead are held in suspended animation, as the term itself suggests: "cemetery" comes from the Greek *koimētērion*, meaning a sleeping place, quite literally a dormitory. Ralph Waldo Emerson's 1855 address at the dedication of Sleepy Hollow cemetery in Con-

38. A recent book on the Memorial notes on its dust jacket: "Now as much a shrine as a monument, the Vietnam Wall has become a national pilgrimage site, a place where certain people are moved to leave votive offerings in a variety so wide they are impossible to categorize. These offerings represent, for the most part, private messages to the Vietnam dead, their meaning known only to their senders." Thomas B. Allen, *Offerings at the Wall: Artifacts from the Vietnam Veterans Memorial Collection* (Atlanta: Turner, 1995). Offerings have included a rusty harmonica, crucifixes, pillows, black lace panties, and a photo of a Viet Cong soldier and his daughter removed from his dead body by the man who killed him, together with a note of apology.

39. Samuel Johnson, "An Essay on Epitaphs," in *Samuel Johnson*, ed. Donald Greene (New York: Oxford University Press, 1984), 98.

cord, Massachusetts, captures much of the nineteenth-century vision of the cemetery as a spot for the communion of the living and the dead.[40] It also introduces us to his vision of communication, in any setting, as essentially communication with the dead: never as the touching of consciousness, only as the interpretation of traces. Sleepy Hollow, he argues, will be a sort of historical archive for the dead to which the living can repair for edification and enjoyment. Emerson had his own reasons to be interested in cemeteries. He had opened the coffin to view the remains of his first wife Ellen Tucker after she had been dead over a year. He also inspected the remains of his beloved son Waldo when they were transferred to Sleepy Hollow in 1857. Waldo had been dead fifteen years.

The lessons Emerson learned from seeing the decomposed remains of the two creatures he loved most are unrecorded.[41] One clue is found in the key essay called "Experience": "The only thing grief has taught me is to know how shallow it is. That, like all the rest, plays about the surface, and never introduces me into the reality, for contact with which we would even pay the costly price of sons and lovers. Was it Boscovich who found that bodies never come into contact? Well, souls never touch their objects. An innavigable sea washes between us and the things we aim at and converse with. Experience drips off our being like the summer showers off a raincoat. Nothing is left us now but death. We look to that with a grim satisfaction, saying, There at least is a reality that will not dodge us."[42] Death is a rather desperate escape hatch from the labyrinth of solipsism, and perhaps what he saw in the decayed remains of Waldo and Ellen was precisely the costly price of sons and lovers.

In his dedicatory address, Emerson celebrates the round of life and death, the recycling of organic substance: "The irresistible democracy— shall I call it?—of chemistry, of vegetation, which recomposes for new life every decomposing article,—the race never dying, the individual never spared,—have impressed upon the mind the futility of these old arts of preserving. We give our earth to earth. We will not jealously guard a few atoms under immense marbles, selfishly and impossibly sequestering it from the vast circulations of Nature." Emerson gives a characteristic critique of possessive individualism, here in terms of the

40. Ralph Waldo Emerson, "Consecration of Sleepy Hollow Cemetery" (1855), in *Miscellanies* (Boston: Houghton Mifflin, 1904), 427–36.

41. John J. McAleer, *Ralph Waldo Emerson: Days of Encounter* (Boston: Little, Brown, 1984), 109.

42. Emerson, "Experience" (1844), in *Selected Writings of Emerson*, ed. Donald McQuade (New York: Modern Library, 1981), 344. The physicist Ruggiero Giuseppe Boscovich (1711–87) influenced both Faraday and Maxwell.

grandiose funerary monuments that proliferated with the embourgeoisement of cemeteries in the nineteenth century. In criticizing "old arts of preserving" Emerson also anticipates some new ones: photography and phonography. Garry Wills suggests that Emerson's address becomes almost a séance.[43] But not quite: a séance suggests a live interchange between the living and the dead, whereas Emerson has something more hermeneutical in mind. He expects no direct reply from the dead; those who visit Sleepy Hollow will be engaged in a form of loosely coupled interpretation. "We shall bring hither the body of the dead, but how shall we catch the escaped soul?" The cemetery will become a "spot tender to our children, who shall come hither in the next century to read the dates of these lives." The next generation will come not for communion but for memory. Emerson renounces the possibility of any soul-to-soul junction between the living and the dead; what is possible is the anamnestic reading of the traces of the dead by the living. To visit the cemetery is to interpret a historical text, not to receive a spirit visitation. Some day "in a remote century, this mute green bank will be full of history: the good, the wise and great will have left their names and virtues on the trees; heroes, poets, beauties, sanctities, benefactors, will have made the air timeable and articulate."[44] *Geist* will be there, if not the souls of the departed. As in the parable of the sower, only one end of the communication circuit will be active.

Emerson does not believe in communication between the living and the dead; he may not believe in communication among the living either. Theodor W. Adorno describes Kierkegaard's doctrine of love as the call to love everyone as if they were dead. Adorno finds this doctrine both noble and wretched—noble because love would then have to be constant and unaffected by rejections or hurt, wretched because love would cease to be a joint journey in which the lover is open to being radically transformed by the beloved.[45] In the same way, Emerson takes communication with the dead as the paradigm for all communication. He never grants any immediate contact. "It is the same among the men and women as among the silent trees; always a referred existence, an absence, never a presence and satisfaction."[46] Emerson does not believe in one-to-one personal sharing either among the living or the dead be-

43. Wills, *Lincoln at Gettysburg*, 75.
44. Emerson, "Consecration of Sleepy Hollow," 430, 436, 430, 435.
45. Theodor W. Adorno, "Kierkegaard's Doctrine of Love," *Studies in Philosophy and Social Science* 8 (1939): 413–29.
46. Emerson, "Nature" (1844), in *Selected Writings of Emerson*, ed. Donald McQuade (New York: Modern Library, 1981), 403.

cause he does not quite believe in either presence or personality. "If I am not at the meeting, my presence where I am should be as useful to the commonwealth of friendship and wisdom, as would be my presence in that place. I exert the same quality of power in all places."[47] To be within touching distance is not to get any closer to another. In a letter to Margaret Fuller, who desired more closeness with Emerson than he felt prepared to give, Emerson wrote of "this porcupine impossibility of contact with men."[48]

For Emerson, the impossibility of dialogue gives us reason to celebrate the universe as a constant transmission to those who have ears to hear. In "Demonology," an 1839 lecture on the variety of spirits then abroad in the land, Emerson criticizes the quest for personal signs in the universe (he is aiming partly at mesmerists, though the point holds for later spiritualists as well). "The whole world," he insists, "is an omen and a sign. Why look so wistfully in a corner?"[49] He enjoins a hermeneutic stance to the cosmos, reading everything as if intended for you. He renounces the search for personal signs, whether of God's benediction or of the survival of loved ones beyond the grave, bravely claiming that it does not matter if the message is even intended as a message, as long as we receive it. The universe, in short, engages only in broadcasting. Whatever meaning we find is left to our power of "creative reading."[50]

For Emerson, communication never involves contact with another, and joyously so. We are released from the obligation to expend our strength on other minds and can bask in the cumulative intelligence of the universe. We find fellowship everywhere and are not so rude as to require any response from those we encounter. In all our conversation we write, and receive, only unanswered letters. In walking through the fields and woods, "I am not alone and unacknowledged. They nod to me and I to them. The waving of the boughs in the storm is new to me and old. It takes me by surprise, and yet is not unknown." To commune with nature is not to enter a terrifying epistemological limbo in which one never knows if one's missives are received, but to feel the presence of a strange and familiar intelligence. Nature, said Schelling, is visible intelligence. For Emerson, it is the hieroglyphic writing of an intelli-

47. Emerson, "Experience," 342.
48. Ralph Waldo Emerson, *The Journals and Miscellaneous Notebooks of Ralph Waldo Emerson,* 7:301. Quoted in MacAleer, *Ralph Waldo Emerson,* 114. Had Emerson read Schopenhauer?
49. Ralph Waldo Emerson, "Demonology" (1839), in *The Early Lectures of Ralph Waldo Emerson,* ed. Robert E. Spiller and Wallace E. Williams (Cambridge: Harvard University Press, 1972), 3:151–71.
50. Emerson, "The American Scholar" (1837), in *Selected Writings of Emerson,* 51.

gence radically unlike one's own. Yet the experience of fields and woods is a genuine encounter, not a projection: "The power to produce this delight does not reside in nature, but in man, or in a harmony of both."[51] This harmony is governed not by notion but by affection and affinity.

Clearly, this is a good recipe for those strong enough to live without need for recognition from an authentically other consciousness, perhaps one of the things Nietzsche found to admire in Emerson. Yet it also invites questions about proof and the avoidance of deception. How can we avoid the flattering deceits of the self and of others? In short, where do we find the proof of reality outside our own private theater of projections? In death, at least, Emerson found one thing that would not dodge him, and his response to skepticism foreshadows later debates about communicative authenticity. In nineteenth-century usage, "media" often meant the five senses, and philosophical skepticism about sensation is a clear forerunner of later skepticism about the reality of the images and reports of the media.[52] Emerson describes "my utter impotence to test the authenticity of the report of my senses." From this, the traditional starting point of philosophical skepticism, he does not conclude that the world is either unstable or unknowable. Instead he draws the protopragmatist conclusion that we are always practically required to act, whatever our epistemological scruples. "Whether nature enjoy a substantial existence without, or is only the apocalypse of the mind, it is alike useful and alike venerable to me."[53] The choice between the world as authentic otherness and as self-projection makes no difference to action. Whether the wall is a figment or not, it still hurts when I run into it. Though we should act as if our choices shape the universe, we must also stand ready to be rudely and gratefully awakened by what Emerson calls "commodity" (the same principle as Peirce's "secondness" or Kenneth Burke's "recalcitrance").

These interruptions by matter can be redemptive. To deny matter would lose the saving touch of otherness. "It leaves God out of me. It leaves me in the splendid labyrinth of my perceptions, to wander without end. Then the heart resists it, because it balks the affections in denying substantive being to men and women."[54] Emerson lists three defin-

51. Ralph Waldo Emerson, *Nature* (1836), in *Selected Writings of Emerson*, ed. Donald McQuade (New York: Modern Library, 1981), 7.

52. John Durham Peters and Eric W. Rothenbuhler, "The Reality of Construction," in *Rhetoric in the Human Sciences*, ed. Herbert A. Simons (London: Sage, 1989), 11–27. Cf. Emerson, "Experience," 343.

53. Emerson, *Nature*, 26.

54. Emerson, *Nature*, 35.

ing horrors the nineteenth century bequeathed to the twentieth: a God-forsaken universe, a self lost in its own labyrinth, and other people depleted of substantive being. Against idealism and materialism, which in their extremes deny the "consanguinity" between nature and humanity, Emerson wants a vision sensitive to the impress of culture on the universe and of the universe on culture. Matter is not only mud; it is the stuff that gives us inklings of God and of others and saves the self from interminable wandering. His idealism wants not to deny matter, but to save it in its multiform appearances. Emerson appreciates the testimonial value of contingencies breaking through the solitary labyrinth of perceptions. In sum, he sees communication as a matter of giving and receiving without any coordination of the two. Whatever linkage occurs is a gift of grace. He allows for the otherness of the world yet refuses to make it account for itself to him.

"BARTLEBY": SCRIVENING AS DISSEMINATION   Emerson thought sincerity was overrated as a virtue if it distracted from honest self-assertion. "In this our talking America we are ruined by our good nature and listening on all sides."[55] Herman Melville's "Bartleby the Scrivener" (1853) is a test of Emerson's faith that one need never receive personal responses from others or the universe.[56] Bartleby is the ultimate impersonality in communication. As a scrivener or copyist, Bartleby inhabits the no-man's-land of writing—and the parallel universe of copies at that. At first he is hired to do a prodigious amount of work for the narrator, an older Wall Street lawyer whose self-righteousness gives an ironic cast to the story, but when asked to read his own work to check its accuracy, he answers, "I prefer not to." The response drives the narrator to distraction, but "I prefer not to" remains Bartleby's reply to all subsequent requests for compliance (32). "You *will* not?" asks the narrator; "I *prefer* not," replies Bartleby (36; emphasis in the original). Bartleby will not say *will*. He can be read as a holy fool who actually practices the injunction to act invariantly regardless of circumstances. As Louis Schwartz has argued, Bartleby may represent the passive resistance of writing itself, a theme the tale shares with the *Phaedrus*.[57] Writing, like Bartleby, gives no answer; cannot be engaged in dialogue; is not "particular," as Bartleby says, of how it is used (58, 59); and is "cadaverous" and

---

55. Emerson, "Experience," 346.

56. Herman Melville, "Bartleby" (1853), in *Piazza Tales* (New York: Elf, 1929), 21–65. Page references hereafter are given parenthetically in the text.

57. Louis G. Schwartz, "Seminar Paper" (paper prepared for seminar on philosophy of communication, summer 1991, University of Iowa).

"ghostly," two terms the narrator repeatedly uses for the scrivener. Bartleby's is a stance of pure dissemination, of letters from the dead. As Socrates complained of writing, it always communicates the same things (*sēmainei isa*) and never acknowledges a query.

The narrator, noting that "nothing so aggravates an earnest person as a passive resistance" (34), puts Bartleby under a prurient sort of surveillance: "Here I can cheaply purchase a delicious self-approval. To befriend Bartleby; to humor him in his strange willfulness, will cost me little or nothing, while I lay up in my soul what will eventually become a sweet morsel for my conscience" (35; cf. 52). The narrator's rage at the remoteness of Bartleby's soul escalates: he first tries to fire Bartleby, gives him an oral eviction notice when he refuses to leave the office, and bribes him to divulge his life story, but nothing can get him to enter into the lawyer-narrator's repressive economics of communication. A nonreactive doppelgänger, Bartleby is quite literally a dead letter: an uncanny shadow of the narrator's moral rigor mortis.[58] Finally the narrator moves to another building, leaving Bartleby alone in the unoccupied chambers: "I tore myself away from him whom I had so longed to be rid of" (56), a line that captures an intertwining of attachment and rejection characteristic of modern dramas like this one. Alfred Kazin called "Bartleby" a "very Existentialist little story."[59] It could be a Sartre play or Bergman film, with its close quarters, agonistic struggle between two people, ambiguity about who is master and who slave, impossible dialogue and inscrutable motives. It is a small step from the agonies of communication explored in the mid-nineteenth century by Melville, Kierkegaard, and Marx to the solipsism of fin-de-siècle idealism and then to twentieth-century existentialism. They all examine media that put us in circuits of communication with the absent.

This singularly resonant tale has sparked a conflict of interpretations. At first the inscrutable Bartleby compels one's attention, but most late twentieth-century readings have focused on the ironies of the narrator's stance, which mingles charity and persecution. Bartleby fits a longer American tradition of literary selves that evade the command to be centered or even human.[60] He refuses to refuse and will not will: he simply prefers not. He is beyond communication. Bartleby would understand Kierkegaard's point that, rather than being misunderstood, "An author

---

58. As Freud has famously shown, part of the uncanniness of the double is the foreshadowing of one's own death: "Das Unheimliche" (1919), in *Gesammelte Werke*, vol. 12 (Frankfurt am Main: Fischer, 1947).

59. Alfred Kazin, "Ishmael in His Academic Heaven," *New Yorker* 24 (1949): 84–89.

60. Richard Poirier, "Writing off the Self," *Raritan*, no. 1 (summer 1981): 106–33.

who understands himself is better served by not being read at all." Bartleby's selfhood has autonomy but no interiority that can be made into an object of power. His otherness drives the narrator to despair and domination, making him an epitome of the chief villains in recent poststructuralist criticism: an agent of pastoral power, who surveys the other's soul in such a way that philanthropy is inextricable from cruelty (Foucault), or a critic who rifles the text, probing its interior, wanting it to give a proper account of itself (Derrida). To recent sensibilities, Bartleby is less a pathological extremity than a rebellious integrity. There can be no communication with such a self: preferring not is a heroic escape from the officious paper power of the lawyer's world.

Bartleby is a martyr to the cold righteousness of dialogism. For a Bruce Ackerman, the refusal to engage in dialogue can only be an act of violence, not a principled moral decision. Consider the power play implicit in his words: "I can use neither force nor reason to impose dialogue on you. All I can do is ask my question and await your reply. If you try to stare me down and impose brute force upon me, I will act in self-defense. If, instead, you answer my questions, I will answer yours, and we will see what we will see. The choice is yours."[61] The choice is ours, in this apparently "free and open encounter," but the choice to opt out of the game will be greeted as a prelude to hostilities. Ackerman's persuasive invitation to chat, despite its protestations otherwise, is backed by a repressive apparatus. Dialogue's supposed moral nobility can suffocate those who prefer not to play along. At their worst, dialogians deploy the inspectionism of the lawyer-narrator in Melville's "Bartleby" under the hegemonic cloak of goodwill.

Am I being too subtle in detecting the workings of power? Is there really something suspicious in an invitation to dialogue? Fair enough, as long as the world is full of rampant poverty and inequality, perhaps the coarser sorts of power, rather than dialogue traps, ought to preoccupy us. Still, the moral tyranny of dialogue blinds us to the nobility of Bartleby, the wisdom of Kierkegaard's Abraham, or the blitheness of Professor Avenarius in Milan Kundera's *Immortality,* all of whom circumvent the demand to account for themselves. In the same way, Jesus did not "dialogue" about the Father's will and, when questioned, would pose counterquestions. He came into the world not to converse, but to testify of the truth to whoever would hear. Though the cosmos does not

---

61. Bruce Ackerman, *Social Justice in the Liberal State,* 371, quoted in Mark Kingwell, *A Civil Tongue: Justice, Dialogue, and the Politics of Pluralism* (University Park: Pennsylvania State University Press, 1995), 61–62.

give answers to our queries, no matter how hard we press, we would be fools to criticize its bad manners. Dialogue can be a wonderful method for enforcing imagination of the other's position and is obviously a far superior mode of handling differences than fisticuffs or nerve gas, but it is not in itself an adequate communicative vehicle for bearing the full varieties of moral experience.

THE PHONOGRAPH AND DISTORTED DIALOGUE The phonograph, like writing, daguerreotypy, and money, is a medium that preserves ghosts that would otherwise be evanescent. Like Bartleby, the phonograph is a copyist; it evoked many of the same anxieties as its predecessors in the art of scrivening. The phonograph, as its name suggests, is a means of writing.[62] Its rearrangements of culture were as imaginatively decisive as writing's effects on the oral world, and its intellectual reception runs along *Phaedrus*-like tracks. Inscription, as Ricoeur notes, spells the removal of utterance from the original situation, the death of the author, and an open-ended audience. The phonograph disembodied and even immortalized sound; exerted a kind of erotic control at a distance; and was as promiscuous in its distribution as it was faithful in its invariant narrative. In a classic 1878 article, Thomas Edison boasted of the phonograph's ability to reproduce sound waves "with all their original characteristics at will, without the presence or consent of the original source, and after the lapse of any period of time."[63] It would be hard to find a clearer statement of the founding dreams of phonography or, for that matter, of any other time-binding medium: fidelity, manipulability, liberation from origin, and the overcoming of time and death. This is Socrates' lament of writing with a positive valence.

In many ways the phonograph is a more shocking emblem of modernity than the photograph. From time immemorial people have been able to preserve images by drawing or painting, but to fix sound events requires an altogether different sort of inscription, namely, the ability to capture the serial flow of time itself. Such inscription occurred first, to date it with exaggerated precision, in 1877 in Menlo Park, New Jersey, in Thomas Edison's laboratories. The succession from the "singing wire" (telegraph), through the microphone, telephone, and phonograph to radio and allied technologies of sound marks perhaps the most radical

62. "Phonograph" was originally Edison's trade name for his device. Bell's model was a "graphophone," and Emile Berliner's model, employing a flat disk, was called the "gramophone," the name that stuck in Europe. Throughout, I use "phonograph" as the generic term.
63. Thomas A. Edison, "The Phonograph and Its Future," *North American Review* 126 (May–June 1878): 527–36, 530.

of all sensory reorganizations in modernity. Except for echoes, hearing disembodied voices has, for most of the history of our species, been the preserve of poets and the mad. The phonograph was one of several sound technologies to democratize this experience, and as with most things democratic, the oracular edge has worn off with use. The phonograph presented a human voice without a human body. The human soul, the breath, had taken up residence in a machine.

This is not to burden a small instrument with too large a historical weight, as media scholars are sometimes wont to do; the aspiration to capture live events and life itself was pervasive in nineteenth-century culture, in panoramas, dioramas, wax museums, anatomical shows, photography, taxidermy and natural history exhibits, pleasure palaces, historicism, magic, and spiritualist acts, culminating in the cinema.[64] Still, the phonograph helped change the meaning of sound, music, and the voice. Music no longer required a live performer; sound could be produced without bodily labor.[65] "Music" as such could take on a life of its own, independent of composers, musicians, or audiences. The phonograph record, as Adorno put it, "is the first means of musical presentation that can be possessed as a thing."[66] Adorno did not say musical notation, but *presentation;* the unique thing was the possession of the performance in a form that enabled the eternal recurrence of the same. Jacques Perriault (overlooking the camera) calls the phonograph "the first technology which actively attempts to conjure up death." Two ruling ambitions in modern technology appear in the phonograph: the creation of artificial life and the conjuring of the dead.[67]

Little wonder the phonograph seemed like a door to the spirit world. Nipper, obedient to "his master's voice" in the famous Victor advertisements, was painted in the Victorian iconography of the loyal dog mourning his departed master.[68] The phonograph had the power to "suppress absence."[69] "Writing," said Freud, with equal relevance to the

64. See Richard D. Altick, *The Shows of London* (Cambridge: Harvard University Press, 1978); Bann, *Clothing of Clio;* Gunning, "Phantom Images and Modern Manifestations" and "Tracing the Individual Body"; and Sandberg, "Missing Persons."

65. The aeolian harp, beloved of the romantics, is an obvious exception, as are music boxes, clocks, and barrel organs. James F. Lastra, "Inscriptions and Simulations: Representing Sound, 1780–1900" (paper given at Sound Research Seminar, Department of Communication Studies, University of Iowa, 21 April 1995), discusses "autographic" sound before phonography.

66. Theodor W. Adorno, "The Form of the Phonograph Record," trans. Thomas Y. Levin, *October,* no. 55 (winter 1990): 56–61, at 58.

67. Jacques Perriault, *Mémoires de l'ombre et du son: Une archéologie de l'audio-visuel* (Paris: Flammarion, 1981), 202, 224.

68. For evidence of this iconography, see Morley, *Death, Heaven, and the Victorians,* 201, plate 1.

69. Perriault, *Mémoires de l'ombre et du son,* 177.

Phaedrus and the phonograph, "was in its origin the voice of an absent person."[70] Count Théodore Du Moncel, the nineteenth-century French expert on all things electric, wrote on hearing an early phonograph: "It is startling to hear this voice—somewhat shrill, it may be admitted—which seems to utter its sentences from beyond the grave. If this invention had taken place in the Middle Ages, it certainly would have been applied to ghostly apparitions, and it would have been invaluable to miracle-mongers."[71] A similar reaction was had to a 1922 radio broadcast of a Caruso recording: "Caruso dead and buried these many months, yet singing to us and perhaps twenty thousand others, down out of the ether on this cold winter's night, all by way of a phonograph and a few feet of wire in Newark, a few feet of wire and a telephone in New York."[72] Charles Sanders Peirce had, characteristically, the most visionary notion of an acoustic archaeology of time: "Give science only a hundred more centuries of increase in geometrical progression, and she may be expected to find that the sound waves of Aristotle's voice have somehow recorded themselves."[73]

All these witnesses suggest that something about the phonograph was unsettling and exciting to early audiences, especially its ability to detach voices and sounds from the organic cycle of birth and death. Once, all sounds had been mortal and particular. With recording, one can build a mausoleum of sound, fixed in a state of suspended animation. As Edison declared, "The speeches of orators, the discourses of clergymen, can be had 'on tap,' in every house that owns a phonograph."[74] Not only could voices speak from the other side, they could also take possession of one's soul and body. A 1896 piece called "Voices of the Dead," in complaining that historical writings about great men are spectral and sterile, provides a great example of how the phonograph could arouse what Walter Benjamin called "the sex-appeal of the inorganic."[75] "Like preserved fruit, however delicious, [the transcripts of the speeches of great men] lack the bloom of life: they are dry and difficult of digestion." The phonograph, however, restores the full juices of the original: "I did not know their spirit until I heard their voice on the cylinder of

70. Sigmund Freud, *Civilization and Its Discontents*, trans. Joan Riviere (1930; New York: Norton, 1961), 43.

71. Théodore Du Moncel, *The Telephone, the Microphone and the Phonograph* (New York: Harper, 1879), 243.

72. Bruce Bliven, "The Ether Will Now Oblige," *New Republic*, 15 February 1922, 329.

73. *The Collected Papers of Charles Sanders Peirce*, ed. Charles Hartshorne and Paul Weiss (Cambridge: Harvard University Press, 1965), 5:542. Thanks to Michael Raine for this passage.

74. Thomas A. Edison, "The Perfected Phonograph," *North American Review* 146 (1888): 647.

75. Walter Benjamin, "Paris, Capital of the Nineteenth Century," in *Reflections* (New York: Schocken, 1978).

a phonograph. The body, the strength, the soft modulation, the emphasis, so faithfully reproduced by this delicate mechanism, the life thus imparted to the words, made them sink indelibly into my soul, showing to me in the fulness of their power, the men whom till then I had known only vaguely. I felt their presence; their spirit pervaded me."[76] This remarkable rhetoric reproduces the queer scenario of Phaedrus reading Lysias's speech: the erotic possession of one body by a remote one. What is preserved is not the soul but the body, in all its strength, soft modulation, and emphasis.[77]

The phonograph's simultaneous promiscuity and invariance—its open address and its inability to tailor its discourse to its audience— came in for praise and blame, quite as Socrates had lamented the publicity of all writing. An 1878 comment about the phonograph complained: "This little instrument records the utterance of the human voice, and like a faithless confidante repeats every secret confided to it whenever requested to do so." The same article captures the positive valence of this invariance, praising the phonograph's "charming impartiality" in its equal readiness to record a diva or a street urchin. The phonograph "never speaks until it has first been spoken to."[78] It prefers not. Beings that abstain from interaction are subjects of laughter, awe, or consternation: Harpo Marx, Poe's Raven, oracles, or Bartleby.[79] In its inability to give appropriate conversational responses, the phonograph spoke like the ominous dead. It achieved the great distortion of dialogue, making the gulf between speech and hearing irreparable, offering the single turn of speech in all its alarming solitude.

Again, the wonder of the phonograph, like its Edison sibling, motion pictures, lay in its ability to capture temporal sequence. Sound, whose being Hegel and many others linked uniquely with temporality, no longer vanished into thin air.[80] The phonograph inscribes the music's happening in time, recording not the score but the performance, not the libretto but the voice. Phonography and film attack the monopoly on the storage of intelligence once held by writing.[81] Thanks to what

76. "Voices of the Dead," 1.

77. Wayne Koestenbaum, *The Queen's Throat: Opera, Homosexuality, and the Mystery of Desire* (New York: Vintage, 1993), explores the unnatural couplings of ear, voice, and machine, the sensual pull of unapproved apertures, in vinyl records and record players.

78. "The Phonograph," *Harper's Weekly,* 30 March 1878, 249–50. Many thanks to Mark Sandberg.

79. The invariance of the phonograph fits Bergson's comic formula, "le mécanique plaqué sur du vivant." See *Le rire: Essai sur la signification du comique* (1899; Paris: Presses Universitaires, 1972), 29.

80. On Hegel and sound, see Joseph Simon, *Das Problem der Sprache bei Hegel* (Stuttgart: Kohlhammer, 1966); see 73ff. on the voice as the cry of finitude.

81. Friedrich A. Kittler, *Discourse Networks: 1800/1900,* trans. Michael Metteer (Stanford: Stanford University Press, 1990), 245.

Adorno called (referring to the long-playing record) a "concentric hiero-glyph," sound was no longer fated to die.[82] Sound is fundamentally an event; it was, at least until the phonograph, always historically embodied, particular, and performative. According to Perriault, "The phonograph was, from its beginning, a means to preserve the voice of missing persons." Edison was almost totally deaf to high-frequency sounds, and he initially wanted to develop the phonograph as a hearing aid, inadvertently inventing "the storage and reproduction of the human voice" in the process. Charles Cros, Edison's major French competitor for the title of inventor of the phonograph, called his version a *paléophone*, a term suggesting a kind of telephone that calls out of the past.[83] Indeed, the phonograph was largely considered first as an improved way to preserve and transmit telephone messages. Telephone or paleophone, sound from far away or the past: the nomenclature reveals the alliance between transmission and recording.

The closest analogue to the strange ontological status of a phonograph is the realm of spirits, who possess continuing intelligence without corporeality. The voices of the dead can be revived from their phonographic limbo without their presence or permission. Oliver Lodge praised the phonograph as an analogy in psychical research. "In the early Edison phonographs, the same machine had to be used for both reception and reproduction; but now a record can be readily transferred from one instrument to another. This may be regarded as a rough mechanical analogy to the telepathic or telergic process whereby a psychic reservoir of memory can be partially tapped through another organism."[84] Lodge conceives memory as a phonograph record cut elsewhere that can be played on one's own player. An effect of modern media, again, is the externalization of the fragile and flickering stuff of subjectivity and memory into a permanent form that can be played back at will. The supposed ease of transfer was paid for with ghostliness.

82. Thomas Y. Levin, "For the Record: Adorno on Music in the Age of Its Technological Reproducibility," *October*, no. 55 (winter 1990): 23–47.

83. Perriault, *Mémoires de l'ombre et du son*, 122, 153, 154.

84. Oliver Lodge, *Raymond, or Life and Death, with Examples of the Evidence of Survival of Memory and Affection after Death* (New York: Doran, 1916), 328.

Dead Letters

Nautch joints are depressing, like all places for deposit, banks, mail boxes, tombs, vending machines.

NATHANAEL WEST, *THE DAY OF THE LOCUST*

Recorded sound suspends dialogue, as Bartleby is an allegory of the difficulty of arriving at a destination in writing. Strangely enough, little research in media history has been done on the original context of communication that is most explicitly hermeneutic: correspondence by letter. Media historians are beginning to take the post office seriously as a key site for understanding the development of communications.[85] The cultural history of the mails is a remarkably rich source for philosophical visions of the varieties of communicative experience.

The notion that the mails involve delivery of a private, specifically addressed message was late in evolving. The current division of genres between personal and public correspondence did not exactly exist in the eighteenth-century newsletter in England and the colonies. The "familiar" letter was distinct from the newsletter, the forerunner of the modern newspaper, but both could be edited for and by the public. Newsletters had very high pass-along rates; they were meant quite literally to circulate among readers who would handwrite additional notices in blank spaces left for that purpose. In a similar way, personal letters in the United States at least could be raided for publication in the newspaper or at least for postmaster-led discussion. Some postmasters in the colonial period apparently freely quoted in their newspapers from love letters and personal correspondence.[86] Not only was content open to stray eyes, but the receipt of mail was itself public because local post offices in the United States routinely kept logbooks on who purchased postage for what mail, since payment was typically made by the recipient rather than the sender before the 1850s. Hence not only were local postmasters well informed on local reading habits, they were privy to much of the news locally in circulation and often monitors, even cen-

---

85. Richard B. Kielbowicz, *News in the Mail: The Press, Post Office, and Public Information, 1700–1860s* (New York: Greenwood, 1989); Menahem Blondheim, *News over the Wires: The Telegraph and the Flow of Public Information in America, 1844–1897* (Cambridge: Harvard University Press, 1994); Thomas C. Leonard, *News for All: America's Coming of Age with the Press* (New York: Oxford University Press, 1995); Dan Schiller, *Theorizing Communication: A History* (New York: Oxford University Press, 1996), chap. 1; and Richard R. John, *Spreading the News: The American Postal System from Franklin to Morse* (Cambridge: Harvard University Press, 1995).

86. John Floherty, *Make Way for the Mail* (Philadelphia: Lippincott, 1939), 38.

sors, of what newspapers local postal patrons would read and what mail they would receive.[87] The post was not a secure channel. Letters then were more like postcards today—both privately addressed and publicly accessible.

Jacques Derrida has famously argued that all mailed correspondence has the implicit structure of a postcard, that the attempt to restrict the reception of a message to one recipient is always undermined by the scatter of all textuality.[88] His argument is historically possible, and striking, however, only under a certain postal system: the historically recent convention of mail as a secure private channel. Since the mid-nineteenth century, postal practices in North America and Western Europe quite explicitly sought to contain the potential for straying missives by giving senders private control over their letters and making the address circuitry much more focused. The key innovations that took place in the two middle decades of the century made the modern private letter possible. The first postage stamp appeared in 1840 in Great Britain, bearing a portrait of Queen Victoria. No longer did one need to see a postmaster to pay for carriage, marking a key step toward impersonality in access. In the 1840s adhesive postage stamps appeared in the United States, first as local, private issues, and in 1847 the first national stamp was authorized by the United States Congress. The first United States patent for envelopes was issued in 1849. By sealing off contents against inspection, envelopes gave letters an entirely new aura of privacy. In 1851 Congress, perhaps motivated to secure linkage with the Pacific Coast in the wake of the 1849 gold rush, passed a flat rate for all letters, not graded for distance as some early rates were. In 1856 all mail in the United States had to be prepaid (as opposed to COD, or cash on delivery), and a registered mail service was founded to help prevent the loss of valuables (perhaps in response to the dangers of the Pony Express), though it was rarely used. In 1858 street drop boxes, introduced in London in 1855, were first used in the United States.

By the late 1850s, then, it was possible to mail a letter sealed in an envelope, paid for with a prepurchased stamp, and dropped into a public box. "No longer did the sender have to come under the scrutiny of the receiving postal employees."[89] No sentinels guarded the gates to the system. Confidentiality was now possible—a necessary precondition

87. Leonard, *News for All*, 13–14.
88. Jacques Derrida, *The Post Card: From Freud to Socrates and Beyond*, trans. Alan Bass (Chicago: University of Chicago Press, 1987).
89. Mathew J. Bowyer, *They Carried the Mail: A Survey of Postal History and Hobbies* (Washington, D.C.: Luce, 1972), 24.

both for the censorious work of Anthony Comstock and for the long history of American mail bombing from late nineteenth-century anarchism through the so-called Unabomber. Here, then, we have a system of public communication, connected to every address in the nation, that allows for the conveyance of private messages in sealed packages. Mail, the circulation system of writing and other lightweight cargo, was no longer locally inspected to the same degree. Stamps, envelopes, and drop boxes made the individual sender in principle sovereign over the letter. The post office had thus achieved something quite like what Augustine or Locke wanted for language: to make an inherently public and plural signifying system into one governed by the private will of the sender. The post office, by accommodating sender-imposed restrictions on receivers, had transformed letters from creatures of dissemination (polygamous address) into creatures of apparent dialogue (tight coupling).

As in Augustine and Locke, the ideal of two distant selves brought into contact via some medium also opened up new dangers and problems of miscommunication, specifically of lost letters. Walt Whitman was one of the few not to be alarmed at the specter of missent missives and the unattainability of a secure channel for communication:

I see something of God in each hour of the twenty-four, and each moment then,
In the face of men and women I see God, and in my own face in the glass,
I find letters from God dropt in the street, and every one is sign'd by God's name,
And I leave them where they are, for I know that wheresoe'er I go
Others will punctually come for ever and ever.[90]

Whitman expresses the older wisdom of dissemination: a letter written to one is written to all. Why search so wistfully, he might ask with Emerson, when the whole universe is a letter? The moral lesson of the friends of dissemination, from Emerson through Derrida, seems to be to live ethically and joyously without any assurance of secure channels. All our communications, like everything else, are subject to the interruptions of contingency.

The pathologies unique to the person-to-person ideal are illustrated wonderfully by "dead letters." In 1825 the United States Postal Service started a Dead Letter Office for sorting and collecting mail with address problems, though the practice of opening undelivered letters had been authorized by Congress during the Revolutionary War.[91] A recent esti-

90. Walt Whitman, *Song of Myself*, stanza 48.
91. John, *Spreading the News*, 77–78.

mate has fifty-seven million items annually ending up in this office.[92] The question why undeliverable letters should be "dead" leads to the heart of my argument. With the poststructuralists and pragmatists, I find the vision of communication as private correspondence proposed by Augustine, Locke, and Mesmer ill conceived. Signs are always open to eavesdropping and what Socrates in the *Phaedrus* called *kulindeisthai*, tumbling abroad. Signs are fundamentally public, that is, capable of multiple junctions of meaning. But not all meaning is by the same token equally public. The source of the privacy of meaning lies not in the interior sovereignty of the mind to arrange meanings at will, but in the mortality of the sender. The pathos of dead letters is not that minds fail to share the meaning of signs but that mortal beings miss getting in touch. The problem of communication is not rupture between spirits but letters that never arrive. It is not a noetic problem (relations between minds); it is an erotic one (relations between bodies).

The ghoulish metaphors start with the term "dead letters" itself. The Dead Letter Office is often called "the morgue of the mails" and "the limbo of undeliverable mail."[93] Limbo is the place of oblivion where the souls remain who cannot enter heaven owing to incorrect addressing (such as lack of baptism). With lost letters, the disposal of the dead becomes critical. An 1852 article on the Dead Letter Office in Washington, D.C., describes a room in the General Post Office where "a body of grave, calm men . . . deal with these mortuary remains" (92). They sort the letters and consign most to the flames after removing money, jewelry, or other items of value. Apparently their charge was not to read the letters for "information" of value, but only to search for enclosures. Only in the case of obviously valuable enclosures were efforts made to return to sender, a policy in contrast to those of the United Kingdom and France.[94] Hence, the article continues, a letter "contains a lock of hair—nothing more; valueless in the hard, unromantic judgment of the law" (93). A lock of hair, of course, was a standard Victorian memento of the dead. In Poe's "The Premature Burial," a bereaved lover goes to his beloved's grave "with the romantic purpose of disinterring the corpse, and possessing himself of its luxuriant tresses," only to find that she is still alive.[95] That this purpose should be "romantic" tells us

92. Charis Conn and Ilena Silverman, eds., *What Counts: The Complete "Harper's" Index* (New York: Holt, 1991), 106.

93. Floherty, *Make Way for the Mail*, 167, 171.

94. Pliny Miles, *Postal Reform: Its Urgent Necessity and Practicability* (New York: Stringer and Townsend, 1855), 65–73. Thanks to Dean Colby for providing a copy of this fascinating reformist tract. Miles had done a stint in the Dead Letter Office.

95. Edgar Allan Poe, *Poetry and Tales* (New York: Library of America, 1984), 668.

much about the way the age was half in love with easeful death and gives added pathos to the way the Dead Letter Office serves as a vast crematorium of the dead and their personal effects.

Enclosures of value are sorted into two categories, "money and minor," the latter including articles "that may be either intrinsically of worth, or presumed to be so, to their owners" (96). Every three months the accumulated letters are "solemnly burned" at a place outside of the city, like the biblical Gehenna, "no human being but their writers knowing how much of labor and pain has been expended upon them, thus to perish by fire and be exhaled in smoke" (94). Dead letters stand in for the oblivion of the dead. The symbolic association of the letter and the body is as least as old as the Torah. Dead letters are, in an Augustinian mode, emblematic of our mortal state, prone to become lost in transit. The trope of dead letters clearly plays on the Christian idea that the letter without the spirit, like the body without the spirit, is only a corpse.[96]

The Dead Letter Office deals with the materiality of communication, not its supposed spirituality. It is the dump for everything that misfires. The need for it to exist at all is an everlasting monument to the fact that communication cannot escape embodiment and there is no such thing as a pure sign on the model of angels. Further, the contrast between items that are "intrinsically of worth" and ones of worth only to the owners reveals the ways that shared histories can in fact fill in the meaning of signs. The sense of familiar letters is often peculiar to the parties and not generalizable to those not privy to the code and history. Like the body, dead letters underscore the inalienability of certain sorts of meaning. A human finger to a torturer is just a piece of meat: but to its possessor it is a potential poem, violin song, or caress. In this way private letters are like bodies, objects of immense value that, when detached from their proper setting, are almost utterly useless: my glasses and my eyes, my shoes and my feet, my notebooks and my brain. To me these things are almost infinitely precious; to almost everyone else they are almost infinitely worthless. The disproportionate value of the body to its owner and to anyone else is the firmest proof that not all meanings are public and general.

96. A *Life* magazine "Picture of the Week" from 1 January 1945 features a pile of undeliverable Christmas packages. The caption: "In 1944, when U.S. casualties were highest, the relics of destroyed lives turned up in many places. In U.S. post offices were packages which had come back from men who could not receive them. Stamped on the packages were the cold official legends: return to sender—killed in action. Return to sender—missing in action." Note the curious locution: The packages "come back" from those who could not receive them, as if the dead could send.

Recognizing that they might possess invisible treasures, the Dead Letter Office advertised items and held periodic auctions. In surveying the lists one faces a spectacle of what Nathanael West's Miss Lonelyhearts, briefly transfixed before the window of a pawnshop, calls the "paraphernalia of suffering."[97] At an 1859 auction, for instance, a main item was jewelry, including no fewer than 504 rings, "many of them plain gold wedding rings."[98] All the packages were sealed, however, so that participants had to wager blind. An 1875 auction boasted a sixty-page catalog of items that had accumulated since 1869. It advertised "8,600 different articles sent through the mails, but unredeemed," including jewelry, books, engravings, charms, corn-crushers and corn-huskers, glasses, needlework, asthmatic fumigators, toothpicks, baby clothes, rosaries, poker chips, crucifixes, and the wings of a bat.[99]

Here the private system of the mail spills its guts. No longer understood as a system of moving items that might be used by any number of recipients in addition to the intended, the postal service's new confidentiality of address allows the trappings of private meaning to pile up. Dead letters reveal the indecipherability of private history. The items accumulated at the Dead Letter Office are hieroglyphics, a lost language both sacred and ghastly, that surely would speak to someone somewhere but is a sealed book to us. They are bodies without spirits to breathe life into them. In a similar way, the morgue itself is filled with personal effects—human bodies—precious only to loved ones. The contents of the Dead Letter Office are melancholy props of an enormous dereliction, that of the unclaimed dead, the unredeemed. As the narrator in "Bartleby" appends in epilogue:

Dead letters! Does it not sound like dead men? Conceive a man by nature and misfortune prone to a pallid hopelessness, can any business seem more fitted to heighten it than that of continually handling these dead letters, and assorting them for the flames? For by the cart-load they are annually burned. Sometimes from out of the folded paper the pale clerk takes a ring—the finger it was meant for, perhaps, moulders in the grave; a bank-note sent in swiftest charity—he whom it would relieve, nor eats nor hungers any more; pardon for those who died despairing; hope for those who died unhoping; good tidings for those who died stifled by unrelieved calamities. On errands of life, these letters speed to death. (64–65)

97. Nathanael West, "Miss Lonelyhearts" (1933), in *The Complete Works of Nathanael West* (New York: Farrar, Straus, and Cudahy, 1957), 63–140, at 104.
98. *New York Times,* 9 December 1859, 3.
99. *New York Times,* 26 December 1875, 22 December 1875.

The narrator wants this reverie to stand as an explanation of Bartleby's malady and, by extension, the fate of all of us who wait for the visitor who never comes, concluding: "Ah, Bartleby! Ah, humanity!" The letter that never arrives: What could better suggest the pathos of communication gone awry? The tunes my wife hums inside her head; the dreams I forget on waking; the conversations children have with their "air friends" when they are alone; the sound of the heartbeat in my ears as I lie upon the pillow; the smell of mammoth meat frozen a mile deep within the glacier; the letters in the pockets of the kamikaze pilot; what the sirens sang to the rowers in the belly of Odysseus's ship; what the colors look like beyond violet and below red; what the jaw-bone felt under the dentist's drill while the nerve was numbed with Novocain; what great works died in the trenches of World War I; what the color, humidity, and temperature are within the thing-in-itself. It is easy to mock such questions as repetitions of the old conundrum whether there is a sound when a tree falls in the forest and no one is there to hear it, but what is the meaning of the letter burned in the Dead Letter Office whose writer does not know it is lost and whose recipient does not know it was ever sent?

COMSTOCK AND THE DANGERS OF POSTAL DISSEMINATION   A later and different response to the disseminatory talents of the mails was the New York Society for the Suppression of Vice, founded in 1872 by Anthony Comstock, which fought for the purity of America's youth against the explosive new dissemination of things erotic. Its president for two decades was, "with exquisite appropriateness," a manufacturer of soap, Samuel Colgate.[100] Already widely scorned in his lifetime for his stern holiness, the source of the term "Comstockery," Comstock makes an even easier target today. Walter Kendrick calls him "the archetype of the Victorian prurient prude," and David S. Reynolds finds in him the epitome of "lascivious repressiveness."[101] A man who boasted of the number of suicides he induced and entrapped people without the least regard for due process cannot elicit much sympathy. Yet his rhetoric (a horror at dissemination) and his position (a special agent at the United States Postal Service from 1873 to his death in 1915) offer a key excavation

100. Heywood Broun and Margaret Leach, *Anthony Comstock, Roundsman of the Lord* (New York: Boni, 1927), 154.
101. Walter Kendrick, *The Secret Museum: Pornography in Modern Culture* (New York: Viking, 1987), 136; David S. Reynolds, *Walt Whitman's America: A Cultural Biography* (New York: Knopf, 1995), 541.

171

site in the history of anxious reflection about the disseminatory power of communications.

In Comstock's mind the new anonymity of the post made for all kinds of iniquitous doings. In 1865 a ban was passed against sending obscene materials through the mails, but with the Comstock Act in 1873 the post office acquired expanded powers of search and seizure. The ascendance of Comstock in the 1870s exemplified a more generally narrowing space for sexual and other kinds of reformers in that decade. Whatever his crimes, Comstock recognizes with special acuteness the ways that sex, of all domains of human life, is the most susceptible to alteration by the simple fact of circulation. Comstock's anxieties about published sexuality teach the larger lesson that when mediation touches the body, it not only magnifies its objects but changes their nature. Like Socrates against Lysias, he was concerned about the souls of young men erotically manipulated at a distance.[102]

A particular object of Comstock's wrath was the privacy of letters. Children could order and receive immoral materials without their parents' knowledge. "Secrecy marks these operations. In the darkness of the attic-room, of basement or cellar, is the favorite salesroom."[103] He welcomed the return of the regime of supervised mails: "We are almost ready to adopt the practice of the Roman Catholics, who in their schools and colleges require all letters to be opened in the presence of a priest or teacher."[104] Long before radio and television, Comstock was alarmed at the permeability of domestic space. "The good men of this country . . . will act with determined energy to protect what they hold most precious in life—the holiness and purity of their firesides."[105]

In 1873 Comstock's desire to weaken the sacrosanct character of the sealed envelope met with resistance from the postmaster, a certain T. L. James, who called the seal of a letter inviolate but did agree that undeliverable items or fictitious addresses would end up in the Dead Letter Office at the end of each month.[106] Indeed, it was precisely the flotsam of dead letters that seems to have convinced Comstock and his cronies of the iniquity of postal circulation. He already had a propensity for a certain aesthetics of bulk. The revelation of obscenity en masse was one of Comstock's chief tactics—he had been a drygoods clerk before his call

102. As Kendrick, *Secret Museum*, notes, Comstock focuses on the souls of boys, quite in contrast to contemporaneous purity campaigns in Europe, which featured the vulnerable souls of girls.
103. Anthony Comstock, *Traps for the Young* (New York: Funk and Wagnall, 1883), 131.
104. Comstock, *Traps for the Young*, 146.
105. *New York Times*, 15 March 1873, 1.
106. *New York Times*, 3 July 1873, 8.

in 1873 and retained what Kendrick calls "the clerkly habit of keeping running totals."[107] When he seized smut, he would typically publish reports of it in tonnage, in a forerunner of today's police genre the drug bust, with its scrupulously weighed contraband. His fetish for accumulation expressed itself in inventories of seized paraphernalia that are a veritable warehouse of late nineteenth-century mechanical reproduction: photographs, stereoscopic and other pictures, catalogs, handbills, watch charms and rings, negative plates, lithographic stones, steel and copper plates, woodcuts, stereotype plates, and "lead moulds for manufacturing rubber goods," among other things.[108]

Comstock had a horror of scattered seed. Half-dime novels, "like the fishes of the sea, spawn millions of seed, and each year these seeds germinate and spring up to a harvest of death."[109] He wrote a marvelously characteristic letter to the editor of the *New York Times* in 1873 complaining about the posting of bills: "There is no place that is free from such posting—every tree, tree-box, lamp-post, awning-posts, hydrants, or telegraph poles. The sheds upon the docks, the docks themselves, and every rock and stone on shore, or above low tide, is covered with some filthy advertisement, contrary to law."[110] The target of his ire here was in part the fact of dissemination itself: the "filthy" content of such posters was magnified by their promiscuously public ubiquity. The focus on the conveyance itself also gave Comstock his modus operandi—he was able to control only "smut" in the mails. The channel gave him his leverage. The Latin word *publicare* meant to publish—and also to confiscate and to prostitute. Comstock's activity represents this primal unity.

From antiquity sex has been seen as a way to spend male substance, but the postal system defined the fear of wild-oat sowing in a novel way: "Comstock found in the postal system a perfect metaphor for this ancient terror: spread throughout the country, indiscriminately accessible, public and private at once, the postal system had (odd as it may sound) something sexy about it."[111] Given this book's argument, it ought not to sound odd at all. Any means of linking distant bodies will be erotic to some degree, and the rhizomatic network of the mails boggles the mind for erotic possibilities, with an inlet and outlet at every address in the nation. Any mailbox was an orifice of the body politic

107. Kendrick, *Secret Museum*, 136.
108. *New York Times*, 15 March 1873, 1; cf. Comstock, *Traps for the Young*, 137.
109. Comstock, *Traps for the Young*, 41.
110. *New York Times*, 17 November 1873, 2.
111. Kendrick, *Secret Museum*, 145.

capable of coming into figurative contact with any other. For Comstock, the fecundity of industrial culture was an abominable substitute for the natural fecundity manipulated by birth control and other "obscene" items. Walter Benjamin chose well when he coined the term "the age of mechanical reproduction."[112] Though his "reproduction" referred largely to photography and cinema, it fits reproduction proper just as well. "Copulation and mirrors are abominable," wrote Borges, "because they multiply the numbers of men." To reproduce likenesses: this is what both birth and modern media do. Comstock's horror was not only sex per se but the female capacity to reproduce new bodies. After all, the language of mailing is all about carriage and delivery; dead letters were routinely called "miscarriages."

THE INVASION OF PRIVACY AS DISSEMINATION   A concern for the reproduction of likenesses was central to the famous 1890 *Harvard Law Review* piece "The Right to Privacy," by Samuel D. Warren and Louis D. Brandeis, which I will treat as a final example of the effort to contain dissemination by the principle of privacy. Comstock was worried about what invaded the home via the mails, Warren and Brandeis about what was extracted from it via the press. "Instantaneous photographs and newspaper enterprise," they write, "have invaded the sacred precincts of private and domestic life; and numerous mechanical devices threaten to make good the prediction that 'what is whispered in the closet shall be proclaimed from the house-tops.'"[113] High-speed photography, they argued, eliminated the implicit contract that had implied consent to the reproduction of one's likeness when one had to sit for minutes before a camera. Now not only the home but private thoughts could be captured in a photo of an inadvertent facial expression. Warren and Brandeis faced what Paul Valéry called "the conquest of ubiquity" and what Benjamin called "the dynamite of the tenth of a second."[114] They were very aware of the historically recent character of their argument: privacy, quite explicitly, emerges as a concern once it is threatened by new media

112. Walter Benjamin, "The Work of Art in the Age of Mechanical Reproduction," in *Illuminations,* trans. Harry Zohn, ed. Hannah Arendt (New York: Schocken, 1968), 217–51. The German essay refers to the age of "technische Reproduzierbarkeit" or technical reproducibility, but the English title of his essay derives from the first published version, in French, in *Zeitschrift für Sozialforschung* 5 (1936): 40–63, which refers to "l'époque de sa reproduction mécanisée."
113. Samuel D. Warren and Louis D. Brandeis, "The Right to Privacy," *Harvard Law Review* 4 (1890): 193–220, at 195. On the photographic context of this essay, see the very interesting article by Robert E. Mensel, "'Kodakers Lying in Wait': Amateur Photography and the Right of Privacy in New York, 1885–1915," *American Quarterly* 43, 1 (1991): 24–45.
114. Benjamin, "Work of Art," 236.

of image and sound recording. For Warren and Brandeis, privacy is a distinctly modern notion resting on new individualizations of the self. Like Comstock, Warren and Brandeis recognized that sex serves as the central fuel for the new media of mechanical reproduction. Their prose is full of new communications overrunning old cultural borders. "The press is overstepping in every direction the obvious bounds of propriety and of decency. Gossip is no longer the resource of the idle and of the vicious, but has become a trade, which is pursued with industry as well as effrontery. To satisfy a prurient taste the details of sexual relations are spread broadcast in the columns of the daily papers." Warren and Brandeis are not the only late Victorian cultural critics to face what Horkheimer and Adorno half a century later would call a "culture industry."[115] Like Comstock, they are concerned both about the lack of discretion in things "spread broadcast" and the centrality of the home in the production cycle. Raw material for the gossip trade "can only be procured by intrusion upon the domestic circle." And once more like Comstock, they worry about seedy appetites' being stimulated by spiraling feedback loops: "In this, as in other branches of commerce, the supply creates the demand. Each crop of unseemly gossip, thus harvested, becomes the seed of more, and, in direct proportion to its circulation, results in a lowering of standards and of morality."[116] The same has been said about movies, comics, radio, television, video games, and the Internet during this century.

———

Socrates wanted to find a secure channel through which philosophical lovers could come together in soul if not in body. Promiscuous couplings, scattered harvests, and deathly speeches into the void were the dangers of communication styles and systems, whether they be Lysias's rational choice theory or writing that suspended connection with a distinctly addressed other. With the post and the press in the nineteenth century, similar worries arose about address defects. The postal service was perhaps the first long-distance person-to-person communication

115. Kenneth Cmiel, "Highbrow/Lowbrow" (paper presented at Organization of American Historians, Chicago, April 1991), and Rochelle Gurstein, *The Repeal of Reticence* (New York: Hill and Wang, 1996), chaps. 1–2. Ironically enough, the Warren family itself was involved in culture industries. Members "manufactured newsprint and led the way in the technical improvements that made cheap and prying dailies possible. They were substantial investors in what one press historian has found to be 'the most audacious' of the major Boston papers, the only one with a gossip column." Leonard, *News for All,* 96.

116. Warren and Brandeis, "Right to Privacy," 196.

medium. Dead letters represent the pathos of the letter that never arrives; Comstock, of the letter that arrives under cover; and Warren and Brandeis, of the private missive that is intercepted and broadcast to the public. All three manifest the ways that person-to-person communication, once recorded and transmitted, can break free of its senders and receivers. By the hyperpublic forums of advertising, catalogs, and auctions, the Dead Letter Office sought to reconnect lost letters and their owners. Comstock sought a return to the—for him—good old days when the mails were open to public inspection. What Warren and Brandeis saw as the solution to the wanton dispersion of personal materials—a legal right to privacy based on the notion of inviolate personality—is, very generally, the age-old solution proposed by those alarmed by dissemination. Socrates' call for face-to-face dialectic is, after all, a way to guarantee the privacy of the teaching. Eavesdropping is always a potential in any communications system in which strangers must handle personal cargo; Warren and Brandeis gave the interception of such cargo a name—the invasion of privacy. Mediation increases the specters haunting transmission and reception, the potential touch of alien hands or inspection by alien eyes. Like Augustine and Locke, they assert a principle of privacy in order to secure the public space against the all too noisy and even silly antics of media and signs, those fallen angels.

In sum, the nineteenth century is a long preparation for the echoes and overlaps of dialogue in the twentieth century. Photos of departed loved ones, letters that may never arrive, disembodied voices that cannot reply—these and many other facts of everyday life add to the haunting of communication. The people who so blithely dream of dialogue as a robust encounter between two sovereign souls forget the harsher, more uncanny fact that all communication via media of transmission or recording (which have come to include our bodies and souls) is ultimately indistinguishable from communication with the dead.

FIVE

The Quest for Authentic Connection, or Bridging the Chasm

If I chance to look out a window on to men passing in the street, I do not fail to say, on seeing them, that I see men . . . and yet, what do I see from this window, other than hats and cloaks, which can cover ghosts or dummies who move only by means of springs? RENÉ DESCARTES, *MEDITATIONS*

Wir wissen wenig von einander. Wir sind Dickhäuter, wir strecken die Hände nach einander aus; aber es ist vergebliche Mühe, wir reiben nur das grobe Leder an einander ab,—wir sind sehr einsam.

[We know little of each other. We are pachyderms; we stretch our hands out to each other; but it is wasted effort: we only rub the coarse leather off of each other. We are very lonely.] GEORG BÜCHNER, *DANTONS TOD*

Chapter 4 provided examples, especially from American literature and cultural history, of how greatly enhanced modes of recording could multiply the opportunities for mishaps and breakdowns. The same is true for transmission. Here again developments in physics provide the right metaphors. In a public lecture, probably given in 1873, James Clerk Maxwell described two schools of thought on action at a distance. One held that action at a distance, strictly speaking, could never occur. In this view it was a mistake to think of distance as empty space, for there was always some "line of communication" (physical chain) such as the ether, however imperceptible, linking the two interacting bodies. The notion of action at a distance was thus simply a misperception of the infinitesimal steps linking, say, the moon's gravitational pull and the ocean's tides. The other school asserted, more radically, that "contiguity is only apparent—that a space *always* intervenes between the bodies which act on each other. . . . so far from action at a distance being impossible, it is the only kind of action which ever occurs." Offering a demonstration of the position that all action is action at a distance, Maxwell pressed two lenses together by means of weights and pulleys and, by shining a light through them, projected onto a screen the pattern of rings that resulted from their mutual interference. From the color of the rings, the distance between the lenses could be calculated. With increasing pressure, the rings still showed a gap. Even when pressed so tight that the lenses could not be separated, the rings still showed that they were not in what Maxwell calls optical or real contact. Bodies, Maxwell summarizes, "even when pressed together with great force . . . are not in absolute contact."[1]

Maxwell's two options regarding action at a distance capture the increasingly bifurcated vision of communication in the nineteenth century. On the one hand there is the dream of spirit-to-spirit contact unimpaired by distance or embodiment, a dream stimulated by animal magnetism, the electrical telegraph, spiritualism, wireless, telepathy, and even more exotic forms of mental action at a distance. On the other is the haunting prospect that even touch is an illusion stemming from our sense organs' insensitivity to the microscopic but infinite distances between bodies and the even greater chasms between souls. The problem of communication becomes not only one of getting messages across the waste expanses traversed by the telegraph wires or the interference-prone "ether" of radio transmission, but one of making contact with the person sitting next to you. Maxwell anticipates not only Einstein's universe, in which distance is an epiphenomenon of the space-time continuum, but also a new sense of the phantom nature of touch in thought and culture. He states a major theme of modernist art and literature: that bodies, even when pressed together with great force, may never be in absolute contact! Maxwell's description of an ever vanishing limit stands in nicely for the wider sense that all action, especially all communicative action aimed at coming into junction with another soul, is action at a distance.

Maxwell's sense of the pervasive distances everywhere is the physical

---

1. James Clerk Maxwell, "On Action at a Distance" (1873?), in *Scientific Papers,* ed. W. D. Niven (Cambridge: Cambridge University Press, 1890), 2:313, 314; emphasis in original. Emerson, recall, made a similar point based on the work of Ruggiero Giuseppe Boscovich, an eighteenth-century physicist. Again, thanks to Professor C. W. F. Everitt for help with Maxwell.

counterpart to "solipsism," a notion coined in the same decade, the 1870s. To be sure, the walled-in self has a long genealogy that stretches back well before the conundrums of communication that start to run rampant in the nineteenth century. Though the philosophical doctrine of solipsism—that nothing exists save the projections of the self—was not named until the 1870s, it is a tendency and potential throughout modern thought generally, and in ancient and modern skepticism specifically. Solipsism, after all, is one of those doctrines that is rarely endorsed explicitly, since overmuch eagerness to advocate it lands one in the performative contradiction of supposing the existence of and possibility of communicating with the antagonist one seeks to persuade, thus apparently refuting the key premise of the doctrine. Solipsism is an incommunicable doctrine about incommunicability, but the more general orientation it names has deep roots. In Calvinist self-inspection or the Lutheran *sola fide,* in Pascal's horror of being a castaway in an arbitrary universe, in the more terrestrial self-portraits of Rembrandt, in the vast literature of confession and religious despair stemming from Puritanism and shaping modern British and American literature, and above all in Descartes's efforts to doubt systematically everything he ever learned, felt, or thought, including his body, senses, surroundings, and even soul, one finds intellectual harbingers of the naked self confronting the universe. *Homo clausus,* argues Norbert Elias, is the distinctive style of European selfhood in the past four centuries or so, a personality claustrophobically involuted and walled off from other people and the world.[2] The cosmic loneliness that knows no connection with others and the suspicion that the world is only an airy figment waiting to vanish with the coming madness, revolution, or apocalypse are defining modern moods.

The suspicion that each of us dwells in a heart-shaped box is a product not only of a frenzied philosophical imagination but of lived conditions—in architecture, religion, the organization of work and leisure, public and private, and—as I am arguing—the structure of communications. In a world in which we routinely "communicate" with others whose bodily presence is out of reach and out of sight, where delivery is never assured, the anguish of dubious contact can take hold.[3] "Communication" once meant explicitly the problem of getting messages across a distance via immaterial means. Once applied to the face-to-face

2. Norbert Elias, *The Loneliness of the Dying* (New York: Blackwell, 1985).
3. See, for instance, Dorothy Parker, "A Telephone Call" (1930), in *Fifty Best American Short Stories, 1915–1939,* ed. Edward Joseph Harrington O'Brien (Boston: Houghton Mifflin, 1939), 333–39.

setting, "communication" continues to evoke chasms to be bridged and disturbances in contact. In the quest for remote contact across media, the full bizarreness of modern eros emerged. I take eros to be the attractions and repulsions between bodies, sexual attraction being only one critical part. I follow Plato in understanding eros as the force fields between bodies that do not touch; sex has to do with bodies that touch in specific ways. The intellectual history of "communication" is a record of the erotic complications of modern life. The sense that we cannot touch other minds (communication breakdown) was inspired by settings in which people could not touch other bodies (distant communication). If communication was once the problem of distant minds, by the late nineteenth century it was the problem of proximate bodies. "Come here, I want you," said Bell to Watson in the first telephone call, and this utterance is the symbol and type of all communication at a distance—an expression of desire for the presence of the absent other.[4]

The Interpersonal Walls of Idealism

In late nineteenth-century Anglo-American idealism, for instance, the impossibility of communication is played to an intense pitch. Two people "in communication" are constantly figured in the texts of Josiah Royce and F. H. Bradley, the key American and English idealists of the late nineteenth century, as if they were two inmates of separate rooms, in contact with each other only by signals that bar face, voice, or gesture or any other clue of embodiment or personality. The favored architecture of idealism is the closed room containing a subject out of touch with others. (The Turing test, discussed in chapter 6, is a later variant.)[5] As Adorno argues with respect to Kierkegaard, the architectural setting of the bourgeois interior represents the lonely power of the rentier.[6] In a similar way, the recurring idealist image of the closed room gives us a glimpse of the limits of *Homo clausus*. For one thing, this is not *Femina clausa*. Virginia Woolf wrote of a room of her own not as a fait accompli but as something to be desired; the protagonist of Charlotte Perkins

4. Avital Ronell, *The Telephone Book: Technology—Schizophrenia—Electric Speech* (Lincoln: University of Nebraska Press, 1989), 228.

5. Stanley Milgram's famous *Obedience to Authority: An Experimental View* (New York: Harper and Row, 1974) argued that willingness to subject strangers to electrical shocks was correlated with the remoteness of the victim. When "the victim is out of sight and unable to communicate with his own voice" the probability of a higher voltage was greater than with closer proximity. See Milgram, chap. 4.

6. Theodor W. Adorno, *Kierkegaard: Construction of the Aesthetic,* trans. Robert Hullot-Kentor (1933; Minneapolis: University of Minnesota Press, 1989), 40–46.

Gilman's 1892 story "The Yellow Wall-Paper" experiences her confinement in a closed room not as an existential fate but as an insanity-inducing power play of patriarchy.[7] Solipsism may be the luxurious imagining of literate men protected from diapers and dishes by studies whose doors they keep closed.

Consider a scenario from Josiah Royce's *The Religious Aspect of Philosophy* (1885). "Let us suppose that two men are shut up, each in a closed room by himself, and for his whole life; and let us suppose by a lantern contrivance each of them is able at times to produce on the wall of the other's room a series of pictures." Plato's cave here meets the problem of intersubjective knowledge. "But neither of them can ever know what pictures he produces in the other's room, and neither can know anything of the other's room, as such, but only of the pictures. Let the two remain forever in this relation." It is also an allegory of selfhood, the condition of never knowing what pictures we project on other people's walls. One of the men, A, starts to notice the pictures on his wall, conjectures they are pictures from the other room, and seeks some way to affect them "by himself acting in a way mysterious to himself so as to produce changes in 'B''s actual room, which again affect the pictures that the real 'B' produces in 'A''s room. Thus 'A' might hold what he would call communication with his phantom room."[8] In such a state, A and B cannot be in error about each other, since there is no third party to judge the truth or falsehood of their impressions. A could interpret his own projections on the wall as messages from B, and neither would be the wiser. They would never know if they did "hold communication with" each other. Though Royce uses the scenario only as a prop in an argument about the way the possibility of error implicates the absolute, it shows what a fragile thing communication could be in idealist thinking—coordinated solipsism at best.

With F. H. Bradley, one is even more likely to find oneself utterly walled in, at least in occasional terrifying moments. Bradley, the leading late nineteenth-century proponent in England of absolute idealism, argues the insulation of subjective experience in his important *Appearance and Reality* (1893). "The immediate experiences of finite beings cannot, as such come together; and to be possessed directly of what is personal to the mind of another, would in the end be unmeaning." Since there exists no such thing as "direct connexion between souls," such as telep-

---

7. Denise D. Knight, ed., *"The Yellow Wall-Paper" and Selected Stories of Charlotte Perkins Gilman* (1892; Newark: University of Delaware Press, 1994).

8. Josiah Royce, *The Religious Aspect of Philosophy* (1885; Gloucester, Mass.: Peter Smith, 1965), 413–14.

athy (which Bradley explicitly mentions), the only way to communicate is via our bodies, a fact that raises skepticism whether communication between minds ever occurs. "If such alterations of bodies are the sole means which we possess for conveying what is in us, can we be sure in the end that we have really conveyed it?" Other people may be figments: "There is, indeed, a theoretical possibility that these other bodies are without any souls, or that, while behaving as if they understood us, their souls really remain apart in worlds shut up from ours."[9] Bradley works in the Cartesian tradition of allowing the thought that other people might be soulless automatons. As Emerson had complained, idealism risks denying "substantive being to men and women."

In a quotation made famous by T. S. Eliot's *Waste Land* (1922) Bradley gives each person a room of his or her own: "My external sensations are no less private to myself than are my thoughts or my feelings. In either case, my experience falls within my own circle, a circle closed on the outside; and, with all its elements alike, every sphere is opaque to others which surround it. . . . In brief, regarded as an existence which appears as a soul, the world for each is peculiar and private to that soul." The peculiar and opaque quality of each self extends to the outer world. Trees and poems may be just as elusive as raw feelings or percepts. Communication must always remain "indirect and inferential." It "must make the circuit, and must use the symbol of bodily change. . . . The real identity of ideal content, by which all souls live and move, cannot work in common save by the path of external experience."[10] The real identity of ideal content—this is the dream and nightmare of communication, both union and possession. Bradley, however, is quite close to the pragmatist sensibility that communication is always a matter of inference and interpretation; though he envisions insulated consciousness, he does not call us trapped.

William Ernest Hocking, a student of both James and Royce, was not exactly an idealist, but his theologically inclined philosophy dealt extensively with the problem of communication. In *The Meaning of God in Human Experience* (1912), he explored alienation from self and others, arguing that knowledge of other people rests on knowledge of God. In so doing, he sketched some primal scenes of communication breakdown. Echoing Emerson and foreshadowing existential angst, Hocking asserts, "Souls by their own nature, cannot touch each other." At best,

9. Francis Herbert Bradley, *Appearance and Reality* (1893; Oxford: Clarendon Press, 1946), 303, 304–5.

10. Bradley, *Appearance and Reality*, 306, 306–7. The passage is quoted in the notes to section 5, "What the Thunder Said." Eliot wrote his dissertation on Bradley and studied with Royce at Harvard.

efforts at contact are "launches from solitude in the direction of an assumed reality; which reality, if it exists, is no less solitary." He imagines
the reader protesting: "Human communications must be at bottom as
real as we think them to be—no intricate, successful, solitary *pantomime*
of each with himself and Body." All the goods are here: the barred doors,
noisy society, and smothering solipsism, the fear that communication
may be only a more or less well choreographed pantomime *à deux.*

But like Bradley, Hocking does not shut people off from each other.
The body, a necessary but flawed vehicle for Augustine and Locke, has
a similar doubleness for Hocking, who takes the idealist trope of the
wall and installs it in the body. "I have sometimes sat looking at a comrade," he muses, "speculating on this mysterious isolation of self from
self. Why are we so made that I gaze and see of thee only thy Wall, and
never Thee?" Again, there is no "direct connexion" (Bradley) between
minds. "How would it seem if my mind could but once be within thine;
and we could meet and without barrier be with each other?"[11] Hocking,
like Royce and Bradley, offers the kind of thing parodied *ad deliriam* by
Samuel Beckett, the assiduous student of Descartes and taunting master
of the idiom of professional philosophy that he is, namely, the groping
sense of the impossibility of union with the other, the acquired insanity
of philosophy. Other people become machines, cadavers, or hallucina-
tions—in short, hell.

Hocking does not stay in the abyss. In a pragmatist vein, he makes a
case for coupling in the common world: "I can imagine no contact more
real and thrilling than this; that we should meet and share identity, not
through ineffable inner depths (alone), but here through the foregrounds of common experience; and that thou shouldst be—not behind
that mask—but *here,* pressing with all thy consciousness upon me, *containing* me, and these things of mine." Hocking does not flee from eros;
disembodied mind, he argues, would be unintelligible. He is skeptical of
telepathy, because it ignores the critical contribution that embodiment
makes to thinking. "Telepathy would save, presumably, the trouble of
expression; it would save the detour of thought, by which it must journey down into language and back into thought again. It would connect
the two termini directly, without the complex series of irrelevant
means." In contrast to this idyll of wirelessness ("termini" was an early
term for radio receivers), Hocking argues that mediation is productive.
Could we express everything instantly, little but folly and triviality

11. William Ernest Hocking, *The Meaning of God in Human Experience* (New Haven: Yale University Press, 1912), 245, 246, 265.

would spew forth. "In truth, it is no hardship that friends must 'descend to meet'—as Emerson has it: for such descent into physical expression is a progress into valid and active existence." Besides, telepathy would create problems of authentication and interpretation: we would want to make sure who sent the message and what was meant, driving ourselves back to the need to demand further clarification. Thoughts derive their meaning from the "history of the body"; they need a gestation; without bodies, thoughts would consist only of miscarriages, conceptions too early introduced to the world.[12]

The stunt pilotry of a hair-raising but momentary swerve into solipsism is a key part of twentieth-century flights of communication theory. The discourse of late nineteenth-century idealism sometimes can have a fiercely erotic imagination, as we have seen in Hocking, but the sense of the body tends to be hygienic and ethereal, not organic and sensuous. In Charles Horton Cooley, finally, a founding figure in American sociology and philosophically a clear idealist, we find the high point of theoretical disembodiment together, not incidentally, with what is probably the first sustained account of communication in twentieth-century social thought: chapters 6–10 of his *Social Organization* (1909), significantly subtitled *A Study of the Larger Mind.*

Cooley's 1894 dissertation on the political economy of transportation (his father, a judge and legal theorist, was the first chairman of the Interstate Commerce Commission) holds the pregnant sentence: "Transportation is physical, communication is psychical."[13] Today "psychic" has come to refer to paranormal powers, a legacy of psychical research. Like the psychical researchers and anyone using a telegraph, telephone, letter, or radio, Cooley faced the problem of communication in the absence of the communicant.[14] Cooley reveals the inner affinity of the two senses of "communication": communication as transfer or transportation and as the communion of psyches. In his language, communication means both "fellowship in thought" and "the destruction

12. Hocking, *Meaning of God,* 266, 257, 258.
13. Charles Horton Cooley, *The Theory of Transportation* (Baltimore: American Economics Association, 1894), 70.
14. Cooley makes liberal use of fluid and ether metaphors. In his article "The Process of Social Change," *Political Science Quarterly* 12 (1897): 63–81, he calls language "a fluid whole, every part of which in some way feels and responds to the motion of every other part. In this fluid are propagated an infinite number of movements of thought and action. . . so far as men have like natures that come into sympathy through communication, they really form a sort of fluid in which impulses are propagated by simple suggestion or contact" (72, 80). For other examples of such metaphors, see Josiah Royce, *The World and the Individual* (New York: Macmillan, 1901), 2:220; Herbert Spencer, *The Principles of Sociology,* 3d ed. (New York: Westminster, 1896), 536; and Robert Ezra Park, *The Crowd and the Public,* trans. Charlotte Elsner (Chicago: University of Chicago Press, 1972).

of distance."[15] Both involve bypassing the flesh. Cooley does not lament the increasing irrelevance of physical presence for communication; he embraces the phantasms of the living. His vision is brilliantly in step with changing communicative conditions.

Cooley argued that communication makes geography irrelevant. "In transportation place relations and the overcoming of obstacles in space are everything. In communication place relations, as such, are of diminishing importance, and since the introduction of the telegraph it may almost be said that there are no place relations."[16] In the Augustinian tradition writ large, Cooley welcomed communication as a liberation "from the gross and oppressive bonds of time and place." Like Harold Adams Innis and Marshall McLuhan half a century later, Cooley made media the movers of social change: "Social influences act through a mechanism; and the character of their action depends upon the character of the mechanism." This is almost "the medium is the message." Like the Canadians, he found in communications a non-Marxist engine of history. His notion of media is almost as broad as McLuhan's: "The mechanism of communication includes, of course, gesture, speech, writing, printing, mails, telephone, telegraphs, photographs, the technique of the arts and sciences—all the ways through which thought and feeling can pass from man to man." Here is no "shock of body against body," as Marx described the class struggle, or "the struggle for survival," as Darwin described the history of life on the planet; communication for Cooley is mind made concrete in culture. Like Charles Sanders Peirce, Cooley sought to tell a tale of evolution that was friendly to the higher forces—intellect, sympathy, and above all, love. "Since communication is the precise measure of the possibility of social organization, of good understanding among men, relations that are beyond its range are not truly social, but mechanical."[17] This sentence crystallizes the vision of communication he shared with his fellow progressives, his teacher John Dewey above all. He had a vision of a world in which people would communicate as freely as the ghosts, but he rarely faced the harder questions that James never forgot: breakdown and authentication.

Despite Cooley's fondness for metaphors of touch and closeness, the body per se has no essential privilege as a carrier of personality: in social life "sensible presence is not necessarily a matter of the first impor-

15. The term "fellowship in thought" is used by Charles Horton Cooley, *Social Organization: A Study of the Larger Mind* (New York: Macmillan, 1909), 63.

16. Cooley, *Theory of Transportation*, 70.

17. Cooley, "Process of Social Change," 78, 73, 74, 76.

tance." Cooley blames materialistic thought for making humans into "a lump of flesh." Instead, "the imaginations which people have of one another are the solid facts of society," and the study of mutual imaginations "must be a chief aim of sociology." A person can be "more truly present" in letters, literature, or fantasy than "in the flesh." The face of a friend is no different from any other symbol: "It starts a train of thought, lifts the curtain from an intimate experience. And his presence does not consist in the pressure of his flesh upon a neighboring chair, but in the thoughts clustering about some symbol of him."[18] Cooley's great strength is his pragmatic insistence on the signs that mediate our relations; his great failing is his Victorian insistence that embodiment does not matter.

Cooley locates the marks of personality in what "each of us unconsciously communicates through facial and vocal expression." Personal signifiers consist of "ghosts of expression" such as the look on the face and the grain of the voice. Cooley gives us a theory of communication fit for an age of photography and phonography when personal traces can take new incarnations apart from "the person." Since our personal signs are detachable from our bodies, Cooley obviously allows for communication with the dead. This is not just an afterthought; it is an explicit part of his doctrine. The imagined, the mediated, and the dead may be as socially alive as those whose flesh presses on the furniture. "In order to have society it is evidently necessary that persons should get together somewhere; and they get together only as personal ideas in the mind. Where else? What other *locus* can be assigned for the real contact of persons?" Here again, "place relations" have disappeared. The real contact of persons does not occur in matter; Cooley has learned Maxwell's lesson about the phantom nature of touch. "What, indeed, would society be, or what would any one of us be, if we associated only with corporeal persons and insisted that no one should enter our company who could not show his power to tip the scales and cast a shadow?"[19]

Like William James, Cooley sees a tyranny in policing bodies as the price of admission to society. Under our skins we are all ghosts, and we ought to extend the same hospitality to all our fellow ghosts. Some of the dead, he argues, are "more real in a practical sense than most of us who have not yet lost our corporeity."[20] Caesar, though long turned to clay, may be a more gripping presence to a reader than a pedestrian

18. Charles Horton Cooley, *Human Nature and the Social Order* (New York: Scribner's, 1902), 95–96, 120, 121, 117.
19. Cooley, *Human Nature and the Social Order*, 106–7, 113, 119, 123.
20. Cooley, *Human Nature and the Social Order*, 119.

bumped into on the street. Cooley, good late nineteenth-century soul that he is, theorizes society so that it allows for fellowship with spirits. Indeed, for him spiritual intercourse is the model of all communication. The flow of personal traces, not the presence of bodies, is the key. Reading, reverie, the phonograph, and film connect people as much as touch. He invites us to commune with the quick and the dead, the fictional and the historical. Cooley's social reality is already virtual reality. With the looking-glass self comes the looking-glass other. Our care and communion must be catholic, encompassing the inhuman, living or dead, old or young, substantial or spectral. Society—or community— can arise wherever there is a way to exchange symbols. Distance and death avail not. Face-to-face is here theorized in the shadow of communication at a distance.

In Cooley, communication is indistinguishable from simultaneous projection. Lacking the full-fledged account of the sign process of Peirce or Royce, or the behaviorist check of the whole pragmatist tradition that always asks if we do, in fact, cooperate, Cooley makes communication indistinguishable from a solipsistic pas de deux. He saw the "ghostly element between people" as clearly as Kafka ever did but was happy to gambol and gibber with the spirits in ways that Kafka was not. He was a privileged Protestant in Ann Arbor, not a bilingual Jew in Prague. The genius and madness of Cooley's sociology lies in his insistence on the waning of place in communication or, more specifically, his indifference to mediation, especially to the mother of all media, the body. In flight from the materialism of Spencer and Huxley, Cooley etherealizes society into a hall of fun-house mirrors, or sign flows without bodies.

Just as he posits a continuity between imaginations, he posits a commensurability between the local community and the new scale of social organization in twentieth-century America. Once the body is made spiritual, geography and distance no longer limit sociability. The dispensability of the body allows both spiritual intercourse between two people and coherent mass communication among many. Cooley valorizes in "communication" a certain style of sociability that, he thinks, can be enlarged without limits. Cooley is often thought of as a celebrant of intimacy, of the hearth, family, or gang—the "primary group" as he called it. Yet his celebration of the face-to-face association of intimates is a generalization of the style of mediated communication in which bodies and place are insignificant and "ghosts of expression" are key. For Cooley, the mediated becomes the natural condition. All the hearing, seeing, writing, and imagining aids that were developed to connect people far off get reimported into the face-to-face context. Helen Keller serves him as the discoverer of communication: being sensorily handicapped becomes the general condition. We are all blind and deaf to the larger social world; but new kinds of communication will make us whole again. In Cooley's most rapturous rhetoric, "the new communication has spread like morning light over the world, awakening, enlightening, enlarging, and filling with expectation."[21]

Cooley's vision of communication as the relationship—essentially— among ghosts has a certain relevance for the weird forms of sociability that invite our fellowship in television, radio, print media, and the cinema, in which actors act, announcers broadcast, journalists write, politicians orate, never knowing who their audience will be. Further, Cooley manages to circumvent the uncanniness of proximate bodies, the ickiness of the other, the recognition that there are hair and moles on the arms and perhaps sweat in the armpits and that the person is breathing, metabolizing, and secreting even as we speak. His sociology is perhaps the ultimate achievement in late Victorian social thought: it gives us a way to conceive of society without bodies.[22]

Fraud or Contact? James on Psychical Research

"Believe me, I am not rubbish."
MRS. PIPER'S HODGSON CONTROL TO WILLIAM JAMES

The problem with spiritual intercourse is that it leaves the question of contact open-ended and even undecidable. William James, one of Cooley's heroes, was one of the most thoughtful explorers of this no-man's-land. Communication as the direct transfer of cognitions from one ego to another was for him beyond the realm of normal psychology. His forgotten work in psychical research is marked by his characteristic themes and wit. James was, after all, a founder of the American Society for Psychical Research, and psychical research is not peripheral but in many ways is at the center of his thought. The three postulates Kant deemed unprovable but necessary for a rational and moral life—that nature is governed by law, that the will is free, and that the soul is immortal—are constantly interrogated in James's psychical research and in his philosophy more generally.[23] Psychical research, at its Jamesian best, not only was about paranormal phenomena, but ultimately was

21. Cooley, *Social Organization*, 88.
22. For another view of Cooley's sociology in the context of Victorian culture, see Steven Marcus, "Human Nature, Social Orders, and Nineteenth Century Systems of Explanation: Starting in with George Eliot," *Salmagundi* 28 (winter 1975): 20–42.
23. I accept the interpretation of James as neo-Kantian in many respects.

an attempt to answer the questions: What can I know? What should I do? For what may I hope? Kant believed that rational answers could be provided, but never, like Baron Münchausen, could one pull oneself through the circle of one's own cognitions. For Kant, one could not act rationally without presupposing principles of causality, morality, and immortality. (For James the order was reversed: one had first to act as if and maybe then the principles would follow.) Attempts to venture beyond the knowable would only reproduce what was already within rather than discovering what was beyond.

But psychical research, like the development of post-Kantian idealism before, did not always find Kant's strictures satisfactory. Once in a blue moon and under special conditions, thought many psychical researchers, one could cross over into lands that Kant deemed forever off-limits. Communication was one chief principle of crossing. As the British physicist Sir Oliver Lodge concluded after thirty years of psychical research, "Occasional communication across the chasm—with difficulty and under definite conditions—was possible."[24] With a quote from the *Symposium*, Lodge argued that "there is no real breach of continuity between the dead and the living; and that methods of intercommunication across what has seemed to be a gulf can be set going in response to the urgent demand of affection,—that in fact, as Diotima told Socrates . . . LOVE BRIDGES THE CHASM."[25]

Whether such metaphysical breaches were in fact possible remained, for James, an open question. James was a permanent fence-sitter about psychical phenomena and was too credulous for some tastes.[26] He took the longing to rupture the limits of mortality as a chief document of the human will to believe without ever quite committing to the objective possibility of such rupture. But he defended his exploration of "wild facts" as the properly scientific stance. His inquiries focused especially on "Mrs. Piper," as she has become immortalized in psychical research. James first met Eleonore Piper in 1885 and studied her extraordinary mediumistic talents until his death in 1910. In one of his first encounters with her, James was struck by her remarkable access to confidential details of his wife's family life: "The medium showed a most startling intimacy with this family's affairs, talking of many matters known to

24. Oliver Lodge, *Raymond, or Life and Death, with Examples of the Evidence of Survival of Memory and Affection after Death* (New York: Doran, 1916), 389.

25. Lodge, *Raymond,* 83; emphasis in original. This Platonic *logion* (*Symposium,* 202e) was a favorite in psychical research: Myers quotes it as well.

26. Such as Martin Gardner, "William James and Mrs. Piper," in *The Night Is Large: Collected Essays, 1938–1995* (New York: St. Martin's Press, 1996), 213–43.

no one outside, and which *gossip* could not have possibly conveyed to her ears." Though at first inclined to think Mrs. Piper had scored only lucky hits, James concluded that she was "in possession of a power as yet unexplained."[27] The ability of the medium to provide evidence from the private sphere was for James a compelling token of some kind of immunity from fakery. The accidental, as Kierkegaard claimed, is just as necessary as the necessary.

Here proof of authenticity, as for other kinds of mediated communication, came in contingent details too trivial to have been faked.[28] James sorted through the "bosh" and "rubbish" of Mrs. Piper's performances for the telltale signs of other minds across the veil.[29] He looked for insignificant trifles as marks of genuine otherness. In short, he sought the soul hidden within the medium. But the ghost in the machine manifested itself only in the realm of private, contingent fact. What cannot be reproduced, especially the body, remains the bastion of communicative authenticity.

James's method for detecting fakes is in line with other methods emerging at the same time. Just as the photograph and the phonograph allowed for new personal phantasms in the late nineteenth century, they also revealed hitherto unexplored worlds, incidentals of motion and action that were never visible before—the gaits of horses and humans, the varieties of human earlobes, or the split-second expressions on the face. Media spelled not only disembodiment, but a new focus on bodily singularities. Carlo Ginzburg argues that a mode of interpretation arose in very late nineteenth-century criminology, psychology, and art history based on the claim that scrutiny of "infinitesimal traces [permits] the comprehension of a deeper, otherwise unattainable reality." By attending to the shapes of ears, varieties of tobacco ash, or types of perfumes, as Sherlock Holmes does, one can identify the criminal; by noting the ways fingers and toes are painted one can sort the works of the assistants (or frauds) from those of the master, as Giovanni Morelli's method of detecting forgeries argued; and by slips of the tongue or the half-oblivion of dreams one can, with Sigmund Freud, lay bare the un-

27. William James, "Report of the Committee on Mediumistic Phenomena" (1886), in *William James on Psychical Research*, ed. Gardner Murphy and Robert O. Ballou (London: Chatto and Windus, 1961), 97; emphasis in original. Like Warren (a fellow Boston elite) and Brandeis, James noted the intrusion on the "sacred precincts" of the home by new kinds of media (mediums).

28. Carlo Ginzburg, "Clues: Roots of an Evidential Paradigm," in *Myths, Emblems, Clues*, trans. John and Anne C. Tedeschi (London: Hutchinson Radius, 1990).

29. William James, "Report on Mrs. Piper's Hodgson Control" (1909), in *William James on Psychical Research*, ed. Gardner Murphy and Robert O. Ballou (London: Chatto and Windus, 1961), 204.

conscious.[30] Such a mode of detection might be thought fetishistic in its concern for inconsequential details were it not so potent a forensic method. "Their most trivial action may mean volumes," said Sherlock Holmes, "or their most extraordinary conduct may depend upon a hairpin or a curling tongs."[31] At the same historical moment when new media are reproducing human presences without fingernails, earwax, perfume, or breath, those details become the site of truth. It is in what transcends or subverts the medium that truth lies.

In a 1908 study, two years before his death, James examined Mrs. Piper's contact with Richard Hodgson, a deceased colleague in psychical research, one of many psychical researchers to enjoy a posthumous career as a spirit control (ambassador to the living from the dead). Was Hodgson's spirit on the other side, dictating through the sometimes fraudulent, often brilliant, and always histrionic Mrs. Piper? Or was it all just "dingy twaddle"? James contrasted "the will to personate," the all-too-human desire on the part of the medium to perform for an audience, with "the will to communicate," stemming from a source genuinely outside the medium's consciousness, possibly including the spirit of a dead person or a multiple personality from her own mind. In spiritualist communication, humbug and revelation were inextricably in league. "Fraud, conscious or unconscious, seems ubiquitous throughout the range of psychical phenomena."[32] James suggested that Mrs. Piper's communication with Hodgson involved an interaction of the two wills: the spirit, "by pressing, so to speak, against 'the light,' can make fragmentary gleams and flashes of what it wishes to say mix with the rubbish of the trance talk on this side." Even spirits had a hard time with communication.[33] The task for the psychical researcher, in turn, was to discern the relative part of "the rubbish-making and the truth-telling wills" in the message. James concluded that there was "a will to say something which the machinery fails to bring through."[34] Here again

30. Ginzburg, "Clues," 101.
31. Arthur Conan Doyle, "The Adventure of the Second Stain," in *The Complete Sherlock Holmes* (Garden City, N.Y.: Doubleday, 1930), 2:657.
32. William James, "Final Impressions of a Psychical Researcher" (1909), in *The Writings of William James: A Comprehensive Edition,* ed. John J. McDermott (Chicago: University of Chicago Press, 1977), 791.
33. In an essay called "On Hindrances and Complications in Telepathic Communication," Eleanor Mildred Balfour Sidgwick quotes a "Myers" spirit, who compared "the difficulties of sending a message" through a medium to "standing behind a sheet of frosted glass—which blurs sight and deadens sound—and dictating feebly—to a reluctant and somewhat obtuse secretary." In *Phantasms of the Living,* ed. Eleanor Mildred Balfour Sidgwick (1924; New York: Arno Press, 1975), 433.
34. James, "Report on Mrs. Piper's Hodgson Control," 206, 206, 204.

proof of authenticity came via something that transcended the apparatus.

Even so, James left open the possibility that the will to communicate never got out of the Kantian circle. To explain Mrs. Piper's apparent ability to speak for Hodgson, James resorted to a complex of radio metaphors. Quite like Kipling's story "Wireless," James posits a special kind of induction. First, the physician turned psychologist reminds us, "all memory processes [are] . . . coordinated with material processes." In life, our bodies are generally the best records of our personalities. But after death the material world remains a repository of each person that has ever been in it, "the cosmos being in some degree, however slight, made structurally different by every act of ours that takes place in it." (Such is just one of the treasures that occur in James's inquiries into mediumistic phenomena.) Thus, just as "the ether of space can carry many simultaneous messages to and from mutually attuned Marconi-stations, so the great continuum of material nature can have certain tracts within it" that sustain the faint signals of historical acts and actors. "The bodies (including, naturally, the brains) of Hodgson's friends who come as sitters, are of course parts of the material universe which carry some of the traces of his ancient acts. They function as receiving stations." An assembly of friends thus forms an archive of Hodgson's traces that are resuscitated "by some sort of mutual induction." The medium simply serves as "a drainage opening or sink" for the spiritual energy thus retrieved from both the physical universe and presence of friends.[35]

In this conceit, one that owes something to the idea of telepathy as the brain waves of the sitters, James is not really thinking of a "live" contact with a remote spirit who signals across the ether. Piper is less a Marconi station than a phonograph playing a record cut years ago. Though he hated what he called Hegelism, James would agree with Hegel that contact with the dead was more a matter of playing the records than tuning the radio. He saw dialogue with the dead as an adventure in hermeneutics, not spirit travel. Psychical research for him was like nineteenth-century hermeneutics: a massive labor of authenticating, eavesdropping, and source criticism. (James was a friend of Wilhelm Dilthey, the great theorist of interpretation.) He saw that transmission is ultimately a subset of recording, not the reverse. When we reach out to others, near or far, living or dead, we are only able to read and guess. All our sendings and receivings are potentially dead letters.

35. James, "Report on Mrs. Piper's Hodgson Control," 208, 209. The notion has a recent echo: "It will be possible to resurrect dead people from the traces they leave in life. A sort of superarchaeology." Hans Moravec, "Interview," *Omni Magazine* 11 (August 1989): 91.

James considered almost all the data of spiritualist practice "philosophy-and-water," the recycled banalities of the *Zeitgeist*. "It is a field," wrote James, "in which the sources of deception are extremely numerous."[36] There is in James's reports, and even more so in lesser researchers, a certain acedia, heroic patience combined with a *tedium vitae*.[37] Such a massive filtration for such a small harvest! Further, a salient fact about communion with the dead is the triviality or silliness of their reports.[38] James was as interested in the hope for contact as in the contact itself, since such hope was one of the key facts of human experience. James kept the door open, hovering somewhere between a physiological reductionism and a warm embrace of the specters.[39] He sorted through the multiple mediations and projections for the will to communicate—the prize that SETI, primate, or AI researchers all seek (chapter 6). He was looking for a recognition of his recognition, a completion of the loop. James made the leap of faith and managed to stay suspended in midair. Some defenders of spiritualism were the clear toadies of collusion: the spirit photographs might well be double exposures, they said, but that doesn't mean the spirits had no hand in them.[40] Though some may see James as waffling in the same way, he saw a larger picture: "Is our whole instinctive belief in higher presences . . . but the pathetic illusion of beings with incorrigibly social and imaginative minds?"[41] Are the sublimest things we do, know, and hope simply projections? James sought to bridge the Kantian gulf by his pragmatic principle that these beliefs make a difference, and that all acting is essentially acting as if.

In my reading James was no humanist defender of the bourgeois ego; his concern was rather to never rule out the possibility of contact with the inhuman—beast or God. In his universe communication was at best a hello across the chasm of otherness, never the *consensus in idem* of two equally matched and rational parties. To abandon the hope of making

36. William James, letter to Carl Stumpf, in *The Thought and Character of William James*, ed. Ralph Barton Perry (Boston: Little, Brown, 1935), 1:248.

37. On acedia, see Walter Benjamin, "Theses on the Philosophy of History," trans. Harry Zohn, in *Illuminations*, ed. Hannah Arendt (New York: Schocken, 1968), 256, and Benjamin, *The Origin of German Tragic Drama* (London: Verso, 1977), 155–57.

38. Lodge's defense: "Humour does not cease with earth-life. Why should it?" Lodge, *Raymond*, 349.

39. Gerald Bruns, "Loose Talk about Religion from William James," *Critical Inquiry* 11 (1984): 299–316.

40. Tom Gunning, "Phantom Images and Modern Manifestations."

41. William James, "Concerning Fechner," in *A Pluralistic Universe* (1909), in *The Writings of William James: A Comprehensive Edition*, ed. John J. McDermott (Chicago: University of Chicago Press, 1977), 529.

junction, even in such a preposterously "mediated" setting as a spiritualist séance, would be to renounce not only open inquiry but also the perhaps equally crucial attempt to enter fellowship with intelligences radically different from our own. James held fast to the idea that human personality can survive the transit through the mediums and media of communication, because he saw that the ability to connect with other beings, whatever their form, was at stake.

James lived in a world in which "communication" took place apart from embodied presence. As dialogue with the living no longer required proximity of their bodies, neither did dialogue with the dead. The question for James is, How can one know that contact has been made with the other side? In other words, the central question of psychical research was the "possibility of communication between discarnate minds and those still incarnate, and vice versa."[42] The question of communication between the embodied and disembodied not only was pressing for the late Victorians, it is a question for anyone who waits for a phone call or goes to the movies. James's situation with regard to Hodgson and Mrs. Piper is structurally identical to the Turing test: he must distinguish a real human being from a simulated one when access to the other's presence is cloaked by an intervening medium. The problems facing contact with spirits are in many ways the same as those with any other kind of communication at a distance. Psychical research is a kind of DX-ing, as it is called in amateur radio: seeking contact with the most distant possible stations. In each case "the sources of deception" are indeed numerous, in which many signals can be reinterpreted as an artifact of the imperfect machinery of transmission or reception. In psychical research, James explored issues at the heart of communication theory: What happens when personal effigies travel apart from the body? When is a message a message? What is a projection from the self and what a recognition of or by the other? Is the order in the world a product of my own world-projecting powers (as Fichte, Schelling, and many romantics thought), or are there authentically other kinds of intelligence? James gambled on the possibility of junction with other intelligences, animal, spiritual, or human. He knew that the question of communication was one of our time's questions of faith.

42. F. W. H. Myers, *Human Personality and Its Survival of Bodily Death*, ed. Susy Smith (1903; New Hyde Park, N.Y.: University Press, 1961), 29.

Reach Out and Touch Someone: The Telephonic Uncanny

Cooley thought that communication had made the old scale of distances obsolete. He and his contemporaries lived in a universe in which ghostly effigies of human personalities were beginning to swim everywhere. He saw nothing uncanny or suspicious in mediated communication. Subsequent developments in media culture raised the question just how much the body could remain an indifferent presence to communication. Touch, as it happens, could not be suppressed forever.

Take the telephone, for instance. The telephone, after fits and starts, has solidified its use as a means of staying in personal touch with individuals who are not immediately at hand, while wireless technologies (radio and television) have largely gone in the opposite direction of having a diffuse and general addressee. In principle, both telephone and wireless technologies can be either a central exchange for many voices (party lines or radio broadcasting) or a means of point-to-point contact (cellular phones or ham radio). The issue is not so much the inherent properties of the medium as the social constellation of speakers and hearers that became enforced as normative. Radio became the carrier of messages aimed for low-resolution address, and the telephone, of those for high-resolution.

In the dawn of telephone systems, the personal touch was omnipresent. Every call was placed with the aid of a human operator, and up to the 1880s there were no telephone *numbers:* operators simply used the names of subscribers to track the slots on the switchboard. It took the Bell system several years, in fact, to persuade all its customers to switch to numbers. Even then many local exchanges had prefixes based on a sense of local geography—Pennsylvania 6–5000, for example. Even so, the idea of confidential conversation heard only by two people was slow in coming, just as it was in the mails. One technical problem resolved early was how to get only one specific telephone in a networked system to ring, for all would ring when one was called. The telephone, like all media of multiplication (transmission and recording), was essentially a public medium. Just as Warren and Brandeis in the 1890s sought to establish a right to privacy and the anonymously posted letter arose in the 1850s, telephone managers in the 1890s and early 1900s sought to secure private channels of contact between unique addresses.[43] The task

---

43. See Michèle Martin, *"Hello, Central?" Gender, Technology, and Culture in the Formation of Telephone Systems* (Montreal: McGill-Queen's University Press, 1991).

again was to domesticate the plurality of media by the singularity of "communication."

Before automated switching, the routine medium of routing telephone calls was the switchboard operator. We have met this figure before—passive, neutral or feminine gender identity, servicing an apparatus of message delivery—in the spiritualist medium and in Bartleby the scrivener. An Ontario newspaper in the 1890s reported on operators: "The girls then, are automata. . . . They looked as cold and passionless as icebergs," and an early training manual prescribed that each "operator must now be made as nearly as possible a paragon of perfection, a kind of human machine, the exponent of speed and courtesy; a creature spirited enough to move like chain lightning, and with perfect accuracy; docile enough to deny herself the privilege of the last word."[44] These descriptions have the virtue, at least, of explicitness: the operator's body—her voice, gestures and fatigue—was, like that of typists as well, a key site of psychotechnical discipline.[45] The telephone operator antedates the cyborg, a plastically gendered creature formed of electrical wiring and the organic body.[46] Like spiritualist mediums, operators inhabit a profoundly liminal space. The female body hidden at the heart of a national communications network, appearing only in impersonal voice, is an archetypal figure. In popular culture the operator was often treated as a heroine who, knowing everyone's habits, could bring people together in emergencies: the operator as matchmaker, lifeguard, or angel of mercy. She was always betwixt and between.[47]

Like Diotima's Eros, operators had the job of managing the gaps and ferrying messages back and forth across the chasm. Indeed, there was something sexy about operators, with their voices traveling across the expanses. As an American manager wrote in 1905, "There is something about the sound of the voice of a girl on the wire that sets a young man into a wooing mood."[48] The telephone itself has been sung and la-

44. Martin, "Hello, Central?" 70, 73.

45. See Helmut Gold and Annette Koch, eds., Fräulein vom Amt (Munich: Prestel, 1993), and Friedrich A. Kittler, Grammophon, Film, Typewriter (Berlin: Brinkmann und Bose, 1986), 273–89.

46. Donna J. Haraway, Simians, Cyborgs, and Women: The Reinvention of Nature (New York: Routledge, 1991), and Claudia Springer, Electronic Eros: Bodies and Desire in the Post-industrial Age (Austin: University of Texas Press, 1996).

47. See Herbert N. Casson, "The Social Value of the Telephone," Independent, 26 October 1911, 899–906; "How the Hotel Telephone Girl Sizes You Up," American Magazine, August 1923, 23, 70, 72; "When the 'Hello Girl' Tries Hand at Detective Work," Literary Digest, 5 November 1927, 52–54.

48. Martin, "Hello, Central?" 95. Besides the general point that distance breeds eros, Rick Altman suggests the sexiness of the female voice may owe to the suppression of high frequencies in telephone sound (designed on the model of the male voice), thus tending to make female telephone voices into sultry contraltos.

mented as an agent of romantic coupling and haunting, being a classic go-between for lovers. Marriages were performed over the telephone, as over the radio, an obligatory coming-of-age event for each new medium of distance communication.[49] The arrows of Eros and of electrical circuit diagrams here converge. Note too that the couplet—public radio, private telephone—has made the notion of a radio-sex industry sound laughable, but with 900 numbers there is, alas, a thriving phone-sex business.

Once the switchboard connection was made, there were still address gaps. Without access to the bodily presence of the other, initial interaction on the telephone dramatized the likelihood that one did not know whom one was addressing. In face-to-face interaction we usually know whom we are speaking to, save in cases of imposture or more difficult philosophical questions of identity. Negotiations of identity became routine in telephone etiquette. When my second son was younger, he would call a friend's house and speak to whoever answered as if that person were his friend and knew who was calling. He hadn't yet learned to identify himself or the interlocutor, failing to recognize the need for connection management in a medium that cloaks presence. Different styles of decorum arose to manage the missing persons over the telephone. In the Netherlands, telephone speakers are expected to identify themselves at once: those answering must answer with their names, and the callers must do so as well. In the United States norms of self-identification are far more relaxed, and some callers never bother to identify themselves at all, assuming their voice is recognized. In habitual face-to-face interaction, such work at initial coupling is always implicit; thanks to the media-stimulated dream of wondrous contact, we have grown accustomed in the twentieth century to finding such problems everywhere in communication.

In early telephone culture modes of interaction were sought that dispensed with the need for cues of presence.[50] The telephone could be both a handicap (in its blindness) and a sensory extension (a hearing aid and voice amplification device). A 1915 piece states the telephone's

49. One example of telephone marriage is given in Mary B. Mullett, "How We Behave When We Telephone," *American Magazine*, November 1918, 44–45, 94, at 45. A 1995 *National Geographic* article pictures "first virtual reality wedding" as a physically separated couple "embracing" in virtual reality. And yet the meeting in the flesh cannot be postponed forever: "There was no question about the ending though: a real kiss after the virtual one." Joel L. Swerdlow, Louis Psihoyos, and Allen Carroll, "Information Revolution," *National Geographic Magazine* 188, 4 (1995): 35.

50. Lana Rakow, *Gender on the Line: Women, the Telephone, and Community Life* (Urbana: University of Illinois Press, 1992), 43, treats the relative ineptitude of men in the town of "Prospect" at managing telephone talk.

deficiencies with remarkable economy: "Conversation by telephone is talk shorn of all the adventitious aids that spring from the fact of physical and visual proximity." The undifferentiated totality of the face-to-face setting is redescribed according to the new audiovisual order of silent cinema and pictureless telephones. "There is no flashing glance to 'register,' as the movie actors have it, wrath; no curling lip to betoken scorn; no twinkling eye to suggest whimsicality; none of the charm of personal presence that might give substance to an attenuated argument or power to a feeble retort. The voice must do it all."[51]

The telephone could be strange indeed. In it, the face-to-face setting could be redefined as a communication problem, with its "adventitious aids" of "physical and visual proximity" that had never before been distinct channels. The historian Catherine Covert argued that the telephone served cultural critics as an ordinary baseline against which to measure the weirdness of radio in the years after the Great War. In contrast to the supernatural world of radio was "the quite worldly experience of Americans with the telephone—as a direct connection between human beings."[52] In fact, the telephone evoked many of the same anxieties as radio: strange voices entering the home, forced encounters, the disappearance of one's words into an empty black hole, and absent faces of the listeners. An *Atlantic Monthly* piece from 1920, written in the voice of a neurasthenic woman, notes: "It is bad to hear myself talk on any occasion. It is worse to talk into an empty black hole, without the comfort and guide of a responsive face before me." The telephone's lack of manners also irks her. "It makes no preambles and respects no privacies," rings without regard to how occupied one may be in other tasks, and pulls one into "unexplained encounters" with strangers.[53] Our writer notes the classic features of dissemination; Socrates too was worried about odd encounters and indifference to the personal situation.

The looseness of personal identification lies at the core of the telephone's eeriness. Even today, there is nothing quite so unnerving as a caller who repeatedly calls and hangs up or who never identifies himself (it is usually a he) and simply breathes into the phone. Such violations of etiquette call forth the primal uncanniness of the medium. Taking "obscene" in the original sense of something appearing that is supposed to be concealed (off-scene), the notion of an obscene phone call is a

51. "On Conversation by Telephone," *Independent*, 10 May 1915, 229–30.
52. Catherine L. Covert, "'We May Hear Too Much': American Sensibility and the Response to Radio, 1919–1924," in *Mass Media between the Wars*, 1918–1941, ed. Catherine L. Covert and John D. Stevens (Syracuse: Syracuse University Press, 1984), 202.
53. "Telephone Terror," *Atlantic Monthly*, February 1920, 279–81.

THE QUEST FOR AUTHENTIC CONNECTION

redundancy. In ways that foreshadow recent concerns about how loosened markers of personal identity allow abusive discourse in cyberspace, such as the tirades known as "flames," commentators attributed telephone rudeness to the loss of instantaneous recognition in the face-to-face setting.[54] In the words of one 1918 writer, "There are men who, as someone has put it, take advantage of their 'low visibility' over the telephone to act as they never would if face to face with you."[55] The relative anonymity of the Internet, it is similarly argued, allows people to get away with vituperative modes of discourse they would never dare in person.

The telephone also contributed to the modern derangement of dialogue by splitting conversation into two halves that meet only in the cyberspace of the wires. Dialogue, despite its reputation for closeness and immediacy, occurs over the telephone in a no-man's-land as elusive as writing itself. The effect of such flayed discourse has been compared to schizophrenia and to crosscutting in film editing.[56] Mark Twain caught both schizoid and comic dimensions in his satire "A Telephonic Conversation":

Then followed that queerest of all the queer things in this world—a conversation with only one end to it. You hear questions asked; you don't hear the answer. You hear invitations given; you hear no thanks in return. You have listening pauses of dead silence, followed by irrelevant or unjustifiable exclamations of glad surprise or sorrow or dismay. You can't make head or tail of the talk, because you never hear anything that the person at the other end of the wire says.

The piece then offers an account of one such "conversation," a premise for Twain to indulge in a series of droll nonsequiturs, such as:

Pause.
It's forty-ninth Deuteronomy, sixty-fourth to ninety-seventh inclusive. I think we ought all to read it often.
Pause.
Perhaps so; I generally use a hair-pin.[57]

---

54. Mark Dery, ed., *Flame Wars: The Discourse of Cyberculture* (Durham: Duke University Press, 1994).
55. Mullett, "How We Behave When We Telephone," 45.
56. Ronell, *Telephone Book*; Frank Kessler, "Bei Anruf Rettung!" in *Telefon und Kultur: Das Telefon im Spielfilm*, ed. B. Debatin and H. J. Wulff (Berlin: Volker Spiess, 1991), 167–73.
57. Mark Twain, "A Telephonic Conversation," in *"The $30,000 Bequest" and Other Stories* (1880; New York: Harpers, 1917), 204–8.

The subtext of the story, corroborating other comments of the period, is the contrast between masculine gruffness and abruptness on the phone and feminine talkativeness; it is the male narrator, for instance, who is asked to ring the central office for a female member of his household.

Two one-sided conversations that couple only in virtual space: this is the nature of speech on the telephone. Naturally, the question arises whether such coupling ever occurs. In Dorothy Parker's early 1930s monologue, "A Telephone Call," a woman pleads frenziedly with God to have a man friend call, but in the course of the monologue he does not; the title of the story names what never takes place. Waiting for a call that never comes exemplifies not only the loneliness of the neglected lover but the whole problem of how to know that one has made contact at all; it is not by accident that the monologue is addressed to God. Parker gives us a neat communication circuit: she places a call that seeks as its answer another call. The voice of desire seeks another voice of desire. Aldous Huxley's "Over the Telephone" from the same era reverses the gender of the supplicant: a young poet mentally rehearses his grandiloquent invitation to a woman friend to attend the opera, imaginatively taking the entire evening to its happy conclusion as the lovers kiss in his flat. When after many mishaps the operator finally makes the connection with the woman, however, he stumbles hopelessly and she declines owing to a previous engagement: "Despairingly, Walter took the receiver from his ear. The voice squeaked away impotently into the air like the ghost of a Punch and Judy show." The breach in telephonic communication, like that of the planned date, is marked as an erotic failure, squeaking impotently into the air.[58] Such an attempt at "communication" is at best a situation of hermeneutic rupture, two sides barred from each other by some deep distance.

KAFKA AND THE TELEPHONE The spookiest of all explorers of the telephone, and of "communication" as two monologues that may never connect, even in imagined space, was Franz Kafka. All hermeneutics is the art of reading texts by an unintended audience; it is a mode of eavesdropping. Facing the dead, or a partner who cannot, will not, or does not respond, can leave one in a tizzy of guesswork. Mediated communication, as by the telephone, teaches us that we are always eaves-

---

58. Parker, "Telephone Call," 333–39; Aldous Huxley, "Over the Telephone," in *The Smart Set Anthology,* ed. Burton Rascoe (New York: Reynal and Hitchcock, 1934), 122–28.

dropping. How is the voice of Parker's monologue to know what the lack of a call signifies—rejection, a lost number, or nothing at all? All that separates desolation from elation is a phone call. The exploding of dialogue into two remotely linked halves makes the validity of interpretation obscure. The inability to distinguish inner projections from outer messages flourishes in conditions where interpreters have to bear the weight of the entire communication circuit. This inability, psychologically conceived, is called paranoia; socially conceived, we should call it mass communication. Those who have ears to hear will hear. Kafka is our guide to these conditions.

In a short parable called "The Neighbor," Kafka extends the idealist architecture by making the walls too thin rather than too thick.[59] The narrator, a young businessman, tells how an identical office adjacent his own is rented by another young businessman named Harras, whose business is mysterious but seems the same as his own. The two never meet, only brush past each other on the stairs. Their only relations are mediated and imagined; they never actually converse with each other. The walls are so miserably thin, however, that everything can be heard in the neighboring office. Even worse, on the common wall of the two offices, the narrator has a telephone; even if it were placed on the opposite wall, Harras could still hear everything. Ever unsure whether the neighbor is listening, the narrator adopts a roundabout style of speech in his dealings over the phone and studiously never mentions the names of customers. Yet he is sure he is still betraying secrets. "If I really wanted to exaggerate—as people often do, to make things clearer to themselves—I could say: Harras needs no telephone, he uses mine."

Harras is no wiretapper. This is a story of a doppelgänger and a telephone, both of which involve enigmatic splittings of identity and conversation. Harras (as the narrator surmises) eavesdrops on the ghosts that proliferate in the space between the two termini of the telephone conversation. Thus he is able to outsmart the narrator: by figuring out who and where the person on the other end of the line is, Harras speeds through the city and meets the customer before the narrator is even off the phone, working against him (or so fantasizes the narrator). In a new twist on telephone harras-ment, Harras uses the telephone not simply to breathe or threaten, but to transport his person as fleetly as electrical speech. The parable is not only a meditation on surveillance and the

59. Franz Kafka, "Der Nachbar," in *Beschreibung eines Kampfes: Novellen, Skizzen, Aphorismen aus dem Nachlaß* (Frankfurt am Main: Fischer, 1989), 100–101.

futility of coded speech to conceal secrets, but a fantasy on the comparative advantage of presence. Kafka catches the horror of speaking on the phone when one's double—the proxy of the voice—goes streaking through the wires to appear in the presence of the telephone partner. Anyone who has ever used a phone to discuss a sensitive matter knows how your double can arrive on the other end and work against you. The narrator's paranoia—literally, the sense of other minds—is appropriate to a system of mechanically multiplied personal tokens.

Another telephone scene occurs in the beginning of Kafka's posthumous *The Castle* (1926). "K" enters a village inn and finds himself accosted by a representative of the Castle, a vaporous entity whose identity remains permanently veiled throughout the book and thus functions as an allegory of infinity and bureaucracy. Haughtily K claims to be "the surveyor," summoned by the Castle, and the representative checks twice with the Castle by telephone. On being recognized by the Castle the second time, K reflects that this is propitious (since it gets him off the hook from the representative, who had wanted to banish him from the country) but also unpropitious (because it means the Castle is on to him and is giving him the chance to make his next move). K does not know, cannot know, whether he has been recognized or is only party to a fabrication.

This interpretive wavering before an enigmatic answer is a fundamental experience in the modern world: carrying on a fencing match either with a partner who seems to be responding but whose motives are inscrutable or with one whose responses can never be verified as responses. Modern men and women stand before bureaucracies and their representations or wait by telephones in the same way that sinners stood before the God who hides his face: anxiously sifting the chaos of events for signs and messages. The *deus absconditus* (hidden god) of theology no longer hides in the farthest corners of the universe; his successor has moved into the infernal machines of administration. Dante's vision of the place beyond the heavens was a kaleidoscopic reflection of spheres against spheres, a multifoliate rose of infinitely refracted light. K, like the rest of us, peers into a place where the reverberations are not optical but informational. (Game theory, uniquely appropriate for twentieth-century organizational culture, is the scientized form of this experience.) K does not know whether the permission to stay in the village is a mandate from the Castle itself, from some sleepy bureaucrat on the other end of the line trying to cover a possible failure to note K's arrival, or from the representative himself, fascinated by K's haughty certitudes. K must interpret the gestures from the Castle (if they indeed come from the Castle at all) with the same attentiveness with which augurs once monitored the sky above the *templum* for the flight of birds or the fall of stars. He must follow them with the falsificationist rationality of the modern scientist, carefully peeling away alternative hypotheses, checking the data for clerical errors, strenuously trying to avoid fudging the data with his own unconscious visions, wondering if the instrument was flawed or tapped the right information. To survive in the modern world, men and women must become diviners of inscrutable others, interpret the moods of secretaries, the words of department heads, the decisions of deans and CEOs, and shake-ups in the organization of the Kremlin, White House, or Vatican as if they were the language of some hidden, murky, remote god, content to speak only in darkness and in dreams.

Walter Benjamin once said that there are two wrong ways to read Kafka: naturally and supernaturally.[60] The point is Kafka's astounding ability to hover between the two, infinitely postponing a decision. He is the greatest theorist of organizational communication of this century. As Benjamin says, "The world of offices and registries, of musty, shabby, dark rooms, is Kafka's world."[61] Kafka is the premier existential student of bureaucracy, better than Max Weber at interpreting the dark weight of official maneuvers. Kafka's world is not quite a world of conspiratorial deceptions and evil lies that might in principle be uncovered; it is a world in which the ultimate source of all messages is hidden. He knows what is at stake in deciding what is a message, what is a projection, and what is some strange undecidable charade of people in mutual collusion who do not know it or never admit it. In bureaucratic mazes, how is one to know if the memo is a disclosure or a ruse, signal or noise? K, a surveyor, one who must read the marks of ownership, never knows if such marks express a coherent design or if whatever design exists is only a paranoid projection of an overactive interpreter.

The signs are all around us; they simply refuse to tell us how to read them. We hesitate, caught between the fear of being paranoid ("everything's a message") and the fear of missing a revelation if we act as if nothing is a message. The inability to make certain whether a sign is a projection of the self or an utterance of the other, an interpretive artifact or an objective pattern in the world, confronts a variety of social types:

60. Walter Benjamin, "Franz Kafka," in *Illuminations*, ed. Hannah Arendt (New York: Schocken, 1968), 127.
61. Benjamin, "Franz Kafka," 112.

wizards who read tea leaves or entrails, believers who receive answers to prayers, takers of the Turing test who wager on whether the conversant is a human or a smart machine, and anyone who talks with another person on any passionate, painful, or delicate topic.

Small wonder the Kabbalah should be so intriguing a model to theorists of interpretation.[62] For Kabbalah is in part the reading of intent in things where no meaning was intended—"to read what was never written," in one of Benjamin's favorite lines. As Borges notes, it is easy to ridicule the idea that every letter of the text of the Hebrew Bible was willed, so that one may find truth in numbers, acrostics, and anagrams. According to Borges, the Kabbalist vision of Scripture was of a text in which the collaboration of chance was nil. The ridicule lies in this: We see people confusing their own prodigious interpretive powers with the mind of God, confusing the statistical regularities of Hebrew consonants with divine order. The lesson of Kabbalah is to refuse contingency. Mystical styles of reading—fate, handwriting, and so on—refuse to accept the idea that the world could be meaningless. Every dot of an *i,* fall of a leaf, flight of a bird, the pattern that a snail makes, the floating fractals of clouds—are all a secret language. In one of Borges's stories, "The God's Script" the spots on a jaguar's back hold the magical name that gives its possessor all power and the key to the universe. Such readers risk absurdity—the fate of all of Kafka's heroes, quixotic battlers against castles.

The question of who owns meaning has been raised in literary theory over the past quarter century: the reader's creativity, the author's intent, the text itself, the interpretive community, the canon, or the transaction of reader and text? Or is meaning available only for lease? This question, however, is much bigger than theory; it is a question on which life and death hang in a mediated world. The question asks: Does nature speak, does God speak, does fate speak, do bureaucracies speak, or am I just making all this up? Where do projections of my self end and where do authentic signals from the other begin? Is all meaning the spider spinning of my own fertile cogitations? Can the object itself ever break through the veil? Are all the whisperings of spirit, the designs in the

---

62. See Harold Bloom, *Kabbalah and Criticism* (New York: Seabury, 1975); George Steiner, *After Babel: Aspects of Language and Translation* (New York: Oxford University Press, 1975), chap. 2; Susan A. Handelman, *The Slayers of Moses: The Emergence of Rabbinic Interpretation in Modern Literary Theory* (Albany: SUNY Press, 1982), chap. 8; Handelman, *Fragments of Redemption: Jewish Thought and Literary Theory in Benjamin, Scholem, and Levinas* (Bloomington: Indiana University Press, 1991); and Robert Alter, *Necessary Angels: Tradition and Modernity in Kafka, Benjamin, and Scholem* (Cambridge: Harvard University Press, 1991).

entrails, the answers to prayers just so much alienated human energy? Is communication anything but overlapping monologues? Did she ask me to come to her, or am I just imagining it? Did he really say he would call?

Kafka ponders the strange communication circuit of the telephone to reveal potentials for trouble in face-to-face interaction that often are skillfully kept out of sight. He explores the twilight zones in which the signal-to-noise ratio approaches zero or infinity. In both "The Neighbor" and *The Castle,* the telephone foregrounds potentials for schizophrenia, paranoia, dissimulation, and eavesdropping that lurk in everyday speech. The common world may be habitual and sound, but breakdown allows all the primal uncanniness to return. In a blackout, or the telephone's suddenly going dead, or the static caught between the stations, we discover the gaps, not the bridges. To quote a thinker whose sensibility is often akin to Kafka's, "Pathology, with its magnification and exaggeration, can make us aware of normal phenomena which we should otherwise have missed."[63]

The historicity of Kafka's insights is beyond doubt. He dwelled in a zone where the level of message scatter was unbearable, though he died (1924) before the full splendor of radio's bazaar could be appreciated. Today most communications are voices crying in the wilderness. Turn on the radio or television and you will instantly discover a limbo of missed connections: pitch artists waxing earnest about "rock-hard abs" or engagement rings, newscasters describing the latest trauma to life and limb, songsters lamenting lost love in the musical dialects of opera and country. The paraphernalia of dead letters is no longer on display only at auctions: it is the daily stuff of public communication in our time. There are so many kinds of voices in the world, said Saint Paul. Or as Sherlock Holmes sniffed concerning the "agony columns" (personals) in turn of the century London newspapers: "'Dear me!' said he, turning over the page, 'what a chorus of groans, cries, and bleatings! What a ragbag of singular happenings! . . . Bleat, Watson—unmitigated bleat!"[64] Unmitigated bleat mixed with the rare voice of truth crying in the wilderness: this is the formula for so much of modern communications, in spiritualism, the broadcast ether, and much of what we say to each other.

63. Sigmund Freud, *New Introductory Lectures on Psycho-analysis,* Great Books of the Western World, ed. Robert Maynard Hutchins, vol. 54 (1932; Chicago: Encyclopaedia Britannica, 1952), 830.

64. Arthur Conan Doyle, "The Adventure of the Red Circle," in *The Complete Sherlock Holmes* (Garden City, N.Y.: Doubleday, 1930), 2:904.

Radio: Broadcasting as Dissemination (and Dialogue)

For ye shall speak into the air.
1 COR. 14:9 KJV

In the 1920s and 1930s the radio was undoubtedly a leading source of unmitigated bleat. Radio's early history stages, with some starkness, all the issues facing communication in our time: the longing for an assured delivery and the desire to touch over long distances.

The radio signal is surely one of the strangest things we know; little wonder its ability to spirit intelligence through space elicited immediate comparisons to telepathy, séances, and angelic visitations. At any point on the earth's surface in the twentieth century, silent streams of radio voices, music, sound effects, and distress signals fill every corner of space. In any place you are reading this, messages surround and fly past you, infinitely inconspicuous, like the cicadas in the *Phaedrus,* who sing of things we cannot hear with our unaided ears. The remarkable property of the radio signal (discovered in the 1890s, the same decade when Warren and Brandeis wrote of privacy) is its inherent publicity. Electromagnetic signals radiate "to whom it may concern"; they are no respecters of persons, and they rain on the just and the unjust.

Early developers found the omnipresent quality of the radio signal a defect, seeing only dialogue as a legitimate form of communication. Like the phonograph, radio technology was first conceived as a means of point-to-point communication. Marconi was characteristic of his generation in thinking of the new technology as a wireless telegraph. But the telegraph had single termini; the airwaves did not. The looming obstacle, as with the mails before envelopes and anonymous sending and with the party line years of the telephone, was the lack of confidentiality. Anyone with a receiver set potentially had, as the parable of the sower put it, "ears to hear." Reception of the signal was inherently open-ended. As the adman Bruce Barton wrote in 1922, "Radio telephone messages can never be secret. They go out in all directions; and anyone with a machine tuned to the proper wave length can hear what you are saying to your partner in New Orleans or your sweetheart in Kenosha."[65] The inability to bar unintended recipients was a major hindrance to the profitability of wireless telegraphy and, after the audion tube in 1907, wireless telephony as well. The quest for a confidential channel, some-

---

65. Bruce Barton, "This Magic Called Radio: What Will It Mean in Your Home in the Next Ten Years?" *American Magazine,* June 1922, 11–13, 70–71, at 70.

times called "syntony" or "selectivity," was a preoccupation of early radio engineers.[66] Wanted was person-to-person connection, not a party
line.[67] The quest for "private service on a party line" was an aim for both
telephone and radio in this period.[68] Sought was the electromagnetic
equivalent of the postal envelope. The term "listening in," the eventual
verb for describing audience behavior in commercial radio, even borrowed the notion of eavesdropping on party lines, as if radio audiences
were overhearing messages not originally intended for their ears.[69]

An exhibit of the principle that cultural preconception shapes the
uses of technology as much as its internal properties do, radio "broadcasting" was not embraced until wireless technology had been in use
for a quarter of a century.[70] The origins of the term are obscure, but all
fingers point to an agricultural use not far from the *Phaedrus,* the parable
of the sower, and the nervous metaphors of Comstock and Warren and
Brandeis: the scattering of seeds. In nineteenth-century American literature, "broadcast" was most often used as an adjective meaning scattered.
In *Tom Sawyer,* "A sweep of chilly air passed by, rustling all the leaves
and snowing the flaky ashes broadcast about the fire." Thoreau wrote
that "Nature strews her nuts and flowers broadcast, and never collects
them into heaps" (*A Week on the Concord and Merrimack Rivers*). Whitman's *Leaves of Grass* praises the United States for being "essentially the
greatest poem. In the history of the earth hitherto the largest and most
stirring appear tame and orderly to their ampler largeness and stir. Here
at last is something in the doings of man that corresponds with the
broadcast doings of the day and night." The term *broadcasting* did not
at first refer to any organized social practice. The free character of things
broadcast naturally fit the radio signal's tendency to stray.

The discovery of radio as an agency of broadcasting is often attributed to David Sarnoff, future head of the National Broadcasting Company. In a now famous 1915–16 memo Sarnoff described the wireless
as a household music box.[71] The "ether" would be filled not with the

66. Hugh G. J. Aitken, *Syntony and Spark: The Origins of Radio* (New York: Wiley, 1976), and "Radio Wave Band for Every Country," *New York Times,* 23 August 1921, 4.
67. The development of cryptography before and during World War II made it technically possible to destine messages to a specific address via the airwaves. Alan Turing played a key role in this
in Great Britain, as did Claude Shannon in the United States.
68. Phrase taken from "To Stop Telephone-Eavesdropping," *Literary Digest,* 17 October 1914, 733.
69. Covert, "'We May Hear Too Much,'" 203.
70. See Susan J. Douglas, *Inventing American Broadcasting* (Baltimore: Johns Hopkins University
Press, 1987), and Susan Smulyan, *Selling Radio: The Commercialization of American Broadcasting, 1920–
1934* (Washington, D.C.: Smithsonian Institution Press, 1994).
71. David Sarnoff, "Memorandum to E. J. Nally," in *Documents of American Broadcasting,* ed.
Frank J. Kahn (Englewood Cliffs, N.J.: Prentice-Hall, 1984), 23–25.

cacophony of amateur operators making point-to-point transmissions, but with music "broadcast" to a nation of listeners—who would then want to purchase Westinghouse radio sets. One obstacle, of course, to the development of radio as pure broadcasting was the question of how to make money from a communication circuit that seemed to be a continuous potlatch or gift to the public.[72] Sarnoff lit on the idea that desirable programming would fuel acquisition of radio hardware; he had not yet discovered the eventually victorious, lamentable practice of advertiser support for programs. Sarnoff saw the ether's lack of privacy as an opportunity rather than an obstacle. The lack of a specific addressee, he thought, would be the specialty rather than a defect of radio, speaking to the great audience invisible.[73] Sarnoff's memo was a dead letter in its impact on his Westinghouse superiors, though in retrospect it seems prophetic. Maybe, like Socrates, they were suspicious of forms of communication whose reception was open-ended and whose addressees were anonymous.

World War I saw power wrested from radio amateurs by the military, the state, and large corporations. The amateur vision of the ether as a cacophonous public forum in which anyone could take part was losing ground by the 1920s and was preserved largely in the efforts of noncommercial broadcasters, themselves pushed decisively aside by the early 1930s.[74] Herbert Hoover, who as secretary of commerce was probably the chief agent in making American radio a corporate, federally regulated entity, spoke in 1922 against the wireless as a means of person-to-person contact: "The use of the radio telephone for communication between single individuals, as in the case of the ordinary telephone, is a perfectly hopeless notion. Obviously, if ten million subscribers are crying through the air for their mates they will never make a junction."[75] Like Socrates' concerns about writing, Hoover was worried about the inability of "broadcasting" to achieve "junction." The Iowa-born, Stanford-trained engineer is not usually thought of as a particularly erotic thinker, but here eros looms, trying as ever to "bridge the chasm." Imagine the myriad crisscrossing of radio telephone voices crying for their loves, lost in transit, incomplete passes, the very air full of undelivered longings. Ah, Bartleby! Ah, humanity! Saint Paul's warning to the Corin-

72. Smulyan, *Selling Radio.*

73. Daniel J. Boorstin, *The Americans: The Democratic Experience* (New York: Vintage, 1973), 391.

74. Robert W. McChesney, *Telecommunications, Mass Media, and Democracy: The Battle for the Control of U.S. Broadcasting, 1928–1935* (New York: Oxford University Press, 1993).

75. Quoted in Richard A. Schwarzlose, "Technology and the Individual: The Impact of Innovation on Communication," in *Mass Media between the Wars, 1918–1941*, ed. Catherine L. Covert and John D. Stevens (Syracuse: Syracuse University Press, 1984), 100.

thians who practiced glossolalia without interpreters could be motto of every broadcaster: You will be speaking into the air (1 Cor. 14:9). Like Paul, Hoover wanted to control the confusion of tongues.

Eventually radio became officially defined as an agent of public communication. The key question in the 1920s and early 1930s was its regulatory status: Was radio a common carrier or something else? This question involved the old couplet of dialogue and dissemination. "Common carriage" was a nineteenth-century category that included shipping lines, elevators, and above all railroads. The Interstate Commerce Act (1887) gave the Interstate Commerce Commission (ICC) jurisdiction over "common carriers," which were ceded a "natural monopoly" in return for which they had to offer all comers equal service and submit their rates to the ICC for approval. The Mann-Elkins Act (1910) and the Transportation Act (1920) expanded the definition of "common carrier" to include "transmission of intelligence by wire or wireless," thus placing the telegraph and telephone under ICC jurisdiction.[76]

But radio had difficulty fitting the point-to-point model. Heather Wessely captures the contrast well: "Rail transport is not a service designed with a potential terminus in every household."[77] Radio spoke into the blue yonder. A key case before the ICC, *Sta-Shine Products Co. v. Station WGBB* (1932), raised the question whether radio broadcasts entailed a "transmission of intelligence." Should the ICC treat radio stations as common carriers, thus regulating advertising rates? The decision declared radio outside the ICC's jurisdiction, since "no service is performed at the receiving end by the broadcasting company, similar to the service performed by common carriers." Broadcasting lacked "the boy in the blue uniform who rings the door bell and who brings the message itself." Common carriers saw to it that people receive their cargoes or messages, but broadcasting made no effort to ensure delivery. "Unless one has a radio receiving set properly attuned, he will never get and is not expected to get the intelligence, whether it be instruction, entertainment, or advertising, sent out from the broadcasting station."[78] By the standards of common carriage, broadcasting was a deformed

76. The relevant documents can be found in Bernard Schwartz, *The Economic Regulation of Business and Industry: A Legislative History of U.S. Regulatory Agencies*, 5 vols. (New York: Chelsea House, 1973). Congressman James R. Mann also wrote the Mann Act of 1910, prohibiting "the transportation of women across state lines for immoral purposes." His legislation dealt with all sorts of common carriers.

77. Heather A. Wessely, "Culture, History and the Public Interest: Developing a Broadcasting Service for the United States" (manuscript, Department of Communication Studies, University of Iowa, 1993), 54.

78. *Sta-Shine Products Company, Inc. v. Station WGBB of Freeport NY* 188 ICC 271 (1932); quotations from 276, 277–78.

communication circuit, since the "transmission of intelligence" was left to chance.

The conclusive definition of broadcasting was left to the jurisdiction of a New Deal agency, the Federal Communications Commission (FCC). The contrast between broadcasting and common carriage became a cornerstone of United States broadcasting policy in the Communications Act of 1934. According to section 3(h) of the act, "A person engaged in radio broadcasting shall not, insofar as such person is so engaged, be deemed a common carrier."[79] Common carriers operate point-to-point, deliver their goods to a definite address, and must be accessible to anyone and accountable for the tariffs they charge. A common carrier is characterized by "the separation of the content from the conduit" and lacks editorial discretion over the messages private people send.[80] Thus, if you shout obscenities into a phone, the phone company is exempt from prosecution; if you do so into a radio microphone, the station may have to answer to the FCC. Common carriers must be message blind and sender blind, but never receiver blind. Broadcasters, if not quite audience blind, see their audiences through a glass darkly.[81] Broadcasting, as legally defined, involves privately controlled transmission but public reception, whereas common carriage involves publicly controlled transmission but private reception. The two models possess striking symmetry. A common carrier offers universal access to transmission and restricted access to reception, whereas broadcasting offers restricted access to transmission and universal access to reception. Like Socrates in the *Phaedrus,* common carriage seeks to guarantee the delivery of the seed; like Jesus in the parable of the sower, broadcasting focuses on scattering the message to all (even if the actual reception is spotty).

The Communications Act of 1934 thus installed the ancient notion of dissemination in the heart of a modern technology in the guise of "broadcasting." As it developed, however, the term acquired a double sense. In its generic use, it refers to transmission over the air, but "broadcasting" as a legal term refers not to the diverse practices of the airwaves but to an idealized configuration among speakers and audiences. It con-

79. As Justice White put it in 1979: "The language of § 3 (h) is unequivocal; it stipulates that broadcasters shall not be treated as common carriers." *FCC v. Midwest Video Corporation,* in *Documents of American Broadcasting,* ed. Frank J. Kahn (Englewood Cliffs, N.J.: Prentice-Hall, 1984), 364.

80. T. Barton Carter, Marc A. Franklin, and Jay B. Wright, *The First Amendment and the Fifth Estate: Regulation of Electronic Mass Media* (Mineola, N.Y.: Foundation, 1986), 395.

81. This legal distinction may in part be a post hoc version of the division of labor agreed upon in 1926 between RCA and AT&T, leaving the former with the air/broadcasting and the latter with wires/telephony. See Noobar R. Danielian, *AT&T: The Story of Industrial Conquest* (New York: Vanguard, 1939).

jures visions of the agora, the town meeting, or the "public sphere"; broadcasting is supposed to be more a town crier summoning citizens to assembly than a midway barker inviting the curious to spend their nickels on the freak show. By defining broadcasting in terms of the public interest, the 1934 Communications Act articulated a vision of the audience—a civic one, the audience as disinterested public—that fit the technology's lack of confidentiality and gave a lofty lineage to a set of practices that owed as much to the circus as to the polis. In fact, by the 1930s, commercial broadcasters had developed a number of techniques for routing audiences and managing the junction. The brief shining moment of dissemination was washed over by a flood of dialogism.[82]

"THEY WILL NEVER MAKE A JUNCTION" William James had compared the brains of sitters at séances to Marconi stations that pick up and amplify impossibly faint and distant signals of departed minds, just as Rudyard Kipling had compared very early radio communications to a séance. The question in both realms was similar: authentication in psychical research, identification and intimacy in early radio. The issue was how to make sure you reach the one you really want to reach. Throughout the interwar years, theorists and practitioners of radio recognized its strange ability, like the telephone, to put speaker and hearer in "contact" without physical presence or personal acquaintance. Radio carried what Rudolf Arnheim in 1936 called "voices without bodies" and breached limits of space, time, and audibility that had once seemed natural. Organizing radio's connection to the bodies of the communicants was a chief prerequisite of its naturalization into daily life. Without attempting anything close to a cultural history of broadcasting here, I will argue that securing mainstream acceptance for radio required means to close the obvious gaps of distance, disembodiment, and dissemination. Hence the history of commercial radio in the interwar years is of central interest for understanding the twentieth-century obsession with communication breakdown and its remedies. This history is a kind of moving meditation on how to reduce radio's uncanniness quotient.[83]

The distance between speaker and audience in radio replayed idealism's separate rooms and telephony's severing of a conversation into two disconnected halves. DX-ing in particular, the quest for a signal from remote stations and still a common sport among ham radio opera-

---

82. Thus far I have used "dialogism" to mean the ideology that dialogue is the morally supreme form of communication. Here I use it in a different sense, closer to Mikhail Bakhtin, to refer to the multiple voices that layer discourse.

83. My account will regrettably be limited largely to United States sources.

tors, reveals something about the curious ontology of the radio signal and the longings associated with communication at a distance. Communication afar is always erotic in the broad sense—a yearning for contact. The key call in DX-ing is "CQ," from the phrase "seek you." One fictional account of a 1924 family's DX listening describes it as "a sacrificial rite." A son adjusts the dials with excruciating precision to a spot where he hopes to catch the signal of a distant station; instead he hears emanations from the great beyond: "Out of the air comes the sizzle of static. The carrying wave of station after station whistles shrilly, cheerful mischievous devils signaling to presumptuous mortal man from somewhere in the empyrean." It is an evident challenge to find the one true signal, in spite of interference from other stations, the weather, and celestial beings. "Now he catches the murmur of a voice so faint and far that it might be in sober earnest a message from another world."[84] Such "DX-fishing," with its goal to hear the call letters of far-off stations, was a kind of quest for extraterrestrial intelligence *avant la lettre:* the search for the distant transmission amid the shrieks and pops of space. "Behind the music one still hears a wailing of winds lost somewhere in the universe and very unhappy about it."[85] In the early years of radio static was often heard as a sign of distant worlds; "celestial caterwauling," Bruce Bliven called it.[86] Another commentator noted, "The delicate mechanism of the radio has caught and brought to the ears of us earth dwellers the noises that roar in the space between the worlds."[87] Like Dorothy Parker's telephone call to God, or William James's quest to discern the will to communicate, DX-ing is an allegory of faith in our times.

Radio's gaps between transmission and reception could mean comic mockery as well as rites of supplication. As with the telephone, radio invited a new decorum for behavior in conditions of mutual absence.[88] The invisibility and domestic setting of the radio listening experience made for loosened norms of attentiveness compared with those that

84. Bruce Bliven, "The Legion Family and the Radio: What We Hear When We Tune In," *Century Magazine,* October 1924, 811–18, at 814. On the numinous overtones of early radio static, see Douglas, *Inventing American Broadcasting,* 304–5.

85. Bruce Bliven, "The Ether Will Now Oblige," *New Republic,* 15 February 1922, 328.

86. Bliven, "Ether Will Now Oblige," 328. A wonderful account of the literary and metaphysical aspects of radio static is James A. Connor, "Radio Free Joyce: *Wake* Language and the Experience of Radio," *James Joyce Quarterly* 30–31 (summer–fall 1993): 825–43.

87. A. Leonard Smith, "Broadcasting to the Millions," *New York Times,* 19 February 1922, sec. 7, 6, quoted in Douglas, *Inventing American Broadcasting,* 304.

88. The most sensitive students of the social contract between audiences and broadcast events are Daniel Dayan and Elihu Katz, *Media Events: The Live Broadcasting of History* (Cambridge: Harvard University Press, 1992), esp. chap. 5, and Paddy Scannell, "Public Service Broadcasting and Modern Public Life," *Media, Culture, and Society* 11, 2 (1989): 135–66.

had developed in bourgeois theater. Bruce Bliven noted in 1924 that most political orators, if aware of "the ribald comments addressed to the stoical loud-speaker" of the home receiver, would seek other jobs. "The comments of the family range from Bill's, 'Is *that* so!' down to Howard's irreverent, 'Aw, shut your face, you poor hunk of cheese!'"[89] Home listening allowed oratory to be received in a mood of chronic flippancy. Likewise, one could exit live performances midstream without embarrassing anyone. "If the whole audience 'signed off' (disconnected the instruments) Miss Altenbrite would be none the wiser, and would send her trills just as sweetly through ninety thousand square miles of night."[90] More serious questions were raised in England about whether radio audiences should wear hats or sit when hearing an address from the queen.[91] In each case the question was, How binding is a relationship that lacks any contract of mutuality? What kind of moral or political obligation can ethereal contact compel? What is "communication" without bodies or presence?

Anxieties about contact were not confined to the receiving end; senders also faced the prospect of barriers to communication. Having to speak into a soulless microphone was a common complaint in the 1920s and 1930s from entertainers used to performing before live audiences. The microphone replaced the faces and souls of the listeners. In a 1924 radio address, Herbert Hoover worried again about the lack of junction, complaining about having to speak into "the deadly inexpressive microphone. . . . We need a method by which a speaker over the radio may sense the feelings of his radio audience. A speaker before a public audience knows what hisses and applause mean; he cuts his speech short or adjusts himself to it."[92] Critic Gilbert Seldes in 1927 noted the queasy feeling of the radio performer before an invisible audience in even more graphic terms: "The microphone, which seems so alive with strange vital fluids when you begin, goes suddenly dead; you think that somewhere in the next room the operator has cut off the current; that everywhere everyone has tuned out. You wonder who these people are who may be listening, in what obscurity, with what hostility. And when you listen to the radio yourself, you know no more."[93] Seldes was concerned, like other critics of dissemination, about the loss of "strange vital flu-

89. Bliven, "Legion Family," 817.
90. Bliven, "Ether Will Now Oblige," 329.
91. Scannell, "Public Service Broadcasting."
92. Radio Talk by Secretary Hoover, 26 March 1924, box 48, Herbert Hoover Presidential Library; quoted in Wessely, *Culture, History and the Public Interest,* 44–45.
93. Gilbert Seldes, "Listening In," *New Republic,* 23 March 1927, 140–41.

ids," the current's being turned off, the enigma of the missing audience. He found himself in the position of speaker to the dead. His concerns—the unknown listeners, the lack of interaction, the speaking into the air—replicate the larger fears of solipsism and communication breakdown raging through the art, literature, and philosophy of the interwar years.[94] Indeed, the philosophical concerns of a Bradley or Hocking, that the other may be utterly inaccessible, recur in the mundane setting of the radio studio. Broadcasting restages the scenario of idealist philosophy: communicating deaf and blind through impermeable walls. Both broadcasters and audiences ran the risk of sending dead letters to each other. The twentieth century is full of discourses produced in what Paul Ricoeur would call situations of exploded dialogue.

COMPENSATORY DIALOGISM   How to compensate for the fact that people could be in touch without appearing "in person" was an acute question in the early history of radio and its development into a huge commercial entertainment empire. New forms of authenticity, intimacy, and touch not based on immediate physical presence had to be found. The hunt for communicative prostheses—compensations for lost presences—was vigorous in the culture of commercial radio in the 1920s and 1930s. Broadcasters quickly recognized the risk of alienating the affections of listeners and invented diverse strategies to replace what had apparently been taken away: the presence of fellow listeners, a conversational dynamic, and a personal tone. Commercial broadcasting was quite self-conscious about overcoming the listener's sense of being stuck in a mass audience without mutual interaction or awareness, with one-way flow of communication and anonymous styles of talk. New discursive strategies were designed to compensate for the medium's structural lacks. The aim was to restore lost presence.

"The pivotal fact," writes Paddy Scannell, "is that the broadcasters, while they control the discourse, do not control the communicative context." That the site of reception lies beyond the institutional authority of the broadcaster "powerfully drives the communicative style and manner of broadcasting to approximate to the norms not of public forms of talk, but to those of ordinary, informal conversation." He stunningly argues that radio broadcasting marked not the beginning but the end of mass communication as the address of large undifferentiated

94. See Douglas Kahn and Gregory Whitehead, eds., *The Wireless Imagination: Sound, Radio, and the Avant-Garde* (Cambridge: MIT Press, 1992).

audiences.[95] Intimate sound spaces, domestic genres, cozy speech styles, and radio personalities all helped bridge the address gap in radio. In clear contrast to the regulatory language of the FCC, which stipulated that all broadcasting be done in the public interest, one observer noted that on the radio you "are not speaking to the Public. You are speaking to a family much like the families that live on the next block."[96] A 1931 article in the *Journal of Home Economics* put it bluntly: "Radio is an extension of the home."[97] Little wonder the light domestic drama and the soap opera have been the staples of broadcasting: like their audiences, the genres are set in living rooms. If official policy defined radio as a public space, those who actually used the new medium knew better. The styles of address in radio talk that evolved in the United States were a far cry from the stump orator or the Enlightenment public sphere. The heroes of radio in the 1930s were crooners, comics, and avuncular politicians, people who knew how to "reach out and touch" their audiences. The system's lifeblood was advertising, and audiences were its product. Some kind of interaction with them was crucial. Audience ratings and radio research aimed to play Eros by bridging the chasm.[98] The fostering of "we-ness," dialogical inclusion, and intimate address have remained at the core of broadcast discourse to this day.

The glad-handing joviality of much of American commercial radio culture in the 1930s and beyond was not, of course, a natural outgrowth of the technology but a cultural adaptation to specific political economic conditions. Broadcast culture could have remained starkly impersonal; up to the mid-1920s, for instance, most announcers were literally anonymous, known largely by code names, in what was a conscious policy of station owners to suppress radio "personalities" (lest their fame lead to greater salary demands, as of course occurred).[99] Announcers could have remained in the paradigm of telephone operators, passive

95. Paddy Scannell, "Introduction: The Relevance of Talk," in *Broadcast Talk*, ed. Paddy Scannell (Newbury Park, Calif.: Sage, 1991), 1–9, at 3.

96. Morse Salisbury, "Writing the Home Economics Radio Program," *Journal of Home Economics* 24 (1932): 954–60, at 957.

97. Morse Salisbury, "Signs of the Times," *Journal of Home Economics* 23 (1931): 847.

98. Paul F. Lazarsfeld and Frank N. Stanton, "Introduction," in *Radio Research, 1941* (New York: Sloan, Duell, and Pearce, 1942), vii, make this point explicitly. On the historical centrality of the ratings to the broadcasting industry, see Eileen R. Meehan, "Heads of Households and Ladies of the House: Gender, Genre, and Broadcast Ratings, 1929–1990," in *Ruthless Criticism: New Perspectives in U.S. Communications History*, ed. William S. Solomon and Robert W. McChesney (Minneapolis: University of Minnesota Press, 1993), 204–21.

99. Erik Barnouw, *A Tower in Babel: A History of Broadcasting in the United States to 1933* (New York: Oxford University Press, 1966), 163–67.

channels for connecting other people, which was in fact more the model for the BBC. Instead, a policy of "unmitigated bleat" ensued.

One prong of the policy was a new chatty tone. Intimate forms of talk were to replace the harsh open-air soapbox voice. "The normal tone of transmission," wrote Rudolf Arnheim, "has to be that of a light, intimate conversation between broadcaster and listener." Many speakers "bellow through the microphone to an audience of millions," but Arnheim seriously doubted that radio appealed to the millions as masses: radio "talks to everyone individually, not to everyone together. . . . the radio-speaker should proceed softly and as if 'à deux.'" Arnheim prescribed bonhomie rather than bombast.[100] One writer said of educational radio, "I don't want a lecture, I just want a chat in my everyday language."[101]

Dialogic forms were another technique of simulating presence. In such techniques as crooning, direct address of listeners, dramatic dialogue, "feuds" between stars, fan letters, fan clubs, contests and promotional giveaways, or radio comedy, the remote audience was invited to become an imaginary participant in the world of the characters and of its fellow auditors. Radio comedy discovered the live studio audience and the stooge as solutions to the lack of live rapport. The in-house audience was a sounding board for the comic, and the stooge served as "straight man" for gags, both incorporating an internal circuit of sending and receiving in the broadcast. Since a mutual loop of talk could not be achieved with the dispersed listeners, it was simulated within the radio program. Radio programs not only transmitted voices but pretended to receive them back from the great audience invisible. Entertainers learned how to work one end of the telephone line when the other was piped into the millions. The ventriloquistic technique of keeping up both sides of the conversation persists in broadcast discourse. Perhaps the best emblem of such dialogism is the immensely popular comedy duo of the late 1930s and 1940s, Edgar Bergen and Charlie McCarthy. Two voices in dialogue, both produced by the same body. Two characters, one of them a dummy. It would be hard to find a more perfect symbol of radio's communication circuit.

Finally, techniques were explored to provide listeners with a sense of membership in a live audience. As Hadley Cantril and Gordon W. Allport noted in their very astute *Psychology of Radio* (1935), "No crowd can exist, especially no radio crowd, unless the members have a 'lively

---

100. Rudolf Arnheim, *Radio* (1936; New York: Arno Press, 1986), 71, 72.
101. Salisbury, "Signs of the Times," 851.

impression of universality.' Each individual must believe that others are thinking as he thinks and are sharing his emotions." A "consciousness of kind" had to be raised, via "social facilitation," such as the sound of laughter, applause, interaction, coughing, ahems, heckling, or other audible signs of a live assembly. Tapping into the older contrast between crowds and publics, and anticipating the more recent notion of imagined communities, they argued that radio audiences were distinctly "consociate" rather than "congregate" assemblies: united in imagination, not in location. But they also noted that a very different "social contract" prevailed in each type of collectivity; they did not forget the insuperability of touch.[102]

Ironically, the concept of "mass communication," as minted in the 1950s, suggests only the ways that mass media seem to fall short of face-to-face talk: vast audiences, one-way messages, and impersonal address.[103] What it misses is the very lifeblood of commercial media culture as we have come to know it. The early history of broadcast talk consisted largely in the attempt to create a world in which audiences would feel like participants. Today both the programming and reception of most commercial media, in the United States at least, actively cultivate a sense of intimate relations between persona and audience. Media culture is a lush jungle of fictional worlds where "everyone knows your name," celebrities and politicians address audiences by first names, and conversational formats proliferate. The conventional concept of "mass communication" captures only the abstract potential for alienation in large-scale message systems, not the multiple tactics of interpersonal appeal that have evolved to counter it.[104] Early broadcasters saw "mass society" looming and tried to stop it.

HOC EST CORPUS, HOCUS-POCUS But it could not be stopped entirely. Despite the many compensations to make up for the loss of face-to-face communication, including a tonal shift toward snugger modes of address and the simulation of personal interaction, the relationship of body to body could not be restored fully over the ether any more than a telephone marriage could be consummated by wire. A creepy surplus remained. The unease about the new spectral bodies of broadcasting

102. Hadley Cantril and Gordon W. Allport, *The Psychology of Radio* (New York: Harper, 1935).

103. Charles R. Wright, *Mass Communication: A Sociological Perspective* (New York: Random House, 1959), 11–14, offers a classic definition of "mass communication" in this way.

104. Donald Horton and Richard R. Wohl, "Mass Communication and Para-social Interaction: Observations on Intimacy at a Distance" (1956), in *Inter/Media: Interpersonal Communication in a Media World*, ed. Gary Gumpert and Robert Cathcart (New York: Oxford University Press, 1982), 188–211.

could not always be suppressed. A few genres—horror drama, for instance—played radio's uncanny potential to the hilt. The Shadow knew that under commercial broadcasting's carefully wrought artifice of intimate familiarity lurked the loneliness of the long gaps, the eerie calls of distant voices, and the touch of oozing ectoplasm, strange flesh from afar. American radio in the 1920s and 1930s was explicitly a "live" medium, and the effort to breathe life into the spirits emerging from the loudspeaker after a long journey often involved the strangest of resurrectionist techniques.

Liveness in radio was the effort to break the connection between death and distance. The term "live" arose as life's uncontested dominion, its naturalness, ended. The *Oxford English Dictionary* gives such phrases as "two live plants in flower pots" (1856), a locution presumably motivated by plants such as immortelles, flowers that retain their color after death, and "live cattle" (1897), presumably in contrast to the slaughtered. In both cases, "live" explicitly contrasts with something dead. "Live" could also mean "containing unexpended energy," as in a live shell, cartridge, or match. A "live wire" carried electrical current and could provide power or shocks. An 1875 dictionary of mechanics defined a "live-axle," one year before the telephone and two years before the phonograph, as "one communicating power; in contradistinction to a dead or blind axle." Finally, the more recent term "live action" means the filming of actors and events as opposed to animation, titling, or other kinds of image manipulation. "Live" is the prosthetic form of life, something that announces its authenticity against potentially deceptive substitutes. Its fundamental sense is contrastive: "live" means "not dead."

"Live" also means "communicating power," and such is crucial to modern communications. Because life could be simulated by recording and transmitting media, liveness became something eagerly sought. Notions of life were important in the terminology of early moving image technologies: zoetrope, bioscope, vitagraph, cinema (from Greek *kineo*, to move, as in "kinetic"), motion pictures, and movies. By the 1920s, "live" came to mean simultaneous broadcasting. A sociologist in 1928, predicting a greater future for the radio than the phonograph, made the explicit equation of simultaneity with life and recording with death: "The radio does not transmit 'dead' material as does the phonograph, but present and 'living' events."[105] In a "live" performance, the body is present in the flesh. "Live" means that contingency is still possible, that

---

105. E. W. Burgess, "Communication," *American Journal of Sociology* 33 (1928): 125.

the energy is actual, and that a new and singular event can take place. Here again, in the bowels of the new machines of simulation, the old marker of authenticity—the mortal body itself—reappeared.

Freud wrote *Civilization and Its Discontents* in 1929, amid such transformations in the shape of the solo body and the body politic. For Freud, eros and civilization were forever at odds. Eros was the force of coupling and was essentially dyadic, but civilization demanded a larger scope and lowered intensity of affective bonds. "Sexual love is a relationship between two individuals in which a third can only be superfluous or disturbing, whereas civilization depends on relationships between a considerable number of individuals." He could have been talking about the mass address of radio, but he was not. He thought the work of civilization was inevitably to bind individuals, families, nations, and races into larger and larger libidinal units. But the stinger in his story was that an authentically democratic eros was impossible: its price was repression. Nature had loaded the deck against human happiness; the scale of our affections was mismatched with the demands of social order. Civilization sought to rechannel our finite libidinal energy onto its approved objects.

We ought to count Freud as one of the most prescient thinkers of mass communication, of what happens when dyadic form (communication) is technologically stretched to a gigantic degree (mass). His comments on modern media featured the stubborn fact of human embodiment, our twin entanglements in biology and culture. He made a point more commonly associated with McLuhan thirty-five years later, but with a more tragic twist: that media are extensions of the human body. Each medium for Freud was an attempt to cover a human lack, to fill the gap between ourselves and the gods. Telephony has extended our ears, allowing us to hear our distant loved ones, as photography and phonography have substituted for memory. And yet we are none the happier. Finitude recurs with a vengeance. "Man has, as it were, become a kind of prosthetic god. When he puts on all his auxiliary organs he is truly magnificent; but those organs have not grown onto him and they still give him much trouble at times." Freud knew what struggles it took to fit our bodies into the new auxiliary organs of the media.[106]

In addition to the deep reasons for nervousness about radio—its distance, deathliness, disembodiment, and dissemination—there were sound substantive reasons as well. Radio was the latest chapter in Ameri-

106. Sigmund Freud, *Civilization and Its Discontents,* trans. Joan Riviere (1930; New York: Norton, 1961), 39–45. During the writing of the book, Freud wore an irritating prosthesis in the roof of his mouth as a consequence of his throat cancer.

can hucksterism. Resistance to advertising on radio was widespread in the 1920s and 1930s and waning but still strong in the 1940s.[107] Radio called forth not only entertainers and journalists but confidence men whose goat-gland operations and mind cures promised health and rejuvenation to the millions. What Cooley thought had disappeared was back with a vengeance: the need to differentiate between the ghosts and the frauds.

Many of the most successful performers exploited liveness, in the sense of either simultaneity or nondeath, to cut through public anxieties about fakery and duplication in the radio world. A token of the live body was extended across the waves to assure truthfulness. During one of his first fireside chats, for instance, the consummate radio performer President Franklin Delano Roosevelt "suddenly burst forth with 'Where's that glass of water?'" After a pause to drink, he explained to his listeners: "My friends, it's very hot here in Washington tonight."[108] Erik Barnouw's embellished account of the episode calls this "a simple human action that may have been sophisticated showmanship."[109] The gesture was powerful because a "simple human" need was enough to interrupt a presidential address. In the Elizabethan language of the king's two bodies, the body mortal briefly trumped the body politic.[110] By letting his audience in on his thirst and thus revealing the finitude he shared with them, FDR proved his sincerity. He was "one of us." FDR not only wove policies, he interrupted their enunciation to affirm something more profound. Polished words would be too slick. Imperfection was the guarantee of truth in a medium in which the polio-stricken body of the president could be converted into a Voice that reassured Americans everywhere. The intrusion of thirst is a classic reality effect, an undercutting of the medium that actually plays to its strengths. Take, he said, *hoc est corpus meum.*

FDR, like other radio performers who secured the trust or adoration of their audiences, learned—to use James's distinction—to assert the "will to communicate" over the "will to personate." A synecdoche of one's unique human individuality could lift the veil of the commod-

---

107. Smulyan, *Selling Radio,* and Paul F. Lazarsfeld and Patricia L. Kendall, *Radio Listening in America* (New York: Prentice-Hall, 1948), 59–80.

108. "The President Broadcasts: Confronted with Mikes, Cameras, and Radio Engineers, Roosevelt Pauses for a Glass of Water," *Broadcasting* 5, 3 (1933): 8. This outburst is not recorded in the official record of the fireside chats. Thanks to Joy Elizabeth Hayes for advice on FDR and radio.

109. Erik Barnouw, *The Golden Web: A History of Broadcasting in the United States, 1933–1953* (New York: Oxford University Press, 1968), 8.

110. Ernst H. Kantorowicz, *The King's Two Bodies: A Study in Mediaeval Political Theology* (Princeton: Princeton University Press, 1957).

ity.[111] The body and its pain became the last frontier of authenticity, the bedrock immune to fakery, a source of private fact. The flesh provided the ultimate ethos. The religious notion (much older than the mass media per se) that a larger social body could be formed by distributing tokens of an individual body recurs in radio. We ought not to forget that "mass" in "mass communication" can be taken as a noun as well as an adjective.[112]

Like Freud, Theodor W. Adorno thought all such compensations ill-fitting annoyances. There was no more formidable critic of the commercialized culture of sincerity. Simulated community among colisteners or staged interaction between audiences and radio stars were, he thought, so much hocus-pocus (a term that derives from a cynical misunderstanding of the phrase from the Latin Mass, *hoc est corpus*). Adorno's view of media audiences was more subtle than the frequent caricature as brainwashed zombies or infantilized masses. The danger of radio was not its rabble-rousing, but its individualizing ability, its skill at tucking the listener into a cocoon of unreflective security or sadistic laughter. Mass culture did not instill passivity; rather, it shunted enormous energies into shock absorption. Solidarity within the audience was at best a fetish, as was audience participation in the radio world. His rogues' gallery of "regressive listeners" jitterbugging their way into false ecstasy is the epitome of idolatrous interaction with distant objects. The radio ham, for instance, "is only interested in the fact that he hears and succeeds in inserting himself, with his private equipment, into the public mechanism, without exerting even the slightest influence on it."[113] This extraordinary description (an accurate rendering of Adorno's German) complains of the perversion of an authentic and fertile erotic dyad. As in Seldes's description and the *Phaedrus,* the specter of wasted seed recurs. Like Freud, with whom he found much to dispute, Adorno took the dyad as the insuperable site of genuine eros. The libidinal structure of radio, however, could only be either solitary or plural. Ever the Hegelian Marxist, he thought authentic interaction could occur only when one subject encountered another in its objectivity. Radio address had to

111. Allison McCracken, "White Men Can't Sing Ballads: Crooning and Cultural Anxiety, 1927–1933" (manuscript, American Studies Program, University of Iowa, 1998).

112. John Durham Peters, "Beyond Reciprocity: Public Communication as a Moral Ideal," in *Communication, Culture, and Community: Liber Amicorum James Stappers,* ed. Ed Hollander, Coen van der Linden, and Paul Rutten (Houten, Netherlands: Bohn, Stafleu, van Loghum, 1995), 41–50.

113. Theodor W. Adorno, "On the Fetish-Character in Music and the Regression of Listening," in *The Essential Frankfurt School Reader,* ed. Andrew Arato and Eike Gebhardt (1938; New York: Continuum, 1982), 270–99, 286–99, 293. See also Adorno, "Analytical Study of the NBC *Music Appreciation Hour,"* *Musical Quarterly* 78, 2 (1994): 325–77 (written 1938–41).

be structurally insincere owing to the generality of its solicitations. Like Marx on money, Adorno saw in radio a form of pimpery. As Adorno's colleague Leo Lowenthal complained, attempts at personal address involved a slippage between general and individual address: "Especially for you means all of you."[114] Like Socrates, Adorno is concerned about mass eros as one prominent communication disorder.

If Adorno's radio studies exposed the failure to craft symbolic participation at a distance, Robert K. Merton's (1946) study of the all-American singer Kate Smith examined a successful ritual performance. Smith's smashing success at mass persuasion in a one-day war bond drive on 21 September 1943 stemmed, Merton argued, from what audiences perceived as her sincerity. Many Hollywood stars had gone on the air to raise funds for the war effort, but few had achieved Smith's success. Merton borrowed George Herbert Mead's definition of sincerity as a speaker's use of "verbal symbols which evidently affect himself as he intends them to affect his audience. Sincerity provides for a mutual experience."[115] For Merton, Smith was not just staging an interaction; her audience really was getting something from her.

The key to her link with the audience was her "propaganda of the deed." Smith did not exempt herself from the sacrifice she asked of her audience. Her own live radio performance, eighteen hours in a single day, put her body on the line, just as she asked her audiences to put their money on the line. Doing a physically exhausting radio campaign without complaint allayed suspicions of fakery well enough to bind a national audience in a moment of crisis. A recorded performance would have lost the crucially persuasive presence of the live body. If, somehow, it was revealed that it had all been transcribed and her responses to listener calls had been fabricated, Smith's sincerity would have vanished, even if the two performances were identical. The audience may have believed in the metaphysics of presence, but bad metaphysics may still be the basis of persuasive rhetoric. Smith was a sacrificial surrogate who modeled behavior for the listening audience in the best style of ancient expiation. Her lack of sex appeal, Merton found, was also part of her credibility. Kate Smith was not Rita Hayworth; no glamour corrupted her sincerity. The irreality of Hollywood faded, as Merton argued, in the drama of a voice in a race against exhaustion. From the Greeks

114. Leo Lowenthal, "Biographies in Popular Magazines," in *Radio Research, 1942–1943*, ed. Paul F. Lazarsfeld and Frank N. Stanton (New York: Sloan, Duell, and Pearce, 1944), 507–48, 581–85.
115. Robert K. Merton, with Marjorie Fiske and Alberta Curtis, *Mass Persuasion: The Social Psychology of a War Bond Drive* (New York: Harper, 1946), 105.

onward, suffering has been taken as a guarantee of truth; the words of the dying are still given special testimonial value. Pain is often still taken to limit the motive to fabricate.[116] Kate Smith had found the mother lode of communicative authenticity: the body speaking from its pain.

If Adorno punctured incessant manipulation, Merton discovered achievements that transcended it. Merton wanted to save us from anomie; Adorno wanted to save us from abuse. Adorno saw in broadcasting a botched attempt at reconciliation; Merton saw a felicitous suspension of unbelief, a momentary clearing in the cloud banks of cynicism. Characteristically, Adorno eschewed the "pseudoindividualism" of mass appeals, whereas "pseudo-Gemeinschaft" worried Merton; their ideal is evident in what they most fear is corrupted. In sum, conflict versus integration, ideological unmasking versus symbolic togetherness, direct participation versus collective representation—the debate between Adorno and Merton represents the intersection of the two great rival traditions of modern social theory, Marx and Durkheim. For Adorno, solidarity was impossible unless it rested on real interests or personal bonds. Participation required bodily involvement or expenditure. For Merton, mass rituals could be vicarious interactions for which "direct" personal involvement was irrelevant. Adorno and Merton debated, in short, whether mass *communication* was possible. Symbols could be dispersed to vast numbers: the question was the kind of relationships they forged. Merton left judgments of sincerity up to the audience; Adorno thought this stance was a recipe for mass deception. The debate about the social use of radio, much more than the ill-starred collaboration of Adorno and Paul Lazarsfeld, is the key conflict in the history of mass communication theory in this century.[117] The question turns not on administrative versus critical visions of research, but on authenticity versus fakery in communicative ties across distances.

The politics of mass communication theory turn on one's vision of the possibility of media-made community. The question is, Can you take part without being there in the flesh? Can an audience be said to participate in a remote event? The bodily context of all communication

116. Page DuBois, *Torture and Truth* (London: Routledge, 1991); Elaine Scarry, *The Body in Pain: The Making and Unmaking of the World* (New York: Oxford University Press, 1985).

117. The intellectual pivot of debates about the stakes of mass communication research was long the botched effort to fuse the critical theory of Adorno and the empirical research of Lazarsfeld at the Princeton Radio Project, 1938–41. See Todd Gitlin, "Media Sociology: The Dominant Paradigm," *Theory and Society* 6 (1978): 205–53; David E. Morrison, "*Kultur* and Culture: The Case of Theodor Adorno and Paul F. Lazarsfeld," *Social Research* 45, 2 (1978): 331–55; and Elihu Katz, "Communications Research since Lazarsfeld," *Public Opinion Quarterly* 51 (1987): S25–S45.

is inescapable. Merton's argument that symbols working at a distance can afford authentic sociability has an elective affinity with the interests of the media industries, whose economic well-being depends on convincing audiences to trust the sincerity of distant testimonials. Yet Adorno's thesis that all distant relationships are false can give us no antidote to the mutual distrust that eats at us all, for which relationships are untouched by distance (as he well knew)? The analysis of the falsity can be interminable. Adorno's negative dialectics constantly undermines the dream of reconciliation between people—in the name of that dream. Removing false hope is a fine service so long as it does not damage our animal faith, since all action rests on strategic illusion. The decision as to which thinker is right may turn on whether we are more afraid of being suckered by power or deprived of hope.

In the apparently innocuous questions whether Kate Smith can be sincere over the air and whether such a performance can afford a "mutual" experience, then, is found the intellectual and political heart of mass communication theory, the question of mediation—in other words, the possibility of interaction without personal or physical contact. Adorno finds the idea of audience participation in the radio world the worst kind of projection; Merton finds it to be a ritual act of solidarity with real consequences. Merton believed in the possibility, at least on extraordinary occasions, of an expanded social body, joined at a distance. Adorno was suspicious of any attempt to expand the human symbolically or technically. For him no "auxiliary organs," as Freud called media, could heal the body's displacement in mass communication; they were at best clumsy prostheses to restore a bodily wholeness that may never even have existed. Merton's erotics—his vision of how bodies can be coupled—allowed for real communication across distance; Adorno's insisted on the face-to-face, seeing only illusion or perversion in distended ties. In Maxwell's terms, Merton believed in action at a distance; Adorno believed that all immediacy was laced with infinitesimal gaps.

These questions are rich in implication for our public and private lives today. Democracy and eros remain the twin frames for popular reception of each new medium. Talk about the Internet today, for instance, is rife with dreams of new bodies politic (participatory democracy) and horrors of new bodies pornographic (children preyed on). The meaning of communicative connections, large scale and small, is an ongoing conundrum. We continue to play out Maxwell's options: bodies joined at a distance and bodies that, even when pressed tightly together, are not in absolute contact. If success in communication was once the art of reaching across the intervening bodies to touch another's spirit, in the age of electronic media it has become the art of reaching across the intervening spirits to touch another's body. Not the ghost in the machine, but the body in the medium is the central dilemma of modern communications.

S I X

Machines, Animals, and Aliens: Horizons of Incommunicability

Harrowing scenarios in which people come face-to-face with creatures with whom they can have no communication have multiplied enormously in twentieth-century life and thought. To meet abysses of communication at every hand is part of what it means to be modern. Communication as dialogue has consistently been forwarded as the cure for just this ailment, but it is as often the virus itself. Although speech, as Aristotle thought, is perhaps a capacity distinct to the human species, "communication" is not. The prominence of communication as a description for our life with each other marks the breaking open of the dike to admit the floods of the inhuman.

The chief challenge to communication in the twentieth century is contact with beings that lack mortal form. Communication is something we share with animals and computers, extraterrestrials and angels. As beings who not only speak but communicate, we reveal our mechanical, bestial, and ethereal affinities. The concept respects none of the metaphysical barriers that once protected human uniqueness. It easily spans the great chain of being, from DNA to international diplomacy. The question remains what sort of creatures we communicating beings have become. The power of "communication" lies in its ability to extend human interaction across the expanses of space and time; its pathos lies in its transcendence of mortal form. Communication suggests contact without touch. To talk on a telephone is to identify an acoustic effigy of the person with an embodied presence. In "communication" the bodies of the communicants no longer hold the incontrovertible tokens of individuality or personality. Our faces, actions, voices, thoughts, and transactions have all migrated into media that can disseminate the indicia of our personhood without our permission. Communication has become disembodied.

More precisely, the rise of the concept of "communication" is a symptom of the disembodiment of interaction.[1] The intellectual history of this notion reveals a long struggle to reorient to a world in which the human is externalized into media forms. Modern media have altered forever the meaning of anthropomorphism. The large social significance of the media, so often debated throughout this century, lies less in such classic social worries as their effects on children, representation of women, transformation of politics, or diffusion of mass culture than in their rearrangements of our bodily being, as individuals and as bodies politic. Communication places us in affinity with all kinds of monstrous others—and selves.

Contemporary culture and debate are rife with questions about how communication can cross over the gaps of gender, nationality, race and ethnicity, generation, language and culture. Likewise, collective subjects such as "the masses" or "the public" pose peculiar problems of communication. But these gaps, formidable as they are, are all confined to the human world. A concept arising from settings in which the human presence was shielded or mediated, "communication" has invited novel adventures of contact with particularly enigmatic others—animals, extraterrestrials, machines, texts, God—in short, any "being" that gives signs of or simulates intelligence. As the presence of the human body became increasingly irrelevant for "communication," new and alien candidates to communicate with have offered themselves to our fellowship, starting with the nineteenth-century spirits and proliferating wildly since the Second World War. Communication is perhaps the ultimate border crossing concept, traversing the bounds of species, machines, even divinity.

1. This disembodiment is a central theme in Niklas Luhmann, *Social Systems,* trans. John Bednarz Jr. with Dirk Baeker (Stanford: Stanford University Press, 1995), and John B. Thompson, *The Media and Modernity: A Social Theory of the Media* (Cambridge: Polity Press, 1995).

What is at stake in debates about communication is the status of the human being, our place in a universe populated by simians and cyborgs, fetuses and the brain-dead, angels and UFOs, "primitives" and smart machines, the dead and the distant.[2] "Communication" is the term that invites consideration of our relations to these creatures—each marked in some way as "other" to "man," the old center of the humanist universe—if only to say that communication with them is often impossible or dark. Since each of us is, has been, or might become any one of these creatures, communication has become the very field on which to sort out the place of the human in the great network of being. Questions about the inhuman—nature, machines, animals, extraterrestrials—often serve as allegories of social otherness—women, racial and sexual others, the insane, children, the senile, or one's own dear self. Today communication is the preeminent field for carrying out the command, Know Thyself.

Though the therapists (who want communication to build better relationships) and the technocrats (who want to build better systems) have done their best to suppress the truth that communication has surpassed the human shape, every new technique raises more questions of heteropathic identification. The oldest tropes continue to surface in the latest technologies; modernity, as Walter Benjamin argued, always cites prehistory. A recent Hitachi advertisement in *Wired,* a magazine that proudly surfs the cutting edge of technoculture, announces: "Many scientists believe that it will be possible to develop telepathic powers as a practical tool of communication. In the meantime, we offer this alternative."[3] The dead, of course, continue as the *primus inter pares* of strange communicants: "My phone call to a cemetery in Saddle Brook, N.J.," wrote a *New York Times* columnist in 1996, "was answered with: 'You have reached Riverside Cemetery. If you know your party's extension. . . .' Talk about the Internet!"[4]

But empathy for animals is perhaps an equally ancient strange sympathy. In this century the possibility of communication with animals has inspired cartoons, documentaries, agitation and reform, and vast traditions of scientific research. Aliens, likewise, have fueled radio shows, cinema, comics, television, and the tabloid press since at least the 1930s, as well as an international research effort since the late 1950s: SETI, the search for extraterrestrial intelligence. Questions of how to

2. See Donna J. Haraway, *Simians, Cyborgs, and Women: The Reinvention of Nature* (New York: Routledge, 1991).

3. *Wired* 4, 7 (1996): n.p.

4. *New York Times,* 14 July 1996, 17.

come into contact with the text (and with God) are closely linked in at least the Protestant world and remain the founding questions of the study of how to converse in situations where no reply is possible—hermeneutics. With the collapse of the great chain of being, "man" suddenly found many of the distinctions—of species, mechanism, gender, and divinity—that once sustained his status as lord over the earth unprecedentedly permeable. The failure to recognize the paranormal and the inhuman as founding questions for communication theory in our time goes together with the failure to recognize the inhuman when it stares back at you from the mirror. Both are containment strategies, props supporting a dangerously brittle identity.

As Hegel taught, recognition of the other is not a simple matter of perception but involves the founding of the human order. Determining the range of creatures we will communicate with is a political question, perhaps *the* political question. It may be the key question of politics in our century, when we treat animals as if they were human and humans as if they were animals. Polymorphous affiliations lie at the core of our existential and political dilemmas, no less in our love lives than in the absurd violence of a Sarajevo or Rwanda. Tracing all the variants of thought about communication in this century would require another book, but these affiliations underlie them all. Adorno linked the political and existential nicely: "The constantly encountered assertion that blacks, savages, Japanese are like 'animals,' monkeys for example, is the key to the pogrom. . . . The mechanism of 'pathic projection' determines that those in power perceive as human only their own reflected image, instead of reflecting back the human as precisely what is different."[5] I argue, with Adorno, that deliberations about communication are exercises not only in self-knowledge, but in living with the other. The concept of communication has the virtue of refusing to let us think of those tasks separately. The key question for twentieth-century communication theory—a question at once philosophical, moral, and political—is how wide and deep our empathy for otherness can reach, how ready we are to see "the human as precisely what is different."

In what follows, I sketch some of the extremities of communication theory in the mid- to late twentieth century: machines, animals, and extraterrestrials. The deep subtext of the adventures of "communication" in modern thought, I argue, is confrontation with creatures whose ability to enter into community with us is obscure. A detailed look at

---

5. Theodor W. Adorno, *Minima Moralia: Reflections from Damaged Life,* trans. E. F. N. Jephcott (1944–51; London: Verso, 1974), 105.

thinking about communication would have to cover much of twen-tieth-century literature, philosophy, art, drama, cinema, politics, lin-guistics, social science, engineering, and natural science. I can only plead that those who have ears to hear will hear. By exploring our strangest partners, I intend to illuminate the strangeness that occurs in the most familiar settings.

————

René Descartes not only is the philosophical architect, in some sense, of *Homo clausus,* he is also the theorist who makes communication a distinctly human capacity that distinguishes us from animals and ma-chines. The Cartesian boundaries of humanity were animals and ma-chines. More precisely, for Descartes they were the same thing. Animals were very elaborate automatons; so were our bodies. In the *Discourse on Method* he is particularly worried about the simulation of the human. Artificial automatons in the shape of animals, he argues, could easily deceive us, because animals are in effect machines; since we could not test them with speech, the artificial animals—if endowed with sufficient verisimilitude and mimicry—could easily pass as real. Machines, how-ever, made in human form and going through human motions, could always be exposed with two certain tests. "Of these the first is, that they could never use words or other signs, composing them as we do to de-clare our thoughts to others." Even if a machine could utter sounds and say certain phrases if touched in certain places, sort of like a talking doll, it still could not "arrange words in various ways to reply to the sense of everything that is said in its presence, in the way that the most unintel-ligent of men can do." As in the *Phaedrus,* responsiveness in dialogue is taken as a quintessential mark of intelligence. Second, an automaton resembling a human might be able to perform some tasks well—even outperforming humans at them (Descartes mentions the regularity and accuracy of clocks)—but it would lack skill to handle a diversity of tasks. If automatons were tested by a varied set of tasks, "one would discover that they did not act through knowledge, but simply through the dispo-sition of their organs." Descartes thought it "morally impossible" for a single machine to have sufficient subsystems to imitate all the capacities of reason.[6]

These two tests—responsiveness in speech and versatility of action—

6. René Descartes, *"Discourse on Method" and "The Meditations,"* trans. F. E. Sutcliffe (New York: Penguin, 1968), 72–76 (discourse 6).

were also, for Descartes, the dividing lines between humans and animals. Though some animals such as parrots could mime articulate speech, they were incapable of "the expression of thought." Descartes disapproved of the notion "that animals speak though we do not understand their language." Human reason was unparalleled in nature (rationality was, strictly speaking, not natural but divine). The "machine of the human body" was on the same level as the bugs and the clocks, a machine "composed of bones, nerves, muscles, veins, blood, and skin."[7] In one striking flight of fancy, Descartes imagined a body walking about, golemlike, drinking and eating, without a mind, so finely crafted a machine it was; to say the body was a machine was not to deny the splendor and intricacy of its design. Unlike Montaigne or Turing, Darwin or cyborg culture, Descartes had no notion of communicating with beasts or computers, golems or gizmos. He placed us in a different order altogether. To make such borders porous was morally dangerous, he thought, since nothing "leads feeble minds more readily astray from the path of virtue than to imagine that the soul of animals is of the same nature as our own, and that, consequently, we have nothing to fear or to hope for after this life, any more than have flies or ants."[8]

Descartes's epistemology—the "idea" idea we have already encountered in Locke—is part and parcel of his demarcation between species and orders. If the rational world exists only in ideas and humans alone have them (among mortal creatures), then the worlds in which birds and cows and pigs move and breathe are subject to radical doubt if not oblivion. Making interiority the test of sentience or consciousness is a recipe for guilt-free slaughter or abuse of the creatures that lack interiority. Descartes was part of a modernizing army busy suppressing a much more variegated tradition of sympathy between self and cosmos and was clearly in rebellion against popular animism and Scholastic Aristotelianism, both of which posited souls of some sort in all beings.[9] By the nineteenth century the membranes separating humans and beasts, humans and machines start to become permeable again. The question Descartes asks resounds through philosophy down to Alan Turing: How can you tell a human from a fake? What are the distinctive features of humanity? What is the role of the body in our distinctive humanity? Machines and

---

7. Descartes, *"Discourse on Method" and "The Meditations,"* 163 (meditation 6).

8. Descartes, *"Discourse on Method" and "The Meditations,"* 74–76 (discourse 6). All other quotations in the paragraph are from here. Later nihilists would use exactly this argument, such as Raskolnikov in Dostoyevsky's *Crime and Punishment.*

9. Carolyn Merchant, *The Death of Nature: Women, Ecology, and the Scientific Revolution* (San Francisco: Harper and Row, 1980).

animals pose inverse problems: Turing's machine communicates intelligently without a living body, while animals obviously have living bodies but offer no decisive proof of a will to communicate with us.

The Turing Test and the Insuperability of Eros

No engineer or chemist claims to be able to produce a material which is indistinguishable from the human skin.

ALAN TURING, "COMPUTING MACHINERY AND INTELLIGENCE"

The relation between humans and machines has been a poignant one in modern thought and culture, not only owing to industrialism or computers, but since Descartes and Pascal. What Turing asked—How can you tell a human from a machine?—was already Friedrich Nietzsche's question in 1874.[10] John Stuart Mill, in his blistering assault on William Hamilton's philosophy, explored at length the question whether humans could become automatons—a question with perhaps more than a little biographical significance, given Mill's strict utilitarian upbringing. In recent popular culture, robots, malign computers (Hal in *2001*), Toto-like sidekicks (R2D2 in *Star Wars*), androids (Lieutenant Data in *Star Trek: The Next Generation*), replicants (in *Blade Runner*), and the dangerous delights of coupling the body to cybernetic systems spur reflection on digital culture, intelligence, embodiment, gender, political order, and the blurry boundaries of human being.[11]

Alan Turing's 1950 article "Computing Machinery and Intelligence" is a locus classicus for contemplating communication between machines and humans. He starts with an "imitation game" or guessing game whose subject, curiously enough, is sexual difference. A third party must try to tell a man from a woman, both of them are in a different room. The man tries to sound like a woman, but the woman plays it straight. "In order that the tones of the voice may not help the interrogator the answers should be written, or better still, typewritten. The ideal arrangement is to have a teleprinter communicating between the two rooms." The task for the third party is a familiar one for communication at a distance: to discern a body when it is not present. Turing

---

10. Friedrich A. Kittler, *Grammophon, Film, Typewriter* (Berlin: Brinkmann und Bose, 1986), 30.

11. Haraway, *Simians, Cyborgs, and Women;* N. Katherine Hayles, *Chaos Bound: Orderly Disorder in Contemporary Literature and Science* (Ithaca: Cornell University Press, 1990); Anne Balsamo, *Technologies of the Gendered Body: Reading Cyborg Women* (Durham: Duke University Press, 1996); and Claudia Springer, *Electronic Eros: Bodies and Desire in the Postindustrial Age* (Austin: University of Texas Press, 1996).

resurrects the classic idealist scenario of people walled in separate rooms who cannot communicate "in person." Turing was, after all, at Cambridge, the historical center of interest in the ether and psychical research in England. Whatever the echo of this heritage for Turing, he suggests putting the two contenders into a "telepathy-proof room" to prevent any subtle communications from disturbing the effort to make words alone—typed, not handwritten—the carriers of communication. This arrangement "prevents the interrogator from seeing or touching the other competitors, or hearing their voices."[12]

Turing has ruled out sight, hearing, and touch as ways to know another body. Discourse alone, purged of the telltale squiggles of handwriting, will have to suffice. Turing's game presents the primal scene of what Judith Butler calls gender trouble: in the original form of Turing's game, gender is entirely a category of discourse and not of bodies.[13] The aim is to discover the bodily traces in a medium from which they have been evacuated. Quite like Cooley's approach, this is a fantasy of communication without bodies, with nothing being significant but the intelligence itself; and the intelligence would be known by its capacity to respond and engage in dialogue. The gamers are connected not by media that bear bodily witness or utter telltale significances, such as the telephone (which gives tones of voices), film (which gives gestures), or handwritten letters (which disclose the idiosyncratic character of the writer), but by teletyping. Turing represses all signs of embodiment to test if the distinctness of bodies is evident in discourse alone. As carefully as Dr. Albert von Schrenck Notzing inspected the cabinet medium Eva C to prevent concealment of any props, Turing controls access to the body at the other end of communication circuit to enable the manifestation not of ectoplasm, but of its opposite, intelligence. Like Tennyson, Turing wanted a sort of communication "Ghost to Ghost."

The game then substitutes a machine for the man (what happened to the woman is unclear, a question that remains central to the subsequent history of artificial intelligence). "This new problem has the advantage of drawing a fairly sharp line between the physical and the intellectual capacities of a man." The ground on which machines might compete is intelligence, not embodiment. "No engineer or chemist claims to be able to produce a material which is indistinguishable from the human

12. Alan M. Turing, "Computing Machinery and Intelligence," *Mind* 59 (1950): 433–60. All quotations in this paragraph are from 434.
13. Judith Butler, *Gender Trouble: Feminism and the Subversion of Identity* (New York: Routledge, 1990).

skin." For Turing mortality is irrelevant to intelligence. Later he said, dismissing androids, "I certainly hope and believe that no great efforts will be put into making machines with the most distinctively human, but non-intellectual characteristics, such as the shape of the human body."[14] Anthropomorphic affections must be banished. The game is designed to make the respective disabilities of machines and humans irrelevant: "We do not wish to penalise the machine for its inability to shine in beauty competitions, nor to penalise a man for losing in a race against an aeroplane." A similar criterion separates people from machines: "We wish to exclude from the machines men born in the usual manner."[15] He even wants to prevent cloning as a possible way of producing a smart machine; the engineers creating smart machines should all be of one sex, to prevent any natural reproduction. Bodily beauty for Turing is utterly irrelevant to intelligence (a claim that quite distinguishes him from Socrates of the *Phaedrus*). *Physis* and *kallos*—birth, death, and beauty—must be screened out of the contest.

Turing is about the dethroning of "man," or at least about breaching the frontiers between machines and animals, specifically our supposedly unique ability to interact and respond appropriately to questions. Turing is a border blaster. He discounts the theological critique of smart machines that God gave souls to men and women but not to animals or machines. One problem is the depreciation of animals; Turing wants continuity and not a stark break between the ensouled and the mechanical. Further, in constructing machines, just as in begetting children, why might not we be God's colaborers who provide "mansions for the souls he creates"? Turing clearly does not think much of theological objections to intelligent machinery but is simply trying to refute them in their own terms. "We like to believe that Man is in some subtle way superior to the rest of creation." He quotes a critic who would require a machine to "write a sonnet or compose a concerto because of thoughts and emotions felt, and not by the chance fall of symbols" before he would ascribe intelligence to it. This demand makes the criterion of authentic communication something that can never enter into communication—the thoughts and emotions felt by a communicant. Turing has no time for such spiritualist recourse to occult entities. In a pragmatist vein, Turing argues that if shared consciousness is the criterion of success in communication, then communication is impossible, and we get

14. Alan M. Turing, May 1951 radio talk, quoted in Andrew Hodges, *Alan Turing: The Enigma* (New York: Simon and Schuster, 1983), 420.

15. Turing, "Computing Machinery," 434, 435.

stuck in the impasse of solipsism.[16] Instead, all we know takes place in the behavioral daylight of interaction.

Besides, Turing knows that much of what we say consists of "the chance fall of symbols." If machines can imitate people, people can imitate machines. He mentions a testing game used in tutorials called "viva voce" whose aim is to help "discover whether some one really understands something or has 'learnt it in parrot fashion.'"[17] Turing's long experience of school life showed him that machines are not the only ones that simulate intelligence. The presence of the speaker's body is no guarantee that genuine interiority is being tapped.

The Turing test treats indiscernibles as identicals. A smart machine would be proved intelligent by passing: by the inability of the third party to tell the two veiled interlocutors apart. The bodily *Ding-an-sich* is hidden within the machine. The Turing test is in a way a democratic fantasy, in the strict sense that in democracy, in contrast to aristocracy, birth is irrelevant. Turing gives us communication as if bodies did not matter—a perhaps legitimate utopia escaping from a world in which Turing's body and sexual preference did matter, all too painfully much. "The discrete state machine, communicating by teleprinter alone, was like an ideal for his own life, in which he would be left alone in a room of his own, to deal with the outside world solely through rational argument. It was the embodiment of a perfect J. S. Mill liberal." Hodges puts the objection well: Turing "did not meet the problem that to speak seriously is to act, and not only to issue a string of symbols." Human speech exceeds puzzle-solving intelligence, since it is always linked to possibilities of embodied action, which is why questions of ethics, sex, politics, life, and death will elude the machine. If the fear of the Lord is the beginning of wisdom, or if all philosophy is learning how to die, then machines will have difficulty sounding the strength humans draw from their imperfections. Turing is heir to the Cambridge project of discovering the meeting of minds in a medium unsullied by bodiliness, whether it be logic, mathematics, the ether, or telepathy. Turing "had not tackled the question of the channels of communication, nor explored the physical embodiment of the mind within the social and political world."[18] Indeed, he thought channels were ultimately interchangeable, as in his analysis of Helen Keller. Turing depreciates the remarkable work of embodiment that media can perform; "communication" allows him to equate a teleprinter and a breathing human pres-

16. Turing, "Computing Machinery," 443, 444, 445, 447.
17. Turing, "Computing Machinery," 446.
18. Hodges, *Alan Turing*, 425, 421, 423, 426.

ence as doppelgängers. He had learned to equate the proxy sent at a distance with its bodily origin. As Kittler argues, "In the Turing game, so-called man coincides with his simulation."[19]

The body in the works—*corpus ex machina*—is the central enigma of modern communications. Materializing mediums like Eva C and materializing media like the radio sought to foreground the flesh as proof of genuine contact. Turing's scenario of simulating human intelligence via computing machinery took the opposite tack of hiding the uncopyable human skin to reveal the ghost in the machine. Turing stated the central issue with remarkable economy—the presence or absence of bodies in reproducing media. He provides us with an almost mythic narrative of the relation between humanity and the system of body- and mind-extending technical aids. He anticipates the digital age, all communications transformed into *discrete* ones (in either sense of discrete/discreet: on/off signals or the decorum of demurely concealed private facts). He participated in the rewriting of the great chain of being as a code of information, from DNA, a code containing "genetical information," to the world information order that some people still long for.

In sum, Turing's assault on consciousness as a guarantee of communication is admirable, but his veiling of love, attraction, eros, and mortality is troubling. He believes in the possibility of a duplicate without a difference, one reason he is not interested in making a replica of the human epidermis. What is missing in the Turing test—and the whole cultural complex that contemplates the replication of human beings in artificial intelligence—is the desire for the other that Hegel thought raised us out of animality into the homeland of consciousness. As is always true in a good murder mystery (for this is what the Turing test is), the body is hidden. In this case the victim is "man."

THE DISCERNIBILITY OF IDENTICALS   It is the modern Kabbalists, Kafka, Benjamin, and Borges, who know there is always a remainder when a duplicate is made. The fleshly residuum of finitude escapes simulation. It is human frailty, rather than rationality, that machines have difficulty mimicking.[20] Turing thought "the shape of the human body" quite irrelevant to establishing communication, but disability and imperfection may be the only sources of real contact we can claim. By the late nineteenth century it was becoming possible to "appear" without "being

---

19. Kittler, *Grammophon, Film, Typewriter*, 31.
20. Turing does argue that a smart machine might make intentional errors or delay its answers to seem more human. Too much perfection would be a dead giveaway.

there" "in person." Thanks to recording and transmitting media, a principle of duplication entered into what counts as human.

Walter Benjamin's famous "The Work of Art in the Age of Mechanical Reproduction" is in part an analysis of the metaphysics of copying. For him, duplication of artworks strips them of their "aura." The aura is an effect of presence and of distance. His notoriously elusive concept of "aura" is itself about elusiveness: an aura is "the unique perception of a distance, however close it may be."[21] The copy lacks the compulsion and danger of the original. What the original has is uniqueness, permanence, and an authenticating tradition that makes it the bearer of a continuous history. An art print may offer a visually identical image of Rogier van der Weyden's *Portrait of a Lady,* but only the original has cracks in its surface and hangs in the National Gallery in Washington, D.C. The aura attaches to the singular, mortal body of the work in space and time, the canvas and frame that are bearers of contingency. The original *Mona Lisa* is in the Louvre; the Mona Lisa image on a T-shirt inhabits a very different practical universe (it can be worn, sweat in, washed) and is hence unprotected by the prohibitions and "microadjustments" that surround sacred things.[22] An artwork, like a mortal being, has a unique, irreplaceable body from which it cannot be separated without dying in some way.[23] The ambivalence in Benjamin's analysis is famous, for he wants to think he has discovered a means of liberating the oppressed from the politically stupefying spell of art as sacred when he has equally discovered a novel basis for art's status as set apart: its ultimate immunity to reproducibility. Though the form of the work can be doubled, its unique history cannot. Not in glorious and ubiquitous reproduction but in local imperfection lies the proof of authenticity. The aging process is the hardest thing to fake. Mortality and historicity take on a new status as the homeland of truth. The aura dwells in the fingernails and earlobes, as Freud, Sherlock Holmes, and Giovanni Morelli all saw.

Imagine that some novel technical process could replicate the *Mona Lisa* molecule for molecule—the canvas, the paint, and the frame, including the effects of aging and exposure to chemicals, heat, and humidity—such that it would be impossible to tell copy and original apart

21. Walter Benjamin, "The Work of Art in the Age of Mechanical Reproduction," in *Illuminations,* trans. Harry Zohn, ed. Hannah Arendt (New York: Schocken, 1968), 222.

22. Claude Lévi-Strauss, *The Savage Mind* (Chicago: University of Chicago Press, 1966), 10.

23. I pursue these themes more extensively in John Durham Peters, "The Ambivalent Iconoclasm of Kierkegaard and Benjamin," in *The Image in Dispute,* ed. Dudley Andrew (Austin: University of Texas Press, 1997), 9–31.

if they got switched. Still the two works would not at all mean the same thing. One would invite inquiries about the fetching smile, the other about the amazing technique. One would ask us to travel a chain of contagious magic across the distance of time back to Leonardo's time, the other would leave us awed by the technological prowess of our own. The copy would be a spectacle of ingenuity, not a moving or perplexing work of art. It would be a simulation, not an expression. We would have no desire to know the person who made it; it would not sustain fantasies of touching at a distance. We would wonder how it was done, not what it meant. Each would offer its viewers a different invitation: time travel or gawking. One painting would be fit for the Louvre, the other for Disneyland. That hardly anyone would dispute the very different institutional destinies of the two objects reveals what metaphysicians we are, quite appropriately, in dealing with *Geist*. Culture is clearly more than matter in motion; Benjamin alerts us to its delicate ontology, its sensitivity to infinitesimal changes in incarnation. Artworks are not only texts, that is, reproducible fields of signifiers; their origin, afterlife, and material shape all matter profoundly. Identical objects invite radically different hermeneutic stances.

Jorge Luis Borges's story "Pierre Menard, Author of the Quixote," makes the same point. A twentieth-century French *symboliste* poet, one Pierre Menard, learns the rules of chivalry, converts to Catholicism, and studies early seventeenth-century Spanish, all in an effort that can only be described as quixotic: to rewrite the *Quixote* without consulting the original.[24] After Herculean efforts, Menard (re?)produces a few pieces of the text, word for word with the original.[25] That he can write only parts of the text is a comment on the "availability" of texts in different historical moments. After doing all the classic acts of historicism (immersion in source materials, mentalities, language, etc.), but to a logically absurd extreme, Menard still, however, is unable to write the past "as it really was." Historicism stands refuted: Menard produces an identical text eccentric to the original. As the tale's narrator notes, though both texts are "verbally identical," Menard's fragments "are almost infinitely richer" than those of Cervantes. What in 1609 were literary flourishes ("Truth, whose mother is history") resound freshly in the age of Marxism and pragmatism. A sentence's historical setting shapes the range of

24. Allan Megill points out that there was a historical Pierre Mesnard, an early twentieth-century French philosopher with a particular interest in Descartes.
25. George Steiner notes that these pieces happen to be the ones concerned with translation, labyrinths, and Kabbalah—the Borgesian passages: *After Babel: Aspects of Language and Translation* (New York: Oxford University Press, 1975), 70.

its references and resonances. The twentieth-century version is a pains-taking labor of reconstruction rather than a spontaneous outpouring and hence is worthy of novel appreciation.

Whether a copy is richer (Menard's *Quixote*) or poorer (Disney's *Mona Lisa*) than the original, things cultural derive meaning not solely from what can be reproduced—formal patterning, semiotic suggestiveness, or power of statement—but from a tissue of relationships with history, time, and place. Identical objects are never identical. Repetition, as Kier-kegaard noted, is impossible. The births of the two works, contra Turing, are part of their possible interpretations, even of their essence. The one work is haunted by a whole texture of historical ghosts and legends, the other needs to have that aura supplied.

Perhaps we should submit the two *Mona Lisa*s or two *Quixote*s to a Turing test: remove the captions marking authorship and see whether impartial and uninformed witnesses could discern the difference be-tween the two "versions." Clearly, no one could. If the two works were permanently confused, we would be left in the monstrous situation of Borges's cartographers who had built a map the same size as the em-pire.[26] But the Turing test assumes that our knowledge of the history of the painting's or text's embodiment should be irrelevant to our appreci-ation of it. The Turing test, again, explicitly seeks to eliminate attraction to bodies or knowledge of them as a factor in communication. Turing's ambition was to make indistinguishable duplicates of human intelli-gence. But the impossibility of making a precise copy in art holds for humans as well. Eros is the relation of one body to another, and what Turing wants to purge is precisely a faculty of appreciation that depends on the touch of hidden things. Wishing to eliminate any appeal to hu-man superiority based on our deep-seated passion for the shape of the human body, Turing only ends up reaffirming the inescapable anthro-pomorphism that drives our interactions with each other. The Turing test wants to imagine communication as if eros did not matter. But the repressed returns. The skins and faces and bodies of others turn out not to be in the least irrelevant to our interactions with them, at least in interactions among friends, lovers, and families. Turing's fantasy is democratic in that it allows for a mode of sociality in which the bod-ies, parts, and passions of the participants would be utterly irrelevant to their chances for expression. But not all life should be politics, and love is always, as we have seen, anything but democratic; it is usually

26. Jorge Luis Borges, "Del rigor en la ciencia," in *Historia universal de la infamia* (Buenos Aires: Emecé, 1958), 131–32.

madly partial. (Lysias's mistake was to imagine that it could be indifferent.)

Communication conceived of as the project of copying one person's meanings leads to as many inevitable differences as Menard's attempt to reproduce the *Quixote*. If communication for the spiritualist tradition was a problem of transcending bodies so that spirits could connect, by the twentieth century "communication" has become a problem of arranging the ties between distant bodies. The error of the spiritualist tradition was to presuppose what Leibniz called "the identity of indiscernibles." For Leibniz, if two entities share the same properties they can be considered as one, since space is the register of possible coexistences (he has a relational, anti-Newtonian conception of space). The two *Mona Lisas* would be in effect the same painting, since nothing (besides a caption, so little on which hangs so much) could possibly differentiate them. Something like this principle underlies the spiritualist project. Self and spirit proxies are to be identical, such that communication over distances imposes no stretching of soul and body. Angels *are*, after all, their spirit proxies. The dream of communication is the dream of identical minds in concert. Media of transmission and recording, however, drove a wedge between the copy and the original by inadvertently revealing everything that the copy had missed: birth, history, and death. The proxies could become competitors with their origins, the self. The spiritualists missed how the doppelgängers accentuated the hitherto unnoted incidentals of the original—or else celebrated those incidentals in an orgy of ectoplasm, the flesh out of place.

The identity of indiscernibles is a principle perhaps characteristic of the Christian adaptation of Kabbalah, in which Leibniz took an interest; it is certainly characteristic of the longer Christian privilege of the spirit over the letter and of angelic interiorities. The version of Kabbalah reflected in Kafka, Benjamin, and Borges insists, in contrast, on the discernibility of identicals. Between the originals and such doubles as telephone voices (Kafka, "The Neighbor"), photographs (Benjamin, "The Work of Art"), and literary updates (Borges, "Pierre Menard") there is always an infinite gulf. Difference is so pervasive that it appears even— or especially—between exact replicas. In the spaces between identical objects, the impish angels of negation multiply explosively.

Animals and Empathy with the Inhuman

Even more than angels, animals have probably been the chief object for contemplating the human estate. The species barrier has perhaps always been the most permeable of all, at least in imagination. If we believe Hegel, the Garden of Eden was a zoo.[27] The first item of business was the naming of animals, and Adam and Eve had all too little trouble in communicating with a certain snake. From the pervasiveness of totemism in human cultures, it is clear that animals have long served humans as mirrors of self-definition. From Aristotle on, animal societies have been of interest as a comparison point for political theory.[28] According the Greeks, Schiller, Marx, and Arendt, animals have societies (cooperation with conspecifics) but do not have politics (collective determination of right action). In the Judeo-Christian tradition, the ability to communicate with animals has gone together with wisdom and saintliness: King Solomon and Saint Francis. Animals have long served as allegories of human otherness, and quite literally as guinea pigs for the treatment of humans. "After they had accustomed themselves at Rome to spectacles of the slaughter of animals," wrote Montaigne, "they proceeded to those of the slaughter of men, to the gladiators."[29] The condition of animals has long served as a political allegory of the treatment of humans, a founding pathos for the animal rights movement.

But only in the late nineteenth century did scientific efforts to discern animal communication emerge—Darwin, Espinas—sometimes with hilariously embarrassing results in less sophisticated research. Clever Hans, the German horse, could supposedly do simple mathematical calculations by tapping his hoof until he arrived at the desired digit—a mode of communication not unlike that of a spirit rapper. It turns out he simply stopped tapping when his handler's unconscious facial expression and body language cued him that he had arrived at the right answer. His independent intelligence turned out to be a simple mimicry. The Clever Hans syndrome is a favorite cautionary tale in animal communication research about the dangers of projecting ourselves onto animal subjects. It is one of Kafka's worries as well: that the performance of the other is simply a staging for or projection of the self. Clever Hans supplies the classic scenario of miscommunication: a smooth interaction that, it turns out, has radically different meanings for each participant. Wherever the interiority of the other is veiled, questions of projection, otherness, and ventriloquism are acute (as in

27. G. W. F. Hegel, *Lectures on the Philosophy of Religion: The Lectures of 1827,* ed. Peter C. Hodgson, trans. R. F. Brown, P. C. Hodgson, and J. M. Stewart with the assistance of H. S. Harris (Berkeley: University of California Press, 1988), 442.

28. David J. Depew, "Humans and Other Political Animals in Aristotle's *History of Animals,*" *Phronesis* 40, 2 (1995): 156–81.

29. Michel de Montaigne, *Essays II,* Great Books of the Western World, ed. Robert Maynard Hutchins, vol. 25 (1580; Chicago: Encyclopaedia Britannica, 1952), 206.

all situations of first contact). The potential for spectacular miscues is rife when shared history is thin. As Montaigne put it, "The defect that hinders communication betwixt them [animals] and us, why may it not be on our part as well as theirs?"[30]

Through the rich research tradition of ethology (a term first coined by J. S. Mill in his *System of Logic* for the study of human character), such as Lorenz on ducks, Frisch on bees, Marler and Hartshorne on birdsong, Tinbergen on gulls, Holldobler and Wilson on ants, Goodall, Savage-Rumbaugh, and Premack on simians, Lilly on dolphins, Bateson, Sebeok, and Haraway among others as general theorists, much has been done in this century to crack the codes. Thomas Sebeok, a student of "zoosemiotics," likens the interpreter of animal codes to a cryptanalyst, "someone who receives messages not destined for him and is initially ignorant of the applicable transformation rules."[31] This is the familiar hermeneutic problem of the intercepted text. The notion of "communication" allows us to evade the disconnections just as it makes them more central. As Charles Morris wrote in 1946, "All such discussions usually culminate in the question as to whether language is unique to man. Here the issue is in part terminological, since if 'language' is made synonymous with 'communication' there is no doubt that animals have language."[32] On the eve of information theory, Morris gives us a notion of communication indifferent to species boundaries. In a genuine pragmatist moment (which in Morris are often overshadowed by positivist ones), Morris sums up: "The continuity is as real as the discontinuity, and the similarity of human and animal signs-behavior as genuine as the difference."[33] As in mesmerism or telepathy, communication is a concept looser and less material than language or speech, one that lends itself to strange catholicities of blurring.

My story here is not that "man" was once defined by his ability to communicate and that an ever-expanding range of human and inhuman "others" seeking acknowledgment have called this capacity into question; it is rather that "communication" is an adaptation to or symptom of this crisis, a concept that allows for contact without presence, contact that is indifferent to the bodily form of the communicators (animals, people, machines) and even to biology itself (as phonographs capture the voices of the dead or computers have "memory"). The nine-

30. Montaigne, *Essays II*, 215.
31. Thomas A. Sebeok, "Zoosemiotics: At the Intersection of Nature and Culture," in *The Tell-Tale Sign: A Survey of Semiotics*, ed. Thomas A. Sebeok (Lisse, Netherlands: Peter de Ridder, 1975), 88.
32. Charles Morris, *Language, Signs, and Behavior* (New York: Prentice-Hall, 1946), 53–54.
33. Morris, *Language, Signs, and Behavior*, 55.

teenth century pushes "man" toward both animality and mechanism via the assumption by machines of supposed human functions (speaking, memory) and the increasingly permeable intellectual and morphological membrane between humans and animals (always thin in childhood and fairy tales). If the Turing test hides the organism within the machine, the task in animal communication is to find a fellow intelligence in a body of a different shape and species. The task is to find affinities not limited by our anthropomorphic dispositions. "Communication" gives us an image of humanity, not as standing on an ontological ladder betwixt the beasts and the angels, but as a nexus within a biological network and circuit of information flows.

The scholarly literature on animal communication is vast; I simply want to place the twentieth-century project of communicating with animals in the overall argument. The intellectual problem in communication with animals is the sounding of alien intelligences that seem to lack interiority or that cannot acknowledge us in the same medium by which we approach them—a problem similar to contact with nature or the dead (those objects with which we commune rather than communicate). The challenge is to fend off one's own anthropomorphism so as to recognize an otherness that does not know it is other. Against the frank projections of human affairs onto beasts that prevail with domesticated animals, fairy tales, and totemism, Ludwig Wittgenstein teaches a harder doctrine: If a lion could speak, we couldn't understand him. His point—which would stand against Turing as well, who was an occasional but sometimes dissenting attendee at Wittgenstein's Cambridge lectures—was that understanding comes as much from a lived or embodied world of common practices as from symbol-manipulating capacities alone. We would need to live in a lion's body and experience the lion's form of life to understand the lion's speech.

Ethological research shows overwhelmingly that insects, birds, ungulates, simians, and cetaceans, among others, use complicated signaling systems; it has also produced remarkable stories of cross-species bonding and relationships. But the pathos-drenched question of "communication" can probably never be answered in a satisfying way. The whole project is a quest for the liminal space in which our half of the dialogue could find junction with what we imagine is the other half on the part of animals. If the question were simply whether humans and animals can cooperate in a variety of tasks, it would lack urgency; the answer would be obvious. The absence of "communication" has never prevented humans and animals from entering into community with each other. Thousands of years of brute exploitation, and a shorter history of household pets, offer two alternative models besides "communication"—domination and the affectionate projection of human traits. Driving the dream of communication with the beasts is the Hegelian magic, the desire of recognition, Bell's call to Watson: Come here, I want you. No creature has yet stood up to say, I recognize you recognizing me, and I am yours for the taking. The dream is of an alien intelligence that opens itself lovingly to us. But the tokens of friendship should be enough; we ought not to need contact with the soul. Socrates struck the right note concerning the song of the cicadas in the *Phaedrus* (259a–b): "But if they see us in conversation, steadfastly navigating around them as if they were the Sirens, they will be very pleased and immediately give us the gift from the gods they are able to give to mortals." It is precisely in recognizing the impossibility of communication that the blessing comes.

William James saw the elephants and tigers at P. T. Barnum's zoo in 1873. "I could," he wrote, "never hope to *sympathize* in a genuine sense of the word with them. And the want of sympathy is not as in the case of some deformed or loathsome human life, for their being is admirable; so admirable that one yearns to be in some way its sharer, partner, or accomplice. Thus their foreignness confounds one's pretension to comprehend the world—while their admirableness undermines the stoic or moral frame of mind in which one says the real meaning of life is *my* action. The great world of life, in no relation with my action, is so real!"[34] Facing the inhuman, James feels both the impossibility of contact and a yearning for fellowship. He did not vaunt the majesty of human knowledge before the beasts but mourned its inadequacy. Stunned by otherness, he longed to share it in ways other than knowing—sharing, partnership, or complicity. He belongs to a tradition that appreciates how wild affinities destroy epistemological hubris.[35] As Emerson, the tradition's founder, said, "I hold our actual knowledge very cheap. Hear the rats in the wall, see the lizard on the fence, the fungus under foot, the lichen on the log. What do I know sympathetically, morally, of either of these worlds of life?"[36] Transcendentalist thinking

34. *William James: The Essential Writings,* ed. Bruce Wilshire (New York: Harper and Row, 1971), vii.

35. See Richard Poirier, "Writing off the Self," *Raritan* 1 (summer 1981): 106–33, and Anita Kermode, "William James and His Cuttlefish," *Raritan* 2 (winter 1982): 115–19.

36. Ralph Waldo Emerson, "History" (1841), in *Selected Writings of Emerson,* ed. Donald McQuade (New York: Modern Library, 1981), 127.

intuits a secret kinship between the human and the inhuman. "The greatest delight which the fields and woods minister is the suggestion of an occult relation between man and the vegetable."[37] As Thoreau says in *Walden*, I grew like corn in the night. He asks, Shall I not have intelligence with the earth? What is man but a mass of thawing clay? Am I not part vegetable mold myself? Empathy with the inhuman is the moral and aesthetic lesson that might replace our urgent longing for communication.

Communication with Aliens

I firmly disbelieve, myself, that our human experience is the highest form of experience in the universe.

WILLIAM JAMES, *PRAGMATISM*, LECTURE 8

Humans have long imagined themselves in contact with super- and sub-human intelligences; it is a specieswide longing. Before the twentieth century many philosophers had great interest in the inhabitants of other worlds, but as with animal communication, only since the late nineteenth century has the dream of empirical contact with beings not of this planet been pursued as a scientific enterprise.[38] With the modern attack, led by Marx, Feuerbach, Nietzsche, and Freud, on the human imagination as an unwitting maker of all kinds of fantastical others (gods, demons, angels, munchkins, trolls, water sprites, and spirits of all sorts), science has compensated by seeking contact with objective others—animals, aliens, "primitives," the unconscious. In research on extraterrestrial intelligence, as on animal communication, all kinds of strategies have been sought to transcend the inevitability of one-way communication. Any message we receive must decisively prove to be immune to our own fabrications. As in Dorothy Parker's anxious mono-logue, we wait for a telephone call. The quest for contact with aliens is a leading example of the dialectic of enlightenment, the persistence of myth at the heart of the most secular enterprises. Even more, it is an allegory of faith in a disenchanted universe.

The search for extraterrestrial intelligence (SETI), an international sci-

37. Ralph Waldo Emerson, *Nature* (1836), in *Selected Writings of Emerson*, ed. Donald McQuade (New York: Modern Library, 1981), 7.

38. On the philosophical history of such interest, see Lewis White Beck, "Extraterrestrial Intelligent Life," in *Extraterrestrials: Science and Alien Intelligence*, ed. Edward Regis Jr. (Cambridge: Cambridge University Press, 1985), 3–18.

entific effort of varying fortunes since its start in the late 1950s, is perhaps the most sustained examination of communication—and communication breakdown—in late twentieth-century culture.[39] SETI is a child of the twentieth century. The project presupposes knowledge of the speed of light, the measurement of vast distance, the discovery of radio waves, means of sorting signal from noise (such as cryptography and information theory), high-speed computers, and the longing to break through the circle of our own cognitions to touch otherness. The titles of recent articles on SETI tell a tale of communicative pathos: Is anyone out there? Are we alone? An invitation to strangers. Who's there? Still listening. Tuning in to out there. The next voice you hear. Earthlings are figured as Miss Lonelyhearts waiting by the telephone. The literature on SETI, both scientific and popular, is rife with explicit discussion of communication. SETI not only is the project of understanding radio emissions from deep space but is also implicitly a sustained inquiry into our earthly dilemmas about communication. It is a fertile field for exploring the philosophical consequences of storage and transmission capacities across vast expanses of time and space. Perhaps we are interested in communication with aliens because we live among alien communications. Every owner of a radio or television set possesses both a time machine and a teleportation device for alien personages.

Interstellar communication is riddled with astronomical gaps: mind-numbing distances, ranging from four light-years to billions; delays between call and response that could outlast a thousand earth generations; the problem of signal persistence through Doppler shifts, space-time distortion, and signal scatter caused by cosmic dust and gases; and the prospect of such a radical otherness in our interlocutors that their math, their being in time, or their bodies might be like nothing in our ken. Their strangeness could put all other strangeness to shame. They might count with irrational numbers or communicate by modes of being instead of perceptible signals. Any message they send to us might never be recognized as a message. Codes for them might look like nature to us. The whir of the cicadas might be a message they are sending. Their sensitivity to quantities too vast or infinitesimal, or to matter too gross or subtle for the frame of our senses and minds, or even their time scale, might be so queer that no junction could ever be made. If we couldn't understand a lion who spoke, why would we understand an alien?

39. It is also sometimes known as CETI, communication (or contact) with extraterrestrial intelligence.

Across such desperate distance, any evidence of the will to communicate may always be underdetermined, subject to all kinds of alternative explanations.[40]

Extraterrestrial communication, more than any other situation, clearly shows that communication at a distance always comes out of the past. Any "message" received from a distant planet comes from a point already lost to time. If we were to receive a broadcast from a world near Arcturus, say, thirty-eight light-years away, we would hear only what the intelligences there had to say to us thirty-eight years ago. The "now" of reception would be the "then" of transmission. Communication with galactically distant worlds is an archaeological dig. Our dialogic couplings will be wildly asynchronous. SETI, by extremity of exaggeration, reveals what late nineteenth-century spiritualists knew: the unity of communication at a distance and communication with the dead.

Indeed, what psychical research was to the late nineteenth century, SETI is to the late twentieth. In both, highly respected scientists investigate topics that popular culture both abounds in and disdains as frivolous: spirits and aliens. Both draw on extant communications technology and practices. Psychical research owes an immense amount to the telegraph, telephone, and wireless for its imagery, as we have seen, and SETI is the latest step in the wireless imagination. Frank Drake, the founder in 1959 of Project Ozma, the first attempt to eavesdrop or tune in on the broadcasts of distant civilizations, and one of the senior players in SETI, compares any message we might send to faraway worlds to "an interstellar fax."[41] Both psychical research and SETI confront massive but mockingly inconclusive quantities of data with the hope that a junction can be made. Both deal with the most poignant human concerns: mourning, cosmic loneliness, contact with the dead and distant (psychical research) or alien and distant (SETI). Both are moved by faith in the other's existence without the ability to take hold of a sure connection. Both imagine a universe humming with conversations we are unable, for whatever reasons, to tap. As James C. Fletcher, twice the head of NASA and an active supporter of SETI, wrote, "We should begin to listen to other civilizations in the galaxy. It must be full of voices, calling from star to star in a myriad of tongues."[42] Both psychical research and

40. Dennis Overbye, "The Big Ear," *Omni* 13 (December 1990): 44. Frank Drake has suggested that our most likely interlocutors in SETI are immortal beings who have infinite patience to await our response.

41. David Graham, "Intergalactic Conversations," *Technology Review* 96 (February–March 1993): 20–21.

42. James C. Fletcher quoted in Roger D. Launius, "A Western Mormon in Washington, D.C.: James C. Fletcher, NASA, and the Final Frontier," *Pacific Historical Review* 64 (May 1995): 233.

SETI develop innovative methodologies for sorting messages from static, signal from noise. Psychical investigation into telepathy was the origin of randomized design; the experimenter could thus be completely blind to any order created (e.g., in the arrangement of playing cards) so as to bar any unwitting collaboration from his or her own unconscious.[43] Information theory and cryptography, likewise, make SETI conceivable; it is fitting that Stanislaw Lem makes a mathematician with special expertise in statistics the hero of his SETI novel *His Master's Voice* (1968), a brilliantly dizzying meditation on the hermeneutic undecidabilities of a letter from the stars, a text outside any known relationship.[44] Both inquiries have produced methods to restrain the human rage for order, the will to impose meaning on randomness or otherness, and our overzealousness in credulity.

In fact there is a historical link between psychical research and SETI. Oliver Lodge, who in the 1890s wrote of the powers of radio to create direct communication between distant brains and was later an active psychical researcher, was also apparently the first to have the idea of using radio as an instrument of exploration in astronomy. He sought to identify solar radio emissions, but there was too much electrical interference in Liverpool—perhaps owing in part to the sparking of the electrical trams on the streets.[45] His plea for psychical research applies equally well to SETI: "Clearly the conclusion [that the chasm between the living and the dead can be bridged] is either folly and self-deception, or it is a truth of the utmost importance to humanity."[46] Cambridge University, and more specifically the Cavendish Laboratory, was the headquarters not only for many of the late nineteenth-century physicists who both hypothesized the ether and engaged in psychical research, but also of many of the key innovations after World War II in radio astronomy, which completely transformed our understanding of the universe. Since Newton a place of grace and order, the universe of radio astronomy is a Shiva's dance of creation and destruction, spectacular explosions of supernovas, and such unexpected weirdnesses as twin stars, quasars, dark matter, and black holes. The notion to use radio as an instrument of communication rather than of inquiry, however, appeared only in the late 1950s, with Project Ozma.

43. Ian Hacking, "Telepathy: Origins of Randomization in Experimental Design," *Isis* 79 (1988): 427–51.

44. Stanislaw Lem, *His Master's Voice*, trans. Michael Kandel (New York: Harvest/HBJ, 1968).

45. Nigel Calder, *Radio Astronomy* (New York: Roy, 1958), 11.

46. Oliver Lodge, *Raymond, or Life and Death, with Examples of the Evidence of Survival of Memory and Affection after Death* (New York: Doran, 1916), 389.

Reading some of the founding SETI articles from the late 1950s, like messages sent from distant planets forty light-years away, one is struck by how much they assume science is the universal language. In the founding article of SETI, Giuseppe Cocconi and Philip Morrison thought it "highly probable that for a long time [extraterrestrial societies] will have been expecting the development of science near the Sun." Once we receive and answer their signal, we would enter into "the community of intelligence," a sort of intergalactic invisible college.[47] The SETI scientists have a touching confidence that messages from other worlds would be sent by scientists eager to engage in scholarly exchange rather than by mindless bureaucrats, conquistadores, or con artists. Further, underlying early SETI documents is a rather apocalyptically tinged story of technological progress, with the hopes that more "advanced" civilizations could help us skip over intermediate stages without destroying ourselves in the meantime. One scientist even proposed that the apparent silence of the cosmos "may simply be that the mortality-rate for advanced civilizations is too high for them to become abundant in the Galaxy."[48]

Radio begins as a séance, fragmentary messages flying through space, trying to make links with some listener, as in Rudyard Kipling's story "Wireless"; in SETI it ends where it began, in the quest for junction, beaming messages into space, scanning the heavens for proof of intelligible fabrication. The link between DX-ing, spiritualism, and SETI is explicit in the 1997 film *Contact*, based on the Carl Sagan novel by the same name. As a child the heroine, played by Jodie Foster, is an amateur radio operator, who calls "CQ, CQ" into the great beyond. When she is orphaned, her DX-ing becomes a kind of quest for her dead parents. In adulthood she is a beleaguered SETI researcher who finally hits the jackpot—a message that beats out, rap by rap, the sequence of prime numbers from 1 to 100. In the climax, she travels to a distant world where she has a reunion with her father, or rather with an alien presence using her father as a reassuring simulation through which to speak to her. SETI is here figured as a quest for contact with the dead and others across distance. Of course the "contact" she has made leaves no decisive objective evidence except eighteen hours of static-filled tapes, such that the question of the reality of the junction (versus a huge hallucination

47. Giuseppe Cocconi and Philip Morrison, "Searching for Interstellar Communications," *Nature* 184 (19 September 1959): 844.
48. R. N. Bracewell, "Communications from Superior Galactic Communities," *Nature* 185 (28 May 1960): 671.

on her part) is, as always, left naggingly open. The possibility of communication is the twentieth century's version of the mystery of faith.

SETI seeks a true signal amid an infinity of noise; thus by far the most effort has been put into listening rather than sending. Like William James looking for evidence of immortality in the "bosh" of mediumistic performance, K looking for recognition from the Castle, or a lover listening to ten million radio voices for a telephonic message from his or her beloved, SETI faces the vertigo of infinitesimally small odds. The SETI scientist is in a position analogous to that of the radio listener trying to find out whether the voice of Kate Smith or Rudy Vallee is sincere, since he or she must sort out all the potential false sources of noise from the universe. The universe itself emits all manner of radio signals; the first pulsar, for example, was discovered in 1967 and was first thought to be an amazingly insistent radio signal from a remote intelligent civilization. The Cambridge astronomer and Nobel laureate Antony Hewish even hushed up the discovery for six months for fear of causing a public uproar if it really was some kind of distant signal. (It turned out to be a neutron star rotating on its axis at astounding speed.)[49] Indeed, the receipt of an alien signal, especially if it was a declaration of war or the design for a super weapon, could pose a profound question of public relations, not to mention defense; there is even a worldwide pact among researchers not to respond at once if some message does come, lest we inadvertently step into some intergalactic conflict.[50] Radio astronomers are supposed to act initially as what Internet culture calls "lurkers"—those who read messages but do not make themselves known by actually posting one.

SETI recognizes the gaps of which communication is made. Galactic conversation can be nothing but alternating broadcasts. As Stanislaw Lem notes, "When 'questions' were separated from the 'answers' they received by a time that was on the order of centuries, it was hard to call such an exchange 'dialogue.'"[51] Much of SETI's strategy is explicitly the one-way work of eavesdropping. Astronomer Freeman Dyson, a longtime leader in SETI, proposed surveillance as the best course for discerning intelligent life in the universe: rather than DX-ing with the universe (searching for the most distant signal possible), we should inspect the

49. S. A. Kaplan, "Exosociology: The Search for Signals from Extraterrestrial Civilizations," in *Extraterrestrial Civilizations: Problems of Interstellar Communication,* ed. S. A. Kaplan, trans. from Russian (Jerusalem: Keter Press, 1971), 7.

50. Graham, "Intergalactic Conversations," 20.

51. Lem, *His Master's Voice,* 103.

vast archives of photographic data of deep space for evidence of cosmic engineering (specifically so-called Dyson spheres, huge solar power stations that would serve as proof of distant alien intelligence).[52] SETI offers a nice catalog of the pieces that result once dialogue is, in Paul Ricoeur's word, "exploded." There is spying (I receive a signal not meant for me without your knowing it), hailing (I recognize you as a potential interlocutor), recognition (you "copy" my recognition with a counterhailing), and interaction. The enormous elongation of the communication circuit in deep space, like the equally radical extensions of the telegraph or photograph, reveal that the fundamental problem of communication is not adjusting semantics so we mean the same things with words, but figuring out ways to come into fellowship with otherness.

SETI faces a task suited for Kabbalists: scanning an infinite text for the name of names. It must employ search strategies in impossibly vast aggregates. Prophets heard voices from the heavens, but SETI researchers have to contend with the gigabytes of radio emissions naturally produced by the universe, to say nothing of the interference they produce for themselves (the electrical trams of Liverpool, or Clever Hans problems). SETI might rightly take its place among the theological and interpersonal abysses of the twentieth century. Kafka and Borges understand best the stakes of the quest for intelligible order in a pulsating cosmos. Borges's story "The Library of Babel" is a delirium of tedious infinities. This library contains every possible combination of all the letters of the Roman alphabet bound in volumes of 410 pages each. The number of volumes is very large, but not infinite. We know beyond the shadow of a doubt that there is somewhere in the library of Babel the greatest literary work possible with these letters, the Miltonic epic Keats would have written had he lived or sublimities Proust only dreamed of: yet there are billions of variants of this grand work, slightly diminished, and an even greater all but infinity of utter nonsense. We are unable to know if we have found it, since there are a hundred thousand versions perfect in everything but a single typo and a billion slightly blemished versions, and all but an aleph-null of deformed pieces. The absolute confidence that the masterpiece exists—along with every possible masterpiece—goes together with the sure knowledge that it cannot be found. The masterpiece cannot announce itself as such. Somewhere in the library there is even a volume that explicates the order of the library—a catalog—but it too exists in a billion spurious versions.

52. Freeman Dyson, "Search for Artificial Stellar Sources of Infrared Radiation," *Science* 131 (1959): 1667–68. Dyson also has a Cambridge connection: B. A. in mathematics, 1945.

Borges gives us an allegory of inability to connect: theologically, statistically, communicatively. His library is dissemination taken to an infinite extreme. One-to-one contact becomes impossible. Just so, we may know for sure that the animal hurts, but access to that pain is forever barred; we may believe the chances tiny that we are alone in the universe, but the others are so far away. The Library of Babel is an allegory of the minimal odds of our own existence, and still we exist. We seem an exception in the universe, and yet mundanity cloaks us on every side. SETI is an emblem of the hermeneutic giddiness that faces anyone staring into the abyss; our attempts to "communicate" have only made it worse.

One thing that distinguishes SETI from previous attempts to communicate with the heavens is the acute sense of the possibility of error. A 1959 article important in launching the movement nicely stated the grand prize: "indisputable identification as an artificial signal."[53] The issue was how to know a bona fide signal from other worlds—what others since have called "an intelligible beacon"[54] or "a non-random possibly intelligent transmission."[55] To be taken as a message, a signal must have an extremely low probability of being either a random or a natural product. Russian exoscientists made "artificiality criteria" a topic of very sophisticated study, including analysis of the statistical properties of signals.[56] Sought is an unmistakable signature of artifice, of a will to communicate—a concerto, pi to one hundred places, or some other feat of a playful (nonutilitarian) intelligence. Increased capacities of data processing have only escalated the pathos of infinity. Like a Penelope waiting for a rendezvous with an Odysseus she doesn't know if she will recognize, SETI scientists look for incontrovertible tokens. They seek a sign.

The image of the earth alone in the universe is analogous to the idealist's "man" cooped up in his room: both long not to be alone, to find a sign of something that is not a projection of the self. Though we live amid alien human intelligences—music, mathematics, art, and argument—a simple SOS from Tau Ceti would electrify the whole world. It is not only, contra Turing, intelligence or, contra Shannon, information that concerns us in communication, but the body it comes from. What SETI hopes for is the self-consciousness that the other is communicat-

53. Cocconi and Morrison, "Searching for Interstellar Communications," 846.
54. Alan Lightman, "E. T. Call Harvard," *Science* 85 (September 1985): 20–22.
55. Gregg Easterbrook, "Are We Alone?" *Atlantic Monthly,* August 1988, 27.
56. L. M. Gindilis, "The Possibility of Radio Communication with Extraterrestrial Civilizations," in *Extraterrestrial Civilizations: Problems of Interstellar Communication,* ed. S. A. Kaplan, trans. from Russian (Jerusalem: Keter Press, 1971), 103–8. The Eastern Europeans have led the way in these inquiries, in science on the one hand and in literature and cinema on the other.

ing, a sign rather than a signal: nothing would quite thrill like call letters, a break in the flow of programming to "identify oneself" (phrase of Hegelian wonder). Call letters would meet the precise definition of a social sign for George Herbert Mead: a sign used by the self to connect it to others. As one astrophysicist said, "We're looking for the one combination that says, 'Hi there.'"[57] The grand prize of communication at a distance recurs: Come here, I want you.

Otherness turns out, alas, always to be internally defined. In 1959 Cocconi and Morrison offered an elegant and influential argument for using the natural wavelength of the hydrogen atom as the logical frequency to send an interstellar message, assuming that to be a universal constant. But it is a postulate, like the Kantian or Jamesian varieties, that the aliens would also think to broadcast on that wavelength. SETI is a fine example of the post-Kantian problematic of how to recognize authentic empirical inputs within the all-coloring powers of human cognition. Today some scientists fear that the "pollution" of the electromagnetic spectrum by earth's own broadcasting may be so severe that the search may have to shift from radio to the optical band. As interference makes earth-bound scanning impossible, astronomers may either shift to infrared and visible wavelengths or use space stations to scan for signals from deep space.[58] The Drake equation, which gives grounds for calculating the likelihood of intelligent life elsewhere in the universe, estimates the longevity of a communicating civilization at one million years. Perhaps Drake should have calculated instead the span between the discovery of radio and the filling of the spectrum—more like one hundred years in the case of earth history. The shift in strategy from radio to optics is motivated, of course, not by any sense that extraterrestrials might have shifted their signals to a higher frequency but by the capacities of *our* instruments, which always constitute the ceiling on communication. When the aliens in *Contact* communicate with Jodie Foster via her father's persona, they say they are trying to soften the shock of the experience for her, but they end up depriving her of proof of having burst the bubble of solipsism.

The basic assumption of SETI—that a signal must stand in stark contrast to the rest of nature—is based on a shrinkage of the realm of the semiotic. In romanticism, with such thinkers as Ritter, Schelling, or even Kant's notion of a *Chiffenschrift der Natur* (hieroglyphics of nature), nature was once assumed to be a text written in cipher; more anciently it

57. Kent Cullers, quoted in Overbye, "Big Ear," 48.
58. Robert Naeye, "SETI at the Crossroads," *Sky and Telescope*, November 1992, 514.

was assumed to be full of cryptic messages intelligible to the sage or soothsayer. We have seen, since, a recession in the general supply of meaning. In nature we have come to assume that all those obvious but unintelligible and apparently unauthored patterns—sunsets, cries of birds, the guts of a lamb, or the fabric of clouds—are not the work of a conscious intelligence that we can interpret. The pathetic fallacy, animism, and anthropocentrism have all been scared out of us. And so solipsism is inescapable, since the only source of intelligible order is within us. Our lack of confidence in the objectivity of meanings is one key source of the pervasive sense of communication breakdown.

Some exoscientists have not stopped short at receiving messages but have sent messages to space—potentially the ultimate dead letter. Carl Sagan and others designed a message to be sent to outer space with *Voyager* in the 1970s that was supposed to be stripped of any extraneous cultural coding. Twenty-five years later this image already seems an emanation from an alien civilization, with its 1970s hairdos, vision of gender (the man takes the lead in greeting while the woman stands in a pose half demure, half sexy), and race (the couple are clearly white, though whites are not the majority race of the planet). Even in its attempts to transcend itself, a historical moment only reveals its blindness to its own face. By transposing the passage of time to flight across space, SETI offers lessons in the philosophy of history: what is hardest to recapture of the past is not its treasure-house of information about itself but its ignorance of what is most obvious to later observers. The attempt to send a message on a spacecraft is almost amusing, considering just how "hot" our planet has been over the past century in its emissions on the electromagnetic spectrum. Why the aliens should prefer the message on *Voyager* to all the episodes of *I Love Lucy, The Twilight Zone, Gilligan's Island,* or any other signal we earthlings have sent zooming through interstellar space is anyone's guess. SETI scientists at times evince a touching faith that the extraterrestrials would share their preference for Bach or mathematics over rock and roll or Scrabble.[59]

The aliens populate cinema, television, and the tabloids, all of which assume that contact has been made and take it from there with bathos or horror. SETI in contrast scrupulously scrutinizes the alternative hypotheses and wants pure, intelligible other mind, not just patters created by the reader, pulsars, background radiation, or a passing airliner or satellite. Nature and self are systematically excluded as authors: inten-

---

59. *Mother Earth News* 122 (March–April 1990), in its twentieth anniversary issue, sent an open letter to the great blue yonder, apologizing in effect for the bad condition of the planet!

tional otherness must break through. But Plato and Hegel would remind us that if the other has no body whose presence we could desire, then what makes us think minds can make contact? We might even, like Maxwell's glass lenses that never touch, be surrounded by extraterrestrial intelligence, only to never come in contact.

This is indeed the oddest thing about SETI—that we are so plainly surrounded with alien intelligences—bees, whales, porpoises, chimpanzees, DNA molecules, computers, dung beetles, slime mold, even the planet as an ecosystem—but still feel lonely and unable to communicate.[60] How much intelligence and wisdom are found in Chinese civilization, for instance, and how ignorant the West continues to be of it![61] Why do we seek distant alien intelligence when we hardly know what to do with our own? The huge barrier here is the strangeness that we never see: our own faces. We haunt ourselves like aliens. The main ghost that stalks me is my self, the only person whom everyone else knows but I never can. As Peirce wrote, "Facts that stand before our face and eyes and stare us in the face are far from being, in all cases, the ones most easily discerned."[62] Our failure to recognize ourselves fuels our thirst for confirmation from alien intelligences. "It is only when we think of ourselves on the receiving end that imagination seems to fail us."[63] The issue is our failure to enter into a common realm with the other: we are back with all the misfires and distortions that Socrates sketches.

The problem may be less our loneliness than our too stringent sense of communication. If we thought of communication as the occasional touch of otherness rather than a conjunction of consciousness, we might be less restrictive in our quest for nonearthly intelligence. What is the human truth of SETI? That the mundane is only a small pocket of the extraordinary. Of the billions of solar systems, we know of only one so able to support life. An orbit slightly closer to the sun, a tilt of the earth's axis by a few more degrees, or an errant comet all could have made life on earth impossible. Of the five billion years of earth's existence, humanoids have existed for one thousandth of that time. Civilization as we know it (with its writing, war, patriarchy) has existed for one thousandth of that. We are, as the romantics all insisted, the

60. This and many other excellent points are made in Anthony Weston, "Radio Astronomy as Epistemology: Some Philosophical Reflections on the Contemporary Search for Extraterrestrial Intelligence," *Monist* 71, 1 (1988): 88–100.

61. Naeye, "SETI at the Crossroads," 515.

62. Charles Sanders Peirce, "The Law of Mind," *Monist* 2, 4 (1892): 559.

63. Weston, "Radio Astronomy as Epistemology," 91.

great exception to the universe, the rare case, the completion of nature, the way that the universe comes to self-consciousness. The question should be, then, not how we break through the sludge of habit to rediscover the hidden strangeness of things, but how we ever managed to convince ourselves that anything was not a dissemination of intelligence. Boredom is the amazing achievement, not wonder. Our senses can catch only a narrow portion of the spectrum: the cosmic rays, rainbows above or below the range of visible light, or tectonic groans of the earth all elude us. What the moralists have said about the universe, science since Faraday has proved to be empirically true: We are immersed in a sea of intelligence that we cannot fully understand or even sense. Emerson's point about spiritualism applies equally to SETI: Why search so wistfully in a corner when the whole universe is a message? SETI research reminds one of Thoreau's quip about those who tried to measure the depths of Walden Pond: "They were paying out the rope in the vain attempt to fathom their truly immeasurable capacity for marvellousness."[64] In the 1890s William Crookes, Charles Sanders Peirce, Henry Adams, and many lesser spirits were delirious about the chances for human connection via waves naturally emitted from our persons. The hope for brain waves, however, remains constrained by the dullness of our instrumentation; perhaps it is simply our narrow bandwidth that makes telepathy a dream, the privacy of pain a given, and democracy always bounded by the dynamics of a conversation in which only one person can speak at a time.

———

Instead of being terrorized by the quest for communication with aliens, we should recognize its ordinariness. There is no other kind of communication. All our converse with others is via signs, those creatures from outer and inner space. This was a central tenet of Peirce, who led the pragmatist revolt against Cartesian hierarchies. His essay "Some Consequences of Four Incapacities" (1868) directly attacks introspection and Descartes, offers a behavioral understanding of communication, is open to the animal or the inhuman as a potential partner, and relinquishes any claim of special privilege for the human mind—which Peirce, borrowing a line from Shakespeare's *Measure for Measure,* called "man's glassy essence." Not afraid of the charge of animism, Peirce takes human beings and words as continuous. "It may be said that man is conscious,

64. Henry David Thoreau, *Walden* (1854; New York: Norton, 1975), 189.

while a word is not. But consciousness is a very vague term . . . consciousness, being a mere sensation, is only a part of the *material quality* of the man-sign." If words do not have consciousness, in what sense do people have it? Significance, in other words, does not need a live body; a word in itself can radiate meaning, in the same way that a phonograph or photograph can hold thought in objective form. Peirce argued "that a person is nothing but a symbol involving a general idea," and he later drew the even more radical conclusion that "every general idea has the unified living feeling of a person."[65] The criterion of life, then, does not suffice to distinguish humans from signs. "The man-sign acquires information, and comes to mean more than he did before. But so do words." Words mean what people have made them mean, but people mean nothing that words have not taught them to say. Words have their associations and communities, just as people or animals do. "In fact, therefore, men and words reciprocally educate each other; each increase in a man's information involves, and is involved by, a corresponding increase of a word's information."[66]

Peirce's argument is not only a critique of Cartesian high-handedness, or a semiotic animism that ascribes objective reality to meanings, as semantic theorists would fear, but an effort to invite us into a beloved community, one that includes all forms of intelligence as our partners in some way, at least in some future horizon. Though his thinking about evolutionary love and corporate personality ranks among the most wonderful and strange to come from the pragmatist tradition, and though he clearly does believe (in contrast to James) in the ultimate possibility of something like shared brain space, the ascription of independent intelligence to signs might be seen as Peirce's response to a communicative universe in which persons obeyed new laws of motion, scattering themselves into all fields in which signs may play.[67] We play host to signs like alien spores that have taken us over. Instead of taking signs as meaningful because they have an animating mind behind them, it is sounder to think of minds as themselves signs mixed with mortal life. The signs are as conscious as we are; they too have inner lives. Peirce's theory of signs is historically indebted to an age when intelligence can be stored in media.

65. Charles Sanders Peirce, "Man's Glassy Essence," *Monist* 3, 1 (1892): 21.
66. Charles Sanders Peirce, "Some Consequences of Four Incapacities" (1868), in *Philosophical Writings of Peirce*, ed. Justus Buchler (New York: Dover, 1955), 249.
67. A helpful explication and critique is Jürgen Habermas, "Peirce and Communication," in *Peirce and Contemporary Thought*, ed. Kenneth Laine Ketner (New York: Fordham University Press, 1995), 243–66.

Clearly, then, neither Peirce nor James is a defender of some sort of humanism, of "man" as the measure of all things. They recognize, in contrast, our fundamental inhumanity in the sense that we are always more or less than human. They do so with a quality of mercy that other antihumanisms such as behaviorism and poststructuralism often lack. They say not that inner life is a mentalist figment but that interiority appears as an other; that its form is polymorphous; that we find our inner life dispersed pluralistically across the fields of our experience. Inner life is best thought of not as a control panel presided over by a homunculus, but as behavior continuous with all else that we do. The inner and the outer are two sides of the same Möbius strip. We honor, not demean, the riches of inner life by seeing it as one kind of complex behavior not appreciably different from any other we engage in.

The pragmatists teach us that we should care for children, animals, the mad, the deformed, spirits and the dead, aliens and nature not because they potentially have a inner life of reason that can lay claim to our recognition (as Descartes might have it) but because they share our world and our shape. We should relate to animals not because they have minds, but because they have vertebrae, need oxygen, or feel pain. Our obligation to other creatures comes not from our ability to tap into their inner life but from a primordial kinship deriving from a common biological history, as variant forms of intelligent life that God or nature has seen fit to produce. The kinship we share with all creation is written into our bodies before we ever make mental contact (a lesson the pragmatists learned from Emerson and Darwin alike). This is a commonsense fact of compassion rather than an epistemological conundrum of other minds. Against the impasses of solipsism James wrote: "Men who see each other's bodies sharing the same space, treading the same earth, splashing the same water, making the same air resonant, and pursuing the same game and eating out of the same dish, will practically never believe in a pluralism of solipsistic worlds." A behaviorist query—Do we in fact cooperate?—is the question pragmatism poses to the worries about the impossibility of communication. Lovable form trumps abstract impossibilities. "The practical point of view brushes such metaphysical cobwebs away."[68]

This recognition involves a softening of the heart, an admission of the inefficacy of our glassy essence against the awe of strangeness. Interior consciousness ceases to be the criterion of humanness. The refusal

---

68. William James, "The Function of Cognition," in *The Writings of William James: A Comprehensive Edition*, ed. John J. McDermott (Chicago: University of Chicago Press, 1977), 146.

to probe inner life can lead in the more militant direction of depriving all beings of an inner life (some forms of behaviorism) or in the wilder and superior direction of granting an admirable but inaccessible innerness to all creatures, of giving, like Emerson or Whitman, a welcome to the universe—democracy in the best, full sense. A true democracy would have to include a much wider range of creatures than humans, for humans themselves are many creatures. Full democracy would be transspecies, transgender, transrace, transregion, transclass, transage, transhuman: what Emerson called "the democracy of chemistry." Even the dead would be invited.

The problem of communication in the twentieth century arises with much less exotic partners than aliens, animals, and machines, although again it is already a failure of recognition that we think of these creatures rather than ourselves as exotic. All the gaps and breakdowns we find with them we find among ourselves. But they also give us a way to imagine different worlds in which we might dwell. Consider the dolphins. Dolphins have no hands, so they have no works—no weapons, no records, no history, no government, no property, no law, no crime, no punishment.[69] No dolphin is married to any other dolphin, but all dolphins are kin. They are the true idyll of communism as Marx dreamed it. There is no forbidden fruit to expel them from Eden. They are naked and not ashamed. They are some of the aliens among us; women are some other aliens, as are men. So is the self: I am the thing from outer space (the ancients knew this). I am the UFO haunting everything (Novalis, Coleridge, and Emerson all knew this). So the dolphins sing and mate and play and eat and swim. They roll, exempt from the regime of secondness. What collective poetry, oral histories, symphonies of discussions over hundreds of leagues, fondness, relationships they must have. Voices that travel for hundreds of miles, allowing completely asynchronous dialogues. What friendships. What grief at the loss of a fellow to the nets or the killer whales. What philosophical dialogues, with no record but the consciousness of the community that listens. All conversation would be a reading of the archive of the community, as conversational turns traveling across great stretches of water would come to each participant in a unique order. Each response would appear

69. Loren Eiseley, "The Long Loneliness: Man and the Porpoise," in *A Writer's Reader*, ed. Donald Hall and D. L. Emblen (Boston: Little, Brown, 1979), 140–47.

in its true light as a new beginning. Dialogue and dissemination would be indistinguishable. The sea must be the original agora, the place of speech. But the dolphins have no agonistics because there is no drive to besting or individuation; their works of verbal invention are collective compositions. Theirs is a life of sporting firstness. If the hearing capacities of the dolphins are as advanced as our vision, dolphins may be exempt from the hardest argument against democracy: the ability of only one person to speak and be heard at a time. Dolphins can perhaps hear many of their fellows speaking at once; they would not be torn by the unfortunate mismatch between hearing and speaking, which makes democracy ever subject to constraints of scale. The party would be a party always, a polylogue in which everyone spoke and everyone heard. Such is perhaps the vision we should take away from a century's attempt to make contact with alien creatures.

Conclusion:
A Squeeze of the Hand

Come; let us squeeze hands all around; nay, let us squeeze ourselves into each other; let us squeeze ourselves universally into the very milk and sperm of kindness. HERMAN MELVILLE, *MOBY DICK*

Communication is a trouble we are stuck with. Other people and other times may be immune from such worries. Even today, many dwellers on the planet find it easy to live without any such concept. But for the chattering classes of the world's rich societies—and the fact that these words have reached you makes you a member, if only honorary, of such classes—the worry about how to connect with people, near and far, has become a given of our daily doings. In this conclusion I can only tie some threads together. The full working out of the book's implications for thought and life awaits another day.

The Gaps of Which Communication Is Made

To think and speak in fragments of dialogue has become our lot. As Raymond Williams says of the drama of Chekhov, Ibsen, and Strindberg,

I heard, as if for the first time, what was still, by habit, called dramatic speech, even dialogue: heard it in Chekhov and noticed now a habitual strangeness: that the voices were no longer speaking to or at each other; were speaking with each other, perhaps, with themselves in the presence of others. . . . no individual ever quite finishing what he had begun to say, but intersecting, being intersected by the words of others, casual and distracted, words in their turn unfinished.[1]

Williams's syntax mimics the discursive sprawl he has in mind. Failed synapses are a major resource in modern dialogue and life. Twentieth-century drama, from Beckett and Ionesco to the Marx Brothers and Woody Allen, exploits these gaps to disquieting and comic effect, as do the sociological studies of Erving Goffman and Harold Garfinkel. The distortion of dialogue of course is as old as theater—malfunctions in turn taking, miscues extrapolated into gigantic webs of faulty assumptions, the slightest gestures taken as portents and the most obvious signals missed, all with comic or tragic consequences. But the key word in Williams's description is "habit." Broken conversation has become as habitual as it is strange. Twist a radio dial or rustle a newspaper, and you will encounter bits of discourse that never quite connect. Public communications have grown increasingly miscellaneous. As James Clerk Maxwell once asked, What if the book of nature were really a magazine? Crosscutting between distinct lines of plot has become a mark not only of public speech in the newspapers, but of private conversation as well. Whatever dialogue might mean, today it is largely a wash of many sounds. Bakhtin was right to understand dialogue not as a particularly privileged form of ethical and political life, but as a jumble of voices.

That face-to-face talk is as laced with gaps as distant communication is a proposition I take to be both true and historical. The linguistic practices by which we humans caress and harass each other are enormously variable, and those who worry about "communication" belong to a world in which particular forms of talk and relationships have made questions of coupling urgent. But the delay of dialogue was long a potential in letters, prayers, and devotions to the dead. Neither is physical presence assurance that "communication" will occur. You can read poetry to a person in a coma, never knowing if the words are "getting through," but the same doubt is just as relevant in other settings, as any teacher or parent knows. Electronic media have taught us the chasms in all conversation. Conversations, after all, consist of single turns that may or may not link successfully with following turns. To put it a bit archly, dialogue may simply be two people taking turns broadcasting at each other. We tend to resist acknowledging the gaps at the heart of

1. Raymond Williams, "Drama in a Dramatised Society," in *Raymond Williams on Television: Selected Writings,* ed. Alan O'Connor (London: Routledge, 1989), 12.

everyday interchange, even though negotiating them is an accomplishment at which most competent language users are quite expert. But let a pause in a conversation go on too long and the din of the universe starts to fill the spaces, the air pressure mounting rapidly, threatening to suck everyone into the abyss. The gap between sending and receiving is simply made obvious by settings that bar a second turn of response (such as receive-only radio or public address) or in which the central exchange is subject to technical difficulties (such as the telephone or, indeed, the face-to-face). If nineteenth-century historicism and spiritualism took reading as communion with the author, in late twentieth-century poststructuralism interaction with a person has become a reading of textual traces. The image of conversation as two speakers taking turns in order to move progressively toward fuller understanding of each other masks two deeper facts: that all discourse, however many the speakers, must bridge the gap between one turn and the next, and that the intended addressee may never be identical with the actual one.

The Privilege of the Receiver

The other, not the self, should be the center of whatever "communication" might mean. An episode from the life of William James captures the problem well. He had been given charge of a turtle's heart for a popular lecture on physiology by one of his Harvard Medical School professors. The lecturer was demonstrating that the heart would pulsate when certain of its nerves were stimulated, and the pulsations were projected onto a screen in the front of Sanders Theatre. Halfway through the lecture, James realized the heart was not responding, so he took it upon himself, in a sudden and almost automatic response to the emergency, to make the proper motions on the screen by manipulating his forefinger such that the audience would not fail to gain a true understanding of the heart's physiology. Writing many years later—in a final essay on psychical research that was centrally about the balance of fraud and faith in what we can know—James admits that such simulation could be disdained as shameless cheating.[2] Had he acted otherwise, however, the audience would have been cheated of an understanding of physiology. His forefinger had performed humbug in the service of understanding. Confessing his prestidigitation or the demise of the heart would have offered only a secondary truth: the flaws of the appa-

2. William James, "Final Impressions of a Psychical Researcher" (1909), in *The Writings of William James: A Comprehensive Edition,* ed. John J. McDermott (Chicago: University of Chicago Press, 1977), 787–99.

ratus rather than its capacity to project truth. All our knowledge, he suggests, may rest on strategically concealed frauds—or rather, what would be considered frauds by those who still hold to a copy theory of knowledge. The criterion for knowing should not be accurate duplication of the world, but the ability to make our way through with the best aids we can get.

James's scenario in Sanders Theater is enormously rich with central themes in communication theory: projection, verisimilitude, the staging of life, what is good to believe. James stages a primal scene of communication, a crafty counterpart to Plato's cave, that nervously undercuts the long-standing faith that debunking the representations is the road to liberation from the chains. Rather than offering, say, a formula for mass mystification, James has lighted on something morally valuable: where we cannot know the original, we might as well take the best image we can get. More pointedly, communication involves not the direct sharing of truths but the manipulation of effects. Such language sounds ignoble, so let us be clear: James shifts the crux of communication from fidelity to an original to responsibility to the audience. (In this, at least, he is quite close to Socrates' notion of a philosophical rhetoric.) The representation of supposedly unvarnished truth can be just as reckless as outright deception. The dream of angels is dear to anyone who has ever been badly misunderstood, and the spiritualist tradition takes the wishes of the sender as the criterion of happy communication. Herein lies its moral deficiency: the hope of doubling the self always misses the autonomy of the other. Authenticity can be a profoundly selfish ideal.

James proposes the harder task of speaking in such a way that the other person understands rather than that we express the raw truth of our interior. Indeed, as in the mass communication situation of Sanders Theater, so in that of person-to-person: one must often sacrifice the dream of fidelity in representing one's own feelings and thoughts in order to evoke the truest image of them for the other. James offers a higher law: not a social physics of thought transportation but a risky universe in which any speaker must take responsibility for something one can never master—the way one's words and deeds play before the soul of the other. The authentic representation of self or world not only is impossible, it is also never enough. Needed instead is a stoic willingness to go through the motions that will evoke the truth for others. The problem of communication is not language's slipperiness, it is the unfixable difference between the self and the other. The challenge of communication is not to be true to our own interiority but to have mercy on others for never seeing ourselves as we do.

The Dark Side of Communication

The quality of mercy is often absent in popular discussion of communication. There is a kind of righteous tyranny about "communication" that I find troubling. The term can be used to browbeat others for "failing to communicate" when they are opting out of the game. Bartleby, Emerson, and Kierkegaard were all failures at communication—to their everlasting credit. To be accused of "not communicating" is often to be scolded for not providing someone with the response to their demand. Sharing is not a benign concept only. Many have invoked the Latin *communicare* as the origin of a long tradition of sharing talk. The more rarely cited, but equally relevant, Greek term *koinoō* offers a harsher lesson. Like *communicare*, it means to make common, communicate, impart, or share; it also means to pollute or make unclean. Communication crosses the border of inner and outer and can thus be common, just as meaning can be mean. The brutal rigor of this insight is found in a *logion* of Jesus concerning the purity of foods: "Whatever goes into a man from outside cannot defile [*koinōsai*] him, since it enters, not his heart but his stomach. . . . What comes out of a man is what defiles [*koinoi*] a man. For from within, out of the heart of a man, come evil thoughts, fornication, theft," etc. (Mark 7:18–21 RSV). "What comes out of the heart" is not a bad definition of communication as sharing. But such disclosure is here figured as the release of iniquity. To think of the sharing of inner life as an unmixed good rests upon a rather unrigorous account of the human heart.

Communication is a risky adventure without guarantees. Any kind of effort to make linkage via signs is a gamble, on whatever scale it occurs. To the question, How can we know we have really communicated? there is no ultimate answer besides a pragmatic one that our subsequent actions seem to act in some kind of concert. All talk is an act of faith predicated on the future's ability to bring forth the worlds called for. Meaning is an incomplete project, open-ended and subject to radical revision by later events. As Charles Sanders Peirce puts it, "A sign is objectively *general*, in so far as, leaving its effective interpretation indeterminate, it surrenders to the interpreter the right of completing the determination for himself." Since all signs are general to varying degrees, person-to-person converse is like dissemination, closure taking place at the receiving end. Peirce puts it bluntly: "No communication of one person to another can be entirely definite."[3] That we are destined to interpret, and that interpretation will always involve our desires and their conflicts, does not signal a fall from the supposed grace of immediacy; it is a description of the very possibility of interaction. There are no sure signs in communication, only hints and guesses. Our interaction will never be a meeting of *cogitos* but at its best may be a dance in which we sometimes touch. Instead of being an unbearable problem of lonely minds and ghostly apparitions, communication should be measured by the successful coordination of behaviors. All we know, see, hear, and feel of inner life takes shape in words, actions, or gestures, each of which is in some significant way public. The question should be not Can we communicate with each other? but Can we love one another or treat each other with justice and mercy? In our relations one with another animal solidarity is prior to interpretive surety. We can trade words but cannot share our existence. At best, "communication" is the name for those practices that compensate for the fact that we can never be each other.

In this book I have argued that we misspend our hope in seeking some kind of spiritual fullness or satisfaction in communication. The history of thinking about our mutual ties, as well as the history of modes of connection, from writing to the development of electrical media, shows that the quest for consummation with others is motivated by the experience of blockage and breakdown. Once we are stung by miscommunication, it is tempting to imagine communication as an escape from mortal modes. That people long for transcendence or ways to avoid the hurt of misunderstanding is only natural. The danger, rather, is that the immanent work of love and justice will be disdained as nothing but wreckage and refuse. Communication is ultimately unthinkable apart from the task of establishing a peaceable kingdom in which each may dwell with the other. Given our condition as mortals, communication will always remain a problem of power, ethics, and art. Short of some redeemed state of angels or porpoises, there is no release from the discipline of the object in our mutual dealings.[4] This fact is not something to lament: it is the beginning of wisdom. To treat others as we would want to be treated means performing for them in such a way not that the self is authentically represented but that the other is caringly served.

3. Charles Sanders Peirce, "Critical Common-Sensism" (1905), in *Philosophical Writings of Peirce,* ed. Justus Buchler (New York: Dover, 1955), 295.

4. Theodor W. Adorno, "Subject and Object" (1969), in *The Essential Frankfurt School Reader,* ed. Andrew Arato and Eike Gebhardt (New York: Continuum, 1982), 499–500.

This kind of connection beats anything the angels might offer. Joy is found not in the surpassing of touch but in its fullness.

To the therapists and technicians one must concede some things. Certainly errors and mistakes happen in dealing with other people. Certainly people can improve in suaveness, coping, and sensitivity. But the conceit that techniques can correct the painful and happy fact of our mutual difference not only is misguided, it is based on rare scenarios in which the ambiguity of signs can be fatal. Most of the time we understand each other quite well; we just don't agree. The story of Theseus tells us all we need to know. Returning from slaying the Minotaur, Theseus neglected to follow the code he had prearranged with his father, Aegeus. A black sail was to indicate his death, a white one his triumph. Aegeus, seeing a black sail on the horizon and thinking Theseus dead, hurled himself from the cliffs into the sea (thereafter called the Aegean). The moral: Build redundancy into messages on which life and death depend. Communication sometimes masquerades as the great solution to human ills, yet most troubles in human relationships do not come from a failure to match signs and meanings. In most cases except for the most minimal contact, the situation and syntax make the sense of words perfectly clear. Conditions of deprived presence such as letters, the telephone, or electronic mail do, as Kafka knew, provide a breeding ground for the ghosts. But in relations among friends, colleagues, and loved ones, what might be called failure to communicate is more often a divergence of commitment or a deficit of patience. Communication, again, is more basically a political and ethical problem than a semantic or psychological one. As such thinkers as Hegel and Marx, Dewey and Mead, Adorno and Habermas all argue, just communication is an index of the good society. We ought to be less worried about how signs arouse divergent meanings than the conditions that keep us from attending to our neighbors and other beings different from us.

The Irreducibility of Touch and Time

A major theme of the book has been the "condition of infinite remoteness" (Emerson) between people. But because souls cannot touch does not mean that the same sentence rests on bodies. No real community endures without touch. Of all the senses, touch is the most resistant to being made into a medium of recording or transmission. It remains stubbornly wed to the proximate; indeed, with taste, it is the only sense that has no remote capacity (unless eros be such). Touch defies inscription more than seeing or hearing, or even taste or smell (cooking and perfumes are their recording media). Though materializing mediums, telephone promoters, and radio performers all tried to transport touch, their efforts at such cloning always fell eerily short. A very different stance toward touch is found in the argument of some poststructuralists that the body is itself is a text. As fruitful as this insight can be, it risks missing the skin, hair, pores, blood, teeth, eyes, ears, and bones of these texts, and more important, their short life span. Eurykleia's rebuke of Penelope in book 23 of the *Odyssey* holds for those who see the presence of the other as either a wall or a superfluity:

How queer the way you talk!
Here he is, large as life, by his own fire,
and you deny that he will ever get home!
(FITZGERALD TRANSLATION)

Odysseus ultimately proved his identity to Penelope by revealing the scar on his thigh and the privileged knowledge of the bed he had once built her. As a message out of the past and arriving from distant places, he faced all the troubles of authentication. Odysseus's testimonies rested in the parts of his person most resistant to fabrication: scar, personal history, knowledge of intimate places outside circulation. Their singularity attested to their truth. He offered not tropes but trophies.

To view communication as the marriage of true minds underestimates the holiness of the body. Being there still matters, even in an age of full-body simulations. Touch, being the most archaic of all our senses and perhaps the hardest to fake, means that all things being equal, people who care for each other will seek each other's presence. The quest for presence might not give better access to the other's soul, per se, but it does to their body. And the bodies of friends and kin matter deeply. The face, voice, and skin have a contagious charisma. There is nothing so electric or unmanageable as touch: we feast our eyes on each other, kiss, shake hands, and embrace. Whether any of these gestures is a token of affection or constitutes harassment is a matter of interpretation subject to all the same problems as any other signifying act. Touch is no cure for communication trouble: it is more primal, but equally intractable. With his war on "the metaphysics of presence," Derrida is right to combat the philosophical principle that behind every word is a voice and behind every voice an intending soul that gives it meaning. But to think of the longing for the presence of other people as a kind of metaphysical mistake is nuts.

Touch and time, the two nonreproducible things we can share, are our only guarantees of sincerity. To echo Robert Merton, the only refuge we have against communication fraud is the propaganda of the deed. No profession of love is as convincing as a lifetime of fidelity. Despite all the stretching done by recording and transmission media, there are important boundaries to the scale and shape of communication. That our capacity to communicate is limited is a sociological truth; it is also a tragedy. True love—among mortals at least—is communicatively marked by smallness and partiality: it does not parade about publicly or waste itself in gardens of Adonis. The mark of an intimate message is the exclusiveness of its address. (Why else do we feel violated when someone breaks a confidence?) There is no such thing as equal intimacy for all. Amnesty International assigns each local chapter a *single* prisoner of conscience to petition for: philanthropy in general somehow seems false. "Poster children" are a pathetic tribute to our crazy love for individuals.[5] In love, said Kierkegaard, the particular is higher than the universal. The paradox of love is that a neighbor in need exerts a stronger claim on your help than all the hungry orphans in the world. ("One death," in Stalin's brutal insight, "is a tragedy; a million deaths is a statistic.") The face of the other is the strong force. A person late for a meeting on saving the orphans would not be right to walk past the bleeding person in the gutter. The profoundest ethical teachings command love for all people indifferently, and yet time allows genuine intimacy and care for only a few of the planet's inhabitants. We can spend time only with a relative few in the course of a lifetime. We mortals really love only personally, and yet not to love all people is unjust. The paradox of love is its concrete boundedness and the universality of its demands. Because we can share our mortal time and touch only with some and not all, presence becomes the closest thing there is to a guarantee of a bridge across the chasm. In this we directly face the holiness and wretchedness of our finitude.

5. Luc Boltanski, *La souffrance à distance: Morale humanitaire, médias, et politique* (Paris: Éditions Métailié, 1993).

Appendix: Extracts (Supplied by a Sub-sublibrarian)

[Eros] interprets between gods and men, conveying and taking across to the gods the prayers and sacrifices of men, and to men the commands and replies of the gods; he is the mediator which spans the chasm which divides them, and therefore in him all is bound together.   PLATO, *SYMPOSIUM*, 202E (JOWETT TRANSLATION)

But let your communication be, Yea, yea; Nay, nay; for whatsoever is more than these cometh of evil.   MATT. 5:37 KJV

But now ye also put off all these; anger, wrath, malice, blasphemy, filthy communication out of your mouth.   COL. 3:8 KJV

Thou art an elm, my husband, I a vine,
Whose weakness, married to thy stronger state,
Makes me with thy strength to communicate.
WILLIAM SHAKESPEARE, *COMEDY OF ERRORS*, 2.2.172–74

But Man by number is to manifest
His single imperfection, and beget
Like of his life, his Image multipli'd,
In unity defective, which requires
Collateral love, and dearest amity.
Thou in thy secrecy although alone
Best with thyself accompanied, seek'st not
Social communication, yet so pleas'd,

Canst raise thy Creature to what heighth thou wilt
Of union or communion, deifi'd.
JOHN MILTON, *PARADISE LOST*, 1667 (ADAM SPEAKS TO GOD BEFORE MEETING
EVE)

The Comfort and Advantage of Society, not being to be had without Communication
of Thoughts, it was necessary, that Man should find out some external sensible Signs,
whereby those invisible Ideas, which his thoughts are made up of, might be made
known to others. JOHN LOCKE, *ESSAY CONCERNING HUMAN UNDERSTANDING*,
1690

Besides, the communicating of ideas marked by words is not the chief and only end
of language, as is commonly supposed. There are other ends, such as the raising of
some passion, the exciting to or deterring from an action, the putting the mind in
some particular disposition. GEORGE BERKELEY, *THE PRINCIPLES OF HUMAN
KNOWLEDGE*, 1710

No quality of human nature is more remarkable, than that propensity we have to
sympathize with others, and to receive by communication their inclinations and sentiments, however different from or even contrary to, our own. . . . Hatred, resentment,
esteem, love, courage, mirth, and melancholy; all these passions I feel more from
communication than from my own natural temper and disposition. DAVID HUME,
TREATISE OF HUMAN NATURE, 1740

The great pleasure of conversation, and indeed of society, arises from a certain correspondence of sentiments and opinions, from a certain harmony of minds, which like
so many musical instruments coincide and keep time with one another. But this most
delightful harmony cannot be obtained unless there is a free communication of sentiments and opinions. We all desire, upon this account, to feel how each other is
affected, to penetrate into each others bosoms and to observe the sentiments and
affections which really subsist there. ADAM SMITH, *THEORY OF THE MORAL SENTI-
MENTS*, 1759

A common passion and interest will, in almost every case, be felt by a majority of the
whole; a communication and concert results from the form of the government itself;
and there is nothing to check the inducements to sacrifice the weaker party, or an
obnoxious individual. JAMES MADISON, *THE FEDERALIST*, NO. 10, 1787

Poetry ever communicates all the pleasure which men are capable of receiving: it is
ever still the light of life. PERCY BYSSHE SHELLEY, *A DEFENCE OF POETRY*, 1821

We come to them who weep foolishly and sit down and cry for company, instead
of imparting to them truth and health in rough electric shocks, putting them once

more in communication with their own reason. RALPH WALDO EMERSON, "SELF-RELIANCE," 1841

Because everyone knows the Christian truth, it has gradually become such a triviality that a primitive impression of it is acquired only with difficulty. When this is the case, the art of being able to *communicate* eventually becomes the art of being able to *take away* or trick something away from someone. SØREN KIERKEGAARD, *CONCLUDING UNSCIENTIFIC POSTSCRIPT,* 1846

She approached the door that formed the customary communication between the house and garden. NATHANIEL HAWTHORNE, *THE HOUSE OF THE SEVEN GABLES,* 1851

Children come a-berrying, railroad men taking a Sunday morning walk in clean shirts, fishermen and hunters, poets and philosophers, in short, all honest pilgrims, who came out to the woods for freedom's sake, and really left the village behind, I was ready to greet with,— "Welcome, Englishmen! welcome, Englishmen" for I had had communication with that race. HENRY DAVID THOREAU, *WALDEN,* 1854

Two beings, or two millions—any number thus placed "in communication"—all possess one mind. PARLEY PARKER PRATT, *KEY TO THE SCIENCE OF THEOLOGY,* 1855

A member of our household came in and asked me to have our house put into communication with Mr. Bagley's, down-town. MARK TWAIN, "A TELEPHONIC CONVERSATION," 1880

The communication of impressions of any kind from one mind to another, independently of the recognized channels of sense. FREDERIC W. H. MYERS, 1882 (DEFINITION OF "TELEPATHY")

Transportation is physical, communication is psychical. CHARLES HORTON COOLEY, *THE THEORY OF TRANSPORTATION,* 1894

When I communicate my thoughts and my sentiments to a friend with whom I am in full sympathy, so that my feelings pass into him and I am conscious of what he feels, do I not live in his brain as well as in my own—most literally? CHARLES SANDERS PEIRCE, *THE LOGIC OF MATHEMATICS* 1896

Adult life, under civilized conditions, exaggerates the mystery of our apparent sundering from one another, and forgets that only the community of our meanings, and the fact that we are local centres wherein the ideal unity of the world gets various and

contrasted expressions, enables us to communicate with each other at all. JOSIAH
ROYCE, THE WORLD AND THE INDIVIDUAL, 1899–1901

If a machine can produce etheric waves, capable of cognition and communication,
the same possibility should exist within ourselves. FREDERIC FLETCHER, THE SIXTH
SENSE, 1907

By Communication is here meant the mechanism through which human relations
exist and develop—all the symbols of the mind, together with the means of conveying
them through space and preserving them in time. It includes the expression of the
face, attitude and gesture, the tones of the voice, words, writing, printing, railways,
telegraphs, telephones, and whatever else may be the latest achievement in the conquest of space and time. CHARLES HORTON COOLEY, SOCIAL ORGANIZATION,
1909

That the expression "radio communication" as used in this act means any system
of electrical communication by telegraphy or telephony without the aid of any wire
connecting the points from and at which the radiograms, signals, or other communications are sent or received. UNITED STATES RADIO ACT, 1912

The wireless telegraph does not transmit thought, but simply signals which can be
translated into an intelligible communication. Telepathy, on the other hand, deals
with the direct communication of thought. EDITOR, SCIENTIFIC AMERICAN, 1913

There is no real breach of continuity between the dead and the living; and that methods of intercommunication across what has seemed to be a gulf can be set going
in response to the urgent demand of affection,—that in fact, as Diotima told Socrates . . . LOVE BRIDGES THE CHASM. OLIVER LODGE, RAYMOND, 1916

Der Mensch mit sich selbst kommt nicht weiter in der Kommunikation als mit dem
Anderen. In indirekter Mitteilung wirkt er in seiner Existenz auf sich selbst so gut wie
auf Andere und erfährt rückwärts diese Wirkung. Darum der größte Klarheitsdrang
zugleich Kommunikationsdrang ist und doch alle Klarheit umfaßt ist von dem Dun-
klen, das indirekt ist und bewegt. [Man does not come further in communication with
himself than with the other. In indirect communication he works upon his own existence as well as upon others and experiences this effect in return. For this reason the
greatest impetus for clarity is also an impetus for communication even though all
clarity is surrounded by darkness that is indirect and mobile.] KARL JASPERS, PSY-
CHOLOGIE DER WELTANSCHAUUNGEN, 1919

It is certainly true that problems arising out of the means of communication are of the
utmost importance, and one of the most constructive features of the program of

the League of Nations has been the study given to railroad transit and access to the sea. WALTER LIPPMANN, *PUBLIC OPINION, 1922*

Thus, a language transaction or a communication may be defined as a use of symbols in such a way that acts of reference occur in a hearer which are similar in all relevant respects to those which are symbolized by them in the speaker. C. K. OGDEN AND I. A. RICHARDS, *THE MEANING OF MEANING, 1923*

The use of the radio telephone for communication between single individuals, as in the case of the ordinary telephone, is a perfectly hopeless notion. Obviously, if ten million subscribers are crying through the air for their mates they will never make a junction. HERBERT HOOVER, UNITED STATES SECRETARY OF COMMERCE, 1923

Communication from the dead is presumably of the same nature as telepathic communication between the living. ELEANOR MILDRED BALFOUR SIDGWICK, "ON HINDRANCES AND COMPLICATIONS IN TELEPATHIC COMMUNICATIONS," 1924

Mitteilung ist nicht so etwas wie ein Transport von Erlebnissen, zum Beispiel Meinungen und Wünschen aus dem Inneren des einen Subjekts in das Innere des anderen. Mitdasein is wesenhaft schon offenbar in der Mitbefindlichkeit und im Mitverstehen. [Communication is not anything like a transportation of experiences, such as opinions and wishes, from the interior of one subject into the interior of another.] MARTIN HEIDEGGER, *SEIN UND ZEIT, 1927*

Modern social organization is formed and reformed by its means of communication. Changes in communication may therefore afford indexes of wider and more complicated changes taking place in society. E. W. BURGESS, *AMERICAN JOURNAL OF SOCIOLOGY, 1928*

If communication can be carried through and made perfect, then there would exist the kind of democracy to which we have referred, in which each individual would carry just the response in himself that he knows he calls out in the community. GEORGE HERBERT MEAD, *MIND, SELF, AND SOCIETY, 1931*

It is a question whether the obvious increase of overt communication is not constantly being corrected, as it were, by the creation of new obstacles to communication. EDWARD SAPIR, "COMMUNICATION," IN *ENCYCLOPEDIA OF THE SOCIAL SCIENCES, 1931*

The world is on the threshold of a great forward movement in mass communication—transmission and reception of sound and sight combined. O. E. DUNLAP, *THE OUTLOOK FOR TELEVISION, 1932*

Evidently the more intelligent a company policy, the more necessary is it that there shall be a method of communicating understanding "down the line." ELTON MAYO, *THE HUMAN PROBLEMS OF AN INDUSTRIAL CIVILIZATION*, 1933

The intricate patterns of modern civilization would be utterly disrupted if the channels of communication were long closed, for it is clearly evident that communication lines are the nerve threads through which the organization of the world in all its social aspects is made to function. MALCOLM M. WILLEY AND STUART A. RICE, *COMMUNICATION AGENCIES AND SOCIAL LIFE*, 1934

In the end, works of art are the only media of complete and unhindered communication between man and man that can occur in a world full of gulfs and walls that limit community of experience. JOHN DEWEY, *ART AS EXPERIENCE*, 1934

For over against the convenience of instantaneous communication is the fact that the great economical abstractions of writing, reading, and drawing, the media of reflective thought and deliberate action, will be weakened. LEWIS MUMFORD, *TECHNICS AND CIVILIZATION*, 1934

Mass production necessitated mass distribution which necessitated mass literacy, mass communication and mass advertising. JAMES RORTY, *OUR MASTER'S VOICE*, 1934

Radio is an altogether novel medium of communication, preeminent as a means of social control and epochal in its influence on the mental horizons of men. HADLEY CANTRIL AND GORDON ALLPORT, *THE PSYCHOLOGY OF RADIO*, 1935

And what the dead had no speech for, when living,
They can tell you, being dead: the communication
Of the dead is tongued with fire beyond the language of the living.
T. S. ELIOT, *BURNT NORTON*, 1936

To the extent that the last works of art still communicate, they denounce the prevailing forms of communication as instruments of destruction, and harmony as a delusion of decay. MAX HORKHEIMER, "ART AND MASS CULTURE," 1941

Radio cannot teach. Teaching involves communication of a kind that radio cannot attempt,—a discipline, a concentration, a circumstance that have nothing to do with radio's circumstance. CHARLES SIEPMANN, "RADIO AND EDUCATION," 1941

Regard for the object, rather than for communication, is suspect in any expression: anything specific, not taken from pre-existent patterns, appears inconsiderate, a symptom of eccentricity, even of confusion. THEODOR ADORNO, *MINIMA MOR-ALIA*, 1944

All such discussions usually culminate in the question as to whether language is unique to man. Here the issue is in part terminological, since if "language" is made synonymous with "communication" there is no doubt that animals have language. CHARLES MORRIS, *LANGUAGE, SIGNS, AND BEHAVIOR*, 1946

The theme of solitude and the breakdown of human communication are viewed by modern literature and thought as the fundamental obstacle to human brotherhood. The pathos of socialism breaks against the eternal Bastille in which each person remains his own prisoner, locked up with himself when the party is over, the crowd gone, and the torches extinguished. The despair felt at the impossibility of communication . . . marks the limits of all pity, generosity, and love. . . . But if communication bears the mark of failure or inauthenticity in this way, it is because it is sought as a fusion. EMMANUEL LEVINAS, "THE OTHER IN PROUST," 1947

But in the case of neither the instrumentalities of mass communication nor of atomic energy do the inventors of the instrument dictate the use to which they shall be put. LOUIS WIRTH, "CONSENSUS AND MASS COMMUNICATION," 1948

The word *communication* will be used here in a very broad sense to include all the procedures by which one mind may affect another. This, of course, involves not only written and oral speech, but also music, the pictorial arts, the theatre, the ballet, and in fact all human behavior. In some connections it may be desirable to use a still broader definition of communication, namely, one which would include the procedures by means of which one mechanism (say automatic equipment to track an airplane and compute its probable future positions) affects another mechanism (say a guided missile chasing this airplane). WARREN WEAVER, "RECENT CONTRIBUTIONS TO THE MATHEMATICAL THEORY OF COMMUNICATION," 1949

The ideal arrangement is to have a teleprinter communicating between the two rooms. ALAN TURING, "COMPUTING MACHINERY AND INTELLIGENCE," 1950

The whole task of psychotherapy is the task of dealing with a failure in communication. . . . We may say then that psychotherapy is good communication, between and within men. We may also turn that statement around and it will still be true. Good communication, free communication, within or between men, is always therapeutic. CARL ROGERS, "COMMUNICATION—ITS BLOCKING AND ITS FACILITATION," 1951

For in this world, communication is never an absolute (only angels communicate absolutely); and a deficiency in one point in a given communicative system may show as a proficiency at some other point (somewhat as persons deprived of sight may become more acute in hearing or touch). KENNETH BURKE, "INTRODUCTION," IN *PERMANENCE AND CHANGE*, SECOND EDITION, 1953

Communication is not an "expression" of thoughts or feelings, which then could only be secondary to them; truth itself is communicative and disappears outside of communication. HANNAH ARENDT, "CONCERN WITH POLITICS," 1954

Radio and television catch the mind directly, leaving children no time for calm, dialectic conversation with their books. The view from the screen doesn't allow for the freedom-arousing mutuality of communication and discussion. Conversation is the lost art. JOOST MEERLOO, *THE RAPE OF THE MIND*, 1956

The whole theory of mass-communication depends, essentially, on a minority in some way exploiting a majority. RAYMOND WILLIAMS, *CULTURE AND SOCIETY*, 1958

When we speak of "communications" in a consumer society, we have to think . . . of how other people speak *at* us. STUART HALL, "THE SUPPLY OF DEMAND," 1960

The electric light escapes attention as a communication medium just because it has no "content." MARSHALL MCLUHAN, *UNDERSTANDING MEDIA*, 1964

For true communication entails a communion, a sharing of inner experience. The dehumanization of communication has resulted from its annexation by the media of modern culture—by the newspapers first, and then by radio and television. LEO LOWENTHAL, "COMMUNICATION AND HUMANITAS," 1967

One cannot not communicate. PAUL WATZLAWICK, JANET HELMICK BEAVIN, AND DON D. JACKSON, *PRAGMATICS OF HUMAN COMMUNICATION*, 1967

Your essence, my essence, everybody's essence is hooked together. And there is immediate and total communication with them all the time throughout the whole galaxy. JOHN LILLY, "FROM DOLPHINS TO LSD," 1971

Il est vu, mais il ne voit pas; objet d'une information, jamais sujet dans une communication. [He is seen, but he does not see; he is an object of information, and never a subject in communication.] MICHEL FOUCAULT, *SURVEILLER ET PUNIR*, 1974

Telecommunity is our goal; telecommunications our means. AT&T SLOGAN, 1980s

In the "utopia of reason" created within bourgeois self-understanding, "communication" was represented as standing on its own feet, setting limits to the dynamics of autonomous subsystems, bursting encapsulated expert cultures, and thus as escaping the combined threat of reification and desolation.   JÜRGEN HABERMAS, *THE THE-ORY OF COMMUNICATIVE ACTION,* 1981

Just as he relies on the conventions of logic to deduce the solution to this dilemma, so she relies on a process of communication, assuming connection and believing her voice will be heard.   CAROL GILLIGAN, *IN A DIFFERENT VOICE,* 1982

Acknowledgments

It takes a village to make a book. An accounting of everyone who has contributed in some way to this one would be a census of the communities through which I have had the good fortune to pass. My gratitude goes to all.

A fellowship from the National Endowment for the Humanities in 1995–96 made this work possible. At the University of Iowa, the Department of Communication Studies has generously supported my research, as have the Project on the Rhetoric of Inquiry, the Obermann Center for Advanced Studies, and the Sound Research Seminar. A long string of creative and dilligent research assistants have each left their mark: Eung-Sook Kim, Jean P. Retzinger, Tabitha Yeatts, Lilias Green, John M. Streck, Hsin-i Liu, Jing Wu, and Jung-Bong Choi. Graduate students in my courses at the University of Iowa have been generous in their comments and critiques on drafts of this work.

Important advice and support came from Dudley Andrew, Mary J. Depew, Tom Gunning, Martin Jay, James Lastra, Allison McCracken, Allan Megill, Harold L. Miller Jr., Richard Pruitt, Eric W. Rothenbuhler, Mark B. Sandberg, Carol Schrage, Katie Trumpener, Heather Wessely, and Steve Wurtzler. Peter Simonson offered wonderfully detailed comments on a bulky early version, managing to see a butterfly in the larva. James W. Carey, Mark Poster, and Michael Schudson offered invaluable readings of the entire manuscript and saved me from many traps, something Carey and Schudson have done more times in my career than I can count. An anonymous reader at Chicago offered a salutary corrective. Douglas Mitchell and Alice M. Bennett at the University of Chicago Press made the whole publishing angle a dream. All of these people are exempt from blame for my foibles.

David Depew has come to my rescue again and again. Without Ken Cmiel, the book would be a ghost. Marsha, Ben, and Daniel are my favorite beasts and angels of all.

Index